GALLANT CANADIANS

The Story of

The Tenth Canadian Infantry Battalion

1914 – 1919

"There may have been equally good fighting units,
but there was never one any better."
— Major-General Dan Ormond, CMG DSO

Daniel G. Dancocks

Published by The Calgary Highlanders Regimental Funds Foundation
8th Floor, 840 - 6th Avenue S.W., Calgary, Alberta, Canada T2P 3E8

First published 1990
Copyright © The Calgary Highlanders Regimental Funds Foundation, 1990
Maps: Courtesy of The Calgary Highlanders Regiment. These maps were prepared by Second Lieutenant I.R. Spratley under the direction and command of Lieutenant Colonel A.G. Maitland, CD, Commanding Officer.
Photographs and Drawings © Sources as noted for each photograph or drawing.

Canadian Cataloguing in Publication Data

Dancocks, Daniel G. (Daniel George), 1950 — Gallant Canadians: the story of the Tenth Canadian Infantry Battalion, 1914-1919

Includes bibliographical references.

ISBN 0-9694616-0-7

    1. Canada. Canadian Army.   Battalion, 10th — History.

    2. World War, 1914-1918 — Regimental histories — Canada.

    I. Calgary Highlanders Regimental Funds Foundation.   II. Title.

UA602.C24D36 1990   940.4'1271   C90-090351-1

Printed and bound in Canada.

Distributed by Penguin Books Canada Ltd.
2801 John Street, Markham, Ontario, Canada L3R 1B4

ISBN 0-9694616-0-7

GALLANT CANADIANS
(To the 10th Battalion, C.E.F.)

Gallant Canadians, you've shown the world
You can stand for democracy when her flag's unfurled.
At Ypres, Festubert, at Vimy and Somme,
You brought us glory by work well done.

Gallant Canadians, you heard the call —
The motherland in danger — you gave your all.
How can we forget you men, brave and strong,
Fighting for justice, righting the wrong.

Gallant Canadians, the world won't forget
You died for freedom — we owe you a debt.
The deeds you have done for humanity's cause
Will ring round the world — receive its applause.

Gallant Canadians, well done, the world says:
You fought and suffered in the war's early days.
Historians will write as a nation to come;
Democracy hails you for all you have done.

— poem published by the Calgary *Daily Herald*, 10 September 1918

TABLE OF CONTENTS

FOREWORD

Tradition is important to any military unit and history lends meaning to traditions by explaining them. Through this book we are recording the history of the Tenth Battalion and fulfilling the charge of our Colonel-in-Chief, Her Majesty Queen Elizabeth II, to preserve our history and further our tradition.

Created in 1914, the "Fighting Tenth" as it was widely known, established a reputation as one of the very best Canadian combat units by taking part in every major Canadian action and countless smaller operations. The story of the Fighting Tenth is also the story of the brave men, officers and other ranks alike, who made it such a success — farm lads, clerks, lawyers, accountants, and ranchers — who came from all parts of Canada but primarily from southern Alberta and Manitoba. It is important to understand that the bulk of those who fought with the Tenth were raised from the militia, not the regular forces. This precedent held true for The Calgary Highlanders who served with distinction during the Second World War and, in so doing, lived up to the memory of their Great War predecessor, the Tenth Battalion.

The tradition remains. In the years since World War II, young militia soldiers have regularly volunteered to become full-time soldiers in Canada's forces. One such example was a boy piper in The Calgary Highlanders who rose through the ranks to become the present Chief of Defence Staff, National Defence Headquarters. He is General AJGD de Chastelain, OMM, CD.

The Calgary Highlanders trace some of their most cherished traditions to the Tenth Battalion. These include the oak-leaf shoulder distinction and the toast to "The Glorious Memory of the Twenty-second of April 1915". Both the oak-leaf and the toast commemorate the counter-attack by the Tenth and the Sixteenth (Canadian Scottish) Battalions after the first major gas attack by German troops was mounted near Saint-Julien, Belgium during the Great War. General Ferdinand Foch, who later emerged as the Allied Supreme Commander, considered the Canadian counter-attack "the finest act in the war".

To quote Sergeant Wally Bennett, an active participant in the Battle of Saint-Julien, one lesson learned from this battle is "if you can't defend or counter-attack with a particular weapon, the weapon will be used against you". He noted that millions of tons of gas equipment were carried all over the world during World War II but even in the last most desperate days, neither Germany nor Japan used gas.

With the many recent changes of Perestroika and Glasnost reshaping the Eastern Bloc, we are seeing the results of the "balanced forces" policy in deferring war and maintaining peace. There have been many recorded arms races and all but one or two have ended in active conflict. In the one or two exceptions, the balance of forces was so close that neither side would risk war. The odds are far greater for active conflict than you would gamble at Las Vegas and support the "balanced forces" concept. This is another lesson and a tribute to those who have maintained the balance in the years since World War II for unless those who perpetuate the unit also perpetuate the lessons, the lessons will be lost and only relearned at great expense.

Upon reading this book, one realizes that the story of the Fighting Tenth becomes more awesome with the perspective of time and that the lessons learned from the battles they fought should not be forgotten.

Fred P. Mannix
Honorary Colonel
The Calgary Highlanders

Chapter One

BIRTH OF A BATTALION

(2 September 1914 - 21 April 1915)

The battalion destined to be famed far and wide as "The Fighting Tenth" was created in September 1914.

Canada had been at war since 4 August, but without any say in the matter, a reflection of its semi-colonial status. Like the rest of the British Empire, the young dominion had gone to war the moment hostilities broke out between Great Britain and Germany, when the latter invaded neutral Belgium. However, patriotic enthusiasm swept the country from coast to coast, and recruiting offices were soon swamped.

No one was more enthusiastic about the war and its promise of glory than the egotistical minister of militia and defence, Sam Hughes, a teetotalling Orangeman from Ontario. Hughes scrapped existing mobilization plans, choosing instead to improvise the raising of Canada's first overseas contingent by utilizing its 226 militia units. The result was pure chaos. By the beginning of September, more than thirty thousand volunteers — two-thirds of them British-born — had been assembled at Camp Valcartier, near Quebec City.

Like other Canadian volunteers that historic summer, the Calgarians arriving at Valcartier were still basking in the warmth of a near-frenzied send-off. Two long trains left Calgary on Friday night, 21 August, filled with men representing a number of militia units from central and southern Alberta. Included were the 35th Central Alberta Horse, 4th Field Troop, Canadian Engineers, 17th Cavalry Field Ambulance, and 14th Army Service Corps. The biggest contingent was from the four-year-old 103rd Regiment, Calgary Rifles. Commanded by a trio of lieutenants, C. Geoffrey "Jock" Arthur, W. Ashton Cockshutt, and D. Lee Redman, the three hundred men of the 103rd were escorted to Calgary's Canadian Pacific Railway depot by the regimental mascot, a bull terrier named Pat. There they were greeted by "thousands of Calgarians standing on the platform, waving their hats and cheering," according to the Calgary *Daily Herald*. The enthusiasm of the civilians was matched by the volunteers, "with men hanging out of the windows all down the long line of coaches, waving their caps and cheering every now and then."[1]

Camp Valcartier was something of a disappointment. "It was absolutely breaking new ground," recalled Major Daniel Mowat Ormond, a twenty-nine-year-old militiaman from Portage-la-Prairie, Manitoba. "There was nothing there at all. The brush had to be cut down. There was no latrine, there was nothing."[2] A.W. "Wally" Bennett, a nineteen-year-old clerk from Calgary, arrived at Valcartier on 31 August, a few days after Major Ormond. "There were no buildings — just a wooden platform in the open fields. We lined up and marched about a mile to the camp site. The weather was fine, and while there, in tents, we enjoyed the camp life."[3]

Organizing, equipping, and training Canada's first contingent was a major undertaking. This was understandable, considering that a war effort on this scale was unprecedented in Canadian history. But the inefficient Sam Hughes complicated matters by making it his personal project. The militia minister was a regular visitor to Valcartier, travelling from Ottawa in his private rail car and residing in a specially constructed brick bungalow on the edge of the camp. While there, it was not unusual for Hughes to promote certain officers with a hearty slap on the back or to administer verbal abuse to others in full view of their units.

Organization of the volunteers at Valcartier proceeded by fits and starts. Twelve provisional infantry battalions were authorized on 22 August; each unit was to be an amalgamation of several of the more than two hundred militia regiments represented in camp. The Tenth Battalion listed in Camp Order 28 of that date, was to be composed of two Saskatchewan units and two from Manitoba. These were the 60th Rifles of Canada, from Moose Jaw, and the Regina-based 95th Saskatchewan Rifles, 90th Winnipeg Rifles and the 99th Manitoba Rangers from Brandon.[4] Its allocated strength on the last day of August was fifty-three officers and 1528 other ranks.[5]

However, it soon became apparent that these twelve battalions, organized in three provisional brigades, could not possibly accommodate the vast numbers of men flocking to the colours and still pouring into Valcartier by the trainload. A new organiza-

Lieutenant-Colonel Russell Boyle

The conflict that came to be known as the Great War of 1914 - 18 was sparked by a murder. On 28 June 1914, the heir to the throne of Austria-Hungary, Archduke Franz Ferdinand, was assassinated by Serbian nationalists in Sarajevo, in present-day Yugoslavia. Austria-Hungary used the killing as a pretext to go to war with Serbia, and a complex combination of international treaties and bungled diplomacy, nationalism and jingoism, xenophobia and paranoia ensured that it would not be a localized clash of arms. Austria-Hungary and Serbia were at war by the end of July, and when Russia mobilized to come to Serbia's aid, Germany jumped to the side of its ally, Austria-Hungary. France, allied with Russia, also prepared for war.

The only question mark among the major European powers was Great Britain. Loosely allied to France and Russia in the so-called Entente Cordiale, the British were in no mood for war. As late as 1 August, the British cabinet voted two-to-one against sending France a pledge of support in the burgeoning crisis. At the same time, the foreign secretary, Sir Edward Grey, warned his cabinet colleagues that it might prove to be impossible to stay out of the conflict because "Belgian neutrality might become a factor."

Grey's warning was soon proven correct. Germany's war plans had been predicated on a two-front war, with Russia in the east and France in the west. While conducting a holding action against the numerous but ill-equipped and poorly led Russians, the Germans intended to knock out France with a decisive blow delivered through Belgium. The fatal flaw in this scheme was that Belgium was neutral, and its neutrality had been guaranteed by both Britain and Germany, among others, in an 1839 treaty.

On 2 August, Berlin demanded that Belgium permit free passage of German forces. The Belgian government defiantly rejected the ultimatum the next day, declaring itself "firmly resolved to repel by all means in its powers every attack upon its rights."

The mood in Britain changed overnight. The threat to Belgium was a threat to British honour, and that proved to be a challenge which could not be overlooked. On 3 August, the day that Belgium defied German bullying, Foreign Secretary Grey won a thunderous ovation in the House of Commons when he declared that Britain could not overlook its obligations to defend Belgian neutrality. To do so, he said, would "sacrifice our respect and good name and reputation before the world."

The die was cast. At 8:02 a.m. on 4 August, German troops crossed the frontier into Belgium, and as soon as word of the invasion reached London, the British government delivered an ultimatum to Berlin, demanding the immediate withdrawal of its armies from Belgian soil. The ultimatum expired unanswered at 11 p.m., London time, and twenty minutes later a telegram was dispatched to all British ministries: "War, Germany, act."

tion was instituted on 1 September and revised the following day: sixteen revamped battalions, in four brigades. Thus, all units of the first contingent, including the Tenth Battalion, regard 2 September 1914 as the date of their formation. The First Brigade was entirely from Ontario and comprised of the 1st (Western Ontario), 2nd (Eastern Ontario), 3rd (Toronto), and 4th (Central Ontario) battalions. The Second Brigade, from Western Canada, was made up of the 5th (Western Cavalry), 6th (Fort Garry Horse), 7th (1st British Columbia Regiment), and 8th (90th Winnipeg Rifles) battalions. Three of the Third Brigade's battalions — the 9th (101st Edmonton Fusiliers), Tenth, and 11th (100th Winnipeg Grenadiers) — were from the prairies, while the 12th (8th Royal Rifles) was mainly from Quebec. The Fourth Brigade was composed of the 13th (Royal Highlanders of Canada), 14th (Royal Montreal Regiment), 15th (48th Highlanders of Canada), and 16th (Canadian Scottish Regiment) battalions; all but the 14th were kilted units.[6]

The Tenth Battalion was, in theory at least, an amalgamation of two Western Canadian militia regi-

ments, the 103rd Calgary Rifles and the 106th Winnipeg Light Infantry. Its authorized strength was 1511, all ranks, with the majority — 846 — from the Calgary unit.[7] As a result, the Battalion traced its roots to two cities, which was reflected in its post-war perpetuation by The Calgary Highlanders and the Winnipeg Light Infantry in the reorganized Canadian armed forces. In truth, it was not quite so simple; the Tenth was made up of men from all over Canada. Due to the fact it was one of the last battalions to be constituted, all of its members were taken on strength during the last week in September. However, by the end of the war, it was drawing most of its reinforcements from Alberta, and its home was considered to be Calgary.

Because the 103rd Calgary Rifles and 106th Winnipeg Light Infantry were unable to bring the Battalion up to its provisional strength, the shortfall had to be made up in other ways. Any man who was not a member of another battalion was liable to end up in the Tenth, as Victor Lewis discovered.

The twenty-two-year-old Lewis was from Regina, where he had been a night watchman for the

First photograph: the Tenth Battalion at Valcartier

Sam Hughes, minister of militia and defence (centre),
during a visit to Valcartier, 13 September 1914.

The convoy carrying the First Canadian
Contingent to England, October 1914.
Courtesy National Archives of Canada/PA-22731

S.S. Scandinavian
Courtesy National Archives of Canada/PA-148276

Canadian Pacific Railway. When war broke out, he had enlisted in the 95th Saskatchewan Rifles, but soon afterwards, fell ill and had to be hospitalized. His regiment left for Valcartier without him. Recovering quickly Lewis joined three other men who also paid their own forty-five-dollar train fare to Quebec. As they were getting off the train at Valcartier, an officer called to them: "Where are you boys going?"

One of Lewis's friends, John Somers, replied with his own impertinent question: "What the hell do you want to know for?"

"I'm looking for recruits," the officer replied.

"Well," said Somers, "you've got four right here."

The officer was Lieutenant Stanley Glanfield of the Tenth Battalion.[8]

Not only was the Tenth among the last to be organized, it was considerably different than the provisional unit. According to the nominal roll issued in early 1915, the Battalion was composed of 1124 officers and other ranks, and they were a colourful collection. Less than one-fifth were natives of Canada, while three-quarters were born in Britain. Thirty-one were American-born, and forty-eight were from other parts of the world: Australia, Belgium, Brazil, Denmark, Egypt, Finland, France, India, Malta, the Netherlands, Poland, Russia, Sweden, South Africa, Switzerland, and the West Indies. Half of these men had prior service, representing regiments from all over the British Empire, as well as the Royal Navy and Marines and the United States armed forces. One private, Royal Alexander Willingham, an English-born Texan, had gained his military experience in the Mexican army.[9]

The nominal roll makes for surprisingly interesting reading. There were sixteen Smiths and one Smythe. There was also, perhaps inevitably, a private named Sergeant. Among the brothers were two from Calgary, Basil and Clifford Roughton. While Clifford would later be killed in action, Basil, who was just seventeen when he enlisted, survived the war as a sergeant, only to die in a hunting accident eight months after returning home.* There were several other pairs of relatives in the Battalion including: Privates George and Peter Cumming (father and son); Privates Joseph and William Curtis (brothers); Privates Albert and Ernest Ellis (brothers); Privates Thomas and William Keith (brothers); Privates George and Frank O'Dell (father and son); Privates Fred and George Trim (father and son); Privates Guy and Vay Stephenson (brothers); and Privates William Walpole and William Walpole, Jr. Of these, Peter

Cumming, Joseph Curtis, Ernest Ellis, and William Walpole, Jr. were all killed in action.**

Another notable original was English-born Colour-Sergeant William Alexander, who was destined to play a leading part in the Battalion's blackest chapter.[10] He was the only member of the Tenth to be executed.

The Tenth's first commanding officer was Lieutenant-Colonel John Grant Rattray, a gruff, fifty-year-old, Scottish-born Manitoban. A longtime militiaman, he had commanded the 20th Border Horse, which he had organized in 1910. While in civilian life, he was a land inspector for the Canada Life Assurance Company in Winnipeg. Colonel Rattray had briefly commanded the 6th (Fort Garry Horse) Battalion,[11] before taking over the Tenth. "It was my privilege to organize the Battalion at Val Cartier [sic]," he later commented,[12] but he was not destined to take the unit overseas. Politics cost Rattray his command. A Liberal, he had been politically active in his home province and had apparently crossed swords previously with the Conservative militia minister, Sam Hughes, who dispensed patronage so profligately that it caused his government considerable embarrassment. Rattray met his Waterloo the day Hughes, on horseback and escorted by a large entourage, arrived to inspect the Tenth Battalion on the parade square at Valcartier.

The trouble started as soon as Hughes spied Rattray. "Colonel Rattray," he asked in a loud voice, "what are you doing here?" The colonel tried to explain that it was his duty, but Hughes was not interested. "Get the hell out of here!" he roared, and a humiliated Rattray retreated from the parade square. Hughes ordered the Tenth to get off the square, too, then rode away without inspecting the Battalion. According to Lieutenant Ashton Cockshutt, the unit's officers were "appalled" by this remarkable scene.[13]

Rattray, understandably, was no less upset. "I felt so bitter," he later complained, "at the treatment handed to me by Sam Hughes and some other Tories."[14] However, Rattray's association with the Tenth was far from over.

Major Russell Lambert Boyle, who succeeded Rattray and is generally regarded as the Battalion's first commander, was appointed on 27 September. Over six feet tall, the handsome, moustachioed Major Boyle had been born in Port Colborne, Ontario, thirty-four years earlier. A veteran of the South African War, where he served as a sergeant in the artillery, Boyle had been wounded in the summer of 1900. Returning to Canada with the Queen's Medal and

---

* Five Roughton brothers served overseas during the war. Besides Basil and Clifford, Jim also joined the Tenth, while the other two fought as members of the 31st (Alberta) Battalion.

** Of all the brothers who served in the Tenth, there was no more tragic story than that of Privates James and William Farquhar, who enlisted in the 50th Battalion in Calgary in January 1915. They transferred together to the Tenth on the same day, 6 January 1916, and were killed on the same day, 3 June 1916.

three clasps, he moved to Alberta in 1901, taking up ranching near Crossfield, just north of Calgary. Boyle soon emerged as "an outstanding figure" in the community, serving on the rural municipality's council and school board. Attaining the rank of major, he commanded the Crossfield squadron of the 15th Light Horse from May 1910, subsequently passing the militia staff course and gaining his certificate from the School of Signalling. He was, in short, one of the outstanding militia officers in Canada.[15]

Boyle's second-in-command was thirty-year-old Major Joseph MacLaren.* Born in Dundee, Scotland, he had come to Canada in 1905, settling in Brandon, Manitoba, where he taught physical education and served as a major in the 12th Manitoba Dragoons. The Battalion's adjutant was a fellow Manitoban, Major Dan Ormond, who had acted in that capacity with the 18th Mounted Rifles in his home town of Portage-la-Prairie, where he was a lawyer. The only other major in the Tenth at this time was also from Manitoba: James Lightfoot was a South African veteran who had been with the 106th Winnipeg Light Infantry.

To the officers and non-commissioned officers (NCOs) fell the task of shaping the Tenth Battalion into an efficient fighting force. This was not easy, considering the confusion at Valcartier. The Battalion had trouble even looking like a military unit, because uniforms were in short supply initially. "We were a funny-looking bunch," recalled a young clerk from Calgary, Private Wally Bennett, who arrived at Valcartier wearing a blue suit. As September progressed, Private Bennett and his comrades in the Tenth gradually began to resemble real soldiers. "Some day we'd get a tunic, another day we'd get pants and shirts and shoes and socks," he would remember with a chuckle.[16]

Because the Tenth was among the last to be organized, it was, naturally, among the last to be outfitted. Some of the men were still in civilian clothes when Sam Hughes returned to inspect the Battalion on Valcartier's rifle range on 27 September. Accompanied by the newly appointed commanding officer, Major Boyle, the militia minister rode among the ranks, nodding approvingly until he spotted the mufti-clad newcomers at the rear.

"Who are those men over there with the civilian clothes?" Hughes barked at Boyle.

"Oh," the major explained, "they haven't got uniforms yet."

"Well, bring 'em over!" replied the minister, who saw to it that they were issued uniforms.[17]

They were smart-looking uniforms, too. "Tunics were issued with separate, [blue] shoulder straps, fastened on with button and tapes passed through 2 eye-let holes and tied underneath."[18] Unfortunately, the tight-fitting Canadian-made tunics, with their high, stiff collars, were not appropriate for active service — "dress tunics, they were," pronounced Private Bennett[19] — and they were eventually replaced.

This was, sadly, typical of all the equipment provided for the contingent. It was Sam Hughes's desire that, while the Canadians would be fighting as part of the British army, they should be using Canadian-made goods. Although laudable, his goal was undermined by a combination of shoddy workmanship and poor designs, largely due to Canada's limited industrial capacity in 1914. The troops were issued with several notorious items, including the Oliver leather harness, which had been introduced during the South African War. "Unserviceable," in Private Bennett's opinion,[20] the Oliver was uncomfortable and did not carry nearly as much ammunition as the British webbing. Canadian-made boots were no better; paper soles could not withstand the rigours of campaigning. Then there was the MacAdam shovel, a combination entrenching tool and bullet-proof shield patented by Hughes's secretary. The shovel fell far short of expectations, and was eventually relegated to the scrap heap. Even more serious was the flawed Ross rifle, a .303-calibre repeater with a straight-pull bolt. Championed by the militia minister as "the most perfect military rifle in the World today,"[21] the Ross was originally intended to be shorter, lighter, and cheaper than the British army's Lee-Enfield. However, it had been subjected to so many design changes since its adoption in 1902, that it was now longer, heavier, and more expensive. An admittedly excellent target weapon, its shortcomings as a combat weapon would become apparent soon enough, with sometimes tragic consequences for the men using it. Except for the Ross rifle, all of the contingent's Canadian-made equipment was replaced by British equivalents in early 1915.

A seemingly minor organizational change on 25 September could have had enormous ramifications for the Tenth Battalion. It had been decided that the contingent at Valcartier would be patterned on the standard British division of the day. This meant that only three brigades would be combat units; the fourth would serve as a reinforcement depot for the others. On the twenty-fifth, the Fourth Brigade — commanded by one of Sam Hughes's favourites, Colonel Richard Turner, who had won the Victoria Cross as a subaltern in South Africa — was redesignated the Third Brigade, while retaining the 13th (Royal Highlanders of Canada), 14th (Royal Montreal Regiment), 15th (48th Highlanders of Canada), and 16th (Canadian Scottish) battalions. The original Third Brigade was now the Fourth, and its four battalions, including the

---

* The spelling is an arbitrary choice on the author's part. His surname was also commonly spelled McLaren; indeed, on the Tenth's nominal roll, published in early 1915, he is listed as MacLaren but his next-of-kin are McLarens.

"When Britain is at war, Canada is at war. There is no distinction." So said Prime Minister Sir Wilfrid Laurier in 1910, and it was still true in the summer of 1914, although Laurier was no longer in power. Sir Robert Borden was now the prime minister, but there was at no time any question about Canada's part in war brewing overseas.

As the British Empire's first self-governing dominion, Canada's status was more than a little perplexing. Confederation in 1867 had given Canada the right to control domestic affairs, but London still spoke for the entire Empire in foreign relations. When Britain declared war on Germany on 4 August 1914, Canada, along with the rest of the Empire, was automatically at war.

Canada did have the right to decide the extent of its participation, and the wild enthusiasm with which the war news was received in all parts of the country — including Quebec — left no doubt that Canadians would put forth every effort. This was not surprising, because 1914 Canada was very much a British nation. The British flag, the Union Jack, was Canada's flag, and the monarch, King George V, was the King of Canada. British heroes and traditions and values were cherished and promoted in Canada, which did not even have a national anthem. English lyrics to "O Canada" had been written just a few years earlier, and patriotic Canadians sang "God Save the King" and "Rule Britannia."

No one was more enthusiastic about the war than Canada's eccentric minister of militia and defence, Sam Hughes. Since his appointment following Prime Minister Borden's election victory in 1911, Hughes had worked hard to improve Canada's meagre armed forces. As early as August 1912, he had publicly warned that "war is closer than you dream; the great peril is from Germany," and he had managed to nearly double his department's modest budget in an effort to train and equip the nation's tiny army and navy.

At sixty-one years of age, Sam Hughes was, in the words of one historian, "a man destined to live and die without a single doubt," especially about himself. A powerful figure in the federal Conservative party, the teetotalling, non-smoking Hughes had represented his adopted hometown of Lindsay in the eastern Ontario riding of Victoria North since 1892.

A Methodist and Orangeman, he was also a militia colonel, and had seen service in the South African War at the turn of the century — and claimed that he should have won not one but *two* Victoria Crosses! A former schoolteacher and newspaper proprietor, Hughes was a blustering bully whose methods reinforced the admiration of his friends and the enmity of opponents.

Prime Minister Borden's comments regarding his militia minister were typical. While admitting that much of the time, Hughes "was an able, reasonable, and useful colleague," the prime minister noted that he was often "extremely excitable, impatient of control and impossible to work with," and occasionally "his conduct and speech were so eccentric as to justify the conclusion that his mind was unbalanced."

The war became Sam Hughes's personal project. Mistrustful of professional military men — he believed that "the best soldiers are such men as engineers, barristers, contractors, large businessmen with military training" — Hughes promptly scrapped Canada's mobilization plans, preferring what he later described as "a call to arms, like the fiery cross passing through the highlands of Scotland or the mountains of Ireland in former days." Recruiting offices across the country were swamped by enthusiastic volunteers, ensuring that there was no shortage of manpower, for the time being, and the minister's amateur efforts did no serious harm. Similarly, he got away with another odd decision when he ignored the established Camp Petawawa near Ottawa as the assembly point for the first contingent, and chose instead a non-existent camp near Valcartier, Quebec. It was also Hughes's decision to create numbered battalions at Valcartier. This served the double purpose of side-stepping the doubtful legality of sending militia units overseas and ensuring that all militia units would be represented in Canada's combat formations.

More damaging was his determination to provide the contingent with Canadian-made equipment that was generally inferior in quality to its British counterparts. While it provided work for Canadian factories and lined the pockets of political cronies — creating, for example, a munitions' industry where none existed before the war — Hughes's misguided interference in this regard destined Canadian soldiers to be sent into action with an unreliable weapon, the Ross rifle.

Tenth, were to be excluded from front-line service. The Battalion's prospects appeared disappointing.

Little useful training was conducted at Valcartier; "unsatisfactory" was the way the Tenth's adjutant, Major Ormond, described it.[22] This was hardly surprising in view of the extensive organizational activities which occupied most of September, and were major feats in themselves. But the contingent's days on this Quebec plain were numbered. At the suggestion of the War Office in London, the Canadians were

Colt machine-gun

Courtesy National Archives of Canada/PA-49160

to be shipped to England at the earliest opportunity, for training supervised by British professionals. The Canadian government chartered thirty-one ships of varying sizes, and loading of these vessels began during the last week in September: equipment first, then men and horses.

The Tenth Battalion's turn came on Tuesday, 29 September. After a sixteen-mile train ride, the Battalion marched through the picturesque streets of Quebec City to the docks, where the Allan Steamship Line's 12,099-ton *Scandinavian* was tied up. By six-thirty that evening, *Scandinavian* was ready to sail. On board were the Tenth's forty-three officers and 1051 other ranks, along with twenty-one wagons, eighty-nine cases of rifles, forty-five boxes of small-arms ammunition, and 21,109 sacks of flour, a gift from Canada to the mother country.[23] *Scandinavian* steamed that night for Gaspé Bay, where it would rendezvous with the rest of the convoy and the four British cruisers that would escort it across the Atlantic Ocean.

The convoy sailed on Saturday, 3 October. Carrying the largest armed force to cross the Atlantic to that time, the thirty-two transports* formed in three columns, each headed by a cruiser, with the fourth warship bringing up the rear. *Scandinavian* was the sixth transport in the left-hand column.

The twelve-day journey was pleasant enough. The weather was beautiful until the convoy arrived off the English coast, and the troops were kept busy with a steady diet of physical drill, fatigues, lectures, concerts, and sports. In addition, there were illicit games of crown and anchor enjoyed on their own time. In mid-Atlantic, the escort was reinforced by one of the Royal Navy's newest, fastest, and biggest ships, the battlecruiser *Princess Royal*. She put on a stirring display on Monday, 12 October, receiving the hearty cheers of thousands of excited Canadians as she steamed past the convoy at twenty-two knots with her bands playing "O Canada" and "The Maple Leaf Forever." Watching from *Scandinavian*, Private Wally Bennett called it "a thrilling sight that I'll never forget." The twelfth of October was memorable in another way for Private Bennett; he celebrated his twentieth birthday that day.[24]

The convoy reached England the next day, and on the fourteenth, it sailed into Plymouth Harbour to a wild reception. "With what intense enthusiasm did the people of England welcome us," wrote the Tenth's chaplain, Major William Emsley, a Methodist minister from Pembroke, Ontario, "...how the 'Maple Leaf', 'O Canada', and 'Rule Britannia' thrilled us and were the forewords of a splendid welcome which rose to the heights of friendship and affection."[25] It was here that the Canadians acquired their reputation for poor discipline, a reputation which they were unable to shake for the rest of the war, and the Tenth Battalion apparently did its share to promote this unfortunate image. For the British-born majority in the Canadian contingent, this was a homecoming, and Plymouth's public houses proved an irresistible temptation — especially after Valcartier, which, thanks to the teetotalling Sam Hughes, was a "dry" camp. "They let us off the first day in Plymouth," recalled Private Bennett, who had been born in England before moving to Canada at an early age. "We raided the pubs, where you could get something to eat and drink."[26] The problem was too much drink, and the local newspapers were soon filled

---

* In addition to the thirty-one ships conveying the Canadian contingent, one vessel carried a British regiment, the 2nd Lincolnshire, which had garrisoned Bermuda until its relief by the Royal Canadian Regiment. The convoy grew to thirty-three transports on 6 October, when it was joined by *Florizel* and the battalion-sized Newfoundland contingent.

9

with graphic accounts of drunken, disorderly Canadians stumbling through the streets and wrestling with military police.

On Monday, 19 October, the Tenth departed Plymouth for Salisbury Plain, where it would spend the next five months. The Battalion split in two for the move with the first half disembarking from *Scandinavian* at 4:15 p.m. and marching to Plymouth's North Road Station, where it boarded a train for the five-hour trip to Salisbury. The second half of the unit followed two hours later. Each man carried a full day's rations in his haversack.

This date is significant in another way, for it marks the beginning of the regimental war diary.[27] Writing this account was the duty of the adjutant, and the diary was kept until mid-March 1919.

It was dark by the time the last of the Tenth reached its destination. Arriving at Lavington Station on the northern edge of Salisbury Plain, the two halves of the Battalion marched to Pond Farm Camp, one of four initially provided for the Canadians. Joining the rest of the Fourth Brigade in tents on the gently rolling plain, the men of the Tenth settled down for a short sleep.[28] Some were more comfortable than others, however. Major Emsley, the chaplain, recalled that he shared a tent with the second-in-command, Major Joseph MacLaren; they had no blankets that first night on Salisbury Plain and the two majors "slept literally on English soil."[29]

They were up bright and early the next morning. The Battalion paraded twice on Tuesday, 20 October, its first full day on Salisbury Plain. Following physical drill at 6:30 a.m., parades were held at 9 a.m. and 2:30 p.m. Wednesday was highlighted by section and platoon drill. The weather both days was cloudy and cool.[30]

It rained on Thursday and, although the sky cleared in the afternoon, the rainfall proved to be an ill omen. Rain fell on eighty-nine of the next 123 days at Salisbury. The precipitation, accompanied by cold, violent winds that compounded everyone's misery, was double the thirty-two-year average in this part of southern England. Below a few inches of poor topsoil was a solid block of chalk, which provided little drainage for the record rainfall, and Salisbury Plain turned into a vast pool of mud.[31]

In spite of horrid weather conditions, the Tenth Battalion proceeded with its training programme in view of prehistoric Stonehenge. Although the rain and wind-storms played havoc with other units, which often cancelled their agendas on account of the weather, it is worth noting that not once did the Tenth fail to parade and conduct its prescribed activities. These ranged from musketry to route marches, night exercises to lectures; the lectures included "Night Operations," "Discipline," "Duties of Guards, Sentries, Picquets with reference to prisoners, property, etc.," "Interior Economy," "Care of Rifles," "Entrenchments,"

"Methods of keeping touch by day and by night." There were also brigade and divisional manoeuvres, weather permitting. In all, the Battalion underwent thirty-six hours of training per week, for thirteen weeks.

The Tenth's discipline at Salisbury was exemplary and credit for this must go to the newly promoted Lieutenant-Colonel Boyle, who wasted no time in laying down the law. At the Battalion's first parade, Colonel Boyle took off his coat and threw it on the ground, and then addressed the troops in characteristically tough style. "Now, I'm the same as you fellows," he told them. "I'm just an ordinary private, as far as you're concerned, as far as I'm concerned. There were four men on that boat [who] said they'd like to punch the hell out of me. Now I invite you four men, if you have the guts enough to come up, and we'll have it out right here." No one moved, and Boyle had won the men's hearts. Private Victor Lewis, the former night watchman from Regina, was suitably impressed, calling the colonel "a wonderful man."[32]

Sadly, the Battalion recorded its first fatality at Salisbury. On 8 November, twenty-three-year-old Private Charles Ford — who described himself in his attestation papers as an "Adventurer Gentleman" — died in hospital,[33] possibly the victim of cerebrospinal meningitis. An epidemic of this disease ravaged the contingent, claiming twenty-eight lives.[34] The following day, the Tenth abandoned its sodden tents at Pond Farm Camp for newly constructed wooden huts at nearby Sling Plantation. The spread of sickness was limited by stringent attention to cleanliness, both personal and in their living quarters, and the epidemic's worst ravages were curtailed. However, despite improved accommodations, two more members of the Battalion died before its departure from the plain. They were: a twenty-year-old cowboy, Private Charles Bingham, on 6 January 1915.[35] His cause of death is not known. Forty-nine-year-old Captain Henry Cooke committed suicide on 3 February.[36] All were buried in the cemetery in the village of Amesbury.

Venereal disease was also a problem, although it was not as serious as the meningitis outbreak. Knowing that some soldiers would attempt to conceal these afflictions, Colonel Boyle made it clear that such action would not be tolerated. "It is directed that a soldier who is suffering from venereal disease is to report himself without delay," read the colonel's orders on 14 November. "Concealment of venereal disease will be severely dealt with under the provisions of the Army Act."[37]

The Tenth took part in several formal events in its first month in England. The first was on 24 October, when Field-Marshal Lord Roberts, the elderly hero of the South African War, inspected the Canadians. "I need not urge you to do your best," the eighty-two-year-old soldier told them, "for I know you will."[38] Lord Roberts returned on 4 November, when he

The Tenth Battalion trains at Salisbury, in the shadow of Stonehenge.

accompanied an inspection by King George V and Queen Mary. The King welcomed the presence of the contingent which, he said, "is of inestimable value both to the fighting strength of my Army and in the evidence which it gives of the solidarity of the Empire."[39] Three days later, the Tenth contributed an officer and seven other ranks — Lieutenant George Craggs, Sergeant Herbert Baker, Corporal John Matheson, and Privates Harry Clayton, Harry Atherton, William Stephens, Bertie Collins, and David O'Rourke — to the Canadian party at the Lord Mayor's show in London.[40]

There was disappointment on 4 December, when the general officer commanding (GOC) the Canadian Division, Lieutenant-General Edwin Alderson, failed to appear for a scheduled inspection of the Battalion. "Cancelled after men had moved into position," the war diary sourly noted of the 10:30 a.m. inspection, but there would be other opportunities to meet the middle-aged General Alderson, a career soldier with more than thirty years' experience in the British army.

Christmas was a time of mixed feelings for the men of the Tenth, as it was for everyone in the Canadian contingent. Many Canadian-born soldiers were spending their first Christmas away from their families, but the British-born troops were close to home and able to take advantage of it. All soldiers were granted six days' leave at either Christmas or New Year's with a free train ticket to anywhere in Britain. Private Wally Bennett, for example, spent the holiday with his uncles in Kent.[41] For those who remained in camp on Christmas Day, there was divine service in the YMCA hut between 7 and 10 a.m., followed by dinner at 5:30 p.m., "all ranks messing together."[42]

Among those who attended Christmas dinner was the chaplain, Major William Emsley. That had not been his original intention, because he had earlier applied for and received Christmas leave. He changed his plans when he noticed that his permission papers contained the gentle admonition from Colonel Boyle: "Don't you think the boys will miss you at Christmas?" Applying instead for New Year's leave, he spent Christmas with "the splendid lads of the west," as he referred to them. After dinner, he hosted the colonel and Major McLaren in his room, and these officers expressed their desire to get into action as quickly as possible. "Well, we may all be killed, that's all in the game," said Boyle, "but I'm not afraid of wounds as I heal easily." Holding up his right arm, he remarked that "this arm has been shot through and through. I got it in Mexico and again in South Africa but it is a pretty good arm yet."[43*]

Another reflection of the officers' willingness to see combat was their decision to send a Christmas card to Field-Marshal Sir John French, commander-in-chief of the British Expeditionary Force. The field-marshal's reply from his personal secretary was received on 5 January: "Sir John French wishes me to say that it was particularly gratifying to him to receive your Xmas card and the good wishes expressed as coming from so important a unit of the Canadian Troops, which he is looking forward to having under his command before long."[45]

The Tenth continued its training, but with a serious handicap. It was one of just two battalions at Sling Plantation, and Colonel Boyle complained, "we are duty battalion every other day," which "interferes with training."[46] Work duties included building roads and sidewalks, sanitizing the huts, and disinfecting blankets. The Battalion was further restricted on 7 January, when five officers and 229 other ranks were detailed to Lark Hill, the Second Brigade's winter camp, as a working party. They did not return to the Tenth for nearly three weeks.[47]

---

* Shortly afterwards, Major Emsley departed to take a new post, as a chaplain with Number 1 General Hospital. He never forgot the fond farewell offered by Colonel Boyle: "Put in some good words for me, Major, now and then, and where they will do the most good, will you?"[44]

One of Colonel Boyle's most difficult tasks was the reduction of the Battalion to wartime strength. Its nominal roll, issued in early 1915, shows 1124, all ranks, including forty-four officers. The establishment of a Canadian infantry battalion was thirty-four officers and 929 other ranks,[48] so the Tenth's numbers had to be reduced. This was done in a variety of ways. For example, some men were pronounced medically unfit for active service; on 29 January, sixteen other ranks in this category were dispatched to the base training depot at Tidworth.[49] In addition, officers were subjected to particularly close scrutiny; several, such as Captain Andrew Meikle, were "struck off strength contingent, G.O.C. having no further use for his services." Others, including Captain Charles Yates, transferred to the British army or, like Lieutenant John Collins, to other Canadian units.[50]

Several organizational changes took place while the Tenth Battalion was at Salisbury Plain. One of these involved the formation of a machine-gun section. Each battalion in the Canadian contingent was issued four American-made Colt air-cooled, belt-fed machine-guns. "That's the first time I handled a machine-gun," recalled Private Wally Bennett. "We used to work on it and practise with it, putting it in pieces and tearing it down and putting it together again blindfolded."[51]

The Battalion also reorganized into four companies, but it was a convoluted process. The entire Canadian contingent had come to England in eight-company battalions. On 1 November, they reverted to four companies, but this was overturned later in the month by the War Office, which decreed that all British battalions must have eight companies. Unable to make up its mind, the War Office reversed itself in December, and the battalions had no sooner switched to four companies than they were once again ordered to restore the eight-company organization. The final decision was made in January 1915 in favour of four companies, designated by the letters A, B, C, and D. The Tenth was ordered to reorganize on this basis on 18 January[52] and completed the change on the twenty-first.[53] The company commanders were Captain Charles Robinson (A); Major William Nasmyth (B); Captain Lee Redman (C); and Major James Lightfoot (D).

The infantry was the primary arm of the British army and the Canadians fought as part of the British army during the Great War. As historian Reginald Roy points out, "It fought the battle, captured enemy positions and held them when taken." The battalion was the infantry's basic formation, and it was a complex organization, according to Professor Roy:

[I]ts lowest sub-unit was the infantry section, commanded by a corporal, which consisted of ten men armed with rifles initially and later with some light machine-guns. Four sections were grouped into a platoon commanded by a subaltern officer (Second Lieutenant or Lieutenant) with a small headquarters of a platoon sergeant and a runner. Four rifle platoons were grouped into a company commanded by a major or captain. Company headquarters also contained a Second-in-Command (normally a captain), a Company Sergeant-Major, a Company Quartermaster Sergeant, a Company Clerk, cooks and runners.

Four companies under a battalion headquarters formed the infantry battalion. It was commanded by a lieutenant colonel. His headquarters consisted of the battalion Second-in-Command (a major) who was the Commanding Officer's under study. Routine administration was handled by two captains, the Adjutant and the Quartermaster. The Adjutant was responsible for preparing orders, supervising dress and discipline and all matters dealing with personnel as well as overseeing the Orderly Room which dealt with routine orders and correspondence. He was assisted by an Assistant Adjutant (a lieutenant), an Orderly Room Sergeant, several clerks and the provost sergeant who commanded the Regimental Policemen.

The Quartermaster was responsible for all logistic and supply support for the battalion including food, forage, fuel, arms, clothing, ammunition, equipment and stores. He was assisted by his understudy, the Regimental Quartermaster Sergeant, and controlled the unit cooks, butcher, shoemaker, master tailor and postal non-commissioned officer. He also directed the Transport Officer (a lieutenant) who was responsible for all horsed transport, including the care of the animals, assisted by the Transport Sergeant ....

The Regimental Sergeant-Major was the connecting link between the non-commissioned officers and the men of the battalion and the commanding officer. He was responsible for drill, discipline and deportment as well as supervising all duty rosters and the Regimental Police.

Attached to the battalion headquarters was a Medical Officer from the Canadian Army Medical Corps, with a small staff of medical assistants, and a Chaplain from the Canadian Chaplain Services.[54]

The most important change, as far as the Tenth was concerned, also occurred in January. At the beginning of 1915, it seemed certain that the Battalion was destined to spend the war as a reinforcement unit, but the new year was only a few days old when its fate was dramatically altered. On 12 January, divisional headquarters ordered the Tenth to join the Second Brigade, which was losing its 6th (Fort Garry Horse) Battalion. A dismounted cavalry unit, the 6th had been slated since the middle of December to move to the reinforcement depot for the Canadian Cavalry Brigade, which was being formed at that time. The Battalion was informed of the imminent change as early as 19 December.

The Tenth was not the first choice of the Second Brigade's commander, Lieutenant-Colonel Arthur Currie. In a 4 January letter to General Alderson, Colonel Currie, after surveying the Fourth Brigade's four battalions, put in a claim for the 11th (100th Winnipeg Grenadiers), arguing that it was "the most efficient and best officered battalion in that brigade."[55] When his claim was rejected a few days later, he appealed the decision by writing a strongly worded letter on the sixteenth. "I do not believe the admission of the 10th Battalion to this Brigade would increase the efficiency of the brigade to the same extent as if the 11th Battalion were substituted for the 10th." Currie contended that "in no instance has anyone, outside the 10th Battalion, claimed that the 10th was ever the equal of the 11th," adding that even Colonel Boyle had complained that his officers were an "undersized and generally undesirable lot."[56] Currie's appeal was ignored, and on 20 January, the Tenth was ordered to vacate Sling Plantation and move to the Second Brigade's winter quarters at Lark Hill.[57] The change meant, of course, that the Tenth would be a combat unit. Although Currie was unhappy about the situation initially, he would never have cause to complain about the Battalion's performance on the battlefields of France and Flanders.

However, the Tenth found itself in an administrative limbo for several days. Colonel Boyle, in a 19 January letter to his new brigadier, requested the immediate return of the 234-man work party which had been recruited from the Battalion earlier in the month. "The absence of these men seriously interferes with battalion training and I would like to get them back as soon as possible, more especially as we are again going into the 4 company organization." Boyle was also concerned about his new accommodations at Lark Hill. "I believe that the huts now occupied by the 6th Bn. should be thoroughly cleaned before we move into them."[58] These were not unreasonable requests, but the letter was returned four days later, together with a frosty note from Currie's brigade-major, Lieutenant-Colonel Herbert Kemmis-Betty, suggesting that Boyle address his concerns to divisional headquarters, because the Tenth was not yet under the Second Brigade's jurisdiction.[59]

It was not until Monday, 25 January, that the Battalion formally came under the Second Brigade's orders. In the meantime, the Tenth had completed its move from Sling Plantation to Lark Hill; an advance party under the second-in-command, Major Joseph MacLaren, had shifted to the new quarters on the twentieth, and the rest of the Battalion followed the next day. On 26 January, the Tenth took part in its first field exercise with the Second Brigade, and

Colonel Currie inspected the Battalion on the twenty-eighth.[60] The brigadier's opinion of his newest unit is not recorded.

The change in brigades enabled the Tenth to obtain a brass band. The thirty-two-man band belonging to the 106th Winnipeg Light Infantry had received special permission from the militia minister, Sam Hughes, to go overseas attached to the 6th Battalion, under the mistaken impression that their former militia unit was going to be broken up. When the band realized that this was not going to be the case, every member signed a petition requesting they be allowed to transfer to the Tenth Battalion. "By some misunderstanding at Valcartier we were given to understand [that] the Regiment was to be broken up, but have since found out our old Regiment is still intact, viz., 10th Battalion, and we are most anxious to be returned to the old unit as their Band." Major Lightfoot, a former officer of the 106th, took up their cause, pointing out that the Winnipeg-based regiment had created this band "by the expenditure of much time and quite a considerable sum of money."[61]

Colonel Boyle appealed to the 6th Battalion's commander, Lieutenant Colonel R.W. Paterson. "I am willing to accept the transfer of these men," he informed Colonel Paterson on 12 November, "and would request you to consent to their transfer." Paterson refused, arguing that "we have gone to a very heavy expense in connection with the band, having purchased a number of new instruments and a large amount of new music, and it would be a great hardship at the present time to have them taken from us."[62] Boyle then referred the issue to his brigadier, Lieutenant-Colonel John Cohoe. "I feel that the band rightfully belongs to my battalion," he wrote Colonel Cohoe on 16 November. "The matter has reached such a stage that it can only be finally settled by the intervention of the G.O.C., 1st Canadian Contingent [i.e., General Alderson]."

A considerable delay ensued. Colonel Paterson went on sick leave in late November and early December and his absence tested the patience of divisional headquarters, which sought to resolve the tug-of-war between the two battalions. The conversion of the 6th Battalion to cavalry seems to have been the deciding factor. "It is difficult to see what further use the band will be to the Fort Garry Horse," Major Joseph MacLaren observed on 19 December, "& it will be of inestimable value to this Battalion."[63] General Alderson evidently agreed, and his headquarters subsequently informed the Second Brigade's Colonel Currie to transfer the band to the Tenth Battalion, which in turn was to reimburse the officers of the 6th for "any expenses to which they may have been put for the upkeep of the band."[64] The Tenth and its band, under Sergeant Thomas James, were united in early January. This episode, while minor, may explain Currie's initial prejudice against the Battalion.

An even bigger move awaited the Tenth Battalion and the rest of the newly formed Canadian Division. Throughout January, rumours had been flying that the Division would soon be going to France, and while no one was able to confirm the speculation, there were signs that the Canadians would soon see action. The most convincing indicator was the wholesale replacement of the Division's Canadian-made equipment in favour of British uniforms, leather harness, boots, entrenching tools, wagons, and motor vehicles; only the Ross rifle escaped the purge. Typically, the Tenth was one of the last battalions to be re-equipped, completing the changeover on 9 February.[65]

By then, confirmation of the imminent move to France had been received in the form of a second royal review, staged on Thursday, 4 February. It was a cold, wet, and windy day as the King and Queen, accompanied by their fierce-looking secretary of state for war, the legendary Lord Kitchener, inspected the Canadian Division. The Canadians were arrayed for more than two miles near Knight Down, within sight of Stonehenge. "I bid you God-speed on your way to assist my Army in the field," His Majesty declared in a message read to all units afterwards. "By your deeds and achievements on the field of battle I am confident that you will emulate the example of your fellow-countrymen in the South African War, and thus help to secure the triumph of our arms. I shall follow with pride and interest all your movements. I pray that God may bless you and watch over you."[66]

The Tenth Battalion, like the rest of the Canadian Division, spent the next few days making hectic last-minute preparations. On 7 February, the Battalion received its orders for the move to France,[67] and Colonel Boyle issued firm instructions regarding the conduct of the men: "When this unit moves overseas, the passage across the Channel will be treated by all ranks in all respects like a night march. No noise or lights will be permitted."[68] Two days later, the Tenth completed its issue of British-pattern equipment. That afternoon, the Battalion paraded in full marching order, and each man was issued 150 rounds of ammunition.[69]

The eagerly awaited move to France began on Wednesday, 10 February. Reveille at 4 a.m. marked the start of a busy day for the Tenth. Colonel Boyle departed first, reaching Amesbury at eight o'clock that morning and catching a train for Avonmouth, near Bristol, on England's west coast. The balance of the Battalion followed a few hours later, arriving in Avonmouth shortly before noon. Marching smartly from the train station to the docks, the Tenth boarded the steamer *Kingstonian*, a ship variously described as "an old ferry boat"[70] and "a cattle boat".[71] The men were aboard by the middle of the afternoon, but did not sail until five the next morning.[72]

Kingstonian was cramped, crowded, and uncomfortable. "The capacity of the boat was somewhere around four hundred and thirty passengers," recalled Sergeant Christopher Scriven. "That's all they were allowed to carry, but they packed on ... our own unit plus a small unit of Army Service Corps men",[73] a total of more than a thousand, all ranks.

Fortunately, the voyage to France was uneventful. En route, Colonel Boyle opened his disembarkation orders and found that the Battalion was headed for the port of Saint-Nazaire, on the Bay of Biscay; the most direct cross-Channel route, Southampton to Le Havre, was closed by a submarine scare. *Kingstonian* arrived at the mouth of the River Loire at six o'clock on Saturday morning, the thirteenth, and promptly ran aground on a sand-bar. "When the tide went down," recalled Corporal Charles Hatcher, "the boat was bumping on the sand!"[74] During the afternoon, the ship lost two anchors when it was buffeted by heavy winds, the residue of a severe storm which had swept across the Bay of Biscay on 12 and 13 February, delaying the arrival of the other transports by as much as two days. Finally, at four o'clock on Sunday morning, *Kingstonian* floated free of the sand-bar and docked at Saint-Nazaire soon after.[75]

By now, the men were miserable. Everyone was stiff and sore, and most were seasick, but the bulk of the Tenth did not disembark until the next day. Two platoons, under Lieutenants George Forneret and George Coldwell, disembarked as soon as space was made available on a train departing later that Sunday, rejoining the Battalion on 17 February.[76]

Meanwhile, some of the remaining troops landed the unit in hot water. It did not take long to discover an unguarded supply of rum sitting on the dock within easy reach of *Kingstonian*, and the temptation was too much to resist. "During the night," recalled Private Wally Bennett, the Calgary clerk-turned-machine-gunner, "some of the 10th boys got off the boat and 'tapped' some barrels of rum that were standing on the dock — filling water bottles and canteens with the free flowing rum."[77] However, Sergeant Chris Scriven maintained that the Tenth was innocent, blaming *Kingstonian's* contingent of Army Service Corps troops for raiding the rum. "We never saw any of the rum," Sergeant Scriven claimed, "that was the biggest joke of the lot. No body ever saw the rum. We were disembarked and marched right off the quay — we never ever saw rum or even smelled rum."[78] Divisional headquarters thought otherwise. The Battalion's behaviour was described by one staff officer as "disgraceful," and a fine of 900 francs – about $450 in Canadian funds — was levied.[79] Colonel Boyle strongly protested. "I have previously disputed the contention that the 10th Bn. is the guilty party in this matter," he wrote to the brigadier, Colonel Currie, requesting a court of inquiry.[80] It was held on 23 March, under the 14th (Royal Montreal Regiment) Battalion's commanding officer, Lieutenant-Colonel Frank Meighen. The adjutant, Major Dan Ormond, was among nine officers and fourteen other ranks who were called as witnesses, but the court upheld the fine.[81]

Disembarkation began at 7:30 a.m. on Monday, 15 February. Within an hour, the Tenth had vacated *Kingstonian* and assembled on the dock. From there it was an easy march to Saint-Nazaire's railroad station, where the officers boarded private rail cars. The other ranks, to their distress, discovered that they had traded one set of crowded quarters for another when they were herded onto small box cars with stencilled wording on the sides: "8 chevaux, 40 hommes." At noon, the train pulled out, and the Battalion was on its way to the vicinity of Hazebrouck, in French Flanders. It was a five-hundred-mile, forty-three-hour journey, and the train stopped just once, at Le Mans at midnight. Passing through Hazebrouck on the morning of the seventeenth, the Battalion was billeted by noon in the nearby village of Borre.[82] In the distance could be heard the rumble of artillery fire, and each night the sky was lit by spectacular fireworks displays, but it would be several days before the Tenth experienced its first taste of war.

On Saturday, 20 February, the Tenth was inspected by the commander-in chief of the British Expeditionary Force (BEF), Sir John French. Afterwards, the field-marshal commented approvingly of the Canadians: "They presented a splendid and most soldier-like appearance on parade. The men were of good physique, hard and fit. I judged by what I saw of them that they were well fitted and quite able to take their places in the line of battle."[83] The Canadian Division was attached to III Corps of General Sir Horace Smith-Dorrien's Second Army, one of two field armies in the BEF at this time. In order to indoctrinate the troops, the Division was divided into brigade groups, each attached to a British front-line division for a week. The Second Brigade Group, to which the Tenth Battalion belonged, temporarily joined the British 4th Division near Armentières and Ploegsteert — the latter was quickly dubbed "Plug Street" — from 21 to 28 February. The Tenth moved into the battle zone on the twenty-first, departing Strazeele at noon and marching to Romarin, where it moved into billets late in the afternoon.[84]

The next day, the Battalion received its initiation. During the morning of 22 February, while the Tenth was still in reserve well behind the front lines, two platoons, one each from A and B companies, were put to work digging trenches. They "came under heavy shellfire," according to the war diary. There were no casualties, but the episode marked "the first time the Battalion had men on duty under fire."

That evening, A Company, led by Captain Charles Robinson, moved into the front-line trenches held by the Royal Dublin Fusiliers, while Major William Nasmyth took B Company into the positions held by the Royal Irish Fusiliers. Both companies numbered six officers and 200 other ranks, and all escaped without injury. The next night, it was the turn of C and D companies. A and B companies marched back to billets, and Captain Lee Redman took five officers and 198 other ranks of C Company into the Dubliners' trenches, while Major James Lightfoot and D Company, five officers and 204 other ranks, went into the line with the 2nd Seaforth Highlanders. Again, there were no casualties.[85]

Most of the men shared Lieutenant Walter Critchley's feelings. "I was scared stiff, of course," he later admitted, "the same as everyone else, till you got settled down." Twenty-two-year-old Critchley, a noted polo player in the Calgary area, credited the British veterans for calming his fears. "They were a very hardy bunch," he recalled, "extremely brave men."[86] His batman, Private Victor Lewis, never forgot the words of encouragement offered by these British soldiers. "Come on now, straighten up," they told the newcomers from Canada. "Nothing to be afraid of."[87] Of course, there was much to be afraid of, but these two nights in the front lines proved to be a painless introduction to a new and strange kind of fighting: trench warfare.

Few so-called experts had anticipated this state of affairs. Most had forecast a quick end to the war which had begun on 4 August 1914 with Germany's invasion of Belgium, the violation of whose neutrality brought Britain and her Empire into the conflict on the side of France and Russia. The Germans, fighting a holding action on the Russian front, delivered through Belgium what they intended to be the knock-out blow against the French. The small Belgian army fought bravely but barely slowed the German juggernaut; the French, true to form, launched a series of ill-fated and bloody attacks in Alsace-Lorraine, the provinces lost in the Franco-Prussian War of 1870-71. While the Belgians and French reeled in the face of these reverses, the little BEF, which comprised the cream of Britain's pre-war army, arguably the best in the world at the time, moved into Belgium and fought its first skirmish near Mons on 23 August. Heavily outnumbered, the beleaguered British professionals — firing fifteen rounds a minute and setting the standards of excellence to which all members of the BEF, including the Canadians, would aspire — were soon forced to retire along with the Belgians and French. The Germans advanced towards Paris, only to be checked during the Battle of the Marne in early September.

Like dazed boxers, surprised and perlexed at having their best blows blocked, both sides attacked to exploit the only open flank. This resulted in the famed "race to the sea," which led to a great battle in October and November around the ancient city of Ypres, in Belgian Flanders. The consequences of the First Battle of Ypres were two-fold: it ensured that at least one small corner of Belgium would remain free,

It was supposed to be a short war. Most observers expected that it would be over by Christmas. The prevailing opinion was that the conflict would amount to little more than "six weeks' autumn manoeuvres with live ammunition," as one historian put it. In Berlin in early August, 1914, Kaiser Wilhelm II bade his troops farewell, telling them: "You will be home before the leaves have fallen from the trees."

Germany went to war under the shadow of the Schlieffen Plan. Drawn up in 1905 by Count Alfred von Schlieffen, it called for a holding action against Russia while crushing France with a decisive blow delivered via Belgium. Schlieffen, correctly anticipating that the French armies would rush into Alsace-Lorraine, the provinces which France lost in the 1870-71 war with Prussia, marshalled three-quarters of his strength on the right wing. Rolling irresistibly across Belgium into northern France, this powerful wing would sweep through Paris and scoop up the French forces attacking in Alsace-Lorraine.

Many military historians view the Schlieffen Plan as a masterpiece, a blueprint for certain victory had it been followed to the letter. In fact, according to the American writer S.L.A. Marshall, it was a "logistical absurdity," demanding superhuman efforts from the ordinary German footsoldiers who would have to execute it. While the Schlieffen Plan was modified somewhat by Schlieffen's successor, General Helmuth von Moltke, who weakened the right wing and reinforced the centre to face the expected French attacks in Alsace-Lorraine, it remained essentially intact when the war broke out.

France's master plan was even more flawed. Plan XVII — so called because it was the seventeenth in a series drawn up since 1875 — has been bluntly labelled "a piece of back-stairs jobbery" by the eminent British expert, J.F.C. Fuller. The French planned to do precisely what the Germans expected them to do, throw themselves into Alsace and Lorraine, regardless of what the Germans did.

The first weeks of the war unfolded much as the Germans planned. The tiny Belgian army withdrew into its powerful fortifications in Liège and other centres, only to watch the massive concrete defences reduced to rubble by giant Krupp howitzers. The Belgians retired to Antwerp, and the German juggernaut rolled across the flat countryside towards northern France. The French, in the meantime, stormed into Alsace-Lorraine, just as Plan XVII required them to do. At one point, they reached the River Rhine, but success was both fleeting and illusory. The French infantry, clad in Napoleonic red-and-blue uniforms and relying on their bayonets, were no match for German machine-guns and heavy artillery. By the third week in August, Plan XVII was a shambles, and much of the French army with it, and the French commander-in-chief, General Joseph Joffre, belatedly realized that he was in deep trouble.

It was a German error that saved the French from disaster. As his powerful right wing rolled into France — brushing aside the newly arrived British Expeditionary Force, 100,000 strong — General Moltke changed the direction of its advance. Paris lay at his mercy, but he chose to swing his right-hand armies in front of the French capital and attempt to roll up enemy forces reeling in disarray from their defeat in Alsace-Lorraine. The intended outflanking manoeuvre merely exposed the German flank to a counter-attack by the BEF and a hastily organized French army. The German advance was checked at the River Marne in early September, and by the fourteenth, the invaders had retired behind the River Aisne.

Moltke was sacked as a result of this setback. His place was taken by General Erich von Falkenhayn, who unsuccessfully tried to salvage what was left of the Schlieffen Plan.

The famed "race to the sea" ensued, as both sides tried to take advantage of the only open flank, culminating in the First Battle of Ypres in October and November 1914. The battle not only ensured that one small corner of western Belgium would remain free of German occupation, it also created the infamous Ypres salient, which would be the graveyard of hundreds of thousands of young men from Germany, France, Britain, and their respective empires. As the fighting died down for the winter, an unbroken line stretched from Switzerland to the North Sea, a distance of more than four hundred miles. It would take the generals a long time to realize it, but the war of manoeuvre had ended. In its place was siege warfare, twentieth-century style.

and it created a great bulge known as the Ypres salient, which protruded deep into enemy-held territory. The flat, forlorn salient would be a graveyard for hundreds of thousands of young men from all over the British Empire, not to mention France and Germany.

The Western Front had been born. In the wake of the First Battle of Ypres, the opponents dug in for the winter. From Switzerland to the North Sea, a distance of more than four hundred miles, stretched an unbroken parallel line of primitive trenches. German and Allied soldiers faced each other over no man's lands, a strip of land between opposing trenches and ranging in width from a few yards to a few hundred yards. The shallow entrenchments reflected the conviction of the respective high commands that this was a temporary situation, that open warfare would return with the fine weather in the spring of 1915. The generals were, of course, tragically wrong. Armies numbering in the millions, backed by machine guns and a stupendous terrifying arsenal of artillery. At the same time, they were hampered by inadequate communications and by limited means of transportation which restricted mobility. They were left with no flanks around which to manoeuvre. All this meant that there was only one way to bring this war to a conclusion — attrition.

There was dismay among the men of the Tenth Battalion when they saw the condition of the trenches. The adjutant, Major Dan Ormond, noted that "the rear of the trench would be a foot deep, and then what they'd cleaned out of there and thrown forward would make the parapet. In some places the men had got doors off ruined buildings and had built up mud or sandbags, and then that was looked on as a dugout. It probably was a slight protection from the weather, but no other protection."[88] Mud was everywhere, as combatants all along the Western Front were discovering. However, as Major Ormond pointed out years afterwards, the Canadians "were quite used to it after our experience on Salisbury Plain."[89]

One thing quickly learned was that death was a constant companion. Even between battles, there was the ever-present danger posed by enemy snipers, whose deadly aim the men of the Tenth soon respected and admired. Even deadlier was the German artillery, and the varying calibres of enemy shells were given nicknames. High explosives were dubbed "Black Marias," slang for British police patrol-wagons of the era, "Jack Johnsons," after the American boxer, or "coal boxes." Shrapnel shells were called "whiz bangs" or "Whistling Willies." Trench mortars (*Minenwerfen*) delivered "rum jars." Regardless of the name, the exploding shells caused terrible and often untreatable injuries, decapitating and maiming luckless victims with jagged pieces of steel.

Casualties were not long in coming. On 25 February, thirty-nine-year-old Private Wilson Davis became the first member of the Tenth Battalion to be killed in action, followed the next day by Sergeant Tony Knights, a popular, twenty-one-year-old photographer from Millarville, south of Calgary. During the same two days in the front line, the Battalion lost three other ranks who were wounded: Sergeant Walter Couchman and Privates Alexander Andrews and George Bryan. These were the first of the more than 4500 casualties suffered by the Tenth during the course of the war.[90]

The Battalion's initiation period ended at four-thirty on the morning of 28 February, when C and D companies came out of the line. Reunited, the Tenth learned that it was to rejoin the Second Brigade enroute to a new sector a short distance to the south. The next day, 1 March, the Battalion marched to Armentières, where it met the brigade in column of route. That afternoon, the Tenth took up billets in the village of Bac-Saint-Maur.[91]

The following afternoon, the Battalion was addressed by the divisional commander, General Alderson. For many men of the Tenth, this was their first close look at the fifty-five-year-old British officer. A small man with piercing eyes and a walrus moustache, Alderson was a veteran of thirty-six years in the army. Not very imaginative, he was nevertheless ideally suited to the task of turning the Canadian Division into an efficient fighting force. In his speech, he informed the troops that they were about to be entrusted with their own front-line sector (the Division was to join IV Corps in General Sir Douglas Haig's First Army) and offered some fatherly advice, urging the men to exercise caution and common sense in the trenches. "To lose your life without military necessity," he told them, "is to deprive the State of good soldiers." He concluded with a prediction that the BEF would soon be saying: "The Canadians never budge."[92]

The same day, the Tenth moved further south, to new billets in Fleurbaix. The Battalion would spend most of the month of March in this neighbourhood.

Its first tour of duty came three days later. On the night of 5 - 6 March, the Battalion took over front-line trenches near La Boutillarie. The trenches were "all correct," according to the war diary, and aside from the "usual shelling," nothing unusual happened during its three-day stay.

There were more casualties, of course. Lieutenant George Craggs, who had led the Tenth's detachment in the London parade in early November, had the dubious distinction of being the first officer casualty when he was wounded on the eighth. Eight other ranks were also injured, and one, Private Harry Adshead, later died in hospital. Even after the Battalion was relieved, on the evening of 8 March, it was shelled in its billets in Fleurbaix, and two more privates were wounded.[93]

Wednesday, 10 March, was an exciting day. The Tenth Battalion stood to arms as the British launched their first major offensive of the war, at Neuve-Chapelle, adjacent to the Canadian sector. Although the Canadians were not called into action, they did provide small-arms and artillery fire to distract the defenders facing them. The Tenth took part in this operation when it returned to the front lines.

The Battalion suffered heavy casualties due to enemy shelling during the next two days. Fourteen men were wounded, including Lieutenants Seymour Norton-Taylor and Alexander Thomson and Company Sergeant-Major Duncan Stuart. Private Adrien Vulleumier, a native of France, died of his wounds five days later.[94]

Although the Battle of Neuve-Chapelle started well, it ended in failure for the BEF. For the Canadians, it had dire implications. Their diversionary assignment revealed alarming problems with the Ross rifle, which jammed during rapid firing in combat conditions. Two of the Tenth's company commanders, Major Lightfoot and Captain Robinson, pinpointed the British-made ammunition as the culprit. "This ammunition sticks and it requires more than normal force to extract the cartridges; in many cases the men having to push the bolt back by using a foot."[95] Their comments were relayed to the Second Brigade's commander, General Currie*, who immediately urged an investigation, warning that "a serious interference with rapid firing may prove fatal on occasions."[96]

The men of the Tenth quickly lost confidence in the Canadian-made weapon. Many, at the earliest opportunity, traded their Ross rifles for Lee-Enfields left behind by British casualties. "When we got hold of one," a veteran recalled of the Lee-Enfield, "we had to keep our eye on it; in fact keeping our eye on it wasn't in it — we had to fasten it to our belt, or as sure as wink it would be swiped and a Ross put in its place."[97] Possession of the British rifle was strictly forbidden. In late March, Colonel Boyle ordered that all Lee-Enfields "are to be handed into Ordnance. No man in the Battalion is to be in possession of one." More emphatic instructions followed a few days later: "All L.E. rifles *must* be handed into Q.M. Stores by 9:00 A.M. tomorrow morning. Same will be replaced by Ross rifles."[98]

The Tenth was relieved on the evening of 14 March by the 8th (90th Winnipeg Rifles) Battalion, but its relief came too late for Lieutenant George Forneret. A few hours before the 8th arrived, a shell exploded near him in one of the trenches. He was unmarked, but his company commander, Major Lightfoot, observed that the incident "appears to have un-nerved Lt. Forneret to such an extent that a short time afterwards he reported sick." The subaltern collapsed on the way to see the medical officer, Captain George Gliddon, who concluded that Forneret was "suffering from Nervous Shock" and sent him to hospital.[99] In an era in which shell shock was not recognized as a valid medical problem, this must have been humiliating for young Forneret, who never returned to the Battalion.

Coming out of the front lines, the Tenth spent four days resting in Fleurbaix. Among the handful of men court-martialled for minor disciplinary problems, most of which concerned drunkenness and disorderly conduct, was Private Charles Bloxham. On 17 March, Bloxham was caught breaking into a Fleurbaix liquor store which had been placed out of bounds. In his defence, he claimed that he had merely climbed into the garden behind the store and, unable to find his way out, had been forced to break into the building. His record was against him, as he had been one of the soldiers implicated in the Saint-Nazaire rum episode.

Although he was sentenced to ninety days' Field Punishment Number One, in which a man was tied by the wrists and ankles to a wagon wheel for a prescribed number of hours, Bloxham would soon redeem himself.

The Battalion returned to the front lines on the evening of the eighteenth for another four-day stint. The one casualty was Private Thomas Burrow, an English-born veteran of the 103rd Winnipeg Light Infantry, who was fatally wounded.[100]

Routine ruled life in the trenches. Each morning, a half-hour before dawn, the troops stood-to, in anticipation of possible attack. This was followed by breakfast — thick slices of bread fried in bacon fat were a staple — cooked over an open fire, a practice abandoned later in the year due to a scarcity of firewood and to the fact that the smoke drew enemy fire. Movement in the trenches was kept to a minimum during daylight hours, the troops trying to catch a few winks in their primitive dugouts or attempting to clean themselves and their quarters. This was an exercise in futility, since lice were a well-established fact of life in the trenches. Dusk brought another stand-to, followed by a hot meal — stew, biscuits, and tea were typical menu items — and a quarter-ounce tot of "Service Rum, Diluted." With darkness came activity, as Sergeant John Matheson, a thirty-year-old Scottish-born banker from Medicine Hat, described in the following 20 March letter home:

> All our movements are made at night of course. Some nights it is quite exciting, bullets flying around in all directions. We have to do all the fatigue work during the night — packing rations and firewood, barbed wire, etc., into the trenches. … The German trenches are only four hundred yards from us at this point. The most exciting duties at present are when we go out in front of the trenches on listening patrols, endeavouring to find out what work is going on around the enemy's trenches; also improving our own wire entanglements and patching them up after being cut by the enemy. Of course we do this work at night on our hands and knees. There is a possibility of our being seen, in which case it's pretty warm work.[101]

Another nighttime activity was to shore up the trenches when they collapsed due to enemy shell fire or bad weather. It was work that required thousands of sandbags and, in the first few months of the war, there never seemed to be enough. "The sandbags were so scarce," recalled Sergeant Chris Scriven, "that we used to listen at night until we could hear a German work party working, and then we used to go out and swipe their sandbags, and the first piece of trench I

---

* Currie, like the other brigade commanders in the Canadian Division, had been promoted to brigadier-general in early March, conforming to ranks in the British army.

ever built was built with stolen sandbags from Fritzie."[102] "Fritz" was just one of the names they called the Germans. Others included "Heinie," "Jerry," "Hun," and "Boche."

The men of the Tenth took advantage of the enemy's close proximity to trade not only bullets but verbal barbs. "I remember one instance," related Private Sydney Metcalfe, "where there was a German hollered across about him living in Edmonton. He mentioned some of the names of the streets and buildings and so forth, and he said he was going back to Edmonton after the war. And the Canadian soldier is not backward in any way in using a little profanity, especially to the Germans, and I would not wish to repeat on here what actually was said [in reply]."[103]

The Battalion's tour of the trenches ended on Monday, 22 March, the day Private Burrow died of his wounds. Ahead were three weeks of rest and training before its return to the front lines and its first great battle. After its relief, the Tenth spent two days in billets in Fleurbaix before marching to Estaires, where it remained until early April. While at Estaires, the Battalion was joined by a draft of seventeen other ranks as replacements for recent casualties. On 30 March, the Tenth began an intensive training programme, which included entrenching, route marches, physical drill, and practice attacks in the formation utilized by the British army at this time: shoulder to shoulder, in waves thirty yards apart, bayonets fixed.[104] The Battalion would soon put its practice to good use.

A change of scenery was in store for the Tenth. On Monday, 5 April, the Battalion vacated its comfortable quarters in Estaires and marched northwards, into Belgium. Billets were provided in the village of Abelle, in Flanders, where the Tenth continued to train. On 10 April, it was inspected by General Alderson; the next day General Smith Dorrien, commanding the Second Army, arrived to inspect the four battalions of the Second Brigade. General Currie, the brigadier, noted in his diary that the "10th showed up very well"[105] — high praise, considering Currie's opposition to the Battalion's transfer to his command. After his inspection, Smith-Dorrien addressed the Canadians, expressing pleasure at their return to his army. He went on to say, as Lieutenant Walter Critchley recalled, "that evidently the Canadians were tired of the quiet life and needed to get into something worthwhile, and that we were going up where the enemy were more truculent. I'll never forget him saying that: 'They [are] more truculent.' And that statement I will back up one hundred per cent."[106]

The Canadian Division was headed for the Ypres salient, which had been created in the hard fighting of late 1914. Few could pronounce Ypres properly, and most Canadians distorted it, like their British brethren, to "Wipers." The Division, moving onto the left flank of V Corps, was to relieve the French 11th Division; two other French divisions would remain on the left of the Canadians while British formations held the line on their right.

The Tenth Battalion was among the first to move into the new sector. On the night of Monday, 12 April, Colonel Boyle and his company commanders — Majors Lightfoot and Nasmyth and Captains Redman and Robinson — joined their counterparts from the Second Brigade's other three battalions in the French-held front lines northeast of Ypres. Two days later, the Tenth moved into the salient. After lunch, the men boarded forty buses which carried them to Vlamertinghe. They marched the rest of the way, across the Canal de l'Yser and through Ypres, with its cobblestone streets and historic Cloth Hall, then through the villages of Saint-Jean and Wieltje and into the front lines accompanied by French guides. The relief was completed by four-thirty Thursday morning.[107]

Initially, the Tenth was one of three front-line battalions holding the Second Brigade's front. It was flanked on the left by the 7th (1st British Columbia Regiment) Battalion and on the right by the 8th (90th Winnipeg Rifles), but the latter unit was relieved by British troops on the night of 16 - 17 April. On the brigade's left was the Third Brigade, which moved into position on 15 - 16 April; the First Brigade remained in reserve in and around Vlamertinghe. At 10 a.m. on 17 April, General Alderson formally took command of the sector and issued a scheme of defence declaring that it was the Division's duty "to hold the front trenches at all costs and in the event of any trench being lost, to counter-attack at once."[108]

Defending these trenches would be difficult, because they were hardly worthy of the name. The Tenth Battalion's position, a 1500-yard front northeast of the village of Gravenstafel, was typical. To begin with, the trenches "were extraordinarily filthy," as the adjutant, Major Ormond, recalled. "Actually, they were paved with dead Germans. When you'd move, bubbles would come up from the dead men. And it was very smelly. There was one place in the trench where there was a hand dangling through the parapet — the men used to shake hands with it!"[109] Ormond described the defences in detail in the war diary:

These trenches were the most remarkable that we had seen up to this time and nothing of the kind have been seen since. The parapet, if such it might be called, varied in height and thickness from none at all to 2 feet, averaging on the top 12 to 14 inches. There were numerous dugouts, and these so filthy that our men could not occupy them.... The wire in front was useless, very little of any kind and a lot of that simply smooth trip wire. It was so meagre that one of the machine gun sections, when carrying a bundle of empty sand bags, walked through the wire and was on

19

Canadians training on Salisbury Plain: (above) bayonet practice and (below) skirmishing order.

his way to the German lines when halted by a German sentry....[110]

Ormond had a similar experience himself. During the Battalion's first night in the line, he and the second-in-command, Major Joseph MacLaren, set out to inspect the position. "We went right through our line before we knew it," Ormond recalled, "and we kept on going, and the first thing we knew, a Boche sentry stopped us, and he was thirty feet away!" The two majors dropped to the ground, separated, and crawled back to their own trenches without further incident.[111]

The most striking physical feature about this area, then as now, is its flatness. Ridges were mere ripples in the landscape, standing no more than fifty feet about the surrounding countryside. The key features in this narrative are Gravenstafel Ridge, between one and two thousand yards behind the Canadian front line and roughly parallel to it, and Mauser Ridge, a mile and a half long, running east-west above Ypres. The Canadian sector, just over 4000

yards in length, ran from Berlin Wood, 800 yards east of the hamlet of Gravenstafel, along the valley of the Stroombeek — a willow-lined creek, one of several in the vicinity. It continued to the Ypres-Poelcappelle road, which marked the junction with the 45th (Algerian) Division. Down this road lay the village of Saint-Julien, and 1000 yards to the west stood a six-acre oak plantation, Bois des Cuisiniers, or Kitcheners Wood. Other notable communities included the village of Wieltje, where the Second Brigade's main headquarters were located, and Pond Farm, the site of General Currie's advanced headquarters, or report centre. Mouse Trap Farm, a few hundred yards southwest of Kitcheners Wood, was the location of the Third Brigade's headquarters. Other important points included Locality C, a partially constructed strongpoint on Gravenstafel Ridge, and the General Headquarters Second Line, or GHQ Line, a reserve position constructed by the British. It consisted of a belt of barbed wire and a series of redoubts and shallow trenches which ran past Mouse Trap Farm and Wieltje and southwards.

The worst part was that fundamental weakness of any salient: the enemy, arrayed on three sides, could rake nearly every square inch of ground behind the British and French lines with shellfire. This advantage was enhanced by the German occupation of higher ground to the east, about Passchendaele, a place which would acquire an infamous reputation later in the war. From this vantage point, the Germans made movement within the salient in daytime virtually impossible, by skillfully employing their superior artillery. The defenders were further hampered by the Canal de l'Yser, which ran across the base of the salient and restricted passage in and out.

The Tenth Battalion found out firsthand what all of this meant to the men in the trenches. Three companies — A, D, and C, from right to left — held the

20

Battalion's front line, with B Company in reserve at a nearby farm. Thursday, 15 April, the first full day in the line, was grim. The troops spent most of their time "trying to keep out of sight of the enemy and not step, sit or lie down in filth left by their predecessors, and in becoming accustomed to the odor of sour ground and dead Germans." The enemy shelled the newcomers heavily, and Major Ormond noted with some bitterness that "when we 'took over' from the French, they informed us that they had lost less than 30 killed and wounded since Christmas; one company had not lost a man...." By the time the Tenth was relieved, on the night of 19 - 20 April, it had lost two privates, George Hall and William Watson, killed, and eleven others wounded, including Lieutenant Alexander Thomson, who had just recovered from being injured in early March, and Private Albert Hawkins, who had joined the Battalion with the draft at Estaires in late March.[112]

Carelessness was one reason for the casualties. As Major Ormond pointed out in the war diary, "our men would persist in looking about" and drawing fire. But they also had a lot of work to do strengthening the defences. On 15 April alone, 2500 sandbags had been brought up after dark and placed along the parapet and in dugouts "before midnight." Still, Ormond despaired of the position's overall weakness. In spite of the Battalion's best efforts, "we did not see how it could possibly be held if a determined effort was made to take it by a strong force."[113]

There were ominous signs that the Germans intended to do just that. The brigadier, General Currie, noted in his diary on 15 April: "Attack expected at night to be preceded by the sending of poisonous gases to our lines and sending up 3 red lights (reported by prisoner who came into French lines). Heavy shelling up to midnight but no attack."[114] Word of the imminent gas attack was received with disbelief and puzzlement at Tenth Battalion headquarters. "We didn't believe it," recalled Major Ormond. "We couldn't imagine civilized people using it [poison gas]. After all, they were bound by The Hague Convention."[115] No one, Canadian, British, or French, really understood what was meant by "poisonous gases," but for several days the German lines along the Ypres salient were shelled in a bid to detect the gas supplies. None were discovered and the Allied defenders relaxed, unaware that the Germans were just waiting for the right atmospheric conditions before launching their attack.

While the high command pondered the possibility of an enemy offensive against the salient, the Tenth Battalion went about the business of shoring up its defences. Clearly, it would be a challenge to hold this sector, but it was one which Colonel Boyle readily accepted. His confidence in the Battalion was evident in a letter written on 16 April:

We are now holding a position in the front line trenches in a very historic locality, where some of the bloodiest fighting of the war has taken place. I am writing in a 'dug-out' just in rear of the front line trenches. It certainly is a hot corner. The artillery on both sides shell at intervals both night and day. However, this battalion has earned the reputation of being able to hold its own, and I guess that we will be able to live up to it....

The German artillery is playing merry hell at this very moment, and the shells are shrieking and howling around, but not doing any particular damage. When they get too nasty, I phone back to our own artillery, and get them to plaster the German trenches in front of my section a bit. This usually brings them to a reasonable state of mind....

Well, I must close for this time. I will send this out with the party which brings up our ammunition and rations tonight.[116]

This was probably the last letter that Boyle ever wrote.

The Tenth's tour of the front lines ended on 19 April, when the Second Brigade rearranged its sector. The Tenth was relieved by the 5th (Western Cavalry) Battalion, while the 7th (1st British Columbia Regiment) on the left was replaced by the 8th (90th Winnipeg Rifles). The 7th moved into close support and the Tenth marched back to Ypres, where it was placed in brigade reserve.

Billeted in a warehouse on the north side of city, the Battalion enjoyed but a brief respite from the harsh reality of war. On 20 April, the Germans began a long-range bombardment of Ypres — the "Wipers Express," so-called, according to Major Ormond, because the screaming one-ton shells reminded the troops of London subway trains.[117] One explosion killed Private Alfred Hulme. When the shelling continued the next day, the Tenth vacated the warehouse and moved to a farm on the northern outskirts of Ypres.[118]

The stage was set for the Battalion's trial by fire.

Chapter Two

GLORIOUS MEMORY

(22 April - 5 May 1915)

O! Canada, Mistress of snows and of mountain,
Tears are the dew of thy prairies to-day;
Thy blood has gushed forth as it were from a fountain,
'Neath Belgium's sweet soil thy noble sons lay.
Gallant the "Charge" that made the world-story,
Fierce were the odds, but they knew not dismay,
Ever their fame will reflect in the glory
Of self-sacrifice, as they fell on the way.
— Private George Gilmore, Tenth Battalion[1]

Thursday, 22 April, was a glorious spring day in the Ypres salient — sunny and warm, with temperatures in the seventies, Fahrenheit. This gentle day marked the start of a heroic but horrifying experience for the men of the Tenth Battalion.

Late in the afternoon, the long-range shelling of Ypres, begun two days earlier, intensified. "The shell fire became so intense," recalled one of the Battalion's machine-gunners, Private Wally Bennett, "that the civilians in the City were forced to flee from their homes, taking with them what they could carry on their backs or what they could haul or push away in wheelbarrows, etc. There were some pitiful sights — civilians with the dead and dying, and their homes being razed to the ground."[2]

Ominous developments were taking place. Private Jack Davis later wrote of seeing "a queer sky" to the left, where the sounds of cannonading and musketry indicated "an attack was in progress."[3] Three of the Tenth's officers, Majors MacLaren and Ormond, and Captain George Gliddon, the medical officer, were enjoying a pleasant ride on horseback along the west bank of the Canal de l'Yser when the furious bombardment broke out in the French sector north of the Canadians. The trio spotted a "cloud of peculiar color (greyish, yellowish, greenish), darker near the ground and lighter in color on top."[4] This, they soon learned, was the poison gas they had been warned about.

Riding hard, MacLaren, Ormond, and Gliddon reached Battalion headquarters in time for a 5:15 p.m. officers' meeting summoned by Colonel Boyle. While the three riders described what they had seen,

the farmhouse was rocked by the nearby explosion of a one-ton shell that fell short of its intended target in Ypres. "The windows of the room in which we were gathered were smashed by the concussion," Ormond recalled.[5] Within minutes, orders arrived from Second Brigade headquarters. The Tenth was to parade at 6 p.m. "in marching order less packs," and report to Wieltje by seven-thirty "for work in the trenches."[6] The meeting broke up as the officers rushed out to round up their men, some of whom, like Private Bennett, were in Ypres, "having a walk around and dropping in having a beer in an estaminet."[7]

There was nervous excitement as the Battalion assembled. Falling in along the road to Saint-Jean, the men sang "O Canada" and "The Maple Leaf Forever," and Sergeant Charles Stevenson reported that they were "feeling as gay as if going to a picnic or a ball game."[8] Additional small-arms ammunition was distributed; each man carried 300 rounds. The unit's strength was 1022, all ranks,[9] but 200 of these were left behind in billets, to form a core around which the Battalion could rebuild in the event of disaster.

It was getting dark as the Tenth Battalion set off on what it proved to be a difficult march. "The road was being shelled," related Private Bennett, "and in places it was pitted with shell holes."[10] According to Major Ormond, "the road was packed with civilians and the French troops coming back — these were Turcos and Algerians. And there were some of them definitely very much distressed by the gas, which we didn't know yet what it was all about. That was the first of the two occasions when I ever saw troops keen to fight.* Our own troops were very much annoyed at

---

* The other occasion was in March 1918, when the Tenth Battalion marched to the aid of the beleaguered British who reeled in the face of that spring's great German offensive.

22

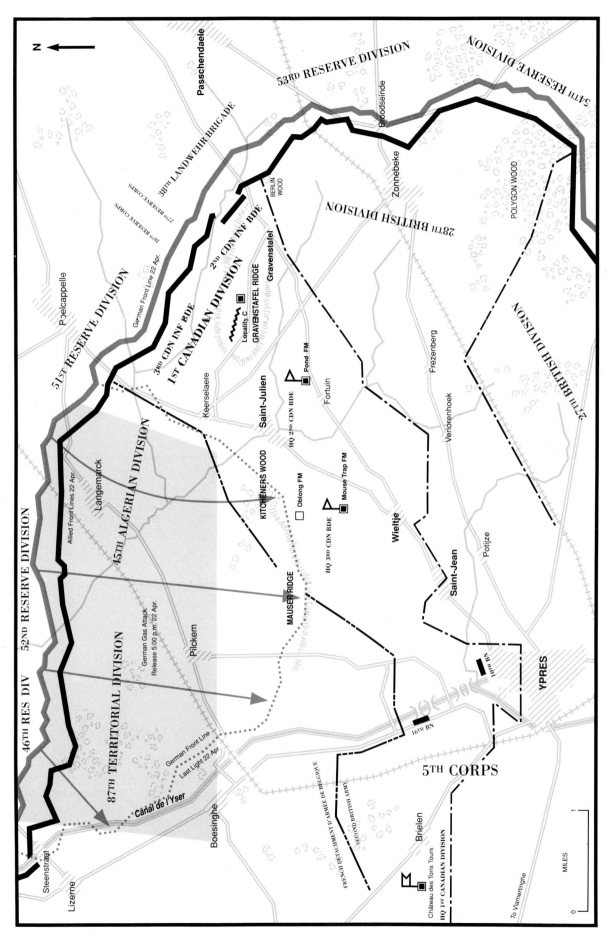

Ypres Salient, April 1915

23

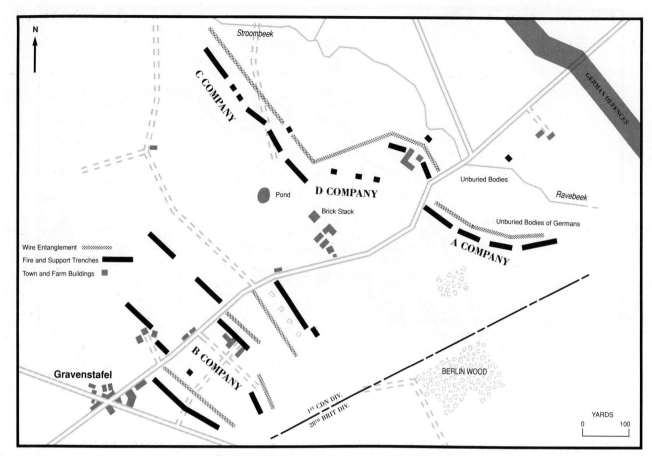

Ypres Salient: Tenth Battalion Sector, 14-19 April 1915

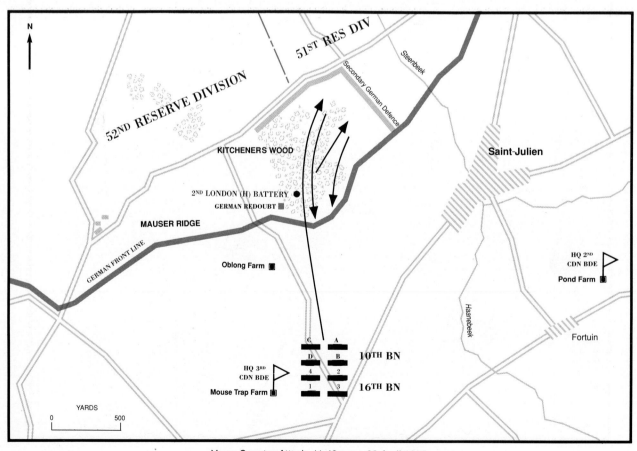

Ypres Counter-Attack, 11:48 p.m., 22 April 1915

24

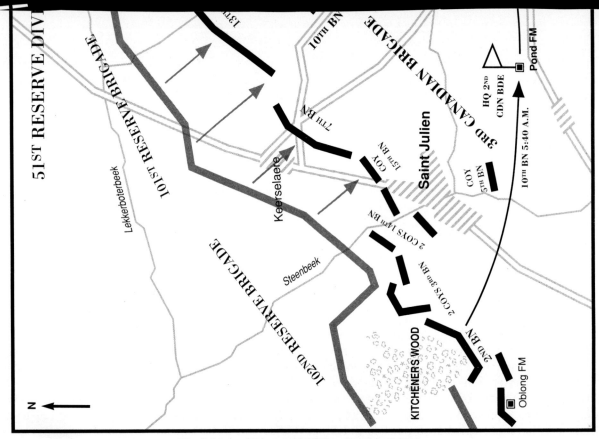

The Defence of Gravenstafel Ridge, 24-25 April 1915

the distress they saw among the civil population, particularly." The road was so crowded that Colonel Boyle and Majors MacLaren and Ormond rode their horses side by side at the head of the column in order to clear a path for the footsoldiers.[11]

The Battalion was witnessing a major military debacle. Attacking behind a cloud of chlorine gas, the Germans had routed the two French divisions holding the northern section of the salient. When the French fled, they opened a hole four miles wide in the Allied lines, exposing the left flank of the Canadian Division and endangering the rest of the salient. Fortunately for the Allied cause, this was strictly a limited operation and the Germans were unprepared to properly exploit a victory of this magnitude. Nevertheless, by early evening on the twenty-second, enemy forces had reached the Canal de l'Yser and the heights known as Mauser Ridge, from which they threatened Ypres and Saint-Julien in the Canadian rear. The Germans neglected to capitalize on their advantage, choosing instead to dig in, rather than continue the advance.

From Wieltje, Colonel Boyle rode ahead to the Second Brigade's advanced headquarters at Pond Farm. Meanwhile, Major MacLaren put the Battalion to work digging trenches in a field outside Wieltje. It

was dark by now, and while no one knew the precise extent of the disaster which had befallen the French, the men of the Tenth knew they were facing a serious situation. "From the sound of the the rifle fire, over to the left," remembered Private Bennett, "the Germans were not far away."[12] At least one man was injured by a stray bullet, but the enemy's fire was not the only problem. "The gas was very bad indeed," wrote Major Ormond, who noted that while the men worked their eyes watered, which was not surprising, considering that gas masks had not yet been invented.[13] "It was some job, since all we had were entrenching tools," recalled Private Jack Davis. "Some of us managed to dig knee deep, then came another order to fall in...."[14]

Colonel Boyle had returned from Pond Farm. The brigadier, General Currie, gave him instructions to take the Tenth and report to the neighbouring Third Brigade, whose left flank was directly endangered by the French collapse. In a note to Brigadier-General Richard Turner, the Third's bespectacled, gentlemanly commander, Currie suggested a defensive role for the Tenth. He proposed that it be deployed in the wide gap between Saint-Julien and the original front line. With the Battalion on the march once again, Boyle, accompanied by Major MacLaren and Ormond and

26

Sergeant A. W. "Wally" Bennett
Courtesy Glenbow Archives, Calgary/NA-4732-1

Scottish) Battalion, which was still en route. Impatient, Turner sent a staff officer, Captain Harold McDonald, to guide the Tenth into an adjacent field. "I regretted placing 10th in front," the brigadier later explained, "but they arrived first, and I prepared them to make the counter[-attack] if necessary alone. Time was urgent."[16]

The Third Brigade issued its final operational orders at 10:47 p.m. "10th and 16th Bns in that order will counter attack at 11.30 p.m.... Attack on frontage of two companies. Remaining 6 companies in close support at 30 yards distance on same frontage."[17] It was a familiar formation, having been practised by the Tenth since its arrival on the Continent; no one questioned its practicality in the face of massed machine-gun fire.

The Battalion, 816-strong, formed up quickly. In the lead, on a 300-yard front, were A and C companies on the right and left respectively. B and D companies were behind, each company in two ranks twenty yards apart, with thirty yards separating each two-company wave. By ten past eleven, the Tenth stood ready and waiting. The 16th Battalion, each of its companies wearing a different kilt, had begun assembling in the same formation directly to the rear. C Company's commander, Captain Redman, observed that the troops "were very quiet, but keen. Discipline was perfect."[18]

the four company commanders, went to Mouse Trap Farm, location of General Turner's headquarters.

There the situation was chaotic. The farm had once been comfortably to the rear; now it was practically in the firing line. The Germans were only a few hundred yards away, and bullets were hitting the moat-enclosed farm buildings. Inside brigade headquarters, C Company's Captain Lee Redman, a darkly handsome, twenty-five-year-old lawyer with the prestigious Calgary firm of Lougheed and Bennett (the former was Sir James Lougheed, grandfather of the future Alberta premier, while the latter was Richard Bedford Bennett, the future prime minister of Canada), noted the surreality which accentuated the tension. "An artillery officer who had completely lost his memory was sitting at the table eating sandwiches and making irrelevant remarks."[15]

Captain Redman and his fellow officers of the Tenth discovered that General Turner, rather than placing the Battalion in a defensive position, had a much different role in mind for it: a counter-attack, the first major offensive operation by Canadian troops in the Great War. Turner had been ordered by divisional headquarters to make the assault on the nearby oak plantation — soon to be famous as Kitcheners Wood — on the east end of Mauser Ridge, overlooking both Saint-Julien and Mouse Trap Farm. To carry out this attack, Turner decided to use the Tenth, along with his own reserve unit, the 16th (Canadian

Captain D. Lee Redman (in uniform of lieutenant
in 103rd Calgary Rifles)
Courtesy Glenbow Archives, Calgary/NA-2362-1

The Germans had been plotting the destruction of the Ypres salient for several months.

The winter of 1914-15 had been quiet on the Western Front, highlighted by the fraternization between British and German soldiers at Christmas — to the mortification on the high commands on both sides. In drawing up their plans for the 1915 campaign, the Germans had decided to take the offensive against the Russians in the east, while maintaining a defensive stance in the west, with spoiling attacks to keep the British and French off balance. One of these minor operations was the attack on the Ypres salient in April.

As early as December 1914, General-Colonel Duke Albrecht of Württemberg, whose Fourth Army was responsible for this sector, had considered a limited, corps-sized offensive against Langemarck and Pilckem, in the northern part of the salient. In January 1915, it was succeeded by a more ambitious plan, which involved the introduction of a chemical weapon, poisonous chlorine gas.

All major powers had been conducting chemical-warfare research, despite international agreements, notably The Hague Convention of 1907, which banned the use of "poison or poisoned weapons" in time of war. While the British had rejected the use of such weapons, both the French and the Germans had experimented with them since the outset of the Great War, with inconclusive results. But Germany's large dye industry provided a considerable quantity of chlorine gas, and scientists had developed a method of employing it on the battlefield. Stored in cylinders until its release, the heavier-than-air gas formed a cloud which, propelled by a favourable wind, was supposed to drift across the enemy lines and incapacitate the defenders.

The original plan had called for a gas attack against the salient's southern sector, which had been taken over by the BEF. Six thousand cylinders were installed opposite the British lines in early March, but, when the necessary wind failed to materialize, the Germans decided to attack the French-held north half of the salient instead. By 11 April, 5730 cylinders were in position along a front of just over three miles. This was strictly a limited operation, designed to test the gas as a weapon and to provide a diversion for German troops departing for the Eastern Front. Because of the operation's limited nature, Duke Albrecht's Fourth Army was not allocated the reserves it would require in the event of success.

It was not until the afternoon of 22 April that the Germans got the breeze they had been waiting for, and their assault on the French was a complete surprise. Two divisions on the immediate left of the recently arrived Canadian Division were routed, and the Germans poured through a gaping hole in the Allied lines. It was one of the few occasions in the entire war that either side achieved a clear-cut breakthrough.

Fortunately for the Allied cause, the Germans failed to take advantage of their victory. For a few tantalizing hours, the salient was theirs for the taking, and with it, four British divisions and most of their artillery and support services. But the enemy allowed this golden opportunity to slip away. The attacking troops followed orders and, having reached most of their immediate objectives, dug in for the night. While the possibility of the Germans reaching the Channel ports was remote — the threat was exaggerated by wartime propaganda and perpetuated by many historians — the fact remains that a crisis of major proportions faced the BEF, including the division of untried Canadians whose flank and rear were exposed by the French defeat on the left.

The German commander, Albrecht, believing that the British position in the salient was untenable, and assuming that Ypres would be abandoned, made the mistake of overreaching himself and his limited resources. Instead of focusing his efforts on 23 April on the destruction of what was left of the salient, Albrecht hoped to score an even bigger victory than the one he had apparently achieved. He looked towards Poperinghe, six miles west of the Canal de l'Yser, as his next objective.

Albrecht committed a cardinal sin when he underestimated his opponents. Reinforcements were rushed to the salient and a series of counter-attacks were staged by Canadian and British units, beginning with the famed assault on Kitcheners Wood by the Tenth and 16th (Canadian Scottish) battalions on 22-23 April. While the British attacks failed to gain much ground, they forced the Germans onto the defensive and thwarted Albrecht's designs.

Late on 23 April, Albrecht was ordered by the German high command to forget about Poperinghe; his primary objective must be the battered, shrunken salient around Ypres. In order to regain the initiative, he resorted to the weapon which had proven so effective against the French. Following a cloud of yellow-green chlorine gas, Albrecht's troops stormed the beleaguered, V-shaped Canadian line on the morning of 24 April. The Germans broke into the Canadian defences, but were unable to smash them, despite the gas and an enormous advantage in manpower, artillery, and position.

The stubborn Canadians suffered grievous losses, but only grudgingly gave ground. More British reinforcements arrived and there were more costly counter-attacks, all of them piecemeal, poorly supported operations. Sporadic fighting continued until the end of May, but the Germans failed to destroy the salient. Their opportunity had vanished by the early-morning hours of 26 April, when the heroic Canadians were withdrawn from the front lines.

Aside from the Canadian stand, poison gas was the legacy of the Second Battle of Ypres. The Canadians, by holding firm in the face of this horrific weapon, robbed it of much of its psychological value; it became, in the words of Canada's official history, "only another of the known horrors of War." Its effectiveness was considerably reduced by the introduction of primitive respirators and, later, by more sophisticated gas masks. Still, both sides continued to use gas until the war ended, in the cloud form employed at Second Ypres, in artillery shells, and in special projectors.

Foul-smelling chlorine was succeeded by phosgene which was colourless, just as rank, and twice as deadly. As well, several irritants were used, notably mustard gas, a colourless blistering agent which caused 90 per cent of British gas casualties. One of the many German victims of British mustard gas was a twenty-nine-year-old corporal in the 16th Bavarian Reserve Infantry Regiment. Temporarily blinded, his face swollen and throat raw, he lived to fight another day. His name was Adolf Hitler.

A grimly determined Colonel Boyle walked among his men. "We have been aching for a fight," he told them, "and now we are going to get it."[19] An admiring private, Algernon Dowty, later called the colonel "one of the bravest men I have ever seen."[20]

It was an occasion for inspiring words. Also present was a chaplain from Montreal, Frederick George Scott, an honorary major who was two weeks past his fifty-fourth birthday. Nominally a member of the 15th (48th Highlanders of Canada) Battalion from Toronto, Major Scott had tagged along with the 16th Battalion as it made its way forward. Now, Scott circulated among the ranks offering words of encouragement: "It's a great day for Canada, boys."[21] The heroic words would soon be matched by deeds.

Colonel Boyle huddled with his officers. "There was sufficient light to see what we had to do," wrote Major Ormond. Five hundred yards to the north stood the shadow-shrouded wood. To the left was Oblong Farm, "and a consultation was held about sending a party to clear it as we were satisfied that this house would contain machine guns but on re-reading the order it was decided that this was not our job and would be attended to by someone else."[22] It was a decision Colonel Boyle would not live to regret.

At eleven-thirty, the Tenth Battalion's officers were joined by their kilted counterparts from the 16th, including the commander, Lieutenant-Colonel R.G. Edwards Leckie. Synchronizing their watches, they agreed to launch the attack as soon as the Canadian Scottish were ready. At this time, Lieutenant-Colonel Garnet Hughes arrived from Third Brigade headquarters. The presence of Colonel Hughes, who was the son of the militia minister, Sam Hughes, and was celebrating his thirty-fifth birthday this day, added little to the preparations. As General Turner's brigade-major, Hughes should have been much more helpful, but he merely pointed out the objective, which everyone could see, and told Colonels Boyle and Leckie to follow the North Star and proceed when they were ready.

The two battalions were to pay dearly for the hurried arrangements. There had been no time for a proper reconnaissance of the ground, and artillery support was negligible; only thirteen British and Canadian 18-pounders were available, and the gunners had no specific targets. Indeed, the element of surprise was the only hope for success in this attack; only time would tell if that would be sufficient.

It was eleven-forty-five by the time the 16th Battalion was finally assembled. At 11:48 p.m., the whispered order to advance was issued. "Believe me, there was some excitement in the ranks," wrote Sergeant John Matheson. "We didn't seem to realize what we were up against."[23] Fifteen hundred Canadians, standing shoulder-to-shoulder, bayonets fixed, started forward on their date with destiny.

The shadowy oak trees loomed in the near distance. "Not a sound was audible down the long waiving [sic] lines but the soft pad of feet and the knock of bayonet scabbards against thighs," Major Ormond later wrote in the war diary, with one eye clearly on posterity. The adjutant, with Colonel Boyle and Major MacLaren, followed the last wave.[24]

Four hundred yards. Aside from the occasional and apparently random bursts of small-arms fire from the wood, there was nothing to indicate that the enemy defenders knew that they were about to be attacked.

Three hundred yards. The Canadians were nearly half-way up the freshly ploughed, barely perceptible slope. "The lines went steadily ahead," wrote Lieutenant William Lowry, "as if they were doing a drill manoeuvre."[25]

And then, trouble. Two hundred yards from the wood, the attackers reaped the bitter harvest sown by the failure to reconnoitre. "A hedge was unexpectedly encountered," related Major Ormond;[26] four to six feet high, with a thick strand of barbed wire threaded through, it was a serious obstacle. "There was no talking, not a word," commented Ormond, in obvious admiration of Canadian discipline, but the snapping twigs and branches and the crunching of dead leaves, as well as the clatter of "entrenching tool[s] and bayonet scabbards and the rifle butts made a great deal of noise."[27] The front rank of the Tenth Battalion broke through the barrier, reformed smartly, and resumed the advance. The following waves did likewise, but the jig was up.

A flare fluttered skywards from the enemy lines. Turning night into day for agonizingly long seconds, the flare revealed the oncoming Canadians in their mass formation.

Moments later, they were engulfed in a storm of machine-gun and rifle fire. Instinctively, they threw themselves to the ground and returned the fire, but they did not lie low for long. "Come on, boys," called D Company's Major James Lightfoot, "remember that you're Canadians."[28] At this, the men of the Tenth gave what Sergeant Charlie Stevenson called "a real British yell,"[29] and charged.

No man who experienced it ever forgot the ensuing scene. "The wood seemed to be literally lined with machine guns," recalled a banker from Medicine Hat, Sergeant Matheson, "and they played these guns on us with terrible effect. Our men were dropping thick and fast."[30] Bullets raked the leading waves of the Battalion not only from the front but from the flank as well, a result of Colonel Boyle's failure to neutralize Oblong Farm to the left. The noise was nearly deafening. "It was almost impossible to be heard," said Captain Redman, the Calgary lawyer who was still at the head of C Company, despite a shattered left arm.[31] The bullets sounded like a "hailstorm on a zinc roof," recalled an unidentified NCO, who noted that "somehow a few of us were missed, while other fellows were cut in half by the stream of lead."[32]

The survivors marvelled at their escape from near-certain death. Sergeant Matheson was "hit by a rifle bullet in the cheek and a piece of shrapnel in the side.... I have bullet holes in my hat, equipment and clothes, but evidently I am slated to do some more evil in this world yet," he wrote soon after the battle.[33] "I went through the charge," related a fellow sergeant, "but with my proverbial luck was not touched. Why, I do not know. Men fell all around me. It was a ghastly sight. Our dead and wounded were lying in heaps."[34] Added another unidentified NCO: "What a life! what an escape! Really I ought to be a stiff — way out there on our battlefield — because I said my prayers and prepared for the inevitable bullet to do its worst, but nothing came except one clean through my hat. I saw

stars with a jerk, thought I was hit, but nothing doing...."[35]

Private David Gordon was not so fortunate. Scottish-born, the twenty-one-year-old Gordon was an accountant in Saskatoon, where he enlisted in August 1914. Travelling to Valcartier as a member of the 105th Saskatoon Fusiliers, he transferred to the Tenth Battalion in late September. Now, Gordon was one of the first to fall, badly wounded by a bullet in the leg.[36]*

The losses were staggering, but the Tenth pressed forward relentlessly. "It charged just as coolly as if it was doing the thing on parade," recalled a proud Lieutenant Lowry.[38]

Not many men were left, but there were enough to reach the objective. Along the southern edge of the wood was a shallow trench dug by the Germans, and Major Ormond estimated that "less than a minute" was required to take it "with bayonet and butt." The trench was, according to Ormond, "filled with dead and wounded," but few Canadians paused to admire their bloody handiwork. The two battalions, by now utterly intermixed, surged into the wood twenty-five yards beyond. Although most of the Tenth's officers, including all four company commanders, were casualties, "the men were thoroughly aroused," to use Ormond's phrase.[39]

More hand-to-hand combat ensued. Dozens of desperate, individual battles took place among the bullet-splintered oak trees which hid a number of sandbagged machine-gun posts. "It was all so mixed up you just didn't know for anything," recalled Private Sydney Cox. "That's where I got the biggest scare of my life. I went into a little bit of a hut there. I went to go in, and a great big German stepped out, and he may've been going to surrender, I couldn't tell you, but I got out of there in a hurry. I pulled the trigger and ran."[40]

Somewhere in the wood, the attack lost direction, veering to the right. This was understandable, considering the confusion and darkness and danger, but Major Ormond later blamed it on the handful of French troops who accompanied the Tenth in the attack. "They were good troops," Ormond said of the red-and-blue-clad Algerians who, the adjutant theorized, were anxious to recapture their line to the northeast and so steered the Canadian attack that way.[41]

It was all over by midnight. The first major Canadian attack in this war had been a success. In less than fifteen minutes, the Tenth and 16th battalions, with little artillery support and only partial surprise, had stormed and seized a semi-fortified position held by seasoned German troops flushed with victory. Major Ormond contended that "hundreds" of Germans

---

* When he recovered, Private Gordon did not return to the Tenth but instead transferred to the British army. As a lieutenant in the 12th Royal Scots, he was killed at the Somme on 1 July 1916.[37]

The Tenth Battalion wins undying fame: the night attack on the wood near Saint-Julien, 22 April 1915.

Courtesy The Times History of the War

"desired to surrender but owing to the fewness of the attackers and the large numbers of the enemy and the fact that some of the enemy continued to shoot, very few prisoners were taken and many lives were lost by the enemy forces." Among the handful of prisoners was a wounded colonel.[42] The captured Germans belonged to two regiments,* the 2nd Prussian Guards and 234th Bavarian, indicating that the Canadian attack had hit the junction of these formations, always a vulnerable point in a defensive position.

One prisoner paid the Tenth Battalion an impressive compliment. He muttered to his captors as he was led to the rear, "You fellows fight like hell."[43]

The Canadians made a surprising discovery. A short distance inside the wood stood four British guns, the 2nd London Heavy Battery, which had been captured by the Germans earlier in an evidently bloody fight. The 4.7-inch guns "were piled high with dead, British, Turcos, and German," related Major Ormond, who felt that "it would have been impossible to have recovered and removed these guns," pointing out "that men hauling [them] would at all times have been under heavy machine gun and rifle fire, and the necessary ropes and tackle were not available...."[44] The disabled guns were later abandoned.

Private Sydney Cox, his nerves still rattled by his close call in an enemy dugout, went looking for the rest of the Battalion. Except for a small group of riflemen, he "couldn't find anybody," and for a while he "thought we were all alone." While searching for some familiar faces, Private Cox and his comrades "found a beautiful horse" in the wood. It was, he recalled, "a lovely pack horse — belonged to a German colonel or something or other — and there the poor devil was tied up, and when I let him go, we didn't know what we were going to do with him. 'Gee, it would be nice to have this to ride!' Lovely animal. I don't know what happened to him."[45]

The immediate task facing the Canadians was to consolidate their gains. It was already obvious that it would be difficult, if not impossible, to hold the wood. They had punched 1000 yards into enemy-held territory, and with both flanks now in the air (exposed and unprotected), Major Ormond said, "we were subjected to fire from all directions except S.E."[46] The fire was hot, indeed. "The trouble there was that you didn't know where you were," recalled Corporal Charles Hatcher, "because the bullets were coming from all ways."[47] Sergeant Chris Scriven, a twenty-three-year-old electrician, agreed. "You couldn't lift your head there, there was — wham! — something'd come at you."[48]

Sergeant Scriven, sent out to reconnoitre, had another brush with death that night. Accompanied by

---

* A German regiment was the equivalent of a Canadian or British brigade.

twenty-nine-year-old Corporal Jack Wennevold, a carpenter from Kenyon, Minnesota, Scriven set out across a field toward a small cluster of trees in hopes of locating the enemy lines. In the middle of this field, they were startled by a flare that was fired right in front of them. Stopping in their tracks, Scriven and Wennevold saw a German officer, holding a flare gun, a mere ten feet away. Incredibly, he failed to spot the motionless Tenth Battalion NCOs, and as soon as the light flickered away, they made a mad dash for safety.

They did not get far. Several shots rang out, and Corporal Wennevold staggered. "I'm hit," he grunted as he fell into Sergeant Scriven's arms.

Scriven was horrified by Wennevold's wound. A bullet had left him "ripped open from stem to stern," across the stomach. The sergeant carried the corporal to the shelter of the trees, where he stuffed field dressings into the wound to staunch the flow of blood, binding the dressings with Wennevold's puttees. Thanks to Scriven, the American survived to make a notable contribution to the Battalion's exploits in the summer of 1917.[49]

On the far side of the wood, the two battalions gradually sorted themselves out. The Tenth, under Major Ormond's supervision, shifted to the left and manned a line along a hedge, while the 16th moved to the right. The position was weakly held and dangerously exposed, and Ormond must have known, even

as he deployed his men, that they would not be able to stay here for long.

After overseeing this manoeuvre, Ormond set out to report to Colonel Boyle. Making his way through the bullet-riddled wood, he returned to the captured trench. There he discovered a furious fire-fight taking place between a small party of Canadians — thirty-four in all, most of them Highlanders belonging to the 16th Battalion — and a German redoubt located in the southwest corner of the wood. "We have you surrounded; surrender," the enemy taunted, in good English.[50]

Major Ormond quickly organized an attack. He detailed Lieutenant William Lowry, still in action despite a bullet wound in the thigh, with "8 or 10" men, to outflank the heavily defended post, while Ormond took advantage of the diversion to lead a frontal assault.

It failed miserably. Lieutenant Lowry quickly deployed his men along the edge of the wood. As he later related, he made them "lie down and familiarise themselves with the ground in front and the location of the German redoubt." Lowry quickly completed his preparations for the attack:

For a few moments all was quiet, the Germans not firing a shot nor throwing any flares. In the redoubt I distinctly heard the levers of machine

Post-war view of Kitcheners Wood

Sergeant Walter Goodfellow (shown as a corporal
in the 103rd Calgary Rifles, June 1914)
Courtesy Glenbow Archives, Calgary/NA-4902-1

guns being worked backwards and forwards testing their action.

Then we opened fire, and the bomb throwers commenced throwing their bombs. I could see that these were falling short. Our rifle fire was ineffectual and weak owing to the jambing [sic] of the bolt in our rifles by the use of British ammunition issued to us. The Germans opened a murderous fire on us with their rifles and machine guns.

Yet with a yell and "at 'em Canadians" we charged, but before we could reach half the distance to the redoubt, practically all our men were mown down. Of my party I think there was only one man besides myself who was not bowled over.... It was useless to go further. I made my way back to the other trench in the blazing light of German flares and rifle fire.[51]

He found that a similar fate had befallen Major Ormond's group. Ormond reported that he had lost "14 to 18" men in a matter of moments.[52] The major called off further efforts, and ordered the survivors to dig a cross-trench, 200 yards long, facing the redoubt. This would minimize the enemy's enfilade fire, which was exceedingly dangerous, as Lieutenant Lowry discovered at that moment. "Just as I ... commenced speaking to Major Ormond," he later wrote, "enemy Machine Gun bullets from the redoubt cut me across the small of the back, slashing my clothing as if done by a buzz-saw and laying me out." But Lowry was far from finished. "Upon ascertaining that I could move, I volunteered to take word back to Headquarters, advising them of our position, and asking for support on our flanks. Major Ormond asked me to do so if I could make it." Lowry set out in the darkness, crawling "over the ground strewn with our wounded and dead." Assisted by a Canadian engineer, he reported to General Turner and Third Brigade headquarters. Only then did he seek medical attention.[53]*

By this time, Ormond was the acting Battalion commander; Colonel Boyle had been severely wounded shortly after midnight. While the time of his injury can be approximated, it is impossible to state with certainty the circumstances of the unfortunate event, because there are at least three versions. The most common states that Boyle, receiving a message from the 16th Battalion, turned on his flashlight and drew fire from a German machine-gun.[54] For a soldier of his experience, that would seem to be a remarkably careless act. Another version came from Corporal Charles Hatcher, who claimed to have been standing beside the colonel when he was shot. "We'd overrun some Germans in a hedge," Corporal Hatcher explained, "and we didn't know they were in the hedge in the dark, and one of these Germans noticed Colonel Boyle — I guess he noticed he was an officer — and he shot him." The Germans in the hedge, said Hatcher, "got the same as the colonel got."[55] Sergeant Arthur Martin also claimed to have been with Boyle. When all of his company's officers were killed or wounded, Sergeant Martin sought out the colonel for further instructions. "I'll come over and have a look," said Boyle, who followed the sergeant towards the wood. En route, the colonel was hit by a burst of machine-gun fire, but retained consciousness long enough to issue orders: "Now, Martin, almost all officers are gone; here's your chance. I want you to get what men you can and charge that wood."[56]**

Whatever the circumstances, there can be no doubt of the results. "The colonel got five bullets from a machine-gun in his left groin — made a wonderful pattern in a radius of two and a half inches," recalled Major Ormond.[58] Major MacLaren, the second-in-command, was in little better shape, having been hit in the leg during the charge. Unable to act in Boyle's place, the major volunteered to assist the colonel to the rear. As Boyle and MacLaren limped into the night, command of the Tenth devolved on the inexperienced adjutant, Dan Ormond.

One of his first tasks was to supervise a withdrawal. Around two-thirty in the morning, the 16th Battalion's Colonel Leckie, the senior officer at the scene, decided that it would be impossible to hold all

---

* Lowry did not return to the Tenth. Instead, he went back to Calgary and raised a reinforcement battalion, the 82nd, which he commanded with the rank of lieutenant-colonel. Three other injured officers, all company commanders, were also promoted: Major Nasmyth raised and commanded another reinforcement unit, the 89th Battalion, while Major Lightfoot did the same with the 222nd Battalion. Captain Robinson later commanded the 187th Battalion and was named an Officer of the Order of the British Empire.

** Sergeant Martin was wounded in the face and shoulder soon afterwards, but he crawled a mile to a dressing station, where he collapsed. When he awoke, he was in hospital in Boulogne. Martin recovered from his injuries and ended the war as a captain in the Tenth.[57]

of the captured ground. He ordered the two battalions to fall back to the trench on the southern edge of the wood. It proved to be a difficult manoeuvre, not because of German shells and bullets, but "because our own fellows wouldn't believe it was us, and they were shooting at us," recalled Private Sydney Cox, who had already had one nerve-racking experience that night. "You would holler at them, and, 'Oh, we've heard that, you can't fool us.' Hardest time trying to convince our own fellows that we were Canadians."[59] However, the troops in the trench were eventually convinced to hold their fire, and the withdrawal was carried out. Left behind were the four British heavy guns recaptured a few hours earlier; Canadian engineers detonated the stockpiles of ammunition before abandoning the battery.

Also left behind were a handful of dead, wounded, and prisoners of war. Perhaps a dozen members of the Tenth were listed as "Missing" as a result of the battle in the wood, and their bodies were never recovered. These included Sergeant Walter Goodfellow, a former member of the 103rd Calgary Rifles, who had been among the first to volunteer for overseas service when the war began. All told, twenty-eight Tenth Battalion men were captured by the Germans. It is a significant statistic, considering that the Battalion lost only thirty-five prisoners in the entire Great War. Two captains, George Coldwell and Thomas Fryer, fell into enemy hands, along with twenty-six other ranks, during the confused fighting on 22 - 23 April. Several, including Captain Fryer, were wounded, and five later died of their wounds: Privates Alexander Birrell, Herbert Bradford, John Roy, Edgar Sculthorpe, and Alfred Wright.

Another private, Alexander Clarke, was injured in both legs, and one was later amputated by the Germans. Repatriated to Canada in August 1916, he bitterly told the Calgary *Daily Herald* that his leg "could have been saved had the German medical assistants given him proper attention. He asserts that they had only one meal a day for several weeks and that consisted of rye bread and soup. For days at a stretch he had no change of bandages or dressing of any kind."[60]

As the Tenth reformed in the trench, Major Ormond found that he had precious little to command. A roll call at six-thirty that Friday morning told the tale in stark terms. Only five officers and 188 other ranks were still standing: "this was what was left out of 816 of all ranks who had gone into action 6 hours before," he later wrote. The 16th Battalion was also sadly depleted, with five officers and 263 other ranks answering the roll call, little more than a third of its strength.[61] Behind these brave few lay a heartbreaking sight. "I looked back across the field we had crossed the previous night," Sergeant Charlie Stevenson recalled, "and I could see what havoc had been wrought on our boys, for all around were the dead bodies of men who, a few hours before, had been singing Canada's national song. They died with it on their lips, but their memory will live for many a day and year to come. For they made a name for the Dominion that will live in history."[62]

The Tenth won undying fame as a result of its counter-attack. While it would be a mistake to read too much into its outcome — the Germans had, after all, already dug in for the night — it was, nonetheless, a significant achievement. Its military merits can be debated, its execution questioned, including the employment of a mass formation in the face of machine-guns, the lack of artillery support, and the sloppy, amateurish arrangements by Third Brigade headquarters. But the fact remains that it was the only remotely successful attack among the many mounted by the Allies in the course of the battle (and the fighting in the salient continued until the end of May, long after the Canadians had departed).

Although the wood could not be held, the Tenth and 16th battalions had displayed a high degree of skill, leadership, esprit de corps and, above all, discipline, and served notice to the enemy that there would be no easy victory here. Ferdinand Foch, a French general who later emerged as the Allied supreme commander, considered the Canadian counter-attack "the finest act in the War,"[63] while General Smith-Dorrien, the Second Army's commander, declared that it "did everything to restore the situation and confuse the enemy," and praised these young Canadians for "maintaining the high tradition of the British Army."[64]

The importance of this action was eventually recognized when, in 1934, The Calgary Highlanders and the Winnipeg Light Infantry, perpetuating the Tenth Battalion in the reorganized Canadian armed forces, and the Canadian Scottish Regiment, perpetuating the 16th Battalion, were authorized to wear a special shoulder badge consisting of an oak leaf and acorn to symbolize that wood near Saint-Julien. Even today, The Calgary Highlanders toast "The Glorious Memory of the Twenty-second of April 1915" in annual mess dinners.

Friday, 23 April, while not quite as dramatic as the previous day, was equally trying. The Germans, believing that the rout of the French had rendered the remainder of the Ypres salient untenable, did virtually nothing to exploit their gas-induced victory, aside from prolonged, punishing bombardments along the V-shaped Canadian line. But the British, rather than pulling out as the Germans expected, resorted to repeated counter-attacks — piece-meal, poorly supported, ill-prepared efforts — to restore the original French position. Canadian and British troops were slaughtered in these brave but bloody attacks at various points along Mauser Ridge, west of the beleaguered Tenth and 16th battalions, which clung stubbornly and defiantly to their trench in front of the wood.

The day began with a tragedy. Shortly after midnight, two fresh battalions, the 2nd (Eastern Ontario) and 3rd (Toronto Regiment), both belonging to the reserve First Brigade, arrived at Mouse Trap Farm, but it was two o'clock before General Turner decided to rush reinforcements to the wood. (Having failed to make the necessary liaison arrangements, it took him that long to learn of the success of his counter-attack.) Turner dispatched three companies of the 2nd Battalion: one shored up the 16th Battalion's right flank, another stormed Oblong Farm on the left of the Tenth, and the last assaulted the troublesome redoubt in the southwestern corner of the wood. The 2nd Battalion was late moving into position and it attacked in broad daylight.

The company that assaulted the redoubt had to cover the same ground crossed by the Tenth and 16th battalions during the night, and the consequences were devastating. In a matter of minutes, the 2nd Battalion troops were cut to ribbons, suffering two hundred casualties. As a horrified Major Ormond recounted, "not more than 10 to 15 ever even got to our trenches."[65] However, the distraction enabled the other two companies to take their objectives on either side of the wood, and a Tenth Battalion machine-gun crew was later dispatched to reinforce a farmhouse held by the 2nd, between the wood and Saint-Julien.

It was "an anxious day" for Major Ormond and his men. "We were bombed and shelled all day," reported the acting Battalion commander, "losing men by 3 and 4 at a time."[66] Movement was often impossible, and the troops had to stay huddled in their shallow entrenchments, benumbed and nearly deafened by the explosions which rocked the ground around them. The parapet was destroyed in countless places, and the occupants showered with dirt and debris.

Survivors in the trench had no choice but to ignore the cries and groans of their wounded comrades, as the slightest movement, either by the injured or by would-be rescuers, drew deadly fire from alert German snipers and machine-gunners. "The enemy shot our wounded unmercifully," Major Ormond complained afterwards, "and with some sort of projectile that set fire to their clothing. These had the velocity of bullets, some exploding in the air — this I observed myself."[67] The Germans, Ormond contended, "shot at all men who attempted to rescue and carry out the wounded." Despite the adverse conditions, the Tenth maintained an aggressive stance, sending two- and three-man teams into the wood "to reconnoitre and keep in touch with the enemy's movements."[68]

Whenever there was a lull in the shelling, Major Ormond put his men to work. Despite the heavy losses, he found that "there were more men than the single trench would hold, so communication trenches were immediately run back towards a slight dip in the ground [and] these proved very useful later on." At the same time, parties from both battalions were charged with upgrading the main trench, which Ormond described as being "1½' to 2' deep, with a good parapet in construction consisting of dirt and sand bags." The major saw to it that the trench was deepened and traverses built to shelter the growing numbers of wounded men.[69]

Among those crouched in the trench, his cap pulled down low (steel helmets would not be introduced for another year), was Private Sydney Cox, who was distressed by the mounting casualties. "They'd make you number every so often," he recalled, "and every time you numbered you were a lower number than you were the time before. You didn't feel so good about that." Private Cox witnessed one death which was quite bizarre. The fellow "just suddenly, in the middle of a word, rolled right forward. Didn't have a bruise on him. And we took every stitch of clothing off him, and we couldn't find a mark. Not a mark. I don't know what killed him."[70]

For a few members of the Battalion, a day-long battle raged near the troublesome enemy redoubt. Following the failed attack organized by Major Ormond and Lieutenant Lowry, Corporal William Baker and a party of bombers engaged the Germans in a fight that lasted for more than twenty-four hours, during which the Canadians were subjected to what Ormond later called "the most severe machine gun fire I have known."[71] When supplies of bombs ran low, the nimble and quick-witted Corporal Baker caught German grenades and threw them back. Baker, who was the sole survivor, was later awarded the Distinguished Conduct Medal (DCM) and the French Croix de Guerre.[72]

The severity of the situation is reflected in some of the urgent messages written by Major Ormond that day. At noon, he wrote to Lieutenant Wilfred "Blackjack" Knowles, who commanded the left of the Battalion's line: "Has a trench been turned off from our left flank yet? If not commence to dig it at once. Have you any communication with our people on our left?" Two hours later he appealed to Lieutenant-Colonel David Watson, the officer commanding the 2nd (Eastern Ontario) Battalion: "Understand that you have Machine guns. We have none on the left. Could you sent [sic] at least one or two?" At 4:10 p.m., he rushed a request to General Turner at Third Brigade headquarters: "Can we possibly get up *tools, wire stakes*, and most important, *Pistols and flares*? We shall require all available stretcher bearers and ambulance." This was followed by an appeal for "an issue of rum.... We need rifle oil badly, rifles are jamming." Another note went to Lieutenant Knowles at five-thirty: "We have to hold to the last." A more complete situation report to Turner followed a few minutes later:

We are holding the German trench from corner of wood.... Our left flank is within 50 yards of

German redoubt full of bombs which they use. We cannot hold the left line unless have flares as we are less than 60 feet from the woods and our patrols cannot hold off a determined attack by bombers. We do need a machine gun so badly, can nothing be done? We have two prisoners with us, one wounded, can you get an escort for him?

Ormond's concern about prisoners was echoed in orders he issued at 5:45 p.m.: "Keep close watch on your prisoners and deal summarily with them if we are hotly attacked. They are cute and need watching."[73]

No assistance was provided by Third Brigade headquarters. Instead Ormond was alerted "to be prepared to make an advance at 7.30 p.m."[74] Thankfully, this attack was cancelled; the Tenth was clearly in no condition to mount offensive operations.

Darkness brought an end to the enemy's bombardment, but there was no opportunity for rest. It was finally possible to fetch the wounded men, who had spent a torturous day in the open, exposed to German snipers and suffering. In addition to the pain of their injuries they suffered from thirst in the hot sunshine. Lieutenant Walter Critchley, the Calgary-area polo player who had turned twenty-three a week earlier, made a number of trips to Mouse Trap Farm seeking ammunition and stretchers. The stretchers, if sent, never arrived, but ammunition and rations reached the weary heroes of the Tenth shortly before midnight.

Thanks to the efforts of Corporal William King, a Battalion signaller, a telephonic link was restored with Third Brigade headquarters. Unsuccessful in maintaining his telephone lines in the wake of the attack on the wood, Corporal King crawled to Mouse Trap Farm just before dawn and was forced to spend the day there. Returning after dark, he strung a new line across the corpse-covered field, and was later awarded the DCM, the second of this battle. As usual, there was much work to be done in the trench, making repairs and improvements. Late in the evening, the troops scrambled for their rifles when the Germans drove the Battalion's listening posts out of the wood, "and it appeared as if an attack was about to be launched against us."[75]

This attack failed to materialize, but a day of hard fighting lay ahead for the Tenth Battalion.

The Battalion was ordered to stand to arms at 3 a.m. on Saturday, 24 April. Within half an hour, it became evident that the Germans were up to something. "Two red rockets and one green was [sic] observed sent up over the enemy lines about 2000 yards to our left," Major Ormond wrote.[76] Around four o'clock that morning, a heavy bombardment broke out to the right, and in the dawn's early light "we observed the greenish yellow grey of the gas to the East."[77]

Thus began what the Canadian official history calls "a great and terrible day for Canada."[78] In a bid to smash the Canadian Division and eliminate the Ypres salient, the Germans had marshalled all of their available forces for a massive converging attack, behind a cloud of chlorine gas, on the slender Canadian line between Saint-Julien and Gravenstafel. In addition to their five-to-one advantage in artillery, the Germans enjoyed a substantial superiority in manpower, with thirty-four battalions facing eight Canadian front-line battalions. The four o'clock attack was stopped almost everywhere by Canadians, who improvised gas masks by holding urine- or water-soaked handkerchiefs over their faces. However, the enemy did succeed in breaking the front of the 15th (48th Highlanders of Canada) Battalion, on the Third Brigade's right, where the gas concentration was thickest and where the defenders were beyond the supporting range of their own artillery. The rupture threatened the entire Canadian position.

Confusion dictated the Tenth Battalion's next move. At Third Brigade headquarters, General Turner, under the mistaken impression that it was the neighbouring Second Brigade which had been driven in, sent orders at four-thirty to withdraw the remnants of the Tenth and 16th battalions, their trenches to be taken over by the 2nd (Eastern Ontario) Battalion. While the 16th reorganized in the GHQ Line, the Tenth was instructed to return to the Second Brigade.

This was not going to be easy, Major Ormond knew. "It was broad daylight," he later wrote. "We were within 100 yards of the enemy machine guns and had to go over a low ridge in full view of the enemy."[79] While the 16th Battalion provided covering fire, the Tenth moved back. The men, crouching and crawling, filed into the communication trenches which extended towards the rear. Summoning every bit of courage, each soldier had to run the gauntlet of menacing machine-gun fire in order to reach safety.

In the case of Private Charley Furnston, it involved a distance of three hundred yards. "We had to crawl all the way," he explained in a letter home to Calgary, "for, believe me, the bullets were flying all around...." Private Furnston eluded the bullets, but a shell got him shortly afterwards; he lived, but doctors removed at least eight chunks of shrapnel from his neck.[80]

A fellow private, Sydney Cox, vividly recollected the withdrawal: "We had to run about fifty feet, jump into a cabbage patch or a wheat field, or something or other there, and you would see three or four [men] run, and they would get one — and then you'd think, 'Well, I'll crawl,' and then you would see three or four crawl, and they would get one. 'No, I'm going to run.' You had to make your mind up which way you wanted to be hit."[81]

Private Charles Bloxham carried a wounded man on his back for more than a mile to the nearest dressing station. Ignoring the heavy shell fire, Bloxham

36

then went back to the Battalion and helped to round up and organize stragglers, for which he was later awarded the DCM. In addition, his March sentence of ninety days' field punishment for attempting to loot a liquor store was rescinded.

Singly and in small groups, the men of the Tenth scrambled to safety. Despite the contrary impression, the withdrawal was carried out "with small loss," according to Major Ormond, who then marched the Battalion to the 2nd Brigade's advanced headquarters at Pond Farm. By now, the Tenth was barely the size of a company, mustering just "3 officers and 171 other ranks."[82]

These few survivors were sent back into action. Arriving at Pond Farm, Ormond reported to his brigadier, who only now learned of the heavy casualties suffered by the unit he had so generously lent to the Third Brigade in its hour of need two nights before. Ormond recalled that "General Currie himself came out and gave the men a cheery word,"[83] then ordered the Battalion to reinforce the company of the 7th (1st British Columbia Regiment) Battalion which was defending critically important Locality C atop Gravenstafel Ridge. "The men responded with a spirit and task that was all that could be desired," Ormond proudly wrote. They were under fire all the way, and the major narrowly escaped serious injury: "I was hit on [the] right shoulder and knocked down, but only bruised." His misery was compounded when he fell into a waterfilled ditch — although he would only admit that "I had to swim" it.[84] Small wonder that he acquired the nickname "Dangerous Dan."

Reaching Locality C before five-thirty that fateful Saturday morning, the Tenth moved onto the left of the 7th Battalion defenders. The trenches, inherited from the French who had previously occupied this sector, were in poor shape. "They were five-man openings, with the dirt thrown forward, and no parados, and it was very hard to dig in," Ormond later complained.[85] To make matters worse, the gas fumes were still "bad," in the major's opinion. "We were almost overcome by gas here and had not Lieut. Critchley given me half his handkerchief which was wet, I should not have been able to carry on."[86] And these were not the only problems. "We at once found that this position was 'in the air'," Ormond noted, "as we had no one except the advancing enemy ... between us and St. Julien," 1000 yards away.[87]

Locality C soon became the focal point of the fighting. The breach in the 15th (48th Highlanders of Canada) Battalion's line had been steadily widened by swarming Germans. While the adjacent 8th (90th Winnipeg Rifles) Battalion, living up to its nickname "The Little Black Devils," resolutely maintained its apparently hopeless position in the Second Brigade's original trenches, British Columbia's 7th Battalion, along with the 13th (Royal Highlanders of Canada) and 14th (Royal Montreal Regiment) battalions were

forced to give ground or face encirclement. Locality C stood directly in the path of the onrushing enemy forces.

Shortly after arriving at this critical point, the Tenth Battalion came under attack. As Lieutenant Critchley recalled, "all we could see was masses of Germans coming up in mass formation. Their officers were still on horseback then. They were just coming right up."[88]

Incredibly, this brave little band of Canadians stemmed the seemingly irresistible grey hordes. Major Ormond described the grim battle which followed:

We stood up on our parapet and gave them three ruddy cheers and shook our fists at them. We gave them everything we had and they figured it wasn't worth while, and they just turned around and went back. They did that again and we did it again. We were quite happy about it. So then they did it a third time. When they went back the third time, we thought we'd won the war.[89]

The Battalion's stand looks even more impressive in view of the difficulties presented by the Canadian-made Ross rifle. It displayed a disturbing tendency to jam during rapid fire when fed .303-calibre ammunition of British manufacture. "Instead of getting off twelve or fifteen rounds a minute, we could only get off two or three," Ormond later lamented. "They were jamming, and men would have to lay down and take their heel to force the bolt out."[90] His soldiers were understandably outraged. "It wasn't even safe to send a fourteen-year[-old] kid out rabbit-hunting in the fields with, never mind going into battle with," commented Sergeant Chris Scriven, expressing the sentiments of most Tenth Battalion veterans who used the Ross rifle. "I laid in a shell hole with four other men for a day and a half, and out of five Ross rifles in that hole, it took four of us to keep one of them working, banging the bolts out."[91] Before the end of this battle, many had thrown away the unreliable Ross and retrieved Lee-Enfields from fallen British soldiers.

When their assaults on Locality C failed, the Germans resorted to deception. At one point, Major Ormond reported, "at least 3000 troops" were spotted nearby.

We could not see who they were, none of the officers could do so, [and] my glasses were full of water. I could not tell color at 150 yards on account of effects of gas. They sent out a white flag, [and] I ordered the men to fire, but the officer in the left trench was sure that they were Turcos.

The party with this white flag were 500 to 700 yards direct to our left. Two men went out to see who these people were, and were surprised by a party closer in, who took them before we could get our people back. During this time the men at the extreme left fired intermittently on the party with the white flag, but as only 3 or 4 could fire, I regret to say no damage was done.

Several men carrying stretchers followed the party of three, and all disappeared into a house, and in a minute we were under a heavy machine gun fire....[92]

There were no further frontal attacks. Instead, "the Boche started to play the piano on us," to use the major's colourful phrase.[93] For the rest of Saturday morning, the Tenth endured a frightful bombardment — "the shelling was really terrific" — and "it seemed impossible that there could be an inch of ground unhit." In Ormond's opinion, it was "the worst that we had seen up to this time, our men were being blown up by 5 and 6 at a time."[94] Ormond called the enemy's artillery "superb."[95]

The Battalion's strength continued to dwindle. Ormond tallied his numbers at 151, including five officers — two more than he had had when he reached Locality C.[96] The story of the additional two officers is the stuff of legend. Thirty-year-old Major Percy Guthrie, a lawyer and provincial politician from Fredericton, New Brunswick, and a member of the 7th (1st British Columbia Regiment) Battalion, was attending to court-martial proceedings at Canadian Division headquarters when the battle broke out. Hearing of the Tenth Battalion's losses, Major Guthrie volunteered his services: "I'll go as a lieutenant, of course." He was joined by Captain Charles "Pat" Costigan, who had been the Tenth's original paymaster but was now serving at divisional headquarters as a field cashier. When the thirty-four-year-old Captain Costigan learned of the need for front-line officers, he promptly locked his pay chest and declared, "There is no paymaster." Costigan, too, served as a subaltern for the time being.[97]

The two officers set out on 23 April. On their way to the Battalion's position, they rescued a pair of wounded British soldiers exposed to German fire and carried them to a nearby dressing station. "Costigan's man was dead on arrival," Guthrie later wrote, "but my chap was not seriously injured and will come around." After dark, they joined the Battalion in its trench along the edge of Kitcheners Wood, where Guthrie had a brush with death. "I felt a chug in the head and some time afterwards discovered that a bullet had grazed my scalp, taking a piece of hair and leaving a nice little hole in my cap."[98]

Accompanying the Tenth to Locality C, Guthrie was appalled by the situation. "The air was absolutely full of whistling bullets," he later related, "and shrieking, whistling and crashing shells." Guthrie marvelled that he escaped injury here. "I had the men on each side of me shot dead — at practically the same instant I saw six men blown to bits a few yards away. I saw arms and legs torn off by shell explosions all along the line. I saw men with eyes protruding, arms dangling and otherwise mangled on all sides of me. In every sense of the word war is indeed Hell."[99]

By noon the situation at Locality C had become almost intolerable. Enfiladed by withering machine-gun fire, and raked by artillery shells from what seemed to be all directions, the Tenth faced bleak prospects by holding this position. Major Ormond realized that it was only a matter of time before the thousands of enemy troops renewed the attack, and with little noticeable artillery support and rifles that "jammed *fearfully*,"[100] it would be impossible to put up more than token resistance. At twelve-fifteen, when he was told that the 7th Battalion company on his right was falling back to a more protected location behind the ridge, Ormond decided to withdraw his command to the road immediately behind Gravenstafel Ridge, "helping down what wounded we could."[101]

Here the major encountered two senior officers, Lieutenant-Colonel W.W. Burland, second-in-command of the 14th Battalion from Montreal, and Lieutenant-Colonel John Currie, commanding Toronto's 15th Battalion. "We consulted," Ormond later wrote, "and I asked for them to come back with us to the hill [i.e., Gravenstafel Ridge], but the general opinion was to retire to the G.H.Q. line, [and] I have not seen them since."[102] He could not know that this was part of a retirement to the GHQ Line by the whole Third Brigade, a move which gravely endangered the Second Brigade's left flank and rear. Only the timely arrival of several British battalions filled the gap and prevented complete disaster for the Canadians.

Major Ormond was wounded soon afterwards. The area behind the ridge was vulnerable to random shell and machine-gun fire, and although the remnants of the Tenth sheltered in some shallow trenches, Ormond was "hit in [the] right leg" shortly before four o'clock in the afternoon.[103] Handing over command of the Battalion to Captain Geoff Arthur, a realtor and former secretary of the Calgary General Hospital Board, the major was evacuated, riding out on a gun limber. Following Ormond's departure, Captain Arthur kept the Tenth in this position until after nightfall.

While the Battalion was making its epic stand near Locality C, one of its machine-gun crews was playing a crucial role elsewhere on the battlefield. The eight-man team under Lance-Corporal George Allan had been dispatched to the 2nd (Eastern Ontario) Battalion, which had reinforced the Tenth and 16th early Friday morning in and around Kitcheners Wood. Corporal Allan's crew was ordered to a farmhouse — dubbed "Doxsee's House," after the 2nd Battalion lieutenant, William Doxsee, who was in charge of the fifteen defenders. It was east of the wood, in an open field seventy-five yards in front of the 2nd's main position. Arriving at six o'clock that morning, Allan set up his Colt heavy machine-gun in a ground-floor window, camouflaging it carefully. A hundred yards away, thousands of Germans could be seen digging in behind a row of hedges.

A day-long fire-fight ensued. The Tenth Battalion gunners, spurning their machine-guns in order to surprise the enemy, opened "fire [on] the Germans behind the hedges, in front, with our rifles," recalled Private Wally Bennett, a twenty-year-old former clerk from Calgary. "They returned our fire, and our men were kept busy during the day, firing through every hole or opening they could find, or make, in the walls."[104]

Conditions in the house were shocking. "The place had been badly shot-up," wrote Private Bennett, "with shell-holes in the roof and walls, windows blown out, doors all battered, and inside was a state of chaos. There were some dead, in the corner, covered with sacks, in one of the rooms." There was no fresh water to be had — the farm's well water was "slimy and rank" — and the men's rations were quickly consumed. Thirsty and hungry, the small garrison of Doxsee's House waited all day for an attack that never came.[105]

Saturday was much different. Beginning shortly after dawn, the Germans stormed Doxsee's House at least half a dozen times. During one lull in the action, Lieutenant Doxsee dashed any hopes of an evacuation, telling his men that his orders were to "hold the house at all cost."[106] Looking around at his grim-faced buddies, Private Bennett knew what the lieutenant's words meant: "I never expected to get out."[107]

The enemy's small-arms fire was deadly. Bennett later wrote that the defenders could move only "by crawling around on our stomachs, as the bullets were coming in through the opening, over our head, and ricocheting around the walls." Casualties mounted

Ross Rifle, Mark III, and (below), excerpt from page of the "Handbook for the Canadian Service Rifle, Ross, Mark III," showing the bolt which caused so many problems for the troops

Courtesy Glenbow Museum, Calgary

7

The *Magazine Opening* B; the *Bolt Stop Seat* C; *Ejector Pin Hole* D; *Bolt Stop Retainer Pin-Slot* E; *Hole for Bolt Stop Hinge Pin* F ; *Notch for Safety Catch* G; *Hole for Bridge Screws* H; *Trigger Opening* I; *Pawl Opening* J; *Ejector Slot* K; *Line showing the location of Ejector Pin Hole* L; *Ejector Spring Seat* M; *Sear Pin Hole* N; *Rear Receiver Screw Hole* O; *Front Receiver Screw Hole in Recoil Lug* P; *Recesses for Bolt Head* Q Q; *Locking Cams* R–R; *Resisting Shoulders* S S; *Location of Unlocking Pin Hole* T; *Gas Vent* U.

On the upper surface of the Front End is stamped the name of the manufacturer and Model of the rifle.

Receiver Screw Front, Fig. 7.

Receiver Screw Rear, Fig. 8.

These two screws secure the Trigger Guard to the Receiver.

The BOLT—Side View, Fig. 9; front view showing bottom, Fig. 10.

steadily, but only the most seriously wounded were allowed to leave — "We needed every man!" At midday Lieutenant Doxsee was hit and killed by a bullet in the head. A saddened Bennett called him "a fine man — and a gentleman. It was hell to see him go like that."[108]

Moved alternately upstairs into the loft, and then back to the groundfloor window, the Colt machine-gun repeatedly repulsed the enemy. The weapon jammed occasionally, the American-made gun having the same problem with British ammunition as the Canadian-made Ross rifle, but Corporal Allan cleared it each time and resumed his deadly fire. The ploughed fields around the farmhouse were soon covered with grey-clad corpses.

Between attacks, reinforcements arrived in the form of a machine-gun crew from the 4th (Central Ontario) Battalion.

The battle for Doxsee's House raged on. Driving off yet another attack, Corporal Allan was killed when a bullet hit him "clear through the top of his head. He dropped on top of me," recalled Private Bennett. "He never knew what hit him!" Recommended for a Victoria Cross, Allan was awarded a posthumous DCM. Bennett took his place behind the machine-gun, and waited for the next assault.[109]

It was not long in coming. Bennett remembered it vividly many years later:

> I watched till they broke through the hedge, and they had over a hundred yards to cross to get to our farmhouse. We saw them breaking through the hedge, with their bayonets fixed, and they were going to come right at us, at the front. And, as near as I can remember, I held my fire, because we were short of ammunition, you know. We couldn't have stopped another attack — we didn't have the ammunition, we'd run out.
>
> So I had to wait until they got through the hedge and let them get a few yards, before I opened up on them. I just cut 'em down. For once, the gun didn't jam. We beat them back — some of them we killed, some of them were lying there kicking, you know, you could hear them [screaming].... Those that could get back, crawled back, and carried some of their wounded with them.[110]

This proved to be the last attack. By now Doxsee's House was practically surrounded, and it was clear that the tiny garrison could not hold on for much longer. Around three-thirty in the afternoon, the order was given to abandon the house. "It was every man for himself," recalled Private Bennett. To get away, they had to cross seventy-five yards of bullet-swept ground in order to reach the 2nd Battalion's trench.

Bennett, carrying the machine-gun, and a few others were among the first to make a run for it, but only two made it. "The bullets were coming both ways — two or three of the others went down," he later related. "And I got near this trench — say, ten or fifteen yards — and a fellow fell down in front of me, wounded. He was hit in the leg. I ran past, put the machine-gun in the trench, crawled back on my belly, got his good leg, and pulled him in[to] the trench. I don't even know who he was."[111]

Bennett's luck would hold. A bullet later ripped through the heel of his boot and he was knocked cold by a shell burst, but he rejoined the Tenth Battalion and got out of this battle unhurt. Only two others from his eight-man crew were so fortunate; the rest were killed or captured.

Even as Private Bennett made his dramatic escape from Doxsee's House, the pitiful remnants of the Tenth were digging in along the road below Locality C. When darkness finally fell, Captain Arthur led his men to the rear, setting off around nine o'clock Saturday evening along with what remained of the 7th Battalion. The 7th had been driven out of its lines earlier in the day northeast of Saint-Julien.

Two more DCMs were won by members of the Tenth during the night. A Polish-born medical orderly, Corporal Samuel Schultz, oversaw the evacuation of every wounded man before he went to the rear, while Private Tom Ross ignored heavy small-arms fire to bring in three injured comrades who would otherwise have been left behind.

Reaching the GHQ Line, these tired, hungry troops enjoyed their first hot meal in two days, then settled down for a well-earned sleep.

But they were to be denied the rest their aching bodies craved. Shortly after midnight, the brigadier, General Currie, arrived from a conference at his main headquarters in nearby Wieltje. Currie had been given instructions to shore up his battered front line, which, remarkably, was still intact even though the Second Brigade's left flank had been up in the air for much of Saturday. The Tenth and 7th battalions — "about 300 men" altogether, in Currie's estimation[112] — comprised the brigade's sole reserve, and the general reluctantly rounded up the troops and led them back towards Gravenstafel Ridge. The ridge was still in Canadians hands, although Locality C was at this time falling to the enemy. Currie amalgamated the two battalions into a composite unit under the 7th's acting commander, Major Victor Odlum,* then personally posted the 7th/Tenth Battalion on the left of the 8th, in a line extending from the ridge to the Hannebeek, a small stream to the west. This position, like those held by the whole brigade, was dangerously exposed, and even now was being raked by German

---

* The officer commanding the 7th, Lieutenant-Colonel William Hart-McHarg, had been fatally wounded during a reconnaissance patrol on 23 April.

bullets. At six-foot-four and 250 pounds, Currie made a fine target as he placed the 7th/Tenth in the line. Private Sydney Cox and his mates "thought he was crazy, standing up there with his red hat on, while we were taking all the cover we could till we got dug in."[113]

It was four o'clock in the morning on Sunday, 25 April, and dawn was already breaking as the composite unit began digging in. Soon after, figures appeared out of the misty semi-darkness, and brisk firing broke out until someone shouted that these were British soldiers from a battalion reinforcing the Canadian line. Major Odlum, a thirty-four-year-old newspaperman from Vancouver, recalled the confused scene:

Although the distance between the two lines was only about 200 yards, the morning was so misty that it was impossible to tell with certainty whether those in front of us were German or our own troops. I ordered firing to cease. One man (name unknown, a man belonging to the 2nd Canadian Battalion and picked [up] with the stragglers) who could speak German, volunteered to go forward and find out who they were. He held up his hands and advanced, shouting out in German. When he had gone about fifty yards he was shot down. It was then quite evident that those in front were the enemy. They soon advanced in considerable numbers, but were held and driven to ground by rifle fire. Both lines then proceeded to dig in.[114]

This was the beginning of a brutal day for the 7th/Tenth Battalion. Its new position was exposed to enfilade fire from the left, where units of the First Brigade had been expected to support the Second. While the Germans launched no direct attacks here, artillery and machine-gun fire played havoc. The "very heavy shell fire," Major Odlum reported, "came from two directions — from the neighbourhood of Passchenda[e]le and from St. Julien," now occupied by the enemy. German machine-gunners had daringly seized a ruined house in the Battalion's left-rear, where they were able to rake the Canadian line with impunity. The position was beyond the range of the Canadian field artillery, which had withdrawn from the Second Brigade's sector during the night.[115]

The casualty count climbed rapidly as the German fire intensified. Private Algernon Dowty, who was wounded here, later wrote his father in Calgary: "I think I am very lucky to have come out of it alive."[116] Not many men of the Tenth would survive to say that.

Major Odlum pleaded with his brigadier for a counter-attack to ease the pressure on his battered

troops.* General Currie, who had no reserves and was waiting impatiently for promised reinforcements which never did arrive, could do little but sympathize and communicate the major's concerns to divisional headquarters. He sent this message at 12:40 p.m.: "Major Odlum in charge of 10th and 7th on left says it is imperative to arrange attack to clear left front. We can only hang on. Can we get any artillery support? ... Where are 1st Brigade units? See nothing of them on our left." Odlum stayed in touch with Currie throughout the afternoon. "At 2 p.m.," the brigadier wrote, "O.C. 7th Battalion reported his men almost all in but would hold on till night. Also that his line fired on from rear, and that nothing could be seen of 1st Brigade on left."[118]

Odlum became separated from the unit later that afternoon. Hearing that British troops on Gravenstafel Ridge had been routed, the major rushed off to help rally them. From there, he proceeded to General Currie's advanced headquarters in the village of Gravenstafel, where he spent the next few hours. In his absence, the 7th/Tenth — now numbering "about 200 men"[119] — reverted to separate commands. The Tenth came under the orders of tall, handsome Major Percy Guthrie, the former New Brunswick politician who had joined the Battalion the previous day.

Major Guthrie's first task was to extricate his men. Shortly after five o'clock in the afternoon, General Currie decided that he could wait no longer for the reinforcements which had been repeatedly promised him but of which there was no sign: "I concluded our position had been judged hopeless and ordered units to retire at dusk...."[120] Currie's orders were dispatched by runner to each of the battalions, British and Canadian, under the Second Brigade's jurisdiction. But the runner sent to the Tenth Battalion failed to arrive, and Guthrie was reluctant to retire without orders, even though the formations on either flank fell back after dusk. The major, accompanied by Private Charles Bloxham, set out for Currie's advanced headquarters in Gravenstafel village, only to find the place occupied by German troops. "We effected our escape hotly pursued by the enemy," but it was after midnight when they finally returned to the Battalion.[121]

Lieutenant Walter Critchley saved the situation. The dependable, twenty-three-year-old subaltern slipped through the enemy in the darkness and, reaching the advanced brigade headquarters, "brought back an order to retire at my discretion," Major Guthrie later wrote. "Without this order I would have maintained my position and been annihilated."[122] Nevertheless, the early-morning withdrawal was completed thanks largely to the darkness and a

---

* One major counter-attack already had taken place that Sunday morning. At five-thirty, five battalions of the British 10th Brigade had stormed Saint-Julien. Within an hour and a half, the British had suffered 2419 casualties, but failed to regain any ground. Walter Critchley, a Tenth Battalion subaltern, later commented that "I have never seen such slaughter in all my life. They were lined up — I can see it now — in a long line, straight up, and the Hun opened up on them with machine-guns. They were just raked down."[117]

41

heavy mist which blanketed the battlefield. "The enemy knew nothing of their movement. They made a successful withdrawal, although at the time completely isolated and outflanked."[123]

Still, Guthrie was far from pleased. "It was a lucky movement, our getting out, as we would have been massacred or captured. I felt rotten about having to give way…. There was nothing else to be done, as our right was left open and our men were worn out. If two new regiments had marched up to our help we need not have given way an inch."[124]

It is impossible to exaggerate the determined spirit displayed by the men of the Tenth. The experience of Private Sydney Cox exemplifies this wonderful attitude. Having survived several close calls during the attack on Kitcheners Wood and the subsequent move to Locality C, Private Cox became separated from the Battalion during the fighting on Sunday and found himself among a group of British soldiers on the ridge. The withdrawal order failed to reach this party after dark, and Cox was appalled when the British, belatedly realizing that they were now cut off and surrounded, proposed to surrender. Cox, arguing vehemently, pointed to a ditch which led — he hoped — to the rear. When they refused to consider his alternative, Cox exploded. "You can surrender if you damn well please, I'm going down the ditch!" All but one of the British followed him, and Cox's luck held. The ditch not only enabled them to elude the Germans who were all round, but led them into the British lines west of the ridge.[125]

By dawn on Monday, 26 April, the Second Brigade's four battered, bloodied battalions had assembled near Wieltje, behind the GHQ Line. But once again, they were robbed of the rest they needed and deserved. Later that morning, the Germans renewed their attacks on the British forces that had relieved the Canadian Division on and around Gravenstafel Ridge. Receiving a report that the enemy had broken through, General Currie promptly marched his weary brigade towards the dangerpoint. The Tenth, which now mustered just two officers and 117 other ranks,[126] led the way with the 8th (90th Winnipeg Rifles) on its right, supported by the 5th (Western Cavalry) and 7th (1st British Columbia Regiment) battalions.

It was another exercise in futility. The reported breakthrough proved to be erroneous, and Currie deployed his four battalions in the open fields near Fortuin, where they remained under severe shell fire. This was "the heaviest yet experienced by the Brigade," according to the brigadier.[127] Fortunately, casualties were relatively light, and the following night — Tuesday, 27 April — the Tenth Battalion joined the remainder of the brigade in a march to the west bank of the Canal de l'Yser.

Withdrawal from the salient was welcomed by the tired troops. "It was certainly cheerful news to us,"

related Private Wally Bennett, the machine-gunner who had finally made his way back to the Battalion, "and we were badly in need of a rest. During the night, our Battalion, or what was left of it, went back through the fields and out along the road through St. Jean and into Ypres," which was a shocking sight, according to Private Bennett. "Shells were bursting in and around the City. Everything seemed wrecked. In some places along the streets, there was only space for one wagon to get through the piles of brick and debris."[128]

The Tenth's few survivors were "a tough looking" lot, Bennett later wrote. "As for myself, I hardly knew my own face: I hadn't seen a razor for about seven or eight days, and my clothes were ragged and torn and still caked with mud!"[129]

The process of rebuilding the Battalion had already begun. On 28 April, nineteen officers and 343 other ranks arrived from England, so hurriedly sent out that none had their identity discs. Together with the two hundred who had been left out of the battle, and the return of numerous stragglers and lightly wounded men, they soon restored the Tenth to nearly full strength. At noon on 29 April, it could muster 910, all ranks.[130]

In the meantime, new duties awaited the Battalion. It was posted, along with the 5th (Western Cavalry), to guard the pontoon bridges on the canal. The two battalions remained there until 5 May, "under most unsanitary conditions," complained General Currie, "owing to the lack of good water and to the fact that the whole area had been soiled by the previous occupation of our Allies [i.e., the French] for several months, and exposed to shell fire practically without intermission during day and night."[131] Guard duty cost the Tenth Battalion three dead and twenty-seven wounded. Among them was Captain George Gliddon, the medical officer, who was wounded by bomb fragments on 4 May; he died in hospital five days later.

Private Victor Lewis was nearly a casualty. Dissatisfied with the rations, he slipped out one night in search of better fare. He found it, in a chicken coop on a nearby farm. As he helped himself to one of these squawking birds, someone — probably the farmer — took a pot shot at him, "and the bullet went through my hat, but it never touched me. I was lucky. I got the chicken anyway."[132]

It was here on the canalbank, while the Tenth licked its wounds, that Private Robert Wilson discovered that he had been injured sometime during the past few days. The thirty-year-old, dark-complexioned Englishman was one of the Battalion's originals, having enlisted from his job as a motorman in Lake Louise the previous August. He had come through the unit's first action apparently unscathed. During this opportunity to rest. "I felt my shirt sticking to my back," he later wrote. "I had been hit by flying splinters of shrapnel." He could not say when he had been hurt, but the injury proved to be minor and Wilson rejoined the Tenth in time for its next action, at Festubert.[133]

The end finally came on the evening of Wednesday, 5 May. Bidding a none-too-fond farewell to the bloodsoaked salient, the Second Brigade departed for billets in Bailleul, sixteen miles west of Ypres. Tenth Battalion set out at 9:45 p.m. on an all-night, "very, very killing march," as a disgusted Lieutenant Walter Critchley commented. "It was a forced march which, really, I think, under the circumstances, was unnecessary. They could have taken it a little easier."[134] Among the footsore soldiers who limped into Bailleul was Private Wally Bennett. "Many of our men couldn't keep up," he recalled, "and were left [sleeping] by the roadside. They came straggling in during the next day."[135]

The battle, officially designated Second Ypres, had been a trying time for the Canadian Division as a whole, and for the Tenth Battalion in particular. The Division's losses totalled a staggering 6037, all ranks. The Tenth lost 718, all ranks,[136] one-sixth of all the Battalion's casualties during the war. The dead included its two top officers, Colonel Boyle and Major MacLaren. After assisting Boyle to the rear, MacLaren was killed on the morning of 23 April, when a shell hit his ambulance as it passed through Ypres.* Boyle died in hospital in Boulogne on the twenty-fifth. His death came as a surprise, according to a fellow patient, Lieutenant William Lowry, who had been hit twice during the first night of the battle. "We did not think he was seriously wounded," Lieutenant Lowry later said of Boyle. "We did not dream he would peg out. He was always ... talking of getting back to his regiment."[138]

Colonel Boyle's death was a grievous loss. He had organized and trained the Tenth, and the Calgary *Daily Herald* was justified in eulogizing him as "one of the most dashing and accomplished officers that Alberta has ever known." There was a tragic footnote, too. The day before he succumbed to his injuries, Boyle's wife, Laura, and their two children, unaware that he was on his death bed in a hospital in France, travelled into Calgary from Crossfield to have their photograph taken, intending to send it to him as a keepsake.[139]

The Tenth Battalion had passed its trial by fire with flying colours. Pointing out that the Battalion had been in almost continuous action for twenty-two days, General Currie later praised "their bravery, stick-to-it-iveness, under the most trying circumstances, their discipline being all that could be desired. The 10th Battalion led the counter-attack and behaved most gallantly, losing their Colonel (Lt.-Col. R.L. Boyle), their second-in-command (Major J. MacLaren), their Adjutant (Major Ormond) and every Company Commander."[140] High praise, indeed, from the man who had opposed the addition of the Battalion to his brigade.

Perhaps the most disappointing aspect was the surprisingly small number of decorations and honours awarded to members of the Tenth in the wake of the battle. This was primarily due to the fact that so few as the officers authorized to make the recommendations survived. "There were many wonderful and brave deeds done by men of the Bn.," Major Ormond explained later, "but all were doing such deeds that one could not be chosen as outstanding above others.[141] His men believed that Colonel Boyle should have won the Victoria Cross, but he received no more than a mention in despatches. Captain Geoff Arthur, the Calgary realtor who briefly commanded the Battalion in spite of a slight wound, won the Distinguished Service Order (DSO). Major Ormond had to settle for a Russian medal, the Order of St. Stanislas, Third Class, with Swords, and Sergeant-Major Robert Good was awarded another minor Russian decoration, the Medal of St. George, First Class. There were six DCM-winners, one of whom, Corporal William Baker, also received the French Croix de Guerre.

And there were other rewards as well. Company Quartermaster-Sergeant Ernest Rickard, who risked his life several times bringing up badly needed bombs,[142] was subsequently promoted to lieutenant, as was Sergeant-Major Good. They were the first NCOs in the unit to be commissioned in the field.[143] Private William Griffiths was able to redeem himself in combat. Sentenced in early March to fifty-six days' Field Punishment Number One for being drunk in the trenches, he served as a runner for Major Guthrie, and "made himself an invaluable asset to the Battalion."[144] The balance of his punishment was rescinded, as was the ninety-day sentence given to the DCM-winner, Private Bloxham, who won additional praise from Guthrie. "I have often said," the major later wrote, " 'give me a Battalion of Bloxhams, with a biscuit and a drink of rum, and I'll get to Berlin.' "[145]

The Battalion had won the admiration and respect of friend and foe alike. Its efforts at Second Ypres were later recognised by three battle honours, "Ypres, 1915 - 17," "Gravenstafel," and "St. Julien." The unit's reputation spawned several nicknames, including "White Gurkhas" (coined by Major Guthrie) and "Terrible Tenth" (sometimes used in newspaper articles), but the most popular sobriquet was also the one that was most fitting: "The Fighting Tenth."

---

* According to Major Ormond, MacLaren and another injured officer were being transported to a dressing station in the back seat of a staff car. A shell presumably passed through the vehicle, silently decapitating the two men while the driver blissfully continued on, delivering the headless corpses to hospital. Only then did he realize what had happened to his passengers.[137]

Chapter Three

"THE GATES OF HELL"

(7 May - 1 June 1915)

Gurkhas come along with me,
Give them Hell and we shall see
If the Hun will fight or flee,
Shouted Guthrie.[1]

The Fighting Tenth was back in action just two weeks after pulling out of the Ypres salient.

By the end of the first week in May 1915, the Battalion had been completely rebuilt. On the fifth, the day it marched to Bailleul, the unit received a reinforcing draft of two officers and 250 other ranks, boosting its strength to 1133, all ranks.[2] Ironically, the Battalion was now bigger than it had been before Second Ypres, but the newcomers did not impress the veterans of the Tenth. "These were men of average physice [*sic*]," notes the war diary, "but green and untried ... very few if them had ever fired a shot, and none had fired their musketry course before being

sent out [from England], nor during their enlistment in November 1914."[3]

Indeed, the Fighting Tenth bore little resemblance to the unit that had so optimistically marched into battle on 22 April. Few officers had survived, which necessitated a drastic change in its command structure. Major Guthrie remained in temporary command of the Battalion, while Captain Arthur was designated second-in-command. (Guthrie recommended Arthur's promotion to major.) Captain Charles Costigan, the former paymaster who had resolutely locked his pay chest and rushed to join the unit in the firing line, became the new adjutant. Each of the four companies

Tenth Battalion officers, 12 May 1915. Within two weeks half of the men pictured here would be dead or wounded.
Top row: Lieutenant Gilbert Todhunter (killed); Lieutenant Robert Good; Lieutenant Wilfred Romeril; Lieutenant Stanley Lewis (killed); Lieutenant Albert Morgan (killed); Lieutenant James Dawson; Lieutenant William Bingham; Lieutenant Frederick Nichol (killed); Lieutenant Alexander Thomson; Lieutenant Ivan Finn (wounded); Lieutenant Ernest Rickard; Lieutenant Osmund Wheatley (wounded).
Middle row: Lieutenant Joseph Simpson; Lieutenant Ashton Cockshutt; Lieutenant George Duncan (killed); Lieutenant Wilfred Knowles; Lieutenant Stanley Glanfield; Lieutenant William Reeve (killed); Captain Robert Stewart (killed).
Bottom row: Captain Allison Day; Captain Harold Snelgrove (wounded); Lieutenant James Still; Captain Edward Ross; Captain Charles Costigan (wounded); Major Percy Guthrie (wounded); Captain Geoff Arthur; Captain Alfred Duck; Major E.J. Ashton (wounded); Lieutenant Walter Critchley.

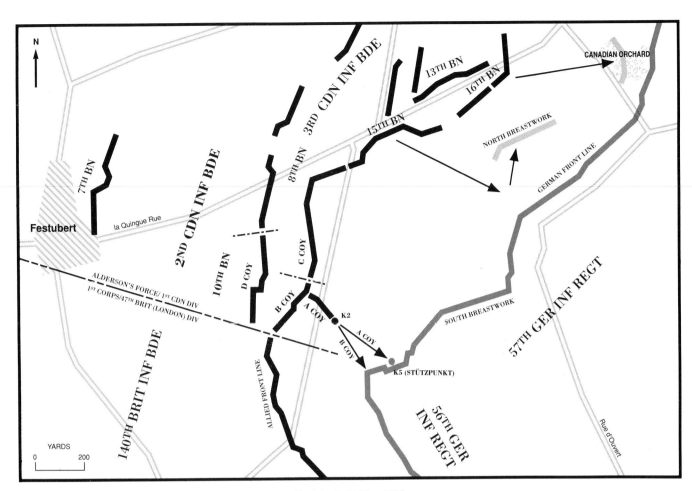

Festubert, 21 May 1915

Returned Tenth Battalion veterans in Calgary, 1916.
Top row: Private Alexander Hayman; Private John Boyd; Private John Niven; Private John Hudgins; Corporal Edgar Cecil; Lance-Corporal James Glover; Private Norman Griffiths; Private Andrew Coats; Private William Hartman; Private John Smith.
Middle row: Sergeant Albert Foreman; Sergeant "Blondy" Bonner; Private Edward Stephens; Private William Tozer; Private Bert Sherman; Private Reginald Farley; Private William Goddard; Private James Wyatt; Private Elsdon Brown.
Bottom row: Lieutenant Ashton Cockshutt; Major Charles Robinson; Major Harold Snelgrove; Lieutenant-Colonel William Lowry; Lieutenant-Colonel William Nasmyth; Major Lee Redman; Lieutenant Albert Harrison; Captain Arthur Martin.

had a new man in charge: Major E.J. "Old Jimmy" Ashton (A); Captain Allison Day (B); Lieutenant Walter Critchley (C); Captain Harold Snelgrove (D).[4]

The Battalion rested, reorganized, and was also re-equipped at Bailleul. Among the unit's few originals who had survived the fighting at Ypres, 149 were found to have armed themselves with Lee-Enfield rifles.[5] "We'd picked up the rifles of wounded Imperial men that we had been with in that area," explained Sergeant Chris Scriven, who, like most members of the Battalion, had been shocked with the unreliable Ross rifle.[6] However, the Lee-Enfields were taken away and replaced with the Ross on 7 May, "much against their wish," according to Private Wally Bennett.[7] All ranks were also issued with primitive gas masks, "a nose and mouth pad of cotton waste wrapped in veiling," with "neutralizing solution for impregnating the pads."[8] These were later replaced with more advanced forms of protection, including the PH gas helmet — a chemically treated flannel head covering with glass eye-pieces — and the box respirator, which closely resembled the modern gas mask. Poison gas, employed by both sides, was to remain a fact of life, and death, for the rest of the war.

The Battalion received warm words of praise from the divisional commander, General Alderson. Addressing the Fighting Tenth on Sunday, 9 May, an emotional Alderson declared that "I have never been so proud of anything in my life as I am of this Armlet with '1 Canada' on it that I wear on my right arm." Recalling his prediction prior to Ypres that the Canadians would some day be reputed as troops who could not be budged from their trenches, he admitted that "I little thought … how soon those words would come true. But now to-day, not only the Army out here, but all Canada, all England, and all the Empire, are saying it of you."[9]

Two days later, the Tenth returned to the training fields. The primary purpose of these exercises was to give the Battalion's many new members a crash course in the basics of company and platoon manoeuvres. But time was short. On the fourteenth, the Battalion bade farewell to Bailleul, marching south to Robecq, then on to Locon on the seventeenth — "Billets very crowded," complained the war diarist. The men reached Le Touret on the eighteenth[10] and in the distance, the rumble of artillery fire signalled the imminence of new fighting.

A joint British and French offensive had begun on 9 May. The French stormed Vimy Ridge and came close to capturing it, while the British attacked fifteen miles to the north, near Festubert, in a bid to outflank the German defences along Aubers Ridge. The terrain around Festubert was ill-suited to offensive operations. Flat and wet, it was intersected by streams and ditches, the latter ranging in size from "mere gutters marked by pollard willows to formidable channels fifteen feet across and five feet deep."[11]

General Haig's First Army was stopped cold, with heavy losses, on the opening day of the offensive, when a brief, inadequate bombardment made no appreciable impression on enemy defences. Haig paused to reorganize before renewing the attack on 16 May with mixed results. When the Germans withdraw that night to take up better positions, the British army commander believed that he had the enemy on the run and ordered new attacks on his apparently crumbling opponent.

The Canadian Division was alerted to be ready to take part in the offensive, and on 18 May, the Third Brigade was attached to the British 7th Division for an unsuccessful assault on a feature which would become famed as the Canadian Orchard. Following this failure, the Canadian Division was ordered into the front line. The Second Brigade, led by the Fighting Tenth and the 8th (90th Winnipeg Rifles), moved onto the right of the embattled Third Brigade on the night of Wednesday, 19 May.

The move was completed by 11 p.m. and Major Guthrie established his headquarters in a small house on the southern outskirts of the ruined village of Festubert. "For an office, dining-room and bed-room," he later complained, "I had an empty turnip bin in one end of a large shed."[12] Three companies held the Battalion's front trenches, with D Company in close support. As one might expect, conditions were far from pleasant. "The trenches we took over we[re] newly captured from the Germans, so they were not in the very best of condition," recalled a machine-gunner, Lance-Sergeant John "Jock" Palmer, who was soon to distinguish himself. The place was "a death trap," in Sergeant Palmer's opinion, and his description was apt.[13] The ground was littered not only with corpses but with wounded men who had been lying neglected in the open for up to a week. A fellow machine-gunner, Private Wally Bennett, who was posted on the extreme left of the Battalion's line, recalled that the "first night we were in the line we heard someone out in front calling for help — and very soon word was passed along the line that a few of our men were going out in front, to see if they could find them. I went out myself, for about half an hour, but could find no one. Later, we heard that our men had brought in a British 'Tommy,' badly wounded, who had been out there for days, hiding in a shell hole, by a stream that ran between the lines."[14]

An abandoned enemy communication trench in no man's land would play a very important part in the coming battle.

As soon as the Battalion took over its assigned front, Major Guthrie went on a reconnaissance mission. Accompanied by Captain Robert Stewart and Lieutenant Wilfred Knowles, he scouted the ground over which his men would soon attack. The trio split up, Guthrie going one way and Stewart and Knowles another. "Personally," the major later wrote, "I got so

German parapet, Festubert

close as to hear the Germans talking in a conversational tone and to see the heads of the sentries along the parapet as they stood with ready rifle peering into the darkness." Stewart and Knowles rejoined him, but not before subduing a sentry. "What happened I need not relate," Guthrie remarked, "but let me advise that a jack-knife is a very useful article for one to have in his kit when scouting." The three officers crawled back to their own line without further incident.[15]

It was undoubtedly this skirmish which prompted the imaginative major to label the Battalion "White Gurkhas," after the feared fighters from India who used their machete-like, razor-edged knives to deadly effect.

The Fighting Tenth attacked the next night. Its objective was an enemy strongpoint known as K.5, from its map co-ordinates, but there was considerable confusion surrounding the operation. The Second Brigade was originally instructed to attack at 6 a.m. on 21 May but, during the afternoon of the twentieth, this order was cancelled by First Army headquarters and the Second and Third brigades were told to launch their assault at 7:45 p.m. — less than five hours' notice!

The Second Brigade's General Currie protested vehemently. Hurrying out to reconnoitre, the bulky brigadier was appalled when he could not even find K.5. His map, issued by the British army, was a horror, printed upside down, with inaccuracies of several hundred yards. In a message to divisional headquarters, he recommended "postponement attack till tomorrow," in order to make better preparations.[16] But General Alderson simply reaffirmed his orders, leaving Currie with no choice but to carry them out. The experience left him angry and bitter. "This was my

first difference with the High Command," he later fumed. "I now know better than ever that I was right, but still I was ordered to make the attack."[17]

Time was at a premium. Conferring with Currie in his dugout headquarters a mile behind the line, Guthrie formulated a plan of attack. After the artillery softened up K.5, two companies would make the assault, jumping off from the enemy's former communication trench in no man's land. The major was under no illusions, for he knew that K.5 was a powerful position. He later described it as "a fort in the German line constructed of concrete and sandbags and in which numerous machine guns were mounted so as to sweep the ground in every direction."[18]

The Fighting Tenth paid the price, as it had done at Ypres, for these hasty arrangements. The preliminary bombardment opened at four o'clock in the afternoon. The Battalion, led by Major Ashton and A Company and supported by Captain Day's B Company, went over the top at 7:45 p.m. The ensuing fiasco is described by the war diary:

> The bombardment preparing for this attack had been quite ineffectual, and had not actually touched K5. The troops detailed for the attack were in open view of the enemy when crossing the gap near K2. The attack had been set for one hour before dusk. The only approach to K5 was through a narrow communication trench which was completely covered by the M.Gun [machine-gun] fire of the enemy. The leading men of the attacking force were all shot down. The O.C. (Major P.[A.] Guthrie), considering any further attempt would only lead to unnecessary loss of life, discontinued the attack.

The ruins of Festubert (1919)

Casualties were not recorded, but the wounded included A Company's Major Ashton, who refused to depart for treatment of two bullet wounds, and the new adjutant, Captain Costigan. As Major Guthrie later told the story, he and the captain had gone into the communication trench, and after the attacking troops had gone over the top, Guthrie started to clamber over the parapet. The irrepressible Costigan pushed him aside, saying, "I'll go, Major, you have a wife and kids." A moment later, the captain was struck by a bullet on the crown of his head, falling back into Guthrie's arms. "I put my hand to his head," the major recalled, "and the blood ran through my fingers and down my sleeve."[19]

The attack had been a shambles, but the Battalion was ordered to try again the following morning. On the left, units of the Third Brigade had finally captured the shattered remains of the Canadian Orchard, while the Second Brigade had only the hundred yards of muddy, bloodstained ground gained by the Fighting Tenth to show for its efforts. The dawn attack initially ordered, was postponed until nightfall, in order to prepare a proper bombardment of the enemy's formidable defences.

Major Guthrie put the time to good use. In drawing up his plans, he made three trips through shell fire to brigade headquarters, "but to give you a list of narrow squeaks I had, would take too much time." At an afternoon conference with his officers, Guthrie finalized the details of the operation. He would again use the communication trench as a jumping-off point, and he would attack with the same two companies as the night before. But this time the assault force would be split in two, the one on the left storming K.5, while the right-hand party cleared the adjacent trenches. "I felt sure the plan I thought of was the best one and the officers taking part thought so too," Guthrie wrote afterwards. "It only remained that K-5 would be reduced [by the artillery] and success was almost assured. If K-5 were not reduced, we all knew what would happen to the party that went up against it."[20]

The barrage opened at 5 p.m., and at 8:30 Friday evening, the Fighting Tenth again went over the top. Major Guthrie, stationed in the communication trench, later called it "the proudest moment of my life. Those brave fellows, with cheers that I shall never forget, dashed forward as one man."[21]

K.5 had not been knocked out. Enemy machine-gun fire soon drowned his men's cheers. Guthrie later wrote that, crouched in the trench, "I felt our men must be creeping forward silently, but groans from the darkness in every direction filled me with fear." The major decided to investigate, and crawled over the parapet, where he found Major Ashton, who had been wounded four times, in addition to the two wounds he had suffered the previous day. The injured major, a

48

Trench scenes in France, 1915

thirty-five year-old, English-born veteran of the South African War, refused to be evacuated and was later awarded the DSO. Realizing that the attack had been stopped practically before it started, Guthrie called to the survivors to follow him in another rush at K.5. But they were "met by a more terrific fire," and Guthrie dove for cover in a shell hole. When a German flare lit up the night sky, he risked a look back. "I saw our brave boys strewn about the field. I shouted again to advance, but no response came to me except groans and shrieks of dying men."[22]

Lieutenant Ivan Finn got closer to K.5 than any other member of the Battalion. He was riddled with at least four bullets and spent the following day lying in full view of the enemy. Before he was rescued, he was further injured by German shrapnel which "ripped open" his side.[23]

While the left-hand party had been stopped in front of K.5, the attackers on the right had more success, clearing the German trench for 225 yards. Private Allan Glasgow, a twenty-three-year-old Irishman who had joined the Battalion following the Second Battle of Ypres, wrote of the assault in a letter home on 27 May: "We captured a trench from the Germans, but they unfortunately could not pluck up nerve enough to wait for us, and the gleam of our bayonets in the moonlight and our Indian yell caused them to beat it in a most undignified manner.... "[24]

Scrambling out of his shell hole, Major Guthrie hurried to the right. Somehow unscathed, he jumped into the enemy trench and found himself face-to-face with a German and a fixed bayonet. The German lunged at him, nicking Guthrie's nose as the major tried to dodge the thrust. Enraged, Guthrie hit the German across the side of the head with his walking stick. "What a joke!" the major marvelled. "I have often laughed over it since. To think I was so angry at that Boche that I forgot to shoot him with the revolver, but whacked him with the stick instead." One of his men bayoneted the German "and joshed his O.C. for being too mad to shoot." A few minutes later, Guthrie had another close call, when he grappled with an enemy officer further down the trench. "I got a lucky hold in the right spot," he recalled, "and the argument was soon over."[25]

Under the major's direction, another 425 yards of the defences were occupied by the Fighting Tenth. After seeing that barricades were built, Guthrie supervised the task of consolidating the hard-won gains. There was much to be done, as he wrote afterwards:

We must, of course, reverse the trench captured so as to have a good front against the German shells in the morning; a new piece had to be built out of sandbags connecting the communication trench with that captured; wire had to be put up; ammunition distributed; rations and water arranged for; front shelters for our reserve bomb supply built,

and last but not least, the care of the wounded and the burial of the dead. Parties were told off for each of the above purposes, so that all the work would be going on at the same time.[26]

Reinforcements rushed to the scene, in the form of Captain Snelgrove and D Company but, while the help was appreciated, inexperienced men sometimes added to the problems. Private Fred Maiden, a young Calgarian who had been among the newcomers to the Battalion in the wake of Ypres, recalled that he had spotted some wires near his machine-gun post in the communication trench, not far from K.5. Having been warned about enemy booby traps, Private Maiden carefully cut the wires, which led to a suspicious-looking mound of earth nearby. Maiden later was horrified to discover he had severed the telephone line to Battalion headquarters![27]

The Fighting Tenth braced for counter-attacks, and the Germans did not disappoint. At dawn on Saturday, 22 May, the enemy mounted the first of four fierce assaults that severely tested the Battalion's mettle. "You could say the counter-attack lasted all day, continuously," recalled Private Sydney Cox. "But they were in the open, we could get at them. We really murdered them there for a while." Supplies ran low, making matters that much more difficult. "We were running out of ammunition," Private Cox remembered years afterwards. "We had no food, we had no water. That's where I got the dysentery, drinking out of shell holes. We had no water, and it was a hot, sunny day."[28]

It was here that the unit's machine-gun section proved its worth. The four Colt heavy machine-guns had been supplied with American-made ammunition and, consequently, "didn't jam so much," according to Private Wally Bennett. Nevertheless, it was Private Bennett's service revolver which saved his life this day. A German soldier, his bayonet gleaming in the sunshine, leaped into the Canadian trench, practically landing on top of Bennett. As his grey-clad adversary attacked, Bennett calmly drew his revolver, "and I got him. Down he went. That was the end of him."[29]

Lance-Sergeant Jock Palmer, a Lethbridge youngster, had a similar brush with death. After repeatedly driving off the enemy, Sergeant Palmer was horrified "when all of a sudden seven Germans jumped over the parapet and made for me. I shot the first two, and the others started back for the trench and I got them in the rear portion. Three of them rolled down dead to the world, and the others fell in the trench."[30]

But the Battalion paid a heavy price for holding this ground. Two more lieutenants, Stanley Lewis and Albert Morgan, both shot in the head, were killed during these furious counter-attacks. Major Guthrie later wrote of them: "Canada could not boast of two men more brave than these."[31]

Even worse than the counter-attacks was the German shell fire. "They shelled the daylights out of

Brigadier-General J.G. Rattray, CMG, DSO

Courtesy Calgary Highlanders

51

us," remarked Private Cox. "I don't know how many hours it kept us, but they really let us have it."[32] According to a twenty-two-year-old Scotsman, Private James Winning, "the place was a perfect inferno for a few hours." Private Winning, who had been with the Battalion since 26 April, was severely injured in one direct hit on the trench. "A piece of shrapnel hit my left foot at the base of the big toe, just glanced off the bone and passed out underneath. The piece was small, otherwise the bone would have been shattered, with more serious results. I was very thankful, indeed, to get off so lightly." Still, the injury ended Winning's war service.[33]

The toll among the officers mounted at an alarming rate. Captain Snelgrove, commanding D Company, "saw his men killed on each side, and faced the music alone until he was blown out of the trench by an explosive shell and damaged seriously." Lieutenant Richard Fairbrother was twice buried by shell bursts, but remained at his post until he was so badly injured by shrapnel that he had to be carried out.[34]

It was no safer to the rear. Major Guthrie returned to his headquarters that morning to write a report on the previous night's operation. His acting adjutant, Lieutenant George Duncan, urged him to get some rest but Guthrie, hearing the sounds of shelling at the front, "felt I was needed up the line." Moments after he departed, two shells hit the house, killing or wounding everyone inside. The dead included Captain Stewart, who had accompanied Guthrie on his reconnaissance mission the first night in the trenches, and Lieutenant Duncan.[35]

During the morning's bombardment, a fifty-yard section of captured trench was completely destroyed, "all of the occupants being killed, so that this portion was abandoned and was not subsequently occupied by either force."[36] Later in the day, the brigadier, General Currie, decided to withdraw the Battalion from a neighbouring section of the same trench, which he judged to be dangerously exposed. The withdrawal was conducted after nightfall, under covering fire provided by the machine-gun section. "When the battalion got nicely away," recalled Lance-Sergeant Jock Palmer, "[the Germans] started a counter-attack, so I put my gun on the parapet and fired eight belts right off.... " Sergeant Palmer's deadly fire drove back the enemy, and he was later awarded the DCM for his heroism.[37]

It was one of four DCMs won by members of the Battalion at Festubert. Twenty-seven-year-old Sergeant Edward Milne took charge of his platoon when the officer and all other NCOs were killed or wounded, "and led it with conspicous bravery and coolness," according to his citation. Another sergeant, Charles Morrison, repeatedly repaired broken telephone wires despite heavy shell fire, and on one occasion brought up a new line into the captured trenches. The other DCM went to Corporal Ralph Brookes for organizing the rescue of a wounded officer trapped in the open.

The Tenth spent three more days in the trenches, enduring heavy shell fire the whole time. Although there was some consolation in watching the capture of K.5, which fell to the 5th (Western Cavalry) and 7th (1st British Columbia Regiment) battalions during the early hours of 24 May, it was on the whole a miserable experience. Private Bennett, whose machine-gun emplacement narrowly missed destruction when a shell exploded nearby, never forgot the pounding he and his mates had endured. "In some places our trenches were blown down with shells, and in daylight our men were compelled to dig down and fill up the gaps, the best we could, so as to keep in communication with other troops — until it got dark, when we were able to work without being seen from the enemy lines."[38]

Major Guthrie was among the casualties. On 25 May, he was on his way to discuss that evening's relief of the Battalion when a shell exploded at his feet. Guthrie and Lieutenant Frederick Nichol, who was with him, survived but both suffered multiple wounds. After picking himself off the ground, "I then got over the stunned feeling and looking down saw that my clothing was torn away and blood gushing from several places," the major recounted. In fact, the thirty-year-old Guthrie had been hit in eleven places, and was later evacuated to England, where he was declared an invalid in December and shipped home.[39*]

The second-in-command, Captain Arthur, assumed temporary command of the Battalion.

That night the Fighting Tenth was relieved by the temporarily dismounted Canadian Cavalry Brigade. This was the first taste of trench warfare for the horse-soldiers, and the brigade's commander, Brigadier General J.E.B. Seely, a former British cabinet minister, issued unusual orders for the relief. Because of the troopers' inexperience, he specified that the outgoing units would remain in the trenches until the entire incoming force was in place. With the enemy shell fire undiminished, this meant that the Tenth would take unnecessary casualties during the takeover by Lord Strathcona's Horse. Infuriated, Lieutenant Walter Critchley stormed out of his trench and set off for Battalion headquarters to protest the

---

* The trip to Canada was another adventure for Guthrie. His hospital ship, *Hesperian*, was torpedoed and sunk, but the major was rescued after being "found floating on the sea supported by his crutches." Promoted to lieutenant-colonel, he raised a Highland unit, the 236th Battalion, which reinforced Canadian combat forces.[40] Colonel Guthrie recruited in the United States and the *New York Herald* later called him "one of the Canadian war heroes who has most aroused the admiration of Americans." (The "dashing" Guthrie was also, according to the *Herald*, "the first recruit in Canada and has been twenty-two times wounded"!)[41] After the war, he emigrated to the U.S., where he became a successful corporation lawyer in Boston.

order which was responsible for needless losses. En route, Lieutenant Critchley ran into another officer, a big man whom he did not recognize. "Who are you?" this officer inquired of the youthful subaltern.

"I'm Critchley, of the Tenth Battalion."

"Where are you going?"

"I'm going back to my headquarters. There's a General Seely – I don't know who the hell he is, but he [has] the stupid idea that we're to stay in the trenches till the Strathconas come in with us. It's creating a very dangerous situation, causing unnecessary casualties, I consider."

"You can go back, Critchley, and move your men out," replied the big officer. "I'm General Seely."[42]*

There were no regrets about leaving Festubert. The official history describes this battle as "the most unsatisfactory engagement" involving Canadian troops in the entire war,[44] and no member of the Fighting Tenth would have disagreed with that assessment. "It was about the worst," opined the DCM-winning sergeant, Jock Palmer. "It was simply the gates of hell opened and everything let loose at once."[45] With only three weeks since the blood-letting at Ypres, the Battalion, like the rest of the Canadian Division, was in no shape to conduct a major battle. Half the infantrymen who fought at Festubert were ill-trained newcomers fresh from Canada via reinforcement camps in England. The artillery, still suffering from shortages of guns and ammunition of sufficient quality to deal with the enemy's impressive field fortifications, proved unequal to the task of clearing a path for the infantry. The foot soldiers again paid the price for hurried preparations and inadequate support which left them exposed to terrible machine-gun fire. If Festubert accomplished one thing, it convinced the generals on both sides that the conflict on the Western Front was siege warfare, with advances to be measured, not in miles, but in mere yards. No gain would ever be commensurate with the expenditure in blood.

The Fighting Tenth's failed attacks on K.5 had been costly: "18 Officers and about 250 other ranks."[46]

The officer losses were disproportionately heavy; the Canadian Division, as a whole, lost ninety-three officers at Festubert. Nearly one in five belonged to the Tenth Battalion, whose casualties in other ranks were less than one-tenth of the divisional total of 2,230[47]. Among the Battalion's dead was Private Frederick Barnes, an English-born bank clerk who was killed on 22 May, eight days shy of his twenty-first birthday.[48] The wounded included Sergeant Charlie Stevenson, a thirty-two-year-old Calgary carpenter who had escaped injury at Ypres only to take a bullet in the arm at Festubert. It was the first of four wounds suffered by Stevenson, who would survive the war as a major.

A six-day rest awaited the Tenth. Following its withdrawal from the front lines, it was billeted in Le Hamel. The Battalion was seriously understrength, a sharp contrast to its situation earlier in May, when it was a hundred men over its establishment. As of 30 May, its four companies could muster barely half their normal numbers: A, 112, all ranks; B, 126; C, 133; D, 105.[49]

Captain Arthur's tenure as acting commander was brief. He handed over his responsibilities to Major Dan Ormond, who rejoined the Battalion on the afternoon of 28 May, having recovered from his shoulder wound of a month earlier.** However, Major Ormond's period of command was just as brief. He was the designated second-in-command; a new commanding officer was on his way from England. In the meantime, Ormond conducted the Fighting Tenth through an inspection by General Currie on the twenty-ninth. The following day he took the company commanders to look at the Battalion's next assigned sector, near Givenchy, just south of Festubert. On Tuesday, 1 June, the Tenth relieved a British battalion, the 17th City of London Regiment, in the front lines. Here, it awaited the arrival of its new commander.

---

* While on this mission, Lieutenant Critchley missed a visit from his father. Sixty-six-year-old Lieutenant Oswald Critchley was the Strathconas' machine-gun officer, and during the relief went looking for his son. Unable to find him, Lieutenant Critchley left a message with a sergeant: "Well, when you see him, give him my love and tell him I'm scared to death!"[43]

As a matter of interest, two of Walter Critchley's brothers were also Strathconas. Cecil, two years older, was the cavalry regiment's adjutant, while Jack, a year younger, was a senior subaltern. Cecil survived the war as a brigadier-general and later was elected to the British Parliament, but Jack died of wounds in March 1917.

** Soon afterwards, Arthur's association with the Tenth ended when ill health forced him to return to Canada. He was formally struck off strength on 11 July. The Battalion's first DSO-winner, Arthur ended the war as a major.

Chapter Four

WAR IN THE TRENCHES

(2 June 1915 - 1 June 1916)

The new commanding officer was no stranger. He was Lieutenant-Colonel J.G. Rattray, the tough, fifty-one-year-old Manitoban who had organized the Battalion at Valcartier, only to be replaced by Russell Boyle before it went overseas. Colonel Rattray had been very much embittered by the experience, but he stayed close to the scene by going to England as a divisional staff officer, before procuring the post of president of the Permanent Board of Enquiry at Shorncliffe. Rattray's appointment as the officer commanding the Tenth took effect on 2 June, the date he joined the Battalion in the line near Givenchy.

No one was more surprised at this development than Rattray himself. "When I saw you last week in

An artist's conception of a Canadian trench raid

Courtesy The War Illustrated Album Deluxe

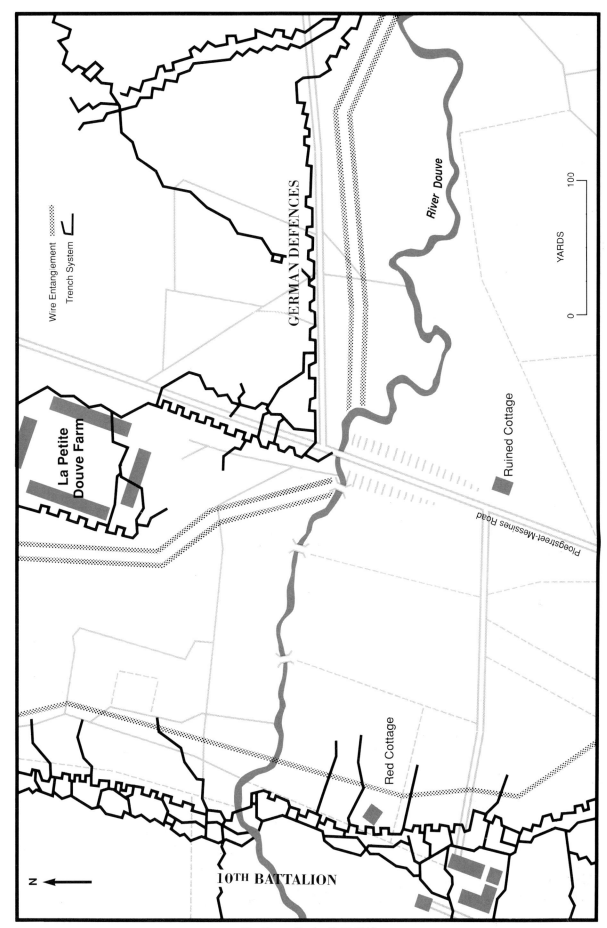

Wire Entanglement
Trench System

GERMAN DEFENCES

River Douve

100

YARDS

0

La Petite Douve Farm

Ruined Cottage

Ploegstreet-Messines Road

Red Cottage

N

10TH BATTALION

The Douve Sector 1915-1916

55

London," he wrote an acquaintance, "I had no idea that I would be in the trenches at the head of the 10th Battalion. When I got back to Shorncliff[e] I found a hurry order for me to go to France at once. I got here on Tuesday. I understood when I left Shorncliff[e] that our Division was resting but I found them very much in the trenches…. I must say there is something quite attractive about it and I am much more used to the shells than I expected to be."[1]

Colonel Rattray had no need to acquaint himself with his second-in-command, Major Ormond, for the two had served together in the Manitoba militia before the war and at Valcartier when the Tenth was organized. But he found it necessary to get to know his other senior officers, including the adjutant, Lieutenant John Graham, and the company commanders, Captain Geoff Arthur (A), Captain Allison Day (B), Lieutenant Walter Critchley (C), and Lieutenant Robert Good (D). Only Captain Day failed to impress him. "His temperament is such that in the trenches he keeps the men in such tension that it is hard on them." Rattray disliked Day's profane language, poor discipline, and, above all, his unreliable reports: "he magnifies small things to suit his own vanity. Everything he does is to show himself as the central figure." Not surprisingly, Day departed later that summer, never to return to the Tenth.[2]

A stickler for detail, Rattray was quick to notice that his Battalion was without its collar badges. Within two days of joining the Tenth, he was badgering divisional headquarters. "Say, where are the $\frac{C}{10}$ badges for this battalion? They have never received the issue…." The colonel insisted that he had seen "some boxes of these" at Salisbury, and demanded to know where they had gone. The badges arrived a short time later.[3]

The Battalion spent five days in the trenches, losing two men killed and fourteen wounded. The latter included Private Charles Coffin, a twenty-six-year-old banker from North Battleford, Saskatchewan, who took a rifle bullet in the lung. Besides suffering broken ribs, Private Coffin contracted pleurisy, which ended his military career later in the year.[4]

Good news awaited the Tenth when it came out of the line on Sunday night, 6 June. During the next week, while billeted in the village of Hinges, the Battalion would exchange its unreliable Ross rifles for the British-made Short Magazine Lee-Enfield, Mark III, which was being issued to the entire Canadian Division. Canadian snipers continued to use the Ross with satisfactory results, but the riflemen of the Fighting Tenth were only too happy to have the Lee-Enfield. "That's the only rifle yet," claimed Sergeant Chris Scriven, who had been one of many to pick up a Lee-Enfield during the Second Battle of Ypres. "I'd rather go out tomorrow with a Short Lee-Enfield than anything they've got right today. Because I'm telling you — mud, sand, anything, that damned old rifle will stay with you. If you know how to use it, it'll stay a long time."[5]

The troops were trained to use the Lee-Enfield during their stay at Hinges, and were also "given a working knowledge of the machine gun" and "taught how to use the several kinds of grenades so that in case of emergancy [sic] every man would be able to use them if necessary."[6] Hand grenades were appallingly primitive in mid-1915. They were called "bombs," and each brigade in the BEF, including the Canadians, had by now formed a company of bomb-throwing specialists. The reason was plain: they were very dangerous weapons, to the user as well as to the intended victims, as Corporal Alexander McGregor related in a letter home to Calgary. They were "made out of old jam cans that are empty of jam, they are filled with some dry gun cotton, then shrapnell [sic], then it is all [w]rapped up in some gunny sa[c]king & placed in an old jam can & a piece of fuse & a detonator put on the end of the fuse & the fuse is then placed in the dry gun cotton & and held their [sic] by a little wire so it won't fall out when its threw by the bomb thrower. They are a very deadley missel [sic] of warfare & are not expensive either".[7] Later in 1915, these homemade devices were replaced by the superior Mills bomb, a metal cylinder filled with explosive.

On Monday, 14 June, the Battalion was inspected by General Alderson. The divisional commander "expressed himself as pleased with the appearance of the men." The following day, the Tenth was ordered "to be prepared to move on an hour's notice as an allied attack was being made in the vicinity of La Basse [sic]."[8] However, it was not involved in this operation, a minor and unsuccessful attack by the First Brigade at Givenchy, on 16 June.

A return to the front lines impended. On 17 June — the date a young lieutenant named Eric MacDonald, a future commanding officer, joined the Battalion — the Tenth marched to La Preol. They then relieved the 2nd Royal Warwickshires on the afternoon of the nineteenth, in the vicinity of Givenchy, near the Canal de la Bassée. The Battalion was "heavily shelled while carrying out this relief," losing two men killed and six others wounded. It was a portent of things to come; by 23 June, it had lost ten more killed and twenty wounded.[9]

One of the victims was Private Ernest Sissons. Wally Bennett, who was now a corporal, recalled that their machine-gun emplacement was only thirty yards from the German lines. "We were so near to them," Corporal Bennett claimed, "that we could hear them talking at night." During the afternoon of 21 June, Bennett later wrote, "I was in the dug-out sleeping. They woke me up — and there was Sissons lying, shot clean through the head — a German sniper got him. It need not have happened, as we had repeatedly told him not to look over the top of the trench, but to use the periscope. But, it was his first trip in the line, hav-

Lieutenant-General Edwin Alderson pins ribbon of DCM on tunic of Lance-Corporal Frank Cox for his part in the Tenth Battalion first trench raid, conducted on the night of 4-5 February 1916. Behind Cox is Private Louis Zuidema, who won the DCM in the same action.

ing just joined our section. [I] suppose they had seen him before, got a rifle fixed, and then let him have it the next time he looked over." Bennett and his machine-gun section buried Sissons behind the line that night.[10]

The Battalion also lost one of its few remaining original officers. After coming through the battles of Ypres and Festubert without a scratch, Lieutenant Ashton Cockshutt was "slightly wounded." The twenty-two-year-old employee of the Cockshutt Plow Company in Calgary never returned to the Tenth. Although he recovered from his wounds and helped to raise the 125th Battalion in his hometown of Brantford, Ontario, Cockshutt was later diagnosed as having tuberculosis. He went back to Calgary and resumed his duties with Cockshutt Plow.[11]

The Tenth pulled out of here on the evening of 24 June, but there was no opportunity to rest. Instead, the Battalion spent the next three nights marching northwards to familiar territory, moving to the neighbourhood of Ploegsteert, where the Canadians had been given their initiation in trench warfare in February. En route, the Tenth was viewed by the brigadier, General Currie, who wrote a kind note to Colonel Rattray: "I congratulate you on the manner in which your battalion marched from Bethune to Estaires on the night 24/25 June and from the latter place to Stangy, night 25/26. They were easily first in

the brigade. Please continue to keep up this good record to-day."[12]

Occupying reserve trenches on the crest of Hill 63, the Battalion faced a test of its endurance. On the last day of June, two companies were sent into the front lines, where the Battalion would spend most of July. According to Wally Bennett, recently promoted to sergeant and responsible for two machine-guns, it was a relatively pleasant place. Nearby was a farm where fresh water could be obtained. "Up in the loft of this place were lots of tobacco leaves, hanging in bunches in the rafters. Here we rolled our own cigars! They were very strong, but nevertheless they were cigars of a kind! The weather during these days in the line was very warm, and it was sure a change … in comparison with what we had been through, in the past, at Ypres and Festubert."[13]

There was plenty of work to be done. "We were building trenches, building fortifications, building barbed-wire protection in front, and all this kind work was going on all the time," recalled Serge Chris Scriven. "If you weren't fighting, you were ing."[14] Major Ormond, the Battalion's second-mand, later described the trenches that we constructed in the summer of 1915:

What you mean by a trench for st siege, warfare is something that a

57

Ploegsteert
Courtesy National Archives of Canada/PA-4479

along standing upright. And when the material was available, they put in what we called 'duck walk' along the bottom. Then you had what was called a 'fire step,' on the enemy's side, so that the men, to use their rifles, could step up, oh, a foot to eighteen inches and fire over the parapet. The parados would be somewhat lower than the parapet. And the top of the trench would range from four feet to six feet wide.

Well, then, off this trench, you had what was called 'dugouts' or 'bivvies' or what-have-you, and they were made of anything that the troops could liberate from what it had been used for before — the doors from smashed-up houses, the wood from stables, all that sort of thing. And then they put sandbags on top of that, and if you got one layer of sandbags on top, it would stop shell fragments and shrapnel and a rifle grenade.

The trenches were made so that three or four men could stand side-by-side and each have a couple of yards. Well, then, you'd put a projection out, so that if a shell burst in one of these what we called a 'bay,' the side-blast would be stopped by these projections. They zig-zagged.[15]

The soldiers, as soldiers somehow seem able to do in all kinds of conditions, made life bearable in what was surely an unbearable situation. Alexander MacGregor, a corporal in D Company, described in detail the preparation of meals in the trenches at this time:

Their [sic] is a ration party goes out every night to [a gi]ven place & meets a transport loaded with pro[visio]ns for the troops in the trenches. They have [to car]ry them in.... It is no fun carrying rations in [throug]h the communication trenches when they [are wet] & mud[d]y & sometimes have 6 in. or a [foot of wat]er in them.

Well after they get back in again the rations are dished out to each man & he has to cook his the best he can. Of course he can always get Bulley [sic] beef or what you would call corn[ed] beef in half lbs. tins & hard tack & tea. But we are mostly sick of that now, though when we are good & hungrey [sic] it tastes fine....

Well when me and my pard gets owers [sic] we start & get a jug of water & that is [what] one of us does & the other hunts around for some wood, then we get ahold of an old pail or, if we can't find anything to build a fire in, we dig a hole about 4 or 5 in. acros[s] & a foot & a half long & 6 in. deep, then we put ower canteen over with the water in for tea. Then one of us gets the stakes [sic] or bacon over the fire in the top half of the canteen & then we get the bread out & the jam or butter... & have a meal....

[S]ometimes a shell disturbs us at work making a meal, if the Huns see the smoke of ower fire, why they drop a shell or shrapnell [sic] over to help us enjoy our dinner.[16]

There was little fighting in this period. Most of the action, aside from ducking snipers' bullets and dodging shells, consisted of patrolling no man's land at night. Two-man listening posts were set up in front of the Battalion's trenches, to warn of enemy activity. It was most unpleasant, according to Corporal MacGregor, "sitting in a space of 4 by 8 made of sacks filled with sand and dirt, which is just big enough to sit up in, with a pair of wet legs, listening to the bullets whistling over every once in a while and in the dark also."[17]

When they were not required to work, the troops passed their time writing letters home, playing cards, or reading British and Canadian newspapers. While personal cleanliness often left a lot to be desired — for lice were omnipresent and mud-free days were rare —

Filling sandbags for construction of a parapet
Courtesy The War Illustrated Album Deluxe

58

the men cleaned and oiled their rifles every day. Indeed, they slept with their rifles, and ate, went to the latrine, and performed all routine duties with them close at hand. A soldier quickly learned that his rifle was his best friend and that there was no better pastime than to look after it.

Colonel Rattray was fascinated by trench warfare. While he was not a brilliant soldier, he never tired of writing letters to his superior officers, offering observations and suggestions. For example, he suggested equipping the men with shotguns for defensive purposes. "A 'Pump' gun of the Remington or Winchester type with 6 cartridges in the chamber loaded with 'Buck' shot would make a very effectual weapon for stopping an infantry attack at close quarters." He was even critical of the way the trenches were constructed. "We dig them too narrow, the sides too straight, and unless the sides are well rivetted [sic] they are going to cave in." Rattray favoured the German method of digging the trenches wider at the top than the bottom, claiming that the British technique settled for "temporary safety at the expense of permanency."[18]

A bomber shows how it's done
Courtesy National Archives of Canada/PA-5328

Rattray's main challenge in the summer of 1915 was to restore the Fighting Tenth to its former level of combat efficiency. It was no easy task, and the colonel was hampered by a shortage of qualified officers. Many of the newcomers, he complained, "are absolutely 'Gun Shy' as we say about dogs in the west. These officers are no use under shell fire."[19] One solution was to promote NCOs who were acting as officers, but his proposal to speed their commissions met with little enthusiasm from Second Brigade headquarters, and Rattray warned General Currie that "if it takes two or three months to get their appointments approved, it will just be that much longer in getting this Battalion into its former efficient condition."[20] His difficulties apparently worsened with the mid-July departure of solid officers such as Captains Geoff Arthur and John Graham, the adjutant, and Lieutenant Robert Good; all were invalided home. By the end of October, the colonel informed his brigadier that "we are actually short 5 captains and 4 subalterns."[21]

The colonel's complaints notwithstanding, the Battalion boasted several outstanding subalterns,

including Eric MacDonald, who arrived in mid-June; Geoff Burbidge, Stanley Kent, and Jack Mitchell, who arrived on 22 July; and Alfred Trimmer, who joined the unit in early October. These five would have a major impact on the Tenth.

Another answer to the problem was to receive better-trained reinforcements. The new men filling the ranks of battle-weakened battalions in France were rarely fit for the task at hand, and combat commanders complained bitterly about the poor training given these men at Canadian bases in England. Rattray did more than complain; he wrote a long letter to his counterpart with the 49th (Edmonton Regiment) Battalion, which at the time was serving as a reinforcement unit for the Tenth. Offering "a few suggestions as to effective training," Rattray stated that the troops "should know how to lay out and dig trenches and dugouts. They live half their time in them so should become conversant with the work, even to the extent of actually living in them in training, doing their cooking, bringing in water and rations and sleeping for a few days." Musketry courses should stress both rapidity and accuracy of fire, as well as care of rifles, and the colonel contended that each soldier should have a "working knowledge" of machine-guns and bombs. He also warned that discipline at the front was demanding, revealing that "a court martial here gave two of my men 1 year each with hard labour, in prison, for being absent from trenches and drunk.... Ordinary absence from billets and drunkenness draws from the commanding officers 21 to 28 days' No. 1 Field Punishment."[22]

July 1915 was a gruelling month for the Tenth Battalion. While the casualties — fourteen wounded — were relatively light, the unit had to endure the incessant strain of front-line duty for an unusually long time. As Major Ormond complained in the war diary on 31 July: "This is the 44th day since rest. 41 days in the trenches or immediately behind, always liable to shell fire, and 3 days of night marches. The men are in every way showing the strain, the percentage going sick has increased to a marked extent."[23] This proved to be Ormond's last entry in the war diary, which was entrusted to the acting adjutant, Lieutenant George Craggs, who in early March ha[d] been the Battalion's first officer casualty. O[n] August, Ormond was assigned to temporarily c[om]mand the 7th (1st British Columbia Regim[ent]) Battalion, when the latter's commander, Lieut[enant] Colonel Victor Odlum – the same officer who [led] the amalgamated 7th/Tenth at Ypres – was [wounded] during a front-line reconnaissance.[24] More th[an] would pass before the man known as "[Ole] Dan" returned to the Fighting Tenth.

Despite Ormond's complaint, it [was] Friday, 6 August, that the Battali[on was] relieved. Its move from the trenches [cost it] five members of the unit who w[ere]

59

The world's foremost military minds were confounded by the situation that existed along the Western Front during 1915. While the Germans maintained a generally defensive posture here, in favour of attacks on the more vulnerable Russians, the British and French sought methods of ending the deadlock and restoring the war of movement with which their generals were more accustomed and for which their armies had been trained.

Most historians are critical of their efforts. "They applied themselves to the task of breaking the German line," observed one writer, "with the intelligence of a group of savages trying to extract a screw from a piece of wood." British generalship, in particular, has been roundly condemned for its apparent lack of imagination, unwillingness to utilize some new weapons and misusing others, and inability to adapt to the changed reality of war. What the critics, both modern and contemporary, forget is that the Great War was very much a transitional war in terms of technology. Communications and transportation failed to keep pace with the killing power of heavy artillery, rapid-firing field guns, and the machine-gun, as well as the unprecedented size of the armies. The Canadian Army Corps, at its peak, was bigger than the armies commanded by either Napoleon or Wellington at Waterloo a century before. To make matters worse, there were no flanks around which to manoeuvre, which necessitated frontal assaults against increasingly sophisti-cated fortifications protected by vast fields of barbed wire. The Western Front was where the main forces of the primary combatants — Germany, Great Britain, and France — were located. As such, it was the main theatre of a war that would continue until one side conceded defeat. In 1915, there were few commanders who appreciated that attrition was the only way this war could be brought to a conclusion.

Sir Douglas Haig was one of the handful who knew the war would be long and bloody. His pre-war studies had awakened him to the massive resources of manpower and technology available to modern industrialized nations at war. "We may well be fighting the Germans in the next few years," he had writ-ten in 1906. "In battle with troops as brave and efficient as the Germans, we shall have to fight long and hard before we can hope for a decision. It will be dangerous to attempt a decisive blow before we have worn down the enemy's power of resistance." The war, when it came, would unfold in several distinct stages, Haig predicted:

The manoeuvre for position.
The first clash of battle.
The wearing-out fight of varying duration.
And the eventual decisive blow, which would give victory.

Haig, a wealthy Scot from a whisky-distilling family, was a corps commander at the start of the war, and commanded the First Army when the BEF expanded to two field armies in the fall of 1914. By the end of 1915, he was the commander-in-chief, a position he held until the war's end.

Before gaining the appointment, Haig had a hand in all three British offensives staged during 1915. At Neuve-Chapelle in March, at Aubers Ridge in May, and at Loos in September, Haig's First Army had enjoyed mixed success. Aubers Ridge, or Festubert, was a debacle, but Neuve-Chapelle and Loos came tantalizingly close to achieving clearcut breaks in the enemy defences. Victory at Neuve-Chapelle was thwarted by the very narrow frontage — less than two miles — and by a notable lack of initiative on the part of the combat commanders who failed to exploit their initial success.

At Loos, early success was negated by the failure to commit the waiting reserves in time. These were under the personal direction of the commander-in-chief, Sir John French, who made the mistake of pub-licly blaming Haig for mishandling them. Haig, who counted King George among his supporters, fought back with a skillful letter-writing campaign which was far more successful than most of his military [eff]orts. French was brought back to England as commander of the Home Forces, and Haig took over the [BE]F.

[T]he biggest British disaster of 1915 took place not on the Western Front but in the eastern [Medite]rranean. In March, the Royal Navy bungled an attempt to force the Dardanelles in a bid to capture [Constan]tinople, knock Turkey out of the war, and establish a sea link with Russia. Convinced that this [was a des]irable alternative to the futility of the Western Front, the British government sent the Army in [to save t]he plan. Landing on the Gallipoli Peninsula, the British, Australian, and New Zealand troops [clung] to their beaches. A quarter of a million casualties later, the British army admitted defeat [and by Janua]ry 1916 had withdrawn.

The French army had an even more miserable time than the British in 1915. "Je les grignote" — "I am nibbling them" — was the way the French commander-in-chief, General Joseph Joffre, summed up his strategy. Far from nibbling, General Joffre was in fact breaking his teeth. Three major French offensives, one in Champagne sandwiched between two in Artois, with Vimy Ridge as the primary objective, cost Joffre's forces hundreds of thousands of casualties. Nicknamed "Papa" by his adoring troops, he sent them into battle with ringing words of encouragement: "Votre élan sera irrésistible!" The French had élan to spare, but it was not enough to get them through the fire of massed machine-guns and artillery. Four hundred thousand fell in the first campaign in Artois; Champagne added 145,000 to the casualty count; the second Artois offensive cost 190,000 men.

There were many lessons to be drawn from these battles, and British and French staff officers studied them exhaustively, searching for answers that would point to victory. The Germans, too, were drawing conclusions about the campaign on the Western Front, and the words of their commander, General Falkenhayn, were significant: "The English troops, in spite of undeniable bravery and endurance, have proved so clumsy in action that they will accomplish nothing decisive against the German Army in the immediate future."

August. Two of these men, Sergeant Thomas Ross and Corporal Charles Maxwell, later died of their injuries.

The toll of the extended tour was apparent. On 7 August, when the Tenth was inspected by the militia minister, Sam Hughes — now an honourary major-general and soon to be knighted — it could parade only 429, all ranks. However, a draft of 212 other ranks joined the Battalion the same day. "These reinforcements were of good physique and well drilled," notes the war diary. "A number of cases however were found to have defective teeth." During the next three days, the Battalion enjoyed "rest and sports with concerts in evening," before returning to the trenches late on 10 August. The short rest had been effective. "Great change noticeable in spirits and bearing of men as result of four day complete rest after 51 days in trenches or immediately behind and always liable to shell fire."[25]

August proved to be a comparatively quiet month. Two tours of duty in the front lines, 10 - 15 August and 20 - 25 August, resulted in one fatality, Private Fred Atkinson; four other ranks were wounded. Between tours, the Battalion was given the honour of representing the Second Brigade during a visit by Etienne Alexandre Millerand, the French minister of war, on the eighteenth. Two companies of the Fighting Tenth were inspected by the war minister although, surprisingly, the event was not considered sufficiently important to rate a mention in the war diary.[26]

The return to the trenches on Monday, 30 August, was more memorable. "Everything quiet," marvelled the war diary. "Absence of artillery activity especially noticeable." The Tenth was relieved on the night of 4 September: "This was the first tour of duty in the trenches in which the Battalion sustained no casualties since its arrival in France in February." The same day, 179 reinforcements arrived. "Men were of good physique," commented the war diarist, "but not very advanced in training." Three relaxing days followed, capped by an inspection on 7 September by General

An assortment of grenades used in the trenches
Courtesy The War Illustrated Album Deluxe

Sir Herbert Plumer, the Second Army's commander. The Tenth's parade strength was 726, all ranks.[27]

Its next tour was much more demanding. The first night, 10 - 11 September, was quiet while working parties "strengthened front line parapets and dug outs." The following two nights, these parties were "hampered" by enemy snipers and machine-gunners who inflicted four casualties, including Private Weldon Clark, who was killed. "On second night," reads the war diary, "after working parties had been withdrawn [we] retaliated on large enemy working party with apparent result of causing considerable casualties." Retaliation had the desired effect. The next night, "our working parties were left undisturbed."[28]

Relieved on the night of Tuesday, 14 September, the Fighting Tenth found itself part of a historic occasion. The Canadian Army Corps was being formed, with the addition of the recently arrived Second Division, under the Third Brigade's former commander, General Turner; on the thirteenth, General Alderson opened his new Corps headquarters. The same day, the Second Brigade lost its commander, General Currie, who was appointed to command the First Division. His place as brigadier was taken by the 8th (90th Winnipeg Rifles) Battalion's Lieutenant-Colonel Louis Lipsett. This appointment was welcomed by the Tenth's Colonel Rattray, who described Lipsett as "a very efficient officer, ambitious, aggressive, and a hard worker."[29] A third division was in the process of being formed, with a fourth to come in 1916, developments which were welcomed by veterans such as Sergeant Wally Bennett. "Let them come, as from the way things were going, it looked very much as if they would be needed."[30]

The opinionated Colonel Rattray was soon involved in a controversy which arose from the creation of the Canadian Corps. The Third Division was to be commanded by the First Brigade's General Malcolm Mercer, who departed in November. In spite of vehement opposition from the new divisional commander, General Currie, Mercer's successor turned out to be Garnet Hughes, son of the militia minister. The younger Hughes performed poorly as General Turner's brigade-major at Ypres, and Currie considered him to be "extremely lucky" but with "practically no experience whatever in military matters."[31] Rattray wholeheartedly supported Currie in this matter. In a long letter to John Dafoe, the fiery editor of the Manitoba *Free Press*, the Tenth Battalion commander made clear his views on Hughes — father and son:

Politics still continues to be very much a factor in the organizing Canadian forces. In this game being played with the lives of men at stake, it is [a] cruel shame to see what is being done. I would like to write more fully must forego doing so, but

the latest perpetration of political imbecility in our appointments to commands is the attempt to appoint Garnet Hughes to command a Brigade. Are the people of Canada going to stand for it? Can't they appreciate what it means to men and homes in Canada? God forbid that after the demonstration of Garnet Hughes' military instinct at Ypres as Brigade Major that he should ever command a Brigade.

Perhaps I am prejudiced. I have ever[y] right to be. I was insulted in season and out, & usually out, alone, in company with a few officers, in conferences with officers and before my Battalion, by Sam Hughes. Deprived of my command and orders given that I was to get nothing; but laying aside all personal hatred and using calm judgement I must say that to stand for the appointment of Garnet Hughes as a Brigadier General is beyond all reason and too many Canadian sons' lives and peace of mind of Canadian homes at stake to take a chance of this kind.[32]

A friendly estaminet, where the troops could enjoy a meal while out of the front lines.

Courtesy National Archives of Canada/PA-4503

These objections notwithstanding, Hughes gained the appointment to command the First Brigade.

The reorganization of the Corps was timely in at least one respect. It spared the Canadians a part in the disastrous Battle of Loos in mid-September. The first major British offensive of the war, it resulted in utter failure and bitter recriminations between the men responsible for it, the BEF's commander-in-chief, Field-Marshal French, and the First Army's General Haig. Their feud climaxed in December, when French was replaced by Haig.

These events were, however, far removed from the Fighting Tenth, which returned to the front lines on Sunday, 19 September. By the time it was relieved on the twenty-fourth, it had endured several punishing artillery barrages; at one point, high-explosive shells destroyed the house adjacent to Battalion headquarters. Fortunately, the casualties during this tour were modest: Private John Martin, one of the English-born originals, was killed, and seven others were wounded, including Corporal William Baker, the DCM-winner from Saint-Julien. The low losses were attributed by the war diarist "to efficacy of deep narrow safety trenches dug behind front line trenches to which troops retired during enemy bombardment."

In any case, the casualties were more than offset by the arrival on 23 September of forty-three reinforcements — "Men of good physique and well trained" — as well as by the return of Captain Charles Costigan, who had recovered from his head wound suffered at Festubert.[33] Curiously, Colonel Rattray was not enthused about Costigan's return, at least not in his present rank. Arguing that he had other men "better qualified" to act as captains, Rattray complained that Costigan, who had just turned thirty-five, should serve as a subaltern because he had "no infantry experience.... He has taken no infantry training but took a Machine Gun course."[34]

The Tenth's next visit to the trenches was bloodier. After five days in the rear, where the men alternated between rest and working parties, the Battalion returned to the front lines on Wednesday, 29 September. Although the daylight hours were generally quiet, the unit's position was bombarded by German artillery, trench mortars, and rifle grenades each night. By Saturday, 4 October, when it was relieved, its losses totalled six dead and fourteen wounded, but the Tenth had proved that it could dish out punishment as well as take it. On the second, after dark, a large group of Germans, "about 200 strong," was detected working in no man's land. It was soon "dispersed by rifle fire, assisted by our trench mortars and rifle grenades."[35]

There was no rest for the Battalion. Removed to brigade reserve on 4 October, it was required to provide working parties to dig trenches and string barbed wire. "No parades," noted the war diary, "as working parties were required both day and night." Lance-Corporal Denis Morris, an original, was wounded on the sixth, while on one of these parties. There was time for a limited amount of training: "Two attack practices over trenches were carried out."[36]

Daring forays by two officers highlighted the Tenth's next tour in the trenches. The Battalion moved into the front lines after dark on Saturday, 9 October and, two nights later, Captain Walter Critchley and Lieutenant Thomas Chutter tested the German defences. Accompanied by a subaltern from Second Brigade headquarters and an unidentified NCO, Captain Critchley and Lieutenant Chutter "went over to German wire in front [of] their fire trench and cut gap 20 feet wide, 12 feet deep. Complete samples of wire and stakes were brought back. Although the party were within 30 yards of German parapet and made considerable noise, one of party falling into shell hole half full of water, no attention at all was paid by Germans." Even more remarkably, Critchley and Chutter repeated the venture the next day, in broad daylight, again without incident.[37]

There was further excitement on Wednesday, 13 October, when the Fighting Tenth took part in a demonstration that was mounted along the entire front held by the Second Army. Designed to test the enemy's reaction to an attack, the carefully rehearsed operation involved the use of smoke bombs, with results detailed in the war diary:

Two officers acquainted with handling of smoke bombs were specially detailed on left flank of front line trenches held by Battalion. All troops were withdrawn from front line trenches to support line 150 - 200 yds in rear or to special safety trenches in immediate rear, except men told off to throw bombs, two or three men per machine gun emplacement and a few sentries.

The bombs were lighted and thrown over at 3.27 P.M., a little in advance of the time ordered, in order to conform with the rest of the line, as at this hour it was noticed that the unit on both left and right had commenced to throw bombs. The bombs lit well and a dense cloud arose and moved slowly across to German lines. Within four minutes from bombs first being thrown German artillery opened fire all along front line trenches with H.E. and shrapnel. The support line and certain communication trenches were also heavily shelled.... This bombardment continued with varying intensity for half an hour and finally ceased at 4 P.M.

As soon as the smoke arose, the enemy lit fires all along the front line trenches opposite, and the bayonets of supporting troops could be discerned moving down communication trenches to the front line from support trenches about 15 yards in rear of front line. At the same time rapid rifle fire was opened from enemy trenches which increased in intensity as supporting troops reached their stations, but at no time was any really heavy volume of fire developed, nor, up to the time that the smoke obscured the view, did the bayonets moving to support appear very numerous ... the enemy could be seen firing at intervals of 8 - 10 feet between each man. The firing was very nervous and ill aimed, most shots going well above our parapet. Fire was opened by enemy with machine guns but not more than two or at the outside three appeared to be employed. Machine gun and rifle fire ceased as soon as smoke cleared away. The enemy did not wear smoke helmets or respirators.

Despite the enemy's inaccurate small-arms fire, the Battalion suffered six casualties, all wounded, including Captain William Bingham, with a fractured skull. At 5:15 p.m., the Germans fired a retaliatory barrage which lasted half an hour. "Orders had been issued to troops not to move from positions taken up during demonstration, with the result that casualties both at this time and during demonstration were comparatively light."

Relieved the next night, the Battalion moved into divisional reserve. After resting for a couple of days, it returned to intensive training on Saturday, 16 October, when it practised assaulting trenches, with "special attention being given to blocking communication trenches and consolidating position captured." A block usually involved improvising a barricade, but the unit experimented with an alternative, placing an explosive in a traverse and causing the wall of the trench to collapse. It was not impressive, according to the war diarist, who noted that the effort required to lay the charge and prepare the fuse "resulted in no more being effected than could have been done with picks and shovels in [the] same time."[38]

A YMCA canteen in the firing zone
Courtesy National Archives of Canada/PA-944

The death of a valued officer marred the Battalion's return to the front lines on the nineteenth. During the relief, the Germans shelled the trenches, wounding six other ranks, and Lieutenant Harold Seccombe hurried forward to take charge of the situation. Struck by shell fragments, Lieutenant Seccombe died the next morning. Colonel Rattray, who could not afford to lose officers of this calibre, called Seccombe's death "a great shock to me. He was one of the brightest and most promising subalterns I had, and I gave him special work to do. He was full of splendid ideas and suggestions and carried out his duties so well that I felt his loss as a personal one."[39]

Sniping and shelling continued on a more or less regular basis for the remainder of the five-day tour,

but by now the men of the Tenth viewed trench warfare with a matter-of-fact attitude. This was true even of relative newcomers such as Lance-Corporal Harold Evans, who wrote home to Calgary to assure his family that the fighting "doesn't bother me at all.... Our billets are five miles back from the firing line, and we take five day spells in the trenches. The noise of the shells passing overhead sounds like a locomotive going at high speed.... The German snipers are very good shots. They have their rifles trained on parapets and loopholes and generally the man who puts his head up is gone. However, our snipers are just as good and do the same thing to them."[40]

Eight more casualties had been incurred by the time the Battalion was relieved in a heavy mist on 24 October.[41] Two of the injuries were unusual: Captain Seymour Norton-Taylor was wounded accidentally, his second war injury, while Private Eli Pilatzke's was self-inflicted. While cleaning his rifle, Private Pilatzke took off the magazine but neglected to set the safety catch. There was a cartridge in the chamber, and the rifle discharged. "Oh, my foot!" he shouted, as his mates scrambled to treat his wound. He recovered and returned to action, but was court-martialled for his carelessness.[42]

After withdrawing to Second Brigade reserve, the Battalion hurriedly prepared for a royal inspection. Three officers and fifty other ranks were selected to represent the Tenth on Wednesday, 27 October, when King George inspected units from the entire Canadian Corps. General Currie, the divisional commander, noted approvingly in his diary: "Everything passed off very well."[43]

By the time the Tenth returned to the trenches on 29 October, the weather had taken a turn for the worse. After a generally fine autumn, it had begun to rain heavily in the latter part of the month; a storm on the twenty-fifth forced the cancellation of the Battalion's working parties.[44] By early November, the effect on the trenches was grim. General Currie complained in his personal diary that "trenches [are] very bad, forts fallen in, subsidiary line ditto."[45] The Fighting Tenth could attest to the terrible conditions. "Owing to wet weather," says the war diary, "trenches, especially communication trenches and reserve trenches, commenced to cave in badly." That was on 2 November; by the early evening of the third, communication trenches were rated as "impassable," thanks to cave-ins and water that was up to five feet deep in places. "All available men at work pumping trenches and repairing parapets and dug outs, although hardly any headway could be made." One trench was temporarily isolated by the rising waters of the River Douve, which bisected the Tenth's front line and flowed towards the enemy's trenches. Usually eight to ten feet wide and three to four feet deep, the Douve was now three times its normal width and twice as deep.[46]

The Battalion was relieved the next night, but the rain was an ill omen. The winter of 1915–16 on the Western Front was grim. Not even Salisbury Plain could adequately prepare the troops for the four months of sustained misery that lay ahead, and no member of the Tenth would forget the experience. "The mud was everywhere," marvelled Captain Walter Critchley, one of the unit's originals. "We lived in it constantly. How any of us survived to come out in good shape is beyond me.... We were wet right through...." It was almost impossible to sleep in the sodden dugouts, with "water dripping on you and rats running over your face." Private Alfred Davis's recollection was similar: "Lot of mud, we had only one suit of clothes and I tell you sometimes we were wet for days. Wet feet was nothing, got used to that...."[47]

It was at this time that the Tenth was introduced to the ravages of trench foot, an ailment not unlike frostbite and resulting from prolonged exposure to wet, cold conditions. During the winter of 1915 - 16, trench foot reached epidemic proportions in the BEF, despite the contention of medical authorities that it could be controlled by proper precautions. They suggested generous applications of whale oil to the men's feet, along with changes to dry socks. The First Division's commander, General Currie, resolved to deal with the matter before it got out of hand. Summoning his twelve battalion commanders, including the Tenth's Colonel Rattray, Currie bluntly declared that he would hold them responsible for cases of trench foot in their units and that he intended to view the malady as a self-inflicted wound. The threat worked, as indicated by the weekly trenchfoot returns issued by the BEF's various army headquarters. "Consistently throughout the winter," a staff officer recalled, "the First Canadian Division was placed very high, more often than not heading the return with the word 'Nil.' "[48] It was a record to which the Tenth Battalion made a proud contribution.

After coming out of the line, the Tenth enjoyed four days of welcome rest. On Sunday, 7 November, the Battalion paraded through the divisional baths at Bulford Camp, and each man luxuriated in a steaming-hot shower which cleansed his mud-caked body, while his uniform was disinfected — although, as always, the lice returned as soon as the soldier went back into the trenches. This was accompanied by an issue of new underwear.[49]

The next day, the Tenth moved into the front lines once more. Things were even worse by now, thanks to the cold, steady rainfall. "All available men by day and night draining trenches, repairing & revetting dry portions and rebuilding dug outs," reads the war diary. Aside from sporadic sniping and shelling, the Germans were quiet, often failing to respond to the periodic Canadian barrages. "The enemy would appear, like ourselves, to be mainly occupied in draining and rendering habitable their trenches," which,

the war diarist noted, "were if anything in worse condition than ours." There was one casualty on this tour: Private John Argent was wounded on 11 November, just nine days after joining the Battalion.[50]

However, the Fighting Tenth was anything but docile. One reason for its aggressive stance was that two platoons and a machine-gun crew from the Royal Canadian Regiment had been attached to the Battalion for training purposes; the RCR was part of the newly formed Third Division, which would join the Canadian Corps in early 1916. On the night of 11 - 12 November, a patrol under Lieutenant Charlie Stevenson discovered an enemy listening post in no man's land and attempted to destroy it. "It was found to be impossible however owing to wire surrounding it and to small bushes among which it was placed. As it was within the main wiring of front line trench it could not be cut off." A sniping post near Le Petit Douve Farm was not so fortunate; pinpointed by a Tenth Battalion patrol, it was "demolished by our artillery."[51]

The relief on Saturday, 13 November, by the 7th (1st British Columbia Regiment) Battalion, was particularly difficult. The River Douve again overflowed its banks and flooded the forward trenches, and a temporary bridge had to be constructed in order to complete the relief.

One member of the Tenth remained behind to take part in a most significant event. During the early-morning hours of 17 November, the 7th, along with the neighbouring 5th (Western Cavalry) Battalion, staged a spectacular raid. Trench raids were not, contrary to popular belief, a Canadian invention, but the Canadians became acknowledged experts in these violent excursions into enemy-held territory. Captain Charles Costigan was selected to lead one of the 7th Battalion's two raiding parties, thirty-five men he trained as intensively "as a coach would a football team." Its part in the raid was vividly described in the Calgary *Daily Herald*:

> Attacking a German trench under any and all circumstances is a serious and difficult problem. The squad was instructed and each man told what to do when one officer, when both officers, when the senior N.C.O. were killed, so that he knew exactly what to do when any or every man in the attacking force was missing.
>
> For several nights the German trench in front of this unit was bombarded, but no infantry attacks were made. Finally one night, when the rain was falling in torrents, exactly at the stroke of 12, the little party stole out of their own trenches, carrying with them a bridge with which they proposed to cross a stream that lay between the two trenches. They crept forward until, within 15 feets of the German trench, they found, to their chagrin, that the barbed wire entanglements had not been completely cut by the artillery.

The little force quietly cut the wires strand by strand, folded them back, fastening the ends, leaving a wide path. So silently did they accomplish this work that not a single German sentry realized that the Canadians were so near. Seeing a large white platform in front of them which looked solid, Capt. Costigan and his brother officer sprang upon it, when, to their horror, it gave way and they were precipitated headforemost into the trench on to the heads of three German sentries. The latter were more surprised than the Canadian officers, and before they could recover themselves, Captain Costigan and his pal had shot two sentries dead and the third, wounded in the leg, ran down the trench screaming for help.

The Germans began to pour out of their dugouts into the trenches, but by this time the rest of the squad had sprung into the trench loaded with bombs. Each of the two ends of this sector of the trench were blocked by Canadians armed with bombs. The artillery kept a circle of fire back of the trench, so that the Germans in this section could get no assistance from any others.

As fast as the Germans came out of the dugouts they were met by the bayonets.... Thirty-five Germans were killed, twelve were taken prisoner, and bombs were thrown in all the dugouts where the Germans refused to come out. In twenty minutes the whole operation was over.[52]

The cost of this enterprise was one man accidentally killed and another slightly wounded. Recommended for a Victoria Cross, Captain Costigan was later awarded the DSO.

Surprisingly, the Germans were little more alert and aggressive when the Fighting Tenth relieved the 7th on Thursday, 18 November. "Considerable amount of sniping during night" resulted in two casualties: Private John Eddie was killed and Private John Brown was wounded. Before the Battalion's relief on the twenty-third, two more of its originals were lost. Sergeant George Evans was fatally wounded on 20 November, while another sergeant, Wally Bennett, was injured when random enemy shell fire destroyed his dugout.[53] "I woke up in the dressing station," he later recalled. "I haven't got a belly button. A piece of shell casing cut it off."[54*] But these incidents were the exception, rather than the rule. "Men moved about freely in open in full sight of enemy, but were not interfered with in any way," says the war diary. On the other hand, the Tenth made life miserable for enemy working parties, on several occasions dispersing them with small-arms fire. The weather was generally cold and misty, and everyone was glad to come out of the line on 23 November. Nearly a month would pass before the Battalion returned.[55]

Two weeks of intensive training lay ahead. On 24 November, the Tenth was shifted from divisional reserve to Corps reserve, departing the First Division's Bulford Camp in the morning and moving to Bailleul. "Billets in farms, at little distance from each other, but companies kept intact or at most divided into two billets near each other." After a day of rest and cleaning uniforms and equipment on the twenty-fifth, the Battalion was put to work. Its training programme was extensive:

Nov. 26th to 29th inclusive
A.M. 8.30–9.00 — Physical Exercise
    9.00–9.20 — Running and Games
    9.30–10.00 — Arm Drill
    10.00–10.25 — Squad & Section Drill under Section Leaders
    10.30–11.00 — Platoon Drill under junior N.C.O.'s
    11.00–11.20 — Platoon Drill under Platoon Commanders
    11.30–12.30 — Company Drill under Company Commanders
Nov. 30th to Dec. 2nd inclusive
A.M. 8.30–9.00 — Physical Exercise
    9.00–9.20 — Running and Games
    9.30–9.45 — Arm Drill
    9.45–9.55 — Clip Loading
    10.00–10.30 — Platoon and Section Drill under N.C.O.'s
    10.35–11.00 — Company Drill under junior Officers
    11.10–12.30 — Route March not less than 3¼ miles to be covered
Dec. 3rd to Dec. 7th inclusive
A.M. 8.30–9.20 — Physical Exercise, running and Games, including 500 yards to be covered at the double (this may be by running around Parade Grounds)
    9.30–10.00 — Arm Drill and Clip Loading
    10.00–10.50 — Company in Attack
        (a) Open order
        (b) Close order as from trenches
        (c) Organized for a bombing attack and blocking
    11.00–12.30 — Route March not less than 3 miles to be covered.[56]

---

* The injury ended Sergeant Bennett's association with the Tenth Battalion, but it did not end his war. After recovering from his abdominal wounds, Bennett served for a short time as a machine-gun instructor in England. Volunteering for front-line duty, he returned to action in March 1916, only to be wounded again during his first trip into the trenches. Declared unfit for further service, he joined Sir Max Aitken, the future Lord Beaverbrook, at the Canadian War Records Office on Lombard Street in London. While there, in 1917, he posed for Richard Jack's famous painting of the Second Battle of Ypres.

The Tenth Battalion at rest, May 1916

Courtesy National Archives of Canada/PA-1, 4, 9

The men were allowed to rest in the afternoons, and by the time the Battalion returned to Bulford Camp, on 11 December, the effect was apparent. "Great improvement in marching and bearing of troops noted as result of rest and routine training," observed the adjutant, Captain George Craggs.[57]

On Thursday, 16 December, the Tenth went into the trenches again. Conditions were as cold and wet as ever, but there had been a notable change in policy. All battalions were allotted longer fronts to hold, and tours were now six days long. But this revision had little effect on the Tenth, which suffered only two casualties, a pair of privates, both wounded on 17 December. German patrols were fairly active in the misty, wet weather, and an ambush in no man's land was planned for the twenty-first. It failed, for the simple reason that "no [enemy] patrols appeared."[58]

Relieved by the 7th Battalion on Wednesday, 22 December, the Fighting Tenth was placed in brigade reserve, where it remained over Christmas. The festive season was paid little heed. The Battalion provided working parties on a regular basis — "50 men by day, 250 by night" — and, as the war diary points out, there was nothing particularly special about the twenty-fifth: "No notice taken of Christmas season other than issue of plum puddings and gifts of cigars and fruit at midday meal." On Boxing Day, a draft of twenty-one reinforcements arrived from England, but seven were "rejected as medically unfit to do duty in trenches."* On the twenty-seventh, the Battalion bathed before returning to the front lines, which meant that the Tenth would spend New Year's in the trenches.[60]

A cynic might have pointed out that the Battalion was little better off at the end of 1915 than it had been at the beginning of the year. Indeed, Salisbury Plain must have looked pretty good to troops mired in mud- and water-filled trenches along the Western Front. Furthermore, the naïveté at Salisbury had now been replaced with the real risk of being killed or maimed. The same cynic might also have mentioned that, aside from minor alterations amounting to mere yards, the Western Front had undergone no change in a year of bloody fighting. But quiet confidence still predominated. Typical were the comments of Colonel Rattray, who believed that "we are much closer to victory than I thought we would be at this time. We have established an artillery superiority, a physical superiority and what is better than either a moral superiority over the Hun. The change during the past month or six weeks has been very marked and our opposing trenches no longer contain the positive, cocksure enemy of six months ago." However, the colonel was intelligent enough to admit that "I am no prophet so will not hazard a guess but it will be some time yet —

likely a year — and much sacrifice and hardship will be experienced before the close."[61]

Public relations also concerned the colonel. Specifically, he felt that his unit was not enjoying a sufficiently high profile. "At the risk of being considered egotistic," he wrote, "I must say that the 10th Batt. is at the present time one of the best in France." Such a claim is hardly surprising, but Rattray believed that the Battalion's exploits were being overshadowed, thanks "to the advertising of men to some other Western Canadian Batt." — almost certainly a reference to the 8th (90th Winnipeg Rifles), famed as "The Little Black Devils." Rattray contended that "a great injustice has been done to this Battalion."[62] The colonel need not have worried. There was still plenty of time left in this war to ensure that the Fighting Tenth enjoyed a reputation second-to-none.

It was a familiar scene when the Battalion returned to the front lines on Tuesday, 28 December. "All available men draining trenches and repairing caved in dugouts." The Germans had been hard at work, too, "giving special attention in the way of putting in MG emplacements, strengthening the parapet and improving the trenches," and on the thirtieth, just before dawn, Lieutenant Stanley Kent and Sergeant Edward Milne crept into no man's land "and took up a position close under the enemy wire," which was fifteen yards wide and extended right up to the parapet. Remaining there all day, undetected thanks to thick mist, Lieutenant Kent and Sergeant Milne "obtained valuable information" which was soon put to use.[63] "As a result of this reconnaissance our artillery fired on large German working party with, it is believed, good results. This is judged by the fact that the German artillery replied vigorously for a while until silenced by our return fire." Three other ranks were casualties that day, including Private Wellington Garbutt, who was killed.[64]

New Year's Eve was highlighted by the enemy's attempt to fraternize. According to the war diary, several Germans "shouted across friendly greetings but soon stopped on receiving no reply."[65]

Colonel Rattray was given reason to celebrate on the first day of 1916. His tireless efforts to improve the Tenth Battalion's combat proficiency paid off in the form of a DSO, which was announced on New Year's Day. "I can assure you that it came as a complete surprise to me," he wrote the Corps commander, General Alderson, who had received a knighthood, "and it is very encouraging to feel that the efforts I have put forth in the past have met with the approval or perhaps I should say recognition by those under whom I work."[66]

---

* "The draft as a whole is unsatisfactory," wrote the medical officer, Captain W.T. Shannon, "general physique below par; minor defects in nearly all; three men required medical treatment on arrival." The seven rejected were declared unfit on account of problems with their teeth and feet.[59]

An unfortunate incident ushered in the new year. On Sunday, 2 January, a ten-man patrol under Lieutenant Vivian Watkins slipped into no man's land after dark. While the patrol worked its way through the enemy's barbed wire, there was a commotion to the rear: Private Robert Green could be seen "going at a stumbling run towards our own trenches." Private Green disappeared, and was later discovered to have been captured by a German patrol. The episode was puzzling, because Green was described as "a good reliable man," until inquiries revealed that "for about three weeks [he] had been very worried over personal affairs and some of his comrades had been on the point of reporting that he was wrong in the head."[67]

Relieved on the third, the Battalion marched into divisional reserve at Bulford Camp, where it promptly prepared plans for its first raid. "A minor offensive, 'cutting out' operation, having been decided upon as the result of reconnaissance during the past tour, in order to obtain information and to upset the morale of the enemy, a special party was chosen for this purpose and detailed to carry out practices over duplicate trenches. The scheme is to be carried out without artillery preparation on the first suitable night — wet or windy — during the next tour in the trenches."[68] However, nearly a month would pass before the proposed raid could be executed.

There was also time for a belated Christmas celebration. "Owing to Battalion being in Brigade Reserve at Christmas time and then in the trenches, this was the earliest opportunity for any celebration," explains the war diary. On 5 January, half the Battalion sat down to a dinner provided by "the Regimental Fund with the addition of gifts from various sources." The other half dined the next day, "on account of limited accom[m]odation."[69]

Pleasantries aside, there were constant reminders of the dangers so close at hand. On 7 January, Lieutenant Hugh Ferguson was instructing his men in the intricacies of grenades when he "was hit by a piece of practice bomb with dry primer which blew back further than usual. Slight wound in calf." Lieutenant Ferguson, a thirty-two-year-old native of Glencoe, Ontario, had joined the Tenth just nine days earlier, but he would return to play a prominent part in the Battalion's success story.[70]

The Tenth was, by now, a much different unit than the one that had come to the Continent almost a year before. Few originals were left, and virtually every officer, except for Captain Costigan, was a newcomer. These included Major Frederick Dingwall; the second-in-command*, as well as three of the company commanders; the sole original was Captain Alexander Thomson, of B Company, recently promoted from lieutenant, the rank he held on his return from the

wounded list on 4 October. The other company commanders were Captain Philip Walker, who had joined the Tenth in the middle of October and who led A Company; C Company's Major Charles Stewart, who had arrived in mid-November; and Captain Allan Conners of D Company. The Battalion's effective strength on 8 January 1916 was thirty-eight officers and 1069 other ranks.[71]

These numbers were maintained by a more-or-less steady stream of reinforcements. With few exceptions, the new men were not impressive. "21 reinforcements arrived of which 3 rejected as medically unfit," the war diarist complained on 17 January. By March, the situation had not improved. "21 reinforcements arrived," reads the war diary's entry for the fifteenth of that month. "Composed of men from a number of units and far from satisfactory in physique. Numerous minor defects." A similar refrain is contained in the entry on the twenty-fourth. "29 reinforcements arrived. Not up to good standard."

Most of them were turned into good soldiers after they joined the Battalion, as one of Colonel Rattray's anecdotes reveals. The divisional commander, General Currie, had witnessed the arrival of one group of reinforcements for the Tenth, and had been less than impressed. But he was pleasantly surprised when he made a return visit. "Rattray," he told the colonel, "I do not know how your Battalion does it, but a draft when sent you seems, in a couple of days, to get your Battalion spirit in marching well, and put on two inches in height."

The colonel was ready with an explanation. "Good officers, good N.C.O.'s and good men who have real pride in a real Battalion can soon put this 'Esprit de Corps' into the new comers," he informed Currie.[72]

The Tenth's next tour was both costly and frustrating. On the way into the line on Sunday night, 9 January, a shell burst wounded another lieutenant, Thomas Chutter. Once in the trenches, intensive patrolling "discovered no signs of enemy patrols," and there was further disappointment when unusually light nights made it impossible to carry out the planned raid. The German artillery was quite active, however, and on the eleventh, "several direct hits" were scored on Irish Farm, which was occupied by eighty-five members of the Tenth. Fortunately only two men were wounded, but five more, including Sergeant Brian Smith, an English-born original, were hurt the following day, when a shell exploded at the rear of a trench with no parados.[73]

The six-day tour ended without further incident on 15 January, and the Battalion withdrew to brigade reserve about Hill 63. While here, working parties were furnished for daylight duty in the rear and for nighttime activities in the front lines. During this

---

* Dingwall's few months as a member of the Tenth were disappointing, both personally and professionally. In poor health, the major spent most of this time on sick leave, and he was eventually invalided back to Canada, where he died in February 1918.

period, two members of the Tenth distinguished themselves. Lance-Corporal Arthur Courtney and Private Harry Conley, both English-born originals from Calgary, were acting as stretcher-bearers at a dressing station when word arrived that a badly wounded member of the Tenth was lying in an exposed area. Although it was the middle of the day, Courtney and Conley volunteered to rescue him. Crawling, they reached the victim, loaded him onto a stretcher, then carried him "over half a mile in the open" to the dressing station, dodging enemy bullets most of the way.[74] Courtney was later awarded the newly instituted Military Medal (MM), the first to be won by a member of the unit.

The Tenth returned to the trenches on Friday, 21 January. The relief of the 7th Battalion was completed by 6:40 p.m., and shortly afterwards, twenty-three-year-old Captain Eric MacDonald led a patrol into no man's land on a special mission. "The party had to proceed very slowly and carefully owing to the night being light, and the ground was very wet." Captain MacDonald's group brought with it a primitive Bangalore torpedo, a ten-foot length of $2^{1/2}$-inch pipe filled with ammonal, which was placed in the enemy's barbed wire. However, it failed to detonate, "due to the ammonal having become damp," and MacDonald safely conducted his men back into the Battalion's lines.[75] It was the first of several ventures in 1916 which would eventually bring MacDonald the DSO.

Another episode the same night ended in tragedy. While patrolling, Lance-Corporal Frederick Aplin and Private James Adamson were fired on by their own sentries. Corporal Aplin was killed in the fusillade. When their comrades discovered their error, they stopped shooting and scrambled out of their trench to retrieve the corporal's body. The movement drew enemy fire, and Private Adamson was fatally wounded in the exchange.[76]

Once again the Fighting Tenth had to postpone its raid. Bright moonlight each night made it too dangerous to undertake, and so the Battalion had to content itself with aggressive patrol work. This, too, was frustrating. Several ambushes were laid in no man's land, "but [the] enemy would not venture outside their own wire." By the time the tour ended, on 27 January, the Tenth had little to show for its thirteen casualties, which included five dead.[77]

Undaunted, the Battalion renewed its preparations for the raid after coming out of the line. Moved into divisional reserve at Bulford Camp, "a special party was again detailed to practice for this" operation.[78] The raid was placed under the command of that daring subaltern Lieutenant Stanley Kent, who, said a proud Rattray, "takes a keen interest in the doings and actions of the Huns."[79] To assist the raiders, a replica of the enemy's position was laid out nearby.[80]

However, it was beginning to appear that the raid was jinxed. As soon as the Fighting Tenth went back into the line, on the evening of Wednesday, 2

February, it was decided that the operation would be launched the next night. At nine-thirty Thursday evening, Lieutenant Kent set out with a wire-cutting party, but nothing was heard from him for six hours. Kent, a twenty-three-year-old banker in civil life, returned with bad news. He had discovered "that the wire had been extended and that an additional strip had been placed in front of the main wire. Also that the Germans appeared to be sending patrols along their wire to ascertain that it was intact." In Kent's opinion, there was not sufficient time to cut gaps in the wire and launch the raid before daylight, and the operation was again postponed.[81]

It finally went ahead the following night. In Colonel Rattray's absence — he was on leave — it fell to Major Charles Stewart, C Company's commander, to decide whether conditions warranted an attempt to launch the raid. When Major Stewart saw that it was "very dark with clouded sky and slight rain at 6.30 p.m.," he gave the green light to D Company's Captain Allan Conners, the officer in charge of the operation.[82] Fifteen minutes later, Lieutenant Kent went out with his wire-cutting party — Sergeant Edward Milne and five other ranks — accompanied by a two-man signalling section and a ten-man covering party under Sergeant James Pringle.

The first of many problems this night arose almost immediately. Lieutenant Kent halted his wire-cutting crew at the enemy's nearest belt of barbed wire, and crawled back to deploy the covering party. He could find no sign of it, and had to send Sergeant Milne and a private to search for Sergeant Pringle and his men. An hour later, Pringle reported to Kent, informing the lieutenant that he had been delayed by a pair of enemy patrols, but that he had posted his party among the shattered willow trees in a ditch that ran through no man's land. Kent must have detected uncertainty on Pringle's demeanour. Before sending him back to the covering party, the subaltern whispered a plea: "Don't fail us, Sergeant, we are absolutely dependent upon you."[83]

As a result of this waste of time, it was nine-thirty when Kent dispatched a telephone message to the trench at his rear: "Covering Party placed, proceeding to cut German wire." To his pleasant surprise, Kent soon found that his cause had been aided by the Germans, who had cut gaps in their own wire. This enabled him to slip through the first belt and set to work on the main barrier, thirty yards beyond. Shortly before eleven, he sent another report to the rear: "All through enemy first wire, 20 yards second wire cut, no more information until wire cutting complete." By now, the rain had ceased, but everyone was soaking wet and smeared with mud.[84]

Meanwhile, all was not well with the covering party. Shortly after ten o'clock, Private Samuel Rider was shot and killed by a German sniper. Soon afterwards, two members of the covering party crawled back to their trenches to report Private Rider's death and to warn that Sergeant Pringle "seemed somewhat excited."[85] Alarmed, Regimental Sergeant-Major Duncan Stuart, a hard-boiled, forty-year-old veteran of the British army, set out to investigate. RSM Stuart, who was multilingual as the result of twenty-two years of service in Africa and the Caribbean, met Pringle in no man's land.

"What is the matter?" he asked the sergeant.

"We have been surrounded and they are all captured," Pringle replied, "also Mr. Kent's party."

"Are you sure of what you are saying?"

"Yes, we have been surrounded and every man captured."[86]

Stuart, having heard no noise and knowing "that our men would never surrender without giving a good account of themselves," placed Pringle under arrest and sent reinforcements — Lieutenant Lewis Younger, Sergeant Arnold Budd, and a half dozen other ranks — which reached the covering party some time after midnight.[87*]

The wire-cutting seemed to be taking forever. It was nerve-racking work, too. After the rain stopped falling, the night was so quiet that Lieutenant Kent sent his signallers away from their post near the enemy wire, fearing that noise from their telephones might give away the game. Sergeant Milne assisted by Private Frank Sixby, carefully cut their way through the wire entanglement, but "within 5 or 6 yards of completion," Private Sixby "developed a cough," and an anxious Kent took his place.[89] While this delicate and important work was going on, several enemy patrols passed by, and one close call was particularly disturbing. Lieutenant Younger, who had taken charge of the covering party, watched and listened as "a German Patrol of 3 men came down on our left flank talking loudly. They came within 30 yards and threw a bomb which landed on our left and immediately retired to their trench, but do not think that they were certain of our position."[90]

Finally, at 3:37 a.m. on 5 February, word was flashed to the fifty-man raiding party waiting anxiously in the Battalion's forward trenches: the wire was cut! Moments later, Sergeant Milne arrived to guide the raiders across no man's land to the covering party's position, where Lieutenant Kent waited with the rest of his wire-cutters. The raiding force reached Kent around four o'clock that morning and, single file, with Kent, Younger, and Milne in the lead, crawled through the German wire.[91]

Trouble lay ahead. Within a few feet of the enemy trench, Lieutenant Kent abruptly but silently signalled his raiders to halt. There, along the parapet, was an enemy working party. "We decided," Kent later wrote, "to wait another 10 minutes in the hope that the working party would quit work and retire to [the] trench, and then we were to advance and carry out our plans as laid down." Failing that, Kent intended "to rush the working party and bring as many back as we could surround." The raiders were in a vulnerable position, strung out in single file, some of them in the wire, most of them lying in the mud between the two belts.[92]

Seven or eight minutes later, they were discovered. A German covering party, "consisting of between 20 and 30 men," blundered into the Canadians, "and then the mix-up started," in Kent's words.[93] In fact, all hell broke loose. "A hand-to-hand combat took place in which rifles, bayonets, revolvers, knob kerries [sic],** bombs and even fists were freely used. The alarm was raised, work party jumped down into the trench, numerous flares were sent up and German sentinels opened fire on our men and their own."[94] Recalled Private Nicholas Purmal: "I opened rapid fire at them and shot two in the breast. Bombs were thrown into them by the rest of our party." Caught in a cross fire, the German covering party was virtually annihilated; Private Purmal saw just one man get away.[95]

Eight prisoners were taken, but none survived. As Lieutenant Kent later wrote, "they [were] very much disinclined to move [and] had to be shot and bayoneted."[96]

The enemy's working party fared little better. Huddled in the supposed security of their trench, they fell victim to several Mills bombs. "The German trench must have been very crowded with the working party and the garrison, so the bombs thrown in probably caused several casualties, as judging from the cries from the trench they must have been effective."[97]

Of course, there was now no possibility of getting into the enemy positions and doing more damage. Lieutenant Kent, acknowledging that it was too dangerous to remain here, ordered his raiders to retire. But it would not be easy, because they were under "an exceedingly heavy fire of machine guns, rifles and bombs ... from the German trenches all round."[98]

The artillery came to their assistance. Captain Conners, a twenty-nine-year-old real-estate and oil broker from Calgary, witnessed the battle from his vantage point on the parapet of his trench and frantically telephoned for help from two field batteries which were standing by for this purpose. The call went in at 5:12 a.m., and twenty seconds later the first 18-pounder shells were screaming overhead and slamming into the German defenses. The effect of this deluge of high explosive and shrapnel was devastating and immediate. The enemy small-arms fire was

---

* Pringle, a twenty-four-year-old Manitoba farmer, was court-martialled for cowardice and sentenced to death by firing squad. The sentence was later commuted to five years' imprisonment, then suspended. Reduced to private, he remained with the Tenth and survived the war, even winning words of praise from his Battalion commander, who remarked that Pringle "has carried on in a most satisfactory manner ... and on at least one occasion he behaved exceptionally well."[88]

** A knobkerry was a club specially designed for use in trench raids.

71

silenced, and within three minutes, Conners informed the gunners that they could cease firing. Afterwards, Major Stewart praised the performance of the 1st and 4th batteries of the Canadian Field Artillery, declaring that their "excellent shooting ... undoubtedly prevented many of the Attacking Party from becoming casualties during their retirement.... "[99]

Dawn was breaking as the raiders scurried into their trenches under Captain Conners's watchful eye. The last man to return was, not surprisingly, the intrepid Lieutenant Kent, who carried in a wounded engineer. Several other injured soldiers were still in no man's land, but most were later rescued. Kent, although he was "almost completely exhausted," scrambled back to assist them, as did Lieutenant Younger. A fellow lieutenant, thirty-two-year-old Alfred Trimmer, was slightly wounded by a rifle bullet while helping bring in a fallen raider. Sergeant Arnold Budd, assisted by Private Frank Cox, carried in three injured men, while A Company's Captain Phil Walker crawled out to help Private Arthur Stewart, who lay severely wounded on the edge of the enemy wire.

However, Captain Conners finally put a stop to their heroic efforts. "There were three men left near German wire," he later wrote, "but these were reported to me as being dead, and as by this time, it was almost broad daylight, I decided it would be useless to go for them." By then, all of the wounded had been rounded up and taken to the regimental aid post for treatment. The more serious cases were started on the journey to more sophisticated treatment further to the rear, at advanced dressing stations, casualty clearing stations, and stationary hospitals on the French coast and in England. The rest of the raiders were ordered back to billets, "where a hot meal was served and a complete suit of dry underclothing issued."[100]

The next night, Lieutenant Younger took a patrol into no man's land to recover the three bodies, but the corpses had been removed. Three nights later, Lieutenant Kent escorted a French officer* to the scene of the operation, "but found all bodies & traces removed, and gaps in wire closed" by the enemy.[102]

The Fighting Tenth's first raid had been, at best, a partial success. Although its main object had been to obtain information, nothing more was learned about the enemy's position than Lieutenant Kent and Sergeant Milne had already observed on their daring daylight reconnaissance mission in late December. But in another way, it had succeeded brilliantly. "It must have been a severe shock to the Germans," Colonel Rattray pointed out upon his return on 7 February, "to have a large covering patrol in the middle of their own wire all but annihilated and that with a comparative small loss to ourselves."[103] The Battalion's casualties amounted to four dead and sev-

enteen wounded,[104] but most of the injuries were minor, "many of the men being cut only in the wire." German losses were estimated at forty-five.[105]

Senior officers were certainly pleased with the operation. "All ranks seem to have behaved very well and achieved a good result in spite of the fact that the luck was against them," noted the brigadier, General Lipsett, "and considering the difficult position in which they were and the heavy fire which they experienced from the German trenches."[106] The First Division's General Currie was so pleased that on the sixth he visited the front lines and "saw party of the 10th who made the attack."[107] The Corps commander, General Alderson, considered "that the 10th Battalion behaved very well in a critical situation."[108]

This minor affair — so minor, in fact, that it does not warrant a mention in the Canadian official history — produced a plethora of decorations. The Military Cross (MC), the first of the war for the Battalion, was awarded to Captain Conners, Lieutenants Kent, Younger, and Trimmer, and RSM Stuart. Sergeant Milne, who was wounded four times in the raid, became the first Canadian soldier in the Great War to win the clasp to the DCM — and was the only member of the Battalion to do so. DCMs also went to Sergeant Budd, Privates Cox and Sixby,[109] and to Private Louis Zuidema, a twenty-seven-year-old Dutch-born original who had been a member of the covering party and was praised for his "great coolness and courage under severe strain and long exposure in a most exposed position."[110] The popular Zuidema survived two wounds and two stripes (privates had a better survival rate than either NCO's or officers) and after the war went back to Calgary, where he ran a corner grocery for half a century.

There was a further honour in store for the DCM-winners. While they were later presented with their ribbons by the Corps commander, General Alderson, all were given a week's leave in London, where King George handed each man his medal.[111]

After the excitement of the raid, the rest of this tour was comparatively uneventful. The Fighting Tenth suffered no further casualties before its relief on the evening of Tuesday, 8 February, when it moved into brigade reserve. Six-day stints out of the line had fallen into a familiar pattern by now. While in brigade reserve, there was little opportunity to rest, the troops taking turns on working parties during the day and at night. Farther back, in divisional reserve, work was a secondary activity; most of the time was taken up in training, sports, concerts, and bath and pay parades, along with the occasional inspection by a visiting general or dignitary. Corps reserve was usually a combination of intensive training, alternated with generous

---

* Lieutenant S. Dallennes, of the 26th Battalion, Chasseurs à Pied, had been attached to the Second Brigade "to study methods adopted by Canadians with regard to patrols at night."[101] In the space of mere months, the Canadians had acquired a reputation for dominating no man's land.

leisure time. Casualties were quite common in the working parties on the front lines and, on 14 February, two privates were wounded, including Arthur Cottam, one of the Battalion's originals from Calgary.[112]

That evening the Tenth went back into the trenches. It was a stormy night, with gale-force winds and light snow. Upon relieving British Columbia's 7th Battalion, the Tenth learned that the enemy was suspected of digging a mine under no man's land. Mining was practised by both sides; the underground tunnels would be filled with explosives and then detonated, destroying the trench above. Patrols the following evening confirmed the mining activity, which was "within 40 feet of the trench." With help from tunneling specialists, a counter-shaft was constructed. Packed with explosives, it was ignited, and "according to mining officer destroyed enemy main gallery."[113]

The Battalion was in a feisty mood. The next night, patrols discovered an enemy listening post in no man's land, but it proved to be unoccupied. Another patrol went out later the same night "and threw bombs into German trench without, however, provoking any fire or hearing any signs of life. Patrol then walked back without being fired on." After two quiet days, the Tenth was able to provoke a reaction from the foe on Saturday, 19 February. Around two in the morning, "we fired 15 rifle grenades into enemy front lines with good effect, judging by the sounds from the trench. The Germans replied with 40. No reply was made owing to lack of ammunition." The Germans were using a new type of grenade; ten failed to explode, and these were handed over to intelligence officers for further study.[114]

The rifle-grenade duel was repeated twenty-four hours later. This time, the Fighting Tenth gained the upper hand, "firing 48 to enemy 25. Enemy appeared highly excited and fired several grenades without drawing pin. These were of the new type and several specimens were secured."[115]

The tour ended that night, and the Battalion moved into divisional reserve. This proved to be a painful experience, literally, when everyone was inoculated against typhoid and paratyphoid on 23 February. "Large number of men feeling effect of inoculation," the war diarist noted the next day, "but very few serious cases." Besides bathing and witnessing the demonstration of a new German weapon, the flame-thrower, the highlight of this period occurred on the twenty-fifth, when the Corps commander, General Alderson, presented decorations to four members of the Tenth. The general pinned the DCM onto the tunics of Sergeants Jock Palmer and Charles Morrison and Corporal William King. He also awarded the DSO to Colonel Rattray.[116]

Tragedy overshadowed the return to front-line duty. When the Fighting Tenth paraded during the afternoon of 26 February, prior to relieving the 7th Battalion, Private Robert Easton was missing. He was arrested on the morning of the twenty-ninth when discovered in the sector of the 5th (Western Cavalry) Battalion. Soon afterwards, while in the custody of that unit, Private Easton "committed suicide, by shooting himself through [the] head."[117]

There was no time to dwell on the episode, because the Battalion was kept busy in the trenches. A British attack was scheduled for 4:30 a.m., on Thursday, 2 March, on a nearby feature known as the Bluff, a low, tree-covered mound on the north bank of the Ypres-Comines Canal. To assist the V Corps operation, the neighboring First Canadian Division was requested to stage a diversion on its front, and the assignment was handed to the Tenth, which accepted it with characteristic relish. "It was decided," Colonel Rattray later explained, "to explode 50 Smoke Bombs about 30 yards in front of our Listening Posts; fire Rifle Grenades; throw Bombs by Catapult into German trenches; concentrate Machine Gun fire on selected points." Other planned distractions included a raft loaded with explosives and smoke bombs, which would be floated down the River Douve. Sixteen gallons of petrol would also be poured on the river and set alight.[118]

The results, while mixed, were most interesting. Promptly at 4:27 a.m., signalled by three Very lights, members of the Battalion bombing party threw their smoke bombs into no man's land. Rifle grenades were fired three minutes later, when the machine-guns also opened fire. In another two minutes, the artillery joined the chorus of fireworks, "with apparently good effect, the shells bursting at a nice height above the enemy's trenches.... It may be assumed that considerable casualties were effected by our artillery."[119]

The floating bomb was the responsibility of the daring Captain Costigan. Assisted by Corporal Percy Witney, the captain lugged the raft out of the foremost trench at four o'clock that morning and dragged it more than a hundred yards along the riverbank. Costigan slid into the water and guided the raft toward the enemy lines. The raft was attached to a cable which Corporal Witney paid out, but the captain decided not to risk letting it float free, "as there were a great number of overhanging boughs" in which it might be caught. "I therefore swam down with it until I could distinguish the German wire." When the smoke-bomb demonstration began, Costigan lit the fuse and swam back towards his own lines. Behind him, the raft exploded with a bright flash and a loud report.[120] Costigan was later awarded the MC and Corporal Witney won the MM, one of five which resulted from the operation; the others went to Sergeant George Nuttall, Corporal Lancelot Rimmer, and Privates A.E. Bartlett and Alexander McCaughan.

The Battalion could be pleased with its efforts. It not only aided the British in their successful attack on the Bluff but the diversion, carried out with no loss to the Fighting Tenth, gave a clear indication of the enemy's reaction to an attack. "The Huns have no sense of humour," noted Colonel Rattray, "and any new demonstration gets his wind up at once. But the taking of everything seriously is a virtue rather than a vice in this war game." The alarm was sounded in the German trenches by "horns and gongs of various kinds," followed by the firing of rifle grenades and machine-guns, along with a colorful array of flares — white, red, and green. The Germans were evidently taken by surprise. "The garrison was either in deep dugouts or in dugouts well in rear of the front line, as it took from 12 to 15 minutes to get any volume of fire from front trenches." It also took about ten minutes for the German artillery to react, and this fire was directed at the Canadian communication trenches and other anticipated avenues of approach. The enemy's small-arms fire drew Rattray's admiration. "Evidently seasoned troops are opposite our front as their rifle fire was well sustained and accurate, being just along the top of our parapet."[121] But, in many ways, the German response was anaemic. It was later estimated that 15 per cent of their shells did not explode and 30 per cent of the rifle grenades were also duds.[122]

By five-fifteen, the excitement was over. The enemy artillery had ceased firing, although flares were fired for some time afterwards.

From the Tenth Battalion's point of view, there were a couple of disappointing aspects to the operation. The use of catapults was an experiment that was not worth repeating. "After firing 7 or 8 bombs respectively each catapult broke, the rubber sling breaking in each case," wrote Lieutenant Lewis Younger, who was placed in charge of the catapults. "I beg to report that the Catapults are very unreliable and practically useless in an action."[123]

Similarly, the plan to set fire to gasoline in the river was not put into effect. Due to the enemy's heavy shell fire along the banks of the Douve, Captain Costigan feared that the three-man party responsible "would certainly have been hit if they had carried out this part of the programme," and he cancelled it on his own initiative.[124] This was not a significant setback. "The idea will keep," commented Colonel Rattray.[125]

The Tenth was relieved two days later. The intervening period was relatively quiet, although the war diary considered that the enemy's artillery was "fairly active." So was the indefatigable Lieutenant Stanley Kent, who discovered a German listening post in no man's land while patrolling on the night of 2 - 3 March. Lieutenant Kent's party knocked out the post with five well-aimed bombs, before returning safely to their trenches.[126]

Winter's last blast highlighted the Battalion's six days out of the lines. While in brigade reserve, the Tenth provided working parties and was treated to a trip to the divisional baths. A snowstorm on 8 March was so severe that it forced the cancellation of all activities, including the work details.[127]

The heavy snowfall caused problems for the unit's return to the trenches the next evening. The Germans had evidently spotted the tracks of the outgoing 7th Battalion, and trained machine-guns and rifles on various points along the route. When the Fighting Tenth marched in, it came under heavy small-arms fire which resulted in the wounding of one man, Private William McGregor, another of the Irish-born originals.[128]

The Battalion was in a rather surly mood, as the Germans discovered to their regret. The first night in the line, a patrol was sent out to investigate "the sounds of mining" under a trench near the Messines-Ploegsteert road, "but no suspicious sounds [were] heard." The following night was more eventful, when a barrage of eighty-nine rifle grenades was used to disperse enemy working parties in no man's land. After dark on 13 March, a patrol clashed with a four-man German party "and were confident they had hit at least 2, [and] probably more, of the enemy." This could not be proved, as the encounter took place within the enemy's wire and a later patrol could find "no signs of German bodies."[129] The same night, Captain Eric MacDonald slipped over the parapet with a small group and carefully placed three Bangalore torpedoes — described as "3 inch iron pipes about 12 feet long filled with aminel [sic]" — in the German wire. The torpedoes exploded as one, and created a considerable gap in the barbed-wire entanglement.[130]

The Tenth's final night in the line was certainly exciting. Captain MacDonald, accompanied by Lieutenant Claud Trotter and ten other ranks, crept into no man's land in a bid to ambush any German working parties which were repairing the damaged wire. Placing Lieutenant Trotter in charge of the four-man covering party, which followed at twenty-five-yards' distance, MacDonald led the remainder in single file. At the edge of the enemy wire, the captain discerned a work party, "about eight to ten strong." Showering them with bombs and raking them with rapid rifle fire, the Canadians quickly routed the enemy, who left behind one seriously injured man. "I found," MacDonald later wrote, "that he had been wounded in three places: twice in the chest and stomach and once in the mouth." Assisted by Corporal Percy Whitney, the captain tried to haul him back to the Battalion's lines, but the German was a very big man, and when the party came under fire — including an artillery barrage by both sides — MacDonald decided to abandon the prisoner, after searching his pockets and taking his rifle, bayonet, shoulder strap, and cap for identification purposes. The patrol returned to its entrenchments without loss.[131] Afterwards, Lieutenant Trotter took a four-man party and searched for the German, "but could find no trace" of him."[132]

Equally adventurous was Major Charles Stewart. The officer commanding C Company set out at two-thirty on the morning of 15 March, after Lieutenant Lewis Younger, who had earlier gone into no man's land intending to harass the enemy with "some rifle grenades," had spotted a German patrol lying in ambush 150 yards in front of the Battalion's trenches. Accompanied by Lieutenant Younger and twelve other ranks, Major Stewart led his party, in extended order, towards the enemy position. After crawling 125 yards, the major spotted his quarry, and the would-be ambushers were themselves ambushed. At Stewart's command, each of his men fired five rounds in rapid succession, and the major "then advanced to investigate results. Strength of enemy patrol estimated at 6 to 8 men, of who[m] 2 or 3 were seen to run back toward their trench." One German, with an "ugly wound in buttocks," was captured and brought back. Stewart's party suffered no losses.[133]

This tour of duty ended on 15 March. The Battalion's casualties came to three dead and seven wounded, for the six days in the trenches. The toll was typical of the steady attrition of trench warfare: even when no major fighting was taking place, front-line units were forced to take losses which eventually began to add up alarmingly.

More honours awaited the Fighting Tenth. Moving into divisional reserve at Bulford Camp, the Battalion was inspected by General Currie on Thursday, 16 March. The divisional commander, "who expressed himself as well pleased" with the unit's appearance and recent performance, singled out and congratulated Major Stewart, Captain MacDonald, and Corporal Witney for their recent exploits on patrol. On the nineteenth, the Corps commander, General Alderson, presented ribbons to the three officers and five other ranks who had won decorations during the Battalion's raid in early February. "Usual instructional classes" made up most of the rest of the six days out of the front lines.[134]

On 21 March, the Tenth was back in the trenches. Although the casualties — seven wounded — on this tour were not unduly bad, the enemy's activity was notable. "Artillery fairly active on front line trenches," says the war diary's entry on 23 March. "Rifle fire and sniping more active than usual." The shooting intensified during the early-morning hours of the twenty-sixth, when the Germans heavily bombarded the Battalion's positions in response to a demonstration by units on the left. "No casualties and little damage" resulted, but it was worse the next day. "At 6 A.M. heavy artillery bombardment was opened on our trenches coinciding with attack by our troops near St Eloi. All calibre shells, H.E. & Shrapnell [sic] used up to 5.9[-inch]." There were no casualties, but one trench took "9 direct hits."[135]

It was raining when the Tenth came out of the line late on Monday, 27 March. Moving into brigade reserve, the men luxuriated in the divisional baths the following day. "General clean up of billets and equipment in preparation for a move." On the twenty-ninth, the Tenth marched into Corps reserve near Godeswaersvalde, and it proved to be a long day. Although actual marching time amounted to only three and a half hours, much time was wasted waiting for guides to lead the Battalion into its billets, which were not reached until after dark.[136]

"Recreation and rest" took up most of the time in Corps reserve. As always, sporting events proved to be popular pastimes, notably football and baseball. On Sunday, 2 April, the Tenth attended church parade with the 8th (90th Winnipeg Rifles) Battalion; before the service, General Alderson delivered a short address to the two units. The same day brought a tragic accident, the latest in a series which dogged the Tenth during early 1916. Private Robert Tomlinson was killed while trying to jump from a moving train at the railroad station in Godeswaersvalde. "How he came to be on [the] train is not known," states the war diary, "but it is presumed he slipped from his billets and boarded it while in motion."[137]

This otherwise pleasant period ended on 4 April, when the Tenth joined the 8th Battalion on a march to Poperinghe. The column was under the command of the latter's Lieutenant-Colonel Harold Matthews. "March was made in good time," the war diarist noted approvingly. "No one fell out." On reaching Poperinghe, the Tenth moved into divisional reserve billets at Nop Factory, adjacent to the town's train station.[138]

The Fighting Tenth was back in familiar territory; the Ypres salient was where it had distinguished itself a year earlier. While the Battalion was marching to Poperinghe, the Canadian Corps was taking responsibility for a new sector, the southernmost part of the salient, which had been held by V Corps. Both the Second and Third divisions received their baptism by fire here, just as the First had been blooded here the previous April; unlike the senior formation, the newcomers to the Corps failed to perform impressively. The Second had a rough time, moving into the Saint-Eloi sector in relief of British troops who had launched an offensive on 27 March, with unfavourable results in prolonged and futile fighting amid adverse conditions. The Third's introduction to trench warfare was not far in the future.

The Battalion's stay in Poperinghe was brief. On 7 April, the men paraded through the divisional baths, and the next day the Tenth moved into the front lines in the vicinity of Hill 60, its height in metres above sea level. "It was not a natural feature," one recent historian points out, "but simply a large heap of soil and rubble from the nearby railway cutting on the rail link between Ypres and Comines, an important rail junction."[139] Hill 60 was considered to be vital if the Allied hold on the salient was to be maintained, but the Fighting Tenth had problems enough relieving the 14th (Royal Montreal Regiment) Battalion in the trenches. Boarding trains at Poperinghe, the Tenth rode the rails to Brielen, then marched into the salient. The Germans welcomed its return to this grim locale with random shelling, but the late arrival of the guides who were to conduct the Battalion into its new positions meant the relief was not completed until two-thirty in the morning of 9 April.[140]

Here the Fighting Tenth endured a steady diet of sniping, machine-gunning, and shelling. It was a far more active sector than the relatively quiet surroundings on the River Douve, where the Battalion had spent the winter. In eight days in the Ypres salient, the Tenth suffered thirty casualties, including six dead. In return, the Battalion was anything but passive, repeatedly dispersing German working parties with rifle grenades. The unit's snipers, too, did deadly work. "Enemy sniping again noticeably decreased," says the war diary on 15 April, "and it is considered that our snipers have now asserted their superiority in this direction."[141]

One of the Battalion's stretcher-bearers performed a fine piece of work. On Sunday, 16 April, Private Lourn Daugherty, an American original from Sleeper, Idaho, was partially buried when a shell burst caused the wall of a trench to collapse. Private Daugherty was rescued, then spotted a man who had been wounded by shell fragments. Dressing the wounds with no thought for his own safety, Daugherty then carried the injured soldier to the nearest dressing station. En route he collapsed, and both men were brought in for treatment. "It was found on examination at hospital that Daugherty was suffering from bad contusions of the back and injured kidneys."[142]

The most notable event of the tour was the destruction of a German mine. There had been plenty of mining activity in the salient, and as soon as the enemy work was discovered thirty yards in front of the Tenth's trenches, Colonel Rattray issued orders for a destructive raid. The intention was to place a camouflet, a specially designed explosive charge which, detonated at ground level, would cause the tunnel to cave in. "It is not expected that a crater will be made," Rattray wrote in his orders, "but some of our parapets may be shaken down," in which case the position was to be "put ... in good repair" as quickly as possible. The operation would take place during the morning of Wednesday, 12 April, in two phases. In the first, the camouflet would be placed in no man's land by parties of A and B companies, at 1:15 a.m. The second phase would see the detonation, at 11 a.m.[143]

Nearly everything went according to plan. The raiding parties slipped over their parapets, prepared the camouflet, and returned without incident. Lieutenant Stanley Kent presented a detailed report of the subsequent explosion:

At 11.00 AM mine was exploded, only a dull dis-tant sound could be heard and the ground shook for some considerable distance round. Some of the sand bags of parapet Trench 44 were dislodged but otherwise no damage was done to our lines. No actual crater was formed but a fissure or tear in the ground resulted, started about 15 yards in front of their trench and running diagonally towards it and partly down emb[ankment] of railway cutting. Wire, sandbags and a large quantity of timber was seen to fly into the air and considerable damage was done to their parapet, chiefly at that point which it crosses the cutting where the sand-bags are heaped up in pool formed in front of their trench. Part of their parados has also disappeared in the shape of a Snipers Post or O.P. which had been discovered at this point some days previously.[144]

There was just one flaw in the operation, and it was responsible for most of the casualties incurred by the Battalion. Five minutes before the camouflet was detonated, a twenty-five man fatigue party and a small group of tunnellers who had all been working nearby blundered onto the scene and drew German shell fire which caused seven casualties, including one fatality. Livid, Colonel Rattray contended that "it should be investigated. This movement ... was responsible for all the serious casualties." The colonel was also unimpressed with the trench-mortar crew assigned to the Battalion. Due to technical difficulties, the two mortars fired only one shell between them, leading Rattray to sourly conclude that "Trench Mortar Officers and crews that understand their business should be placed in charge here."[145]

The camouflet operation was significant in one respect. It marked the first time that the Fighting Tenth wore steel helmets into battle. The helmets were, according to Captain Joseph Simpson, "gladly worn by all ranks." Captain Simpson pointed out that "one man who was wounded in the Head was no doubt saved of very serious wound if not from death by having put it on."[146] A novelty at first, there were not enough to go around, and helmets were issued only to troops in the trenches. The officers were not particularly interested in having helmets, suggested Captain Walter Critchley. "We wore it only as an example to the other ranks," he insisted, "[and] because we were ordered to."[147] The lackadaisical attitude towards the new protective gear is indicated by a Battalion order in early August: "The use of steel helmets for any other purpose other than that for which they are intended is strictly forbidden. It is pointed out that if a structure of steel of the quality used for steel helmets is subjected to the heat of a cooking fire, the protective value of the helmet will be entirely ruined."[148]

A two-week break awaited the Tenth when it came out of the front lines on 16 April, a wet, dreary Sunday. In brigade reserve at Dickebusch, where it remained until the twenty-fourth, the Battalion provided men for working parties, although the burden was eased by a decision on 21 April "that no man should be sent on working party two successive nights." Heavy rain and hostile shell fire made things uncomfortable, and there were several casualties — two killed and four wounded. On 22 April, the anniversary of the Tenth's memorable attack on the wood near Saint-Julien, it rained all day and working parties were cancelled; the "men were allowed to rest."

From Dickebusch, the Battalion moved into divisional reserve at Scottish Lines. Although 500-man working parties were twice provided to lay telephone lines in the vicinity of the advanced divisional headquarters, the week at Scottish Lines was relatively pleasant. It was highlighted by the 28 April inspection by General Sir Douglas Haig, commander-in-chief of the BEF. There were also three gas alarms, during which the troops were "instructed to be ready to put on smoke helmets at first symptoms of actual gas arriving," but the precautions proved to be unnecessary.[149]

"Two clever little pieces of reconnaissance work" followed the Tenth's return to the trenches on Tuesday, 2 May. Both were led by Lieutenant Stanley Kent, who was establishing himself as one of the Battalion's outstanding subalterns. On the first mission, Lieutenant Kent, accompanied by Corporal Charles White and two privates, slipped into no man's land after nightfall on 4 May. The German trenches here were only thirty to thirty-five yards away. Exploring the area and concluding that "nothing unusual was taking place," the party retired, after throwing a bomb which was believed to have caused at least one casualty. Three nights later, Kent went out again with Corporal White and a private to investigate an enemy sap just twenty-five yards from the foremost trench. However, the position was unoccupied, and Kent brought his party back without incident.[150]

Amid generally cool and wet weather, the Tenth reacquainted itself with the steady sniping and shelling for which this sector was rightly renowned. Casualties mounted steadily; by the time the Battalion was relieved on the night of 10 May, it had lost six killed and twenty-three wounded, including Lance-Corporal Frank Cox, who had won the DCM during the raid in early February.[151]

There were more losses while in Second Brigade reserve at Bedford House. A single shell struck the stables on 11 May, killing Corporal Cyril Clack, an original member of the Battalion, and wounding two privates. On the sixteenth, the unit's billets took three direct hits, and the stables were hit twice. Fortunately, only three other ranks were injured; the toll could have been far worse. There were also casualties on the daily working parties. Altogether, nine more men were wounded, one of them fatally.[152]

On Thursday, 18 May, the Tenth moved into divisional reserve at Connaught Lines. Even here, they could not escape the enemy's attention as German aircraft dropped a dozen bombs in the vicinity of the camp before dawn on the twenty-second. Later that Sunday, General Currie inspected the Battalion and offered his congratulations on its "smart appearance and steadiness."[153]

The return to the trenches on 26 May added to the Battalion's lengthening casualty list. By the time it was relieved on the last day of the month, two men had been killed and seven others wounded. There was one positive note, however; the weather was much better. The days were growing longer and warmer, which, in turn, meant dry trenches.[154]

On Saturday night, 31 May, the Tenth vacated its trenches near Hill 60, handing over to the 5th (Western Cavalry) Battalion. Moving into brigade reserve in the GHQ Line, with Battalion headquarters at Swan Château, the unit looked forward to a period of relative quiet. A 325-man working party was organized on Sunday, 1 June, and assigned to various duties in the vicinity. One man, Private A.H. Dodds, was wounded. "Fine day," the war diarist reported.[155]

Monday was equally fine. But it would prove to be anything but quiet. Ahead lay what one veteran would call "perhaps the worst experience of the Battalion" in the entire war.[156]

Chapter Five

"DEAREST MOTHER, DO NOT WEEP"

(2 June - 5 November 1916)

Friday, 2 June, which marked Colonel Rattray's anniversary in command of the Fighting Tenth, opened with a "terrific bombardment," as the colonel described it.[1] It signalled the start of what Captain Walter Critchley later called, with considerable understatement, "a pretty bad show."[2]

The shell fire ushered in a major German attack on the high ground held by the Canadians immediately north of Hill 60. This sector, which was in the hands of the recently arrived Third Division, contained several important features, including the knoll, Mount Sorrel, that lent its name to the battle. As well, there were Hill 61, Tor Top, and Observatory Ridge. Loss of the ridge would give the enemy command of the severely shrunken Ypres salient.

Beginning at six o'clock in the morning, the shelling heralded a crisis nearly as acute as that of April 1915. The Germans had marshalled overwhelming local artillery superiority, saturating the Canadian defences with high explosive. "The enemy position," noted a German report, "was a cloud of dust and dirt, into which timber, tree trunks, weapons and

equipment were continuously hurled up, and occasionally human bodies."[3] When the German infantry assaulted at one in the afternoon, following the detonation of four huge mines, there were pitifully few defenders left to oppose the advance. The 4th Canadian Mounted Rifles suffered 89 per cent casualties around Mount Sorrel and Hill 61, while in Sanctuary Wood, further north, Princess Patricia's Canadian Light Infantry lost more than half its front-line strength. Nor were these the only losses incurred by the Canadians. Two generals were caught during a visit to the trenches; Major-General Malcolm Mercer of the Third Division was killed and the Eighth Brigade's commander, Victor Williams, was wounded and captured. Easily overwhelming isolated pockets of resistance, the Germans drove more than six hundred yards into the Canadian lines, taking most of Sanctuary and Armagh woods before digging in. As in April of the previous year, the road to Ypres lay wide open to the enemy for several tantalizing hours.

The Canadians quickly counter-attacked. The new Corps commander, Lieutenant-General Sir Julian Byng, who had replaced General Alderson on 28 May, ordered that "all ground lost today will be retaken tonight."[4]

The Fighting Tenth was soon given an important part to play, but, comfortably ensconced in its billets about Swan Château, it was slow to recognize the crisis materializing just a few hundred yards away. "Considerable hostile artillery all round various billets," the war diarist noted, "but our billets not shelled. Companies of C.M.R. Battalions belonging to 8th Can Bde were noticed moving forward during course of morning and it was reported that the Germans were attacking Mount Sorrel and Observatory Ridge." It was not until 4:40 p.m. that the Tenth received instructions, sent more than an hour and a half earlier, to occupy the GHQ Line. Seven hours later, when the Battalion had carried out its orders, Colonel Rattray was informed of the proposed counter-attack. The Tenth was to relieve the 7th (1st British Columbia Regiment) Battalion, so that the latter, assisting elements of the Third Brigade, could then participate in the bid to recapture the lost ground. Because the 7th was under the acting command of an inexperienced major named Bernard

Lieutenant-General Sir Julian Byng
Courtesy National Archives of Canada/PA-1284

78

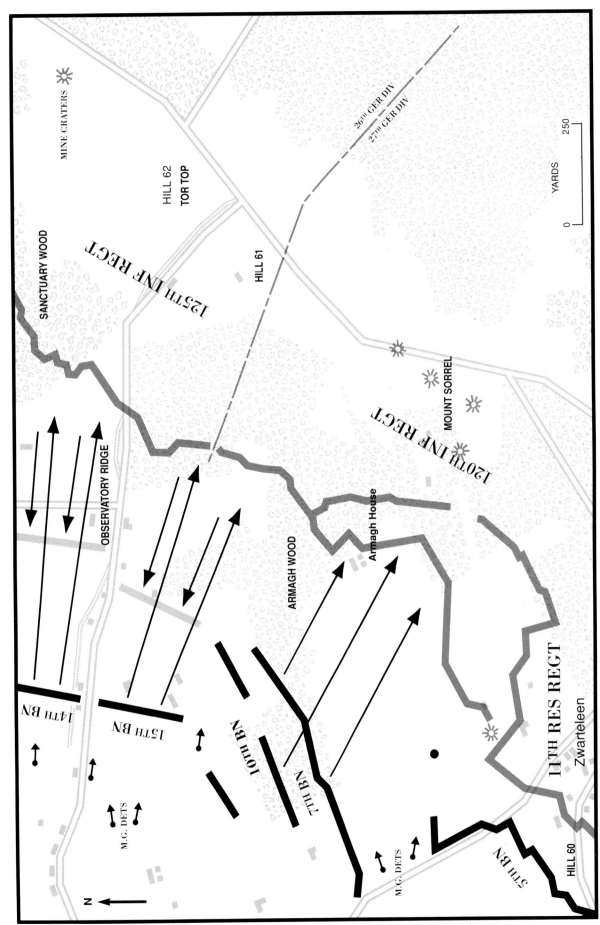

Mount Sorrel, 3 June 1916

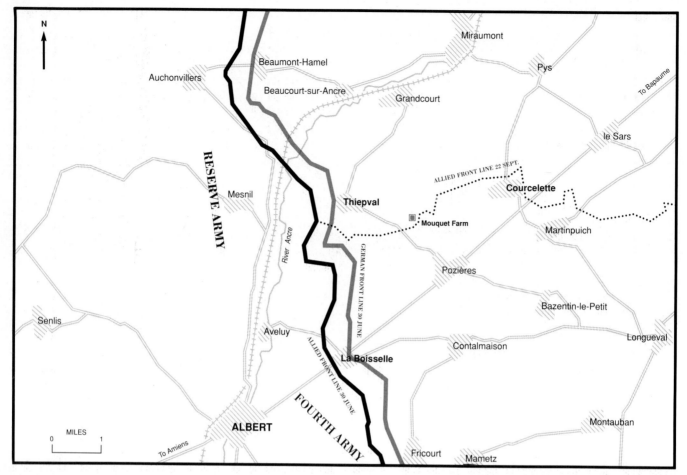

The Somme

Humble, the brigadier, General Lipsett, placed Rattray in charge of the Second Brigade's share of the operation.[5]

This was the test for which the colonel had so painstakingly prepared the Battalion. However, the Tenth's effective strength on 2 June, 959 all ranks, was nearly a hundred below its authorized strength of 1,033.[6]

The situation was very confused. It was after one o'clock on Saturday morning, 3 June, when these orders were confirmed, and it took the Fighting Tenth until two-thirty to carry them out. Colonel Rattray moved his headquarters to a farm, Leicester Square, which offered a better vantage point. En route, he later wrote, "I passed parts of the 14th and 15th Battalions, and as these were to be in the counter attack at dawn and as dawn was breaking, and having had no report from the O.C. 7th, and no preparatory bombardment was going on, no attack was launched at dawn."[7] At Leicester Square, Rattray found the 7th Battalion in nearby trenches, but there was no sign of the unit's headquarters. (The untried Major Humble later explained that he had been forced to move to a new site and had sent a messenger to inform Rattray of this fact, but his man was unable to find the Tenth's commander.)[8] Deploying his own com-

panies in accordance with his orders, Rattray awaited daylight and further developments.

Finally, at 5:11 a.m., he found out what was happening. A captain named Ford arrived at Leicester Square and announced that the 7th was "all ready to carry out the counter attack, and I sent a message of the Brigade advising this and that two companies of the 10th were in a position of readiness to support the counter attack." Shortly afterwards, Second Brigade headquarters replied with details of the impending operation: the bombardment would open at 6:10 a.m., and thirty-five minutes later "six green rockets" would signal the start of the assault. Accordingly, Rattray exercised his prerogative as the operational commander and deployed the 7th Battalion's four companies. Armagh House was the objective, with two companies striking to the right and two to the left. The Tenth's A and B companies would support the assault, and the colonel sent up Major Charles Stewart "to see that the counter attack was properly launched."[9]

But there were serious problems. "The bombardment was delayed for half an hour," Colonel Rattray wrote, "and no green rockets were observed, so it was not until 7.35 a.m. that I received a message to launch the attack and sent forward this order to Major Stewart. At 7.40 a.m. Major Stewart jumped on the

Lieutenant-General Sir Edwin Alderson's days as commander of the Canadian Corps were numbered. The British veteran had long since lost the confidence of the militia minister, Sir Sam Hughes, who had selected him in the first place. "I can see no hope," Hughes huffed in May 1915, "with General Alderson in Command of our boys." Relations between the two men worsened steadily, thanks to Alderson's criticism of the Hughes's beloved Ross rifle. The militia minister rejected the general's complaints, claiming that Alderson did not "know the butt from the muzzle," and after the First Division was re-equipped with the Lee-Enfield in June 1915, it was only a matter of time before Alderson was replaced. The only surprise is that he lasted as long as he did, because Hughes frankly considered him "unfit" to command the Canadian Corps, which had grown to three divisions by early 1916, with a fourth on the way.

A battle in the spring of 1916 set the stage for Alderson's demise. The green Second Division underwent its baptism of fire in late March and early April at Saint-Eloi, in the southern Ypres salient. The operation was ineptly conducted by the divisional commander, Major-General Richard Turner, who had done so poorly at Second Ypres as a brigadier, and by one of his subordinates, Brigadier-General H.D.B. Ketchen. Alderson recommended that Generals Turner and Ketchen both be replaced, but the BEF's commander-in-chief disagreed. Aware of Sam Hughes's meddling, Sir Douglas Haig concluded that "the main point is whether a serious feud between the Canadians and British is greater than the retention of a couple of incompetent commanders." Haig, with Hughes's full support, decided that Alderson would have to go.

His successor was Lieutenant-General Sir Julian Byng. Tall, slim, and a future governor-general of Canada, General Byng was baffled by his appointment to the Canadian Corps. "Why am I sent to the Canadians?" he wondered. "I don't know a Canadian. Why this stunt?" Byng, who arrived at Corps headquarters on 28 May, the same day Alderson departed for England for a vague posting as inspector-general of the Canadian forces there, soon faced his first crisis.

For six weeks, the Germans had been planning a surprise attack on the Canadians holding this sector of the Ypres salient. The main blow, by two divisions of XIII Württemberg Corps, would fall on a narrow front held by the inexperienced Third Canadian Division. Some of the German preparations were detected, but poor weather conditions prevented systematic observation of the enemy's rear areas. Despite warnings from the neighbouring First Division that an attack was imminent, the Third was caught unawares when the storm broke on 2 June. Although it was a limited operation, the Germans had assembled a vast array of artillery to support their attack; Lord Beaverbrook later called the enemy shell fire "the heaviest endured by British troops up to that time." Within hours, key positions in the heart of the Third Division's defences had fallen.

The first Canadian counter-attack, on the morning of 3 June, failed to regain the lost ground, and General Byng wisely paused to properly prepare the next effort. He entrusted it to the able commander of the First Division, General Currie, who gave the Germans a taste of their own medicine in the form of a furious and prolonged bombardment, before sending in his attacking battalions at 1:30 a.m. on 13 June. In less than an hour, Currie's troops evicted the enemy and drove them back to their original lines.

"In a straight fight between Canadians and Württembergers," says the British official history, "the better soldiers won." But Mount Sorrel had been a costly lesson for the Canadians. Their losses between 2 and 14 June totalled 8,000, compared to 5,765 suffered by the enemy.

parapet and gave the men a most encouraging send off, but was struck in the leg by a machine gun bullet."[10]

Launched long after the preliminary bombardment, without proper reconnaissance, and out of co-ordination with the other attacking units the attack failed. In addition to the 14th (Royal Montreal Regiment) and 15th (48th Highlanders of Canada) battalions, both belonging to the Third Brigade, the Third Division's 49th (Edmonton Regiment) Battalion attacked at various times that Saturday morning. The 7th Battalion was soon stopped in its tracks, although

it "went gallantly forward," in Colonel Rattray's words. The two companies on the left were cut to ribbons by a "destructive machine gun fire from Hill 60," while the two on the right ran into a newly installed barbed-wire barrier in Armagh Wood. The Tenth's C Company, led by Captain Edwin Fisher of Calgary, rushed forward to continue the assault on the right, but it, too, was immediately caught up in the enemy's entanglement. Captain Fisher, a member of the Battalion since the previous July and described by Rattray as "a brave, keen, painstaking officer who did splendid work," was killed in the hail of enemy small-

Brigadier-General Frederick Loomis
Courtesy National Archives of Canada/PA-2192

Frederick Buddry and Arthur Hayter hurried out to offer their assistance, braving intense machine-gun and shell fire. Corporal Buddry was wounded while carrying several injured men to safety, but refused to seek treatment. Corporal Hayter, a stretcher-bearer, also helped a number of wounded. Only a severe wound forced him to stop, but not until he had led a group of survivors to the shelter of the Battalion's lines.

At noon, the 7th's Captain Holmes reported to Rattray. "Capt. Holmes was anxious to go out and consolidate, but as I had a message from Brigade that the heavy artillery was going to open fire on Armagh House I told Capt. Holmes to get his men back." The colonel directed that the remnants of the British Columbia battalion should fall back through the Tenth's lines to Battersea Farm. This was duly carried out and, at 1:20 p.m., Rattray informed brigade headquarters that it was safe for the big guns to commence their bombardment.[14]

Unfortunately, when the British heavy artillery opened fire, the Tenth Battalion's positions were the unintended target. Captain Walter Critchley (now in command of the Tenth's front lines and afterwards promoted to major, when Rattray praised his "calm, cool" performance[15]) was horrified as a battery of 4.5-inch howitzers shelled his trench, killing "quite a few of our men," and it was only with considerable difficulty that he was able to redirect the British fire. But Critchley was not bitter about the episode when questioned about it many years later. "You can't blame the artillery for it. The guns are suddenly rushed into terrain before they have time to plot it, and, of course, you've got to figure in those days sometimes the trenches were fifty, sometimes a hundred, sometimes two hundred, yards apart — and that was all, you see, and it means pinpointing it pretty clearly to get accurate coverage."[16]

It is possible that one of these British shells was responsible for ending Private Charles Smith's war. The twenty-year-old Irish-born Smith suffered wounds to his right shoulder and left knee, due to shell splinters. Later declared medically unfit for military service, he was demobilized in 1917, returning to his duties as a clerk at the Canadian Bank of Commerce in Rockyford, east of Calgary.[17]

There was also enemy fire to contend with, and it seemed to grow hotter as the afternoon went along. "During this time there was very little rifle fire but considerable H[igh] E[xplosive] was falling in Armagh Wood but especially in Leicester Square," Colonel Rattray reported. At seven that evening, the colonel was finally forced to evacuate Leicester Square in favour of Fosse Way, behind Battersea Farm, but the Germans stepped up their pressure on the Battalion's front soon afterwards. Around eight o'clock, Rattray related, "the Germans opened up a terrific artillery fire and rifle fire, to which our men replied with rifle

arms fire. By mid-morning, it was clear the operation had failed, and Rattray sent orders to the 7th Battalion's Captain William Holmes, who was in charge of the attack on the left of Armagh House, at 9:58 a.m.: "If you think it impossible to make further efforts without better artillery preparation that you consolidate, then consolidate. Do you want any further troops to assist you? Let me know how situation stands at present time."[11]

While the 7th struggled to solidify its shaky hold in shattered, bullet-riddled Armagh Wood, a sad story was unfolding in the Tenth's forward trench. Major Stewart, hit in the leg by a bullet when the attack began, died at ten-thirty after being struck by shell fragments. "This ended the career of a very capable, efficient and experienced Officer, who if he had been spared would have had a splendid future before him," Colonel Rattray later wrote. "He was brave, daring and gallant, greatly like[d] by all who had the privilege of meeting him."[12]

Stewart was the second Tenth-Battalion major killed this day. The other was Merritt Kimball, an American-born railway contractor from Brooks, east of Calgary. A noted local athlete, Kimball "was killed just before the counter attack was launched," according to Colonel Rattray. "He was a new officer but full of courage and daring."[13]

Two lance-corporals of the Tenth won the DCM here. Witnessing the carnage of the failed attack, fire." The fighting raged "for over half an hour, but no advance was made by the Germans." The enemy mounted another violent bombardment at midnight, and again at one-thirty Sunday morning,[18] but each time they were discouraged by the Battalion's machine-gunners, who responded vigorously to the German fire. Rattray was delighted with their performance: "Many of the machine gunners were using the usual expletives peculiar to the soldiers in anathematizing the Hun...."[19]

During the night, the Tenth was relieved by the 1st (Western Ontario) Battalion. Two A Company platoons, under Lieutenant Alfred Trimmer, were left behind to assist in carrying in the wounded. Lieutenant Trimmer's force remained here until four in the afternoon, before rejoining the Battalion.[20] Trimmer carried out his difficult task with such skill that he was awarded the bar to the MC he had won earlier in the year. He was the first member of the Tenth to be so honoured.

It had been a costly affair. The Fighting Tenth lost five officers and 144 other ranks, killed, wounded, and missing.[21] The toll was unusually heavy, considering that only one company, C, had been actively engaged, and that the dead included Majors Stewart and Kimball, and Captain Fisher. There was a bright side, as Colonel Rattray pointed out. While no ground had been retaken, "the result was that any further advance by the Germans was held."[22]

Licking its wounds, the Tenth withdrew to Dickebusch Huts. The remainder of Sunday, 4 June, was "spent in rest, adjusting rolls, making up complete lists of casualties & lists of deficiencies in kit."[23]

But the opportunity to rest was short-lived. On Monday, 5 June, the Tenth was moved up to Hill 60 to relieve the battered 5th (Western Cavalry) Battalion. Due to darkness and the poor condition of the front lines, this was not completed until after midnight. The 5th had been heavily bombarded here, and its "trenches were severely damaged, in some places completely obliterated." As a result, the Tenth spent Tuesday and Wednesday making repairs, trying to shore up the position in case the Germans attacked. Aside from scattered shelling, it was comparatively quiet both days, and a considerable amount of work was accomplished during daylight hours. While here, the Battalion received 113 reinforcements, a mixed blessing according to the adjutant, Captain George Craggs. "General physique of draft appeared good," the captain commented, "but men very untrained and in very soft condition."[24]

The Battalion was in a difficult position. Hill 60 was threatened from the rear by the enemy's position of Observatory Ridge. The shallow, muddy trenches offered little protection from either the elements or German fire, and the enemy lines were within two hundred yards, making it exceedingly difficult to work. "A Canadian party, moving forward in extended order to take up a task, would be discovered in the light of the flares — up would go the red star shells from the slopes of Sanctuary Wood, and, in a minute or so, crash would come down the enemy barrage."[25] Casualties, though light, rose steadily. Among the Tenth's wounded was a Calgarian, Private Ernest Marles, who was injured on 7 June. Private Marles spent more than a year in hospital, but he never recovered from his wounds. He died on 21 July 1917 and was buried at Noeux-les-Mines Communal Cemetery near Bethune.

By Thursday, 8 June, the action had started to pick up. A patrol of the Fighting Tenth clashed in no man's land with a party of Germans, and Corporal Percy Witney shot at least one of them and recovered the body; the victim was identified as a member of the "11th Res. Prussian Regt. and wore Iron Cross ribbon." Perhaps as a consequence of this clash, the German artillery became more active that day, and in subsequent days. By the time the Battalion was relieved on Saturday, 10 June, it had suffered thirty more casualties. Among the wounded was nineteen-year-old Private William Taylor, who was injured by shrapnel in the right thigh. It was the second time in

Brigadier-General Louis Lipsett
Courtesy National Archives of Canada/PA-7442

Front-line view of Hill 60
Courtesy National Archives of Canada/PA4484

less than two months that Private Taylor had been hit; on 15 April, he had taken a chunk of shrapnel in the left forearm.[26]

It rained heavily on the ninth and tenth, adding to the unit's misery before it pulled out of the line. However, the Battalion could take satisfaction in a job well done, as it handed over trenches "now somewhat in shape."[27]

Few members of the Tenth were aware of what they had accomplished. While the Battalion held critically important Hill 60, the rest of the First Division was preparing for another counter-attack intended to recapture the ground lost on 2 June. As Colonel Rattray later observed, "it must be considered very much to the credit of the Battalion to hold this key position during the time of the preparation for an attack." In addition to the work on the unit's own trenches, there was plenty of activity going on all over the hill. Tunnellers, engineers, and machine-gunners worked feverishly to upgrade the defences in the area, and Rattray commanded "over 1500" men at this time. From Corps headquarters came Brigadier-General Raymond Brutinel, the French-born machine-gun genius, who later said that "the headquarters of the 10th Battalion was the only cheerful and optimistic place that he had met" during his front-line inspection.[28]

Big things were afoot. As mentioned above, the task of restoring the lost line about Mount Sorrel was handed to the First Division's General Currie, who had opposed the original counter-attack because of the hasty preparations: "I had no hopes whatever of the counter-attack regaining the positions and said so at the time".[29] Now, Currie was given plenty of time and, just as importantly, artillery and ammunition to clear the way for the infantry. The assault was delayed by bad weather and eventually scheduled for 1:30 a.m. on Tuesday, 13 June, which gave Currie time to reorganize his brigades. The Fighting Tenth joined the 5th

(Western Cavalry), 14th (Royal Montreal Regiment), and 15th (48th Highlanders of Canada) battalions in the First Brigade, which would remain in reserve while the revamped Second and Third brigades stormed Mount Sorrel. Colonel Rattray thus found himself temporarily under the command of Brigadier-General Garnet Hughes, whose appointment he had so violently opposed; none of the colonel's comments about this undesirable situation survive.

The Tenth had every right to expect a long rest now that it was in reserve. The Battalion had already seen more than its share of action since the first of the month, having supported the 7th Battalion's unsuccessful attack on Armagh Wood, then held the front under difficult circumstances. On the eleventh, after the Battalion came out of the line, another draft of reinforcements, 270 strong, arrived. "Men physically well built but soft and badly in need of training," Captain Craggs noted of the newcomers. "None appeared to have had any instruction in bombs and the majority were unacquainted with Lee Enfield rifle."[30]

But there was no rest in store for the Fighting Tenth. In a driving rainstorm in the early-morning darkness of 13 June, General Currie's counter-attack was, according to the British official historian, "an unqualified success,"[31] regaining nearly all of the lost ground between Mount Sorrel and Sanctuary Wood. As Currie intended, the bombardment orchestrated by the British and Canadian gunners was awesome. It was so noisy, noted one observer, that "no speech was intelligible even to a comrade alongside."[32]

Later in the morning, the Tenth was summoned to relieve the 16th (Canadian Scottish) Battalion amid the shattered remains of Armagh Wood and Hill 61. It would have come as small consolation to the men in the ranks to know that the decision to return the Tenth to the fighting front had come only after much soul-searching at Canadian Corps headquarters. Lieutenant-Colonel T. Birchall Wood, a senior staff officer, remarked: "I do not see how I can look [Colonel Rattray] in the face, as this is the third time that his Battalion has been ordered into this fight."[33]

This was a difficult relief. "On the way to the trenches the Battalion was heavily shelled and this shelling was continued all night with varying intensity," reads the war diary. "The trenches, both our old trenches and those constructed by the enemy were very badly battered by the shell fire to which they had been subjected by both sides, and large stretches had been completely obliterated and blown in." In pouring rain and almost complete darkness, the Tenth could not complete the relief of the 16th Battalion until after seven o'clock the next morning.[34]

The devastation was truly remarkable. "The trench system around was a wreck," says the history of the 16th Battalion. "In places, it was entirely obliterated; in others, a short stretch of the fire step was

In the absence of a supreme commander, the British and French relied on close co-operation to conduct the war. During the first two years of the conflict, the British readily admitted their junior status and acquiesced to French desires, for the simple reason that the French army was so much bigger than the steadily growing BEF. Fortunately, the respective commanders-in-chief saw eye-to-eye on just about everything. "I am *not under* General Joffre's orders," General Haig explained, "but that would make no difference, as my intention was to do my utmost to carry out General Joffre's wishes on strategical matters, as if they were orders."

It was Joffre, therefore, who set the Allied agenda for 1916. His wish was for a joint campaign in the vicinity of the River Somme, due north of Paris, while Haig's preference was for an offensive in Flanders. "Strategically there is no doubt about that being the best place for us to attack," Haig's intelligence chief, Brigadier-General John Charteris, wrote in January. "It strikes direct at the main railway communications of all the German armies. The Germans could not even make good their retreat. A victory, however great, on the Somme would still let them get back to the Meuse." However, when Joffre insisted on undertaking the Somme operations, Haig deferred to his desires.

The plans for a Somme offensive during the summer of 1916 were confirmed at a conference at Chantilly on 14 February. But the Germans upset the Allied timetable by mounting a major attack at Verdun on 21 February. Code-named *Gericht*, "place of execution," it proved to be a coldly calculated battle of attrition, for the Germans knew that the French considered this to be hallowed ground and would defend it at all costs. The bloodbath went on for weeks and months and, while the French army eventually saved Verdun, the cost was heart-breaking. "L'infanterie française n'existe plus," wept one general as he considered the half-million French casualties.

The Germans were bled at Verdun, too, and the butcher's bill resulted in the sacking of the commander, General Falkenhayn. His replacement was a tandem of Field-Marshal Paul von Hindenburg and Chief Quartermaster Erich Ludendorff, who had enjoyed impressive successes on the Eastern Front. Their first decision was to postpone all further offensive activity on the Western Front and launch construction of the elaborate series of concrete and barbed-wire fortifications which came to be known as the Hindenburg Line.

The French, frantic to ease the pressure on the Verdun sector, repeatedly urged Haig to advance the date of his Somme campaign. The dour British commander knew that his armies were unseasoned and ill-trained, and postponed operations for as long as possible. Finally, bowing to Joffre's pleadings, the BEF attacked on 1 July. It was primarily a British effort; the French, drained by their losses at Verdun, were necessarily relegated to a secondary role.

The Somme turned out to be a nightmare. While it succeeded in relieving the pressure on Verdun, the offensive cost the BEF dearly, but Haig was quite prepared to sustain previously inconceivable casualties. The first month's fighting on the Somme resulted in 164,909 dead, wounded, and missing British soldiers — or, as Haig noted, "about 120,000 more than they would have been had we not attacked. They cannot be regarded as sufficient to justify any anxiety as to our ability to continue the offensive." And so the offensive continued. By the time it was halted by bad weather in November, the BEF had lost 419,654 men.

Historians have vilified Haig for prolonging the slaughter on the Somme, portraying him as a blundering butcher. But Haig was handicapped by a number of deficiencies. An estimated one-third of the shells fired by the British artillery failed to explode, and the supply of high explosives required to cut the German wire and smash their defenses was lamentably inadequate, as were the battlefield communications required to control an army of a million men. The technology that produced the tank was not matched by the industrial capability to manufacture it in numbers that could influence the war in a measurable manner.

The German army had suffered heavily in the Verdun and Somme battles. Its losses at the Somme were increased by the policy of counter-attacking at all costs and at every opportunity, over ground which was of no strategical and little tactical value. Haig, an incurable optimist, contended that, because of the Somme campaign, "an appreciable proportion of the German soldiers are now practically beaten men, ready to surrender if they could find opportunity, thoroughly tired of the War, and hopeless of eventual success."

Haig would soon discover that he was terribly wrong; the Germans were far from beaten.

left upstanding giving a resting place to the crumpled bodies of its defenders, whose blood tinged with redness the water at the bottom of the trench. Looking over the battlefield from the height of ground at the final objective, the light of dawn revealed through the blur of rain a dreary waste of desolation — sodden earth, water-logged shell-holes, shattered tree stumps, and limp, bedraggled groups of men cautiously picking their way back over the morass into a curtain of watery mist, which entirely obscured the rear area."[35]

The Tenth was required to spend only a single day in the line this time, but it proved to be a long one. Wounded Canadian and German soldiers were discovered and brought in for treatment, in spite of heavy enemy shell fire which Lieutenant Lewis Younger remembered for the rest of his life. "You know how they said no two shells hit the same place? Well, there were shells landed back here, and a rat came out, and I said, 'That rat'll never get it.' Just half an hour [later], another shell came and hit the hole. Oh, you have no idea how the shelling was."[36] Colonel Rattray later claimed that it was "the most intense artillery fire the Canadians had been subjected to at any time in the war."[37]

Private Thomas Jones undoubtedly would have concurred with his colonel. A shell burst filled his legs with jagged chunks of metal and "threw me into a sort of trench where the men had dug themselves in a while before. I lay there a minute, wondering if I was really hurt, then I unstrapped my pack and put it on the top of the hole in which I was lying. Perhaps I was a good deal dazed and unable to realize how long I really lay there. Anyhow, it seemed only a minute when another shell came along and blew my pack ... to fragments."[38]

In this moonscape of craters and debris, it was difficult to determine the unit's precise position. "The whole ground was so ploughed up with shell fire and a network of old and new trenches battered out of recognition that it was impossible to form more than a rough idea of the position of the trenches and the troops holding them."[39]

Several members of the Battalion performed outstandingly. Twenty-nine-year-old Captain Alexander Thomson, though twice wounded, refused to leave, and supervised the consolidation of the position. Lieutenant Thomas Chutter and Company Sergeant-Major Jack Nuttall captured two unwounded German snipers who had been causing casualties. Major Joseph Simpson, ignoring heavy fire, personally directed movements to shore up the line. Lieutenant Stanley Robertson not only did fine work leading his bombing section on the left flank, but later rescued a wounded officer in no man's land. Major Simpson, Captain Thomson, and Lieutenants Chutter and Robertson won MCs, while Sergeant-Major Nuttall was awarded the DCM.

The Battalion's trial ended that night. Two battalions, the 24th (Victoria Rifles of Canada) and 26th (New Brunswick), relieved the Fighting Tenth during the evening of the fourteenth. The situation was so confused that two machine-gun posts, which had been forced to relocate, were not informed of the relief and the crews did not rejoin the Battalion until the fifteenth. The Germans bade the Tenth a rough farewell, shelling steadily throughout the relief and causing more casualties. Its latest front-line stint had cost the Battalion two officers and ninety-three other ranks, bringing total losses for the Battle of Mount Sorrel to seven officers and 267 other ranks.[40]

Twenty-one members of the Tenth won decorations as a result of the furious fighting here. In addition to the five MCs — including Lieutenant Trimmer's bar — awarded to officers of the unit, other ranks received three DCMs and thirteen MMs. Among them was Private Joseph Milne, a twenty-seven-year-old Calgarian who would be the only man in the Battalion to win the MM three times. Others awarded the MM were Regimental Sergeant-Major Duncan Stuart, MC; Sergeants Sydney Sydenham and Byron Greer; Corporals Walter Brown and Reginald Marvin; Lance-Corporal Albert Nowell and Privates Robert Adamson, H. Eden, Richard Harrison, William Summers, and Leslie Wright.

In Corps reserve at Camp E, the Tenth was treated to the well-merited reward of two weeks out of the front lines. The Battalion bathed twice, and the remainder of the time was devoted to working parties, ranging in size from 300 to 450, and to the apparently successful training of the many new men. It was twice visited by senior officers, on 17 June by the departing

Private Ernest Marles
Courtesy Glenbow Archives, Calgary/NA-4025-16

86

Mount Sorrel, with ruins of Armagh House in foreground (1919)
Courtesy National Archives of Canada/PA-4486

brigadier, General Lipsett, who was being promoted to command the Third Division, and the next day by the Corps commander, General Byng.[41] This was Byng's first close look at the Tenth and he was most impressed. "Rattray," said Sir Julian, after his inspection, "I want you to tell your officers, N.C.O.'s and men how *very very* pleased I am with the Battalion."

This was not puffery on Byng's part, as Rattray later discovered. A few months afterwards, the colonel was approached by Lieutenant-Colonel Edouard Panet, a staff officer of the Fourth Division. "Rattray, what did you do to Byng when he inspected your Battalion?" Panet queried.

"Nothing I know of," Rattray replied, "why?"

Panet explained that after inspecting several units of the Fourth Division, Byng had paid special compliments to one battalion. When a staff officer asked whether it was the best in the Corps, Byng had replied, with characteristic frankness: "No, not quite, the 10th Battalion was a little better."[42]

The Tenth returned to the trenches on Thursday, 29 June and completed the "quiet and quick relief" of the 13th (Royal Highlanders of Canada) Battalion north of Mount Sorrel early Friday morning. It rained that day, and while there was no notable enemy activity, an accident — the "premature explosion" of a grenade — wounded four privates. "Very quiet," says the war diary of the six-day tour, "enemy apparently busy on repairing their own trenches. All available men at work day & night clearing and reclaiming trenches." A heavy rainstorm on Tuesday, 4 July, forced the cancellation of all working parties, and the next day, Ontario's 1st Battalion arrived to relieve the Fighting Tenth. Casualties were modest — fifteen, of whom three had been killed — but they included one of the unit's best officers, Captain Stanley Kent, who was wounded just before the relief; he would be out of action for several months.[43]

The next few weeks were among the most quiet in the Battalion's brief history. Aside from a four-day

tour in early August, the Tenth would not return to the front lines until September. Alternating between brigade and divisional reserve, it was inspected on 18 July by the Corps commander, General Byng, whose comments were again "very favourable." The new brigadier, Frederick Loomis, also inspected on the tenth and nineteenth of that month. Training was a priority, although large working parties, ranging in size from 180 to 427, were detailed to improve the defences on and behind Hill 60. There was some excitement on 25 July when the Germans exploded a mine under the Bluff. The Fighting Tenth stood to arms for two hours, but British Columbia's 7th Battalion needed no assistance in repulsing subsequent enemy attack.

After its tour of the trenches between 7 and 11 August — which cost twenty-six casualties — the Battalion returned to divisional reserve. Marching to Moulle via Hazebrouck, Steenvoorde, and Cassel, the Tenth spent the second half of August in intensive training, suggesting that action was not too far off.[44]

On Wednesday, 23 August, the unit's officers attended a lecture of some significance. Entitled "The Battle of the Somme," it detailed the events of the latest campaign rocking the Western Front. Although it would be apparent only to future historians, the Great War had entered a new phase, begun in February 1916 with the great German attack on the French at Verdun. The two sides had spent most of 1915 feeling each other out, the high commands unable to believe that the end of the war of movement was anything more than temporary. By 1916, the opponents were ready to slug it out in a bid to break the deadlock. Verdun signalled the realization that attrition was the only way this war was going to be won, and the Somme was further evidence of that unfortunate fact.

The concept of the campaign left much to be desired. "The Somme offensive had no great geographical objectives," observed Colonel G.W.L. Nicholson, the Canadian official historian. "Its purpose was threefold — to relieve pressure on the French armies at Verdun, to inflict as heavy losses as possible on the German armies, and to aid allies on other fronts by preventing any further transfer of German troops from the west."[45] The battle was launched on 1 July and General Haig's dream of a breakthrough vanished within hours. In a single day, the BEF suffered a staggering 57,470 casualties, without gaining any appreciable amount of ground or, it seems, inconveniencing the enemy to a great extent. Undaunted, the commander-in chief continued to hurl his forces into battle, and the Germans responded with counter-attacks of equal ferocity and determination.

The lecture attended by the Tenth's officers was timely, because the Canadian Corps would soon be on its way to the slaughterhouse on the Somme. The Battalion's turn came on the morning of Sunday, 27

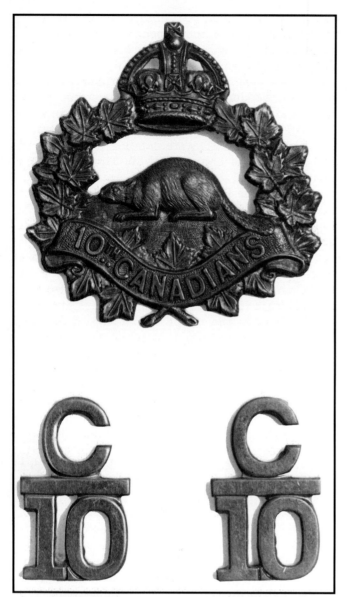

Tenth Battalion cap and collar badges (other ranks)
Courtesy Glenbow Museum, Calgary

would have revealed some distinctive markings. In addition to the CANADA shoulder badge worn since the war's early days, each man in the Canadian Corps was now wearing on his upper sleeve a patch by which his division, brigade, and battalion could be readily identified, depending upon the shapes and colours of the patches. In the case of the Fighting Tenth, the patch consisted of a red rectangle, three inches by two inches, denoting the First Division, surmounted by a two-inch red square, which indicated that it was part of the Second Brigade.[49]

The Tenth had also joined the growing list of Canadian units with regimental badges. Previously, the Battalion utilized the General Service maple-leaf badge, but Colonel Rattray had taken the initiative to adopt a unique design. He selected one which featured a beaver within a wreath of maple leaves, beneath a crown, with a scroll inscribed "10th Canadians" on the wreath and under the beaver. As Dan Ormond later explained, "we have always tried to have the simple name of 'THE TENTH CANADIANS' adopted but have made no effort to have this adopted in an official way.... We have not asked for localization of a name for we have received many good men from all parts of Canada and in fairness to everyone do not wish to localize."[50]

It is difficult to determine precisely when the Battalion received the badges. Colonel Rattray had launched the project as early as 9 November 1915, when he wrote his brigadier, General Lipsett, request-

August, when it began its long, leisurely march southwards. Moving via Candas and Montrelet, the Tenth reached Rubrempré on the thirtieth.[46]

One writer likened the move to "a holiday," and in some respects, it was.[47] "The fields were a mass of green and gold. Flowers bloomed everywhere — a wonderful thing for men who for many months had seen little or nothing of Nature's beauty. There were frequent rests, and the orders for each day provided, as far as possible, that the strength of the troops should not be taxed. It was the desire of the officers that the men should arrive at the Somme in perfect condition...."[48]

To the casual observer, such as a French civilian watching from a nearby farm or standing along the roadside, there was not much to distinguish these Canadian troops from the British soldiers alongside whom they were fighting. For example, the Canadians wore British uniforms and used British equipment, including the Lee-Enfield rifle. A closer examination

Tenth Battalion cap and collar badges (officers and senior NCOs)
Courtesy Glenbow Museum, Calgary

ing approval for the chosen design. The request was relayed to divisional headquarters, which promptly approved it. Rattray then wrote to Canadian Military Headquarters in London, addressing his appeal to Major-General John Carson, personal representative of the militia minister, Sir Sam Hughes. General Carson, replying in late February, told Rattray that battalion badges could not be provided at public expense, but the colonel swiftly assured him that regimental funds would defray the cost, and the badge design was resubmitted to London in March 1916.[51]

Approval came on 18 March. However, the Canadians authorities made it clear that the badge would be permitted only "on the understanding that the unit undertakes to bear the cost of provision."[52]

The new badges arrived within the next three months. While the exact date cannot be pinpointed, research by Barry Agnew, the military curator at the Glenbow Museum in Calgary, has revealed a Battalion order in the middle of June indicating that the new badges were in use, if improperly in a few cases. "It has been noticed in some instances a piece of red cloth has been placed behind the new cap badge. It is to be understood that only dark blue cloth is to be used."[53]

While all ranks wore the regimental badge on their caps, a smaller version was issued to officers for the collars of their uniforms. Other ranks, however, continued to wear the collar badge featuring the letter C over the numeral ten, available since the summer of 1915. It is interesting to note that the badges, while very similar, were not identical. Depending on the manufacturer — at least three British firms, along with at least one in Canada, produced Tenth Battalion badges — the beaver on the regimental badge varied in size and the London firm of Hicks and Son produced a set of officers' badges on which the beaver and scroll were a white metal overlay. As well, the C-over-ten badges were slightly different shapes and sizes.[54]

Their uniforms now adorned with new sleeve patches and regimental badges, the men of the Fighting Tenth faced another test of their mettle. After two days at Rubrempré, the Battalion moved into the battle zone, passing signposts painted with such grim names as "Death Valley" and "Casualty Corner," which merely hinted at the trouble which lay ahead. General Currie, who watched all of his troops, including those of the Tenth, move into the area, was delighted with their appearance. "They behaved themselves in billets, they marched well, wore their clothes and equipment well, conducted themselves like soldiers," he wrote approvingly.[55]

On 4 September, the Battalion took over billets in the battered town of Albert, with headquarters at 102 Rue d'Aveluy. Albert's cathedral had become one of the war's enduring symbols. The statue of the Virgin Mary atop the tower had been knocked askew by a German shell in 1915, and the superstition had arisen that if it fell, the Allies would lose the war; to prevent that from happening, engineers had secured the statue with steel hawsers.

While a group of officers reconnoitered the front-line trenches, two hundred other ranks participated in "Practice Contact Aeroplanes," an early attempt at practical co-operation between flyers and footsoldiers.[56] "The attacking infantry carried flares, mirrors and special signalling panels, and as they advanced they signalled their positions to aircraft assigned solely to tactical observation. The information thus received was then dropped at formation headquarters or sent back by wireless."[57]

The Fighting Tenth soon made its first appearance in the front lines at the Somme, in the trenches near La Boisselle and the Chalk Pits, three miles north of Albert. On Saturday, 9 September, the Tenth took over trenches held by the 8th (90th Winnipeg Rifles) Battalion. The relief was completed in a little over seven hours — "a record for the 1st Divn. in this sector," claims the war diary — at the cost of ten casualties.[58] It was also completed without Colonel Rattray, who had left the Battalion the previous day.

There is not much mystery about the colonel's departure: he had been promoted to brigadier-general and given command of a training brigade in England. The colonel still carried a chip on his shoulder about his treatment at the hands of Sam Hughes, believing that "pull is such that my making good will not be rewarded. It is discouraging at times to take all the chances of trench fighting day in and day out, building up and keeping up our efficient battalion, spending great energies — taking all kinds of chances — recognized as a success in the fighting line but all the time knowing that there is 'nothing to be given you' because Sam Hughes has given these instructions. I often wonder if it is worth while but then I think it over and after all I am not serving Sam Hughes, I am only part of a nation ... and a nation is greater than a man...."[59]

Motor trucks carry Canadian troops from the trenches at the Somme, September 1916

Courtesy National Archives of Canada/PA-705

West Miraumont road near Courcelette, October 1916
Courtesy Glenbow Archives, Calgary/NA-1870-9

It is unlikely that political factors were a consideration in Rattray's removal from his combat command but, if they were, the tough Manitoban could soon console himself with the knowledge that Hughes was on his way out as minister of militia and defence. Rattray's age (fifty-two) was against him, so it seems that he was simply judged unsuitable for active service, that his talents were more appropriate for training new recruits. Not a great field commander, he was, nevertheless, a competent officer. In the space of fifteen months under his command, the Tenth Battalion had further enhanced its reputation.

When Colonel Rattray departed at seven o'clock on the morning of 8 September, the Battalion came under the temporary command of the recently installed second-in-command, Major Alexander Thomson. As a lieutenant, the Scottish-born Thomson had been one of the first officer casualties in the Tenth, in March 1915. Rattray called him "an officer who did not know what fear was",[60] with reason, for Thomson had already won the MC and was about to win the DSO.

Rattray left in the knowledge that his successor would be a man who was known to the Battalion and enjoyed its full confidence. That man was none other than the former adjutant, Major Dan Ormond.

Colonel Rattray had had a hand in Ormond's selection. On 1 January 1916, he had written the divisional commander, General Currie, making a case for Ormond to succeed him in command of the Tenth, if and when the opportunity arose, for whatever reason. "I have not heard directly from Major Ormond and he is unaware that I am writing to you as I have done."[61] Now that the opportunity had arisen, Rattray again urged that Ormond succeed him. In a discussion with Currie, Rattray explained that he had high regard for the former Portage-la-Prairie lawyer, both from their service together with the Tenth and from their pre-war militia days in Manitoba. A sceptical Currie told

Rattray, "You have a higher opinion of Ormond than I have, but I will take your word for it."

Rattray replied confidently, "Ormond will not disappoint you." His confidence was well-founded, as subsequent events would prove.[62]

Major Ormond, who would not arrive until late September, was taking over a unit drastically different from the one he had left a year before. After leaving the Fighting Tenth to take temporary command of the 7th Battalion, Ormond's health declined, forcing him to spend much time in and out of hospital in England prior to his appointment as commandant of the Canadian Pioneer Training Depot. When he returned, he would recognize few of the officers, aside from Major Thomson, the second-in-command, and Major Eric MacDonald, who commanded C Company. The other company commanders were new to him: Major Guy Marriott (A), Captain David Black (B), and Major Allan Conners (D).

Under the acting command of the fearless Major Thomson, the Battalion experienced the hell that was the Somme. The shell-swept terrain was, like Flanders, remarkably flat with few notable features, and those were mainly man-made. One such was the enormous crater near La Boisselle, which was created by a British mine on 1 July and can still be seen today, replete with warning signs about the dangers of unexploded munitions.

Around-the-clock shelling was routine; the casualties, even in so-called "quiet" sectors, were appalling, marked by a steady stream of walking wounded and stretcher-bearers carrying other luckless victims to the dressing stations. Although makeshift cemeteries with rough-hewn wooden grave markers seemed to be everywhere, thousands upon thousands of men on both sides were deprived of a final resting place. They literally disappeared from the face of the earth in this witch's cauldron of high explosive and mud.

As the Tenth would soon discover, the part played by a battalion at the Somme was "insignificant." In the opinion of a veteran-cum-historian, Hugh Urquhart, "Tactically little need be said to describe it. The men marched in over shell swept roads; they waited patiently in the shelled trenches; they advanced a few hundred yards in the 'limited objective' attacks, with barrages in front of them; if fortunate they held their position with heavy casualties; if not, they came back — or such as remained — to their jumping-off trench and had still heavier losses; and they returned to rest billets a shadow of their former selves."[63]

The BEF's immediate objective in this area was the high ground north and east of Albert. German control of the so-called Ancre Heights, which took their name from lazy River Ancre, a tributary of the Somme, precluded a British advance on Bapaume, a key rail centre and one of the primary goals of the offensive. These heights, described by historian

Jeffrey Williams as "a broad plateau, whose wide unfenced wheatfields could be mistaken for the Canadian prairie,"[64] dominated the district's main thoroughfare which ran northeast from Amiens, through Albert to Bapaume. The notable landmarks included the villages of Courcelette and Thiepval, which lent its name to the main ridge. Another, Mouquet Farm was a strongpoint that had resisted no fewer than six Australian assaults in late August and early September.

Anyone clinging to the notion that the Somme was just another place on the Western Front quickly changed his mind. The Fighting Tenth, going into the front line opposite Mouquet Farm with twenty-two officers and 733 other ranks, found itself in the thick of the action. On Sunday, 10 September, the Battalion's first full day in the front line, the Germans mounted no fewer than four attacks. The first was launched at 9:20 a.m., but was quickly broken up by machine-gun fire. "Their cries for stretcher bearers were heard from our lines," says the war diary. Twelve hours of sustained shelling followed before the next assault was mounted. Delivered at 9:30 p.m., it was again routed by the Battalion's machine-gunners. Another attack occurred at 10:05 p.m., and it fared no better than others. The Germans, "estimated at 200 men," were forced "to retire in confusion" in the face of concentrated rifle and machine-gun fire. Undaunted, they tried again at 10:30 p.m. "The occasion was sufficiently serious to warrant a call to our Stokes Gun Battery to barrage in front of Mouquet Farm. Ninety two rounds of ammunition were sent over by this battery." The enemy came no closer than thirty-five yards to the Battalion's trenches. Lieutenant Roy Lutz, who had just joined the unit on 4 September, was killed, and two other officers, Captain Alfred Trimmer, the two-time MC-winner, and Lieutenant Frederick McKenney, were wounded, along with twelve other ranks.[65]

The next day was more typical of the Somme abattoir. Nothing out of the ordinary occurred, but by the

No man's land near Courcelette, October 1916
Courtesy William Ivor Castle/DND/National Archives of Canada/PA-786

time it was over, the Battalion had sustained forty casualties, including five dead and one missing. Rain was falling when the Tenth was relieved that night by the 2nd Canadian Mounted Rifles. Two days in the trenches had cost the Battalion fifty-five men.[66]

Among the dead was a young Irish-born private named Gibson Skelton. A member of the Fighting Tenth since the previous October, he had celebrated his twenty-first birthday on 6 September, just before the unit headed into the trenches. Private Skelton, who was still grieving for his brother killed in action three months earlier, seems to have had a premonition about his own death, as he wrote his mother on the seventh:

> My brother's death brought home to me with force the necessity of being prepared at all times for instant death as he was. One never knows what the next moment may bring forth, and especially here where the 'Huns' used such means of taking life. Should anything happen to me do not weep too much or be heartbroken. Remember that I am in God's keeping, and in what better way could I die than fighting for Him and my country. There is a mansion prepared for every one of us by our Lord, and it will be a very short time until we all meet there, never more to part, and where there is no trouble and sorrow.
>
> Dearest Mother, do not weep, and may the same good God who is caring for me keep and bless you all.
>
> Goodbye for a very short time.

Struck in the abdomen by shrapnel on 11 September, Private Skelton died the same day in the dressing station.[67]

Billeted in and around Albert, the Battalion enjoyed two days of rest before marching to Rubrempré via Warloy. The Tenth remained here, in army reserve, until 16 September. Then, by foot and on bus, it returned to the vicinity of Albert. During this period, ninety-three reinforcements arrived, although the war diary makes no comment on their quality. On the nineteenth, while most of the Battalion bathed, the senior officers went up the front lines to familiarize themselves with the sector for which they would soon assume responsibility. On the twenty-second, a Friday, the Fighting Tenth relieved the 52nd (Ontario) Battalion in the forward trenches, completing the move at 1:54 a.m. the next morning.[68]

It was one of the shortest tours in the Battalion's history. Relieved on Saturday night by the 7th (1st British Columbia Regiment) and 13th (Royal Highlanders of Canada) battalions, the Tenth withdrew to the Chalk Pits, the Second Brigade's support position. But it was a costly day. There were fifty-two casualties, including two company commanders, A's Major Marriott and D's Major Conners. Conners, a twenty-nine-year-old Calgary broker, died of his wounds, while Marriott, a Toronto banker, recovered from his injuries but never returned to the Battalion.[69]

The next two days in the Chalk Pits were little easier. The casualties totalled three other ranks killed and thirty-six wounded.[70] But the tally of dead and injured was certain to grow, because the Battalion was slated to participate in a major attack.

Important events had been taking place elsewhere. The Tenth had actually arrived at the Somme during a lull in the action as the BEF prepared to renew its offensive on 15 September. On that date, the Second and Third divisions, accompanied by tanks for the first time in warfare, and by another innovation, the creeping barrage, captured the village of Courcelette just up the road from La Boisselle. This success by the Canadian Corps inspired the commander-in-chief, General Haig, to order attacks all along the line. Now, the Fighting Tenth was to take part in an operation scheduled for 26 September, a bid to capture long, low Thiepval Ridge, between the villages of Thiepval and Courcelette.

The First Division, attacking with two brigades, Second on the left and Third on the right, was to storm the three main lines of defence on the ridge. These were Zollern Trench, the nearest position; the intermediate Hessian Trench; and Regina Trench, which lay just behind the crest. The Second Brigade's attack would be led by the 5th (Western Cavalry) Battalion on the right and the 8th (90th Winnipeg Rifles) on the left, each with a company of the Tenth attached. Major MacDonald and C Company would support the 5th, while the 8th was aided by Lieutenant Geoffrey Burbidge and D Company. The other two companies, under Major Joseph Simpson, would remain behind in close support.

The Battalion's combat strength was twenty officers and 691 other ranks. Each man carried two Mills bombs and 170 rounds of small-arms ammunition, two sandbags, a shovel or pick, and two days' rations.[71]

Once again, Major Thomson would lead it into action. While the new commanding officer, Major Ormond, had arrived, he deferred to Thomson. Whether he was ordered to do so or exercised his own discretion is not known.

There were casualties even before the assault was launched. Parties of the Tenth, sent up to dig jumping-off trenches before dawn, came under heavy shelling. Among the wounded was Private Samuel Hemphill, who was hit by shrapnel. "The one that got me actually wasn't too close," he later related. "It was quite a bit away. And we were crouched down, and the first thing I knew, I got hit in the left thigh, and that was it."[72] It was a wound that was most valued by any soldier, a "blighty," so called because it was not serious enough to maim yet required convalescence in Blighty, the nickname for England. Private Hemphill, a nineteen-year-old meatpacker from Edmonton, would recover and return to win the MM in 1918.

The attack went in at 12:35 p.m. on Tuesday, 26 September, a clear, cool day. A three-day bombardment preceded the operation, which went poorly on the Canadian front. The Second Brigade's sector was no exception. While the 5th and 8th battalions swiftly overran Zollern Trench and fought their way into sections of Hessian Trench, they could go no farther in the face of heavy fire. The British troops supporting the attack on the left were also running into difficulties, and at two o'clock, Lieutenant-Colonel John Prower, the officer commanding the 8th Battalion, reported that his flank was in the air because Zollern Trench on the left was still in enemy hands. At 2:08 p.m., he committed a portion of his Tenth Battalion forces to the battle.[73]

Lieutenant Geoff Burbidge and two platoons subsequently were part of a remarkable story. The Lieutenant, along, with sixty-five other ranks, rushed to the endangered left, and all were soon engulfed in a storm of small-arms fire. Although they advanced in extended order, the men of the Tenth were cut to ribbons. By the time Burbidge had stormed and captured the enemy positions, he had only eight soldiers left; the rest had been killed or wounded. But the twenty-six-year-old bank clerk from Winnipeg had just begun to fight. Leading his little party through a hail of enemy bullets, he bombed his way along the German trench, well into the neighbouring British zone, before establishing a block and digging in. Burbidge's tiny force held on here until relieved the following night.[74] In the process, it captured "two officers, forty six other ranks, four machine guns, a quantity of bombs, S.A.A., rifles and other equipment."[75]*

One member of Burbidge's D Company was in action for the first time. A veteran of the 103rd Calgary Rifles, seventeen-year-old Walter Loudon had come overseas with the 56th Battalion, recruited by his former regimental commander, Lieutenant-Colonel William Armstrong. Private Loudon, who admitted that he felt "pretty scared," recalled a grisly episode when his platoon captured a section of enemy trench. "We jumped in there, and [the Germans] had their hands up," including an officer who suddenly pulled out a revolver and shot one of his Canadian captors. "He was a perfect pincushion when we were finished," Loudon said of the German. "I think every man had his bayonet in him."[77]

On the right, Major MacDonald led C Company into action that afternoon as well. MacDonald's men

---

* Oddly, the 8th Battalion's Colonel Prower afterwards reported that Burbidge's party carried out its assignment "almost without opposition"![76]

shored up the 5th Battalion's line and captured, in addition to considerable quantities of arms and other stores, "seventy other ranks" in Zollern Trench.[78]

The rest of the Tenth was gradually committed to action during the afternoon. Shortly after two o'clock, Major Thomson instructed Major Simpson to take A and B companies into the jumping-off line used by the 5th and 8th battalions. Simpson completed this move within the hour, and these companies were soon sending troops into the fighting line. At 3:15 p.m., Captain Black, commanding B Company, sent forward two platoons and a Colt machine-gun under Captain William Drewry to reinforce the 5th Battalion. Captain Drewry carried out this move "without a casualty." Just before four o'clock, the 8th Battalion put out another call for assistance, and Thomson ordered Simpson to send up a single platoon; a supernumerary, Major FitzRoy George, took this unit into action.[79]

Throughout the afternoon, the mixed force of Canadians — besides the Fighting Tenth, the captured trenches contained troops of the 5th and 8th battalions and, later, the 7th — endured withering small-arms fire, the worst of it coming from the British sector on the left, where the attackers had failed to take vital surrounding high ground. "As a result," reported the 5th, "the ground between our lines was swept by quite a heavy enfilade fire from enemy Machine Guns."[80] Although the British 11th Division claimed to be holding its objectives, and reported such to General Currie at First Division headquarters, the contrary was clearly apparent to General Loomis and his Second Brigade. On Loomis's instructions, the 8th Battalion and its reinforcing parties threw back a defensive flank on the left. It was not until the next day that the British ended the confusion by taking the ground in question.[81]

In the meantime, the Fighting Tenth had been fully committed to the battle across the brigade's front. A key move came in the late afternoon when Lieutenant Wilfred Romeril, a twenty-six-year-old financial agent from Montreal who commanded A Company, rushed three platoons to the exposed left flank. Lieutenant Romeril was later reinforced by the Battalion's bombers and two Colt machine-guns.[82]

The enemy's small-arms and shell fire was unabated, even with the blessed arrival of darkness, and efforts to bring out the wounded simply added to the casualty count. One of the stretcher-bearers who laboured valiantly amid the death and devastation was Corporal Charles Hatcher, one of the unit's originals. He had just rejoined the Battalion after a lengthy illness, but the Somme marked the end of his war service. "On the way up [to the front], I was carrying a stretcher, and a bullet hit me through the hand. I've got the use of these fingers, but I've got no feeling. So that was my end." Invalided back to Canada within a few months, Hatcher returned to work with the CPR in 1917.[83]

The situation remained fluid on Wednesday, 27 September. A German counter-attack recaptured part of Hessian Trench, but the 7th Battalion drove the enemy out late in the day. With only part of the intermediate objective taken, it was clear that no attempt could be made to capture Regina Trench. By now, the attackers had suffered too many casualties, and the enemy's machine-gun fire was undiminished.

General Loomis was quick to blame the British for his brigade's limited success in this operation. "The fact that the troops on our Left did not succeed in maintaining touch with us, nor in capturing the strong positions which overlooked and commanded our area," he later wrote, "prevented us from giving very much attention to the final objective, Regina Trench."[84] As it turned out, this powerful position remained in German hands until November, when the newly arrived Fourth Division captured it in the culmination of a brutal and bloody battle.

All day on the twenty-seventh, the Tenth fought by companies and platoons, mixed with the 5th, 7th, and 8th battalions. Because of the piecemeal nature of the action, it is difficult to relate with precision the part played by the Battalion. However, it says much for the discipline and quality of all these units that

The statue of the Virgin Mary leans perilously from the top of the cathedral in battered Albert

Courtesy National Archives of Canada/PA-1324

they were able to function effectively in spite of heavy losses and extensive disorganization.

The intense shell and small-arms fire was unforgettable, for veterans and rookies alike. Private Walter Loudon, the seventeen-year old Calgarian who was in combat for the first time, remembered seeing an officer hand a message to a runner, who scrambled over the parapet of the trench. The private, Loudon recalled, went perhaps fifty feet before being riddled by bullets.[85]

Having committed all his men, Major Thomson was left with little to do, and at midafternoon he was ordered to report to Lieutenant-Colonel Hugh Dyer, the officer commanding the 5th Battalion. Colonel Dyer was evidently impressed with the young major, for he placed Thomson in charge of that night's relief on the Second Brigade's right-front.[86] Two battalions, the 1st and 4th Canadian Mounted Rifles, moved into the sector after dark. It was a difficult manoeuvre, as might be expected under the circumstances, and it was not until seven-thirty on Thursday morning, the twenty-eighth, that Major Thomson could inform brigade headquarters that it had been completed.[87] When the twenty-nine-year old major wearily rejoined the Battalion later in the morning, he finally handed over command to the patient Major Ormond.

The Fighting Tenth had, as usual, paid dearly. Its thirty-six hours in action on Thiepval Ridge had resulted in 241 casualties.[88] These included another company commander, the third to fall in three days — B Company's Captain Black, who was wounded. The sole officer to be killed was Captain James Clinkskill, who had been with the unit since 1 September. Sergeant Reginald Marvin, an MM-winner at Mount Sorrel, lost his life during the relief operation.

Under Major Ormond's command, the Tenth rested and recuperated from its brutal battle. The Battalion received 284 reinforcements, all of them other ranks, and in Montrelet, on Sunday, 1 October, two visiting generals heaped praise on the unit. In the morning, after church service, General Loomis "spoke of good work done by the Battalion and made special mention of good work done by Major Thomson, also by the Battalion Runners." That afternoon, General Currie addressed the men and commented on the "good work done by the Division, and by the Battalion."[89]

The weather soon took a turn for the worse. Until now, conditions had been generally good, but October brought heavy rain. The Fighting Tenth was scheduled for bath parade on Monday, 2 October, "but Companies could not be bathed owing to heavy rain making river muddy." It rained every day for the next week, as the Battalion moved by stages back to Albert. It arrived on the seventh, and prepared to move into the front lines once more.[90]

The effect of the rainfall was truly terrible. The Somme battlefield was turned into a sea of "cloying, slippery, slithery, gluey" mud, according to war correspondent Fred McKenzie. "Take the worst kind of clay," he wrote, "pound it into dust four feet thick, then moisten it with rain; make extra pits at intervals by the explosions of very heavy shells; fill these pits with more fluid mud. Have your mud at a temperature just above freezing point. Be compelled to stay in it for a day and more at a time — to stand in it, to wallow in it, even to sleep in it. Then you have some idea of the Somme mud."[91]

The mud was a major cause of failure in two more Canadian attacks on Thiepval Ridge. On 1 October, the Second and Third Divisions, floundering in a veritable sea of mud, slipped and slid up the long, gentle slope, where they discovered that the preliminary bombardment had done little damage to the enemy's barbed-wire entanglements. Hung up in the wire and raked by machine-gun fire, the two divisions were stopped cold. Conditions were little better when, after a week-long delay due to bad weather, the First and Third divisions renewed the assault on Regina Trench on the eighth. The attackers broke through in several places, but were unable to hold on when the Germans resorted to their customary counter-attacks.

The Fighting Tenth, housed around Albert, received orders on 8 October to stand-to and be ready to move into the front lines at short notice. However, because of the unsuccessful operations that day, it was not until Tuesday, 10 October, that the Tenth was sent up to relieve the 1st (Western Ontario) Battalion north of Courcelette. This sector had seen an attack by the 13th (Royal Highlanders of Canada) Battalion and, during the day, eight wounded men of that unit were brought in from no man's land. "The white flag was not used nor was any truce observed by us," says the war diary. That night, the Tenth was in turn relieved by the 44th (Manitoba) Battalion, belonging to the new Fourth Division. Its twenty-four-hour tour had cost the Tenth another twenty-six casualties.[92]

The dead included a young private named Clifford Tyner, whose demise heralded a miraculous escape for a fellow soldier, seventeen-year-old Walter Loudon of Calgary. When Tyner was wounded, Private Loudon hurried to his side and tended to his injuries.

"Have you got a cigarette?" Tyner grunted through clenched teeth.

"No," replied Loudon, "but you can use my pipe."

He handed his pipe to Tyner and then watched in horror as, just seconds later, a shell blew the unfortunate man to pieces. Loudon was unscathed.[93]

Returning to Albert, the Battalion bathed on 13 and 14 October. The following day, the fifteenth, it made its last appearance in the trenches at the Somme. Moving into the line northeast of Courcelette, the Tenth relieved the 8th (90th Winnipeg Rifles) Battalion opposite the Quadrilateral, a heavily wired double line of trenches which had repeatedly resisted capture by the Canadians.

The task of taking it was handed to the Fighting Tenth. Major Ormond was not pleased with the prospects, because he knew that the enemy's barbed-wire entanglements were virtually intact. He sent his scout officer, Lieutenant Tom Baker, on several reconnaissance missions, beginning on the night of 10 - 11 October. When Lieutenant Baker returned to report that the wire was "strong and only slightly damaged," the artillery renewed its efforts to smash it, with indifferent results. Two nights later, Baker and his scouts crawled into no man's land and found "the wire to be in good shape, only cut in a few places." When a patrol under Major Joseph Simpson verified Baker's findings on 14 - 15 October, the artillery, short of high-explosive shells and plagued by duds among the few that were available, arranged another massive bombardment. With the Battalion scheduled to go over the top at dawn on 16 October, Ormond dispatched Baker and his scouts to investigate the wire. It was a bright, moonlit night and any movement drew German sniper and machine-gun fire; the scouts could add nothing to the previous reports.[94]

Ormond was convinced that the Battalion was bound for disaster. He reported to his brigadier, General Loomis, that the Tenth was facing "masses of uncut wire." Loomis was unmoved and confirmed his orders "to attack the next morning at daylight."[95]

It would be a suicide attack, and everyone in the Battalion knew it. German machine-gunners, with clear fields of fire, would devastate the infantry hung up in the barbed wire. "Nineteen out of twenty-one of the Officers going into the attack each secretly handed a letter to the Chaplain to be delivered after the attack," Major Ormond later wrote. "The other two shook dice to find out if they would come out." One of them was the brave lieutenant, Geoff Burbidge.[96]

Fate intervened, in the form of General Currie. Ormond's reconnaissance report reached First Division headquarters during the night, and the Fighting Tenth could consider itself fortunate that Currie was an early-riser. As soon as he read the report, he called off the operation. The cancellation order reached Ormond at 5:05 a.m., just minutes before the Battalion was scheduled to go over the top to near-certain destruction.[97]

Instead of being remembered as a nightmare, Monday, 16 October, was notable for being an unusually quiet day, in terms of fighting at the Somme. "Enemy shelled low ground, on which our left rested, very heavily," says the war diary. "All troops were moved to the right and no casualties were caused in consequence." The day's losses were minimal: four other ranks wounded. That night, the Tenth came out of the line, relieved by the 47th (British Columbia) Battalion, and marched back to billets in Albert.[98]

The Tenth's ordeal at the Somme had ended; the prolonged fighting had cost the Battalion 417 casualties. Sadly, the rewards were not commensurate with the sacrifice, at least as far as the officers were concerned. Of eleven who were deemed by Major Ormond to be "worthy of special mention on account of the most splendid and efficient manner in which they carried out the tasks apportioned to them," only one was decorated: Major Thomson was awarded the DSO. Lieutenant Burbidge was recommended (the 8th Battalion's Colonel Prower praised the former Winnipeg bank clerk, declaring that the manner in which Burbidge "handled the various situations gave me absolutely no cause for anxiety"[99]), but received nothing. The unit's other ranks did much better; three — Sergeant David McAndie, Lance-Sergeant Frederick Shoesmith, and Private Alexander Morin — won DCMs and eighteen others were awarded MMs. They were Sergeants Alexander McLaughlin, John McNeil, and Chester Pettit; Lance-Sergeant David Connell; Lance-Corporals Hugh Caminer and George Vowel; and Privates Ernest Bach, Edward Flynn, Wilfred Longwood, Leonard Mallory, Phil McKenzie, Thomas Milligan, John Milton, Rennie Paget, Albert Parsons, Sidney Robson, Walter Stevenson, and John Temperton.

As a result of the Somme, three battle honours were later awarded the Fighting Tenth: "Somme, 1916," "Thiepval," and "Ancre Heights." Only one other action, in the Second Battle of Ypres, garnered as many battle honours for the Battalion.

On Tuesday, 17 October, the Canadian Corps — except for the Fourth Division, which would remain here for another month — began its departure from the Somme.* It was destined for Artois, to the north, and there were few regrets about leaving this blood-soaked, mud-caked, heart-breaking battleground. "It was straight slugging, just out-guessing the other fellow, and pushing ahead," Major Ormond later said of the Somme. "There was nothing exciting about it."[101]

The Fighting Tenth was among the first units to leave the battle zone, marching out of Albert at 1:45 p.m. on 17 October, headed for Warloy, the first stage in a long move northwards. It rained often along the way, and when the days were clear they were uncomfortably cold. Still, the Battalion made good time. On 22 October, for example, it covered the thirteen miles between Mezerolles and Dernier in six hours. Reaching La Comte on the twenty-third, the troops settled down for four full days of inspections, training, and sports. The war diary notes the "keen interest shown by all ranks [in] football, tug of war, bomb throwing competition &c."[102]

An important ceremony awaited the Battalion. A former Canadian governor-general, the Duke of Connaught, was scheduled to visit General Currie's divisional headquarters at Camblain l'Abbé on

---

* Canadian casualties at the Somme totalled 24,029.[100]

Monday, 30 October, and the Fighting Tenth was chosen to provide the guard of honour. With only two days to prepare, the Tenth had its hands full meeting Currie's stringent requirements for the guardsmen:

1. Hair of every Officer and O.R. to be cut short.
2. All uniforms to be clean.
3. All badges to be complete and uniform.
4. Boots to be in good condition and well blacked.
5. Belts and accoutrements to be clean and brass polished.
6. Men to be uniform in size and as tall as available.[103]

The Battalion moved to Estrée Cauchie on the twenty-eighth, and the next day "suitable men" were selected and rehearsed for the ceremony under the watchful eye of the brigadier, General Loomis. Major Eric MacDonald was named to command the honour guard, which consisted of two officers and 100 other ranks. They did the Battalion proud. After being inspected by the Duke, the guard marched past His Royal Highness, accompanied by the Second Brigade's band.[104] No one was more pleased with the ceremony than General Currie, who told his diary that the Duke "was very gracious and said many kind and flattering things to me. The 10th Battalion furnished a splendid guard."[105]

That assignment deftly handled, more serious matters awaited the unit. The Fighting Tenth was preparing to make its first appearance in the front lines in the new sector. During the last two days in October, parties of officers and NCOs were sent up to look over the trenches and terrain. On Wednesday, 1 November, 700 other ranks enjoyed a bath, and that night officers and NCOs were lectured by the First Division's medical chief on the evils of trench foot. The following morning, the Battalion moved into brigade support near Carency, where it provided large working parties for the next three days.[106]

Some of the veterans might have recognized the area between Festubert and Givenchy, the scene of some of the First Division's earliest fighting. This was one part of the ten-mile front allotted to the Canadian Corps, stretching from Arras in the south to Lens in the north, and straddling the River Souchez. The most significant landmark in this sector was south of the Souchez, a long (seven miles), low (470 feet at its highest point) ridge "of sullen grey, rising softly from the plain below, a monotonous spine of mud, churned into a froth by shellfire, devoid of grass or foliage, lacking in colour or detail, every inch of its slippery surface pitted or pulverized by two years of constant pounding."[107] The ridge was a key point in the German fortifications on the Western Front, and it was about to play an important part in the history of the Canadian Corps in general, and of the Fighting Tenth in particular.

Its name was Vimy.

Chapter Six

A RIDGE NAMED VIMY

(6 November 1916 - 29 July 1917)

The winter of 1916 - 17 was the worst in Europe in twenty-one years. It was cold and wet, with icy winds that penetrated even the thickest clothing. Rivers froze solid; "food, served hot, congealed to ice at the edge of mess-tins before it could be eaten."[1]

The Fighting Tenth moved into the front lines opposite Givenchy on Monday, 6 November. In an unusual daytime relief, completed shortly after noon, two other ranks were wounded. This was, however, a blissfully quiet sector compared to the Somme; only four more other ranks were injured before the tour ended on the tenth. There was plenty of work to be done, as recent heavy rains had been taking a toll on

the trenches, which were literally disintegrating. "All available men in front line working day and night cleaning, rebuilding, and revetting trenches." The Germans did not make things easier, and their snipers, machine-gunners, and trench mortars were increasingly active. Particularly damaging was the fire from the enemy's positions south of the River Souchez along Vimy Ridge, which commanded the Canadian lines.[2]

Repairing the trenches was hard and dangerous work, and there were no complaints when the Battalion came out of the line on 10 November. But aside from a welcome bath the next day at Villers-au-

Models such as this were used in preparation for the assault on Vimy Ridge

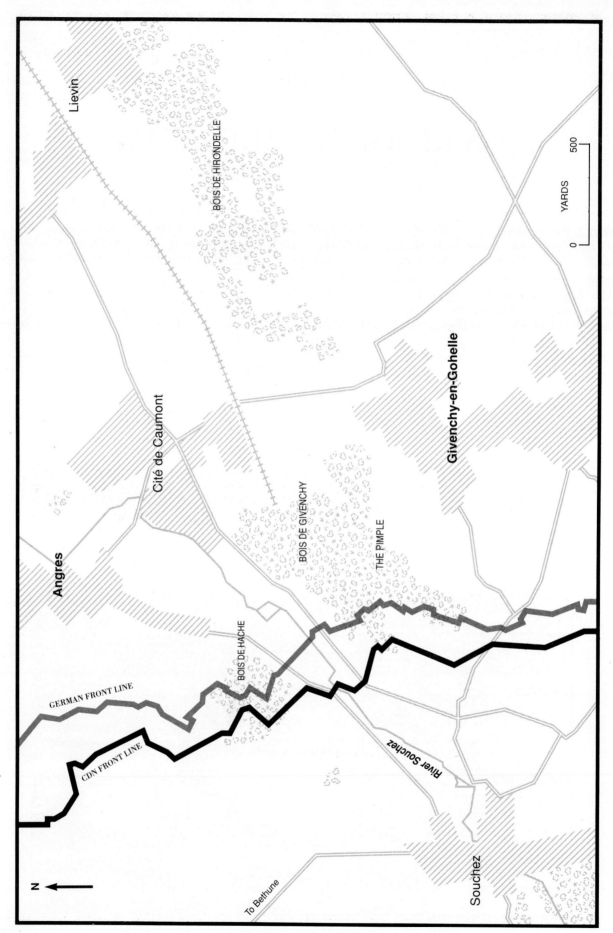

Angres Sector, Winter 1916-1917

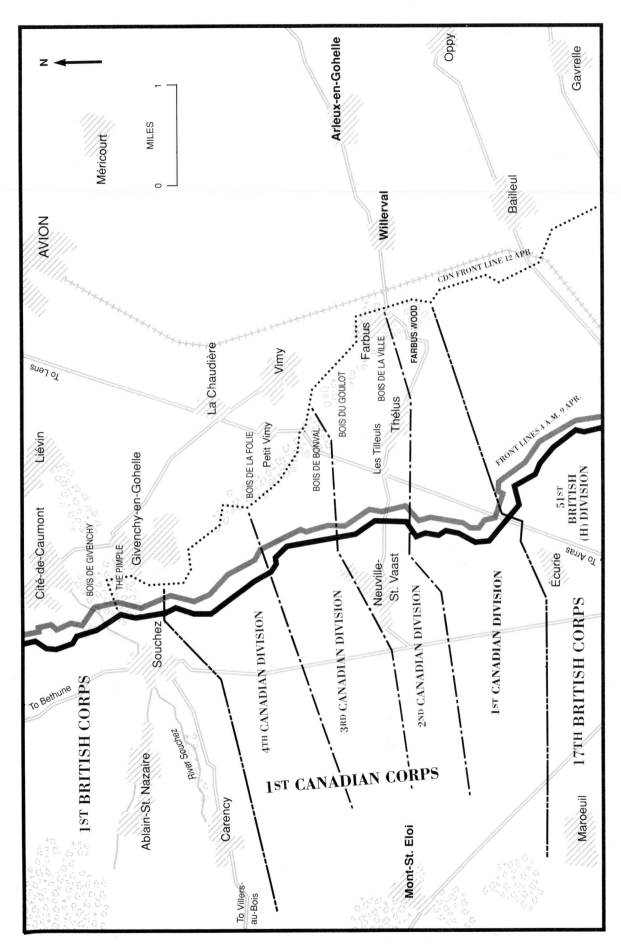

Vimy Ridge: Canadian Corps Operations, 9-12 April 1917

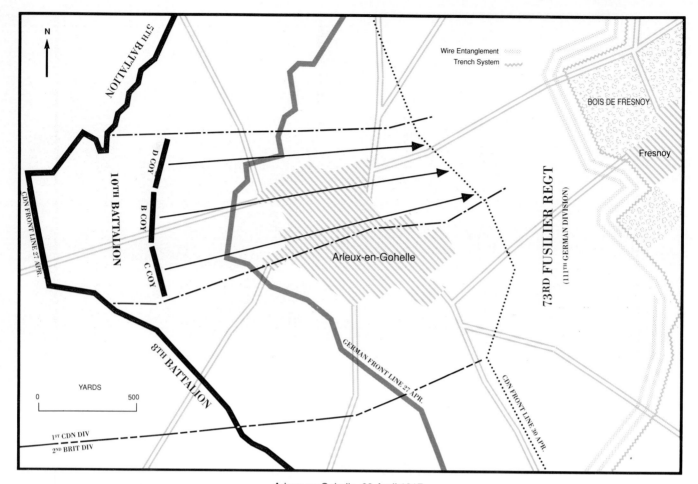

Arleux-en-Gohelle, 28 April 1917

Bois, there was little time for rest and relaxation. Working parties were required on each of the subsequent three days.[3]

The officer commanding the Tenth was a busy man, too. Now a lieutenant-colonel, Dan Ormond was studying the Somme battles and compiling his "views and opinions." In a handwritten, six-page report to the brigadier, General Loomis, on 15 November, Colonel Ormond outlined his thoughts on future offensive operations. He endorsed the use of waves, arguing that "4 waves and the Mopping Up parties can usually cross No Man's Land before Enemy barrage comes down." Early morning was the ideal time to attack: "At the moment after dawn that the First Objective can be clearly distinguished by the attacking force." Each man, he said, should be carrying at least 120 rounds of small-arms ammunition, four bombs, a shovel or pick, forty-eight hours' rations, a waterproof sheet, and empty sandbags. His own role, he realized, was limited once the attack was under way. "For first 15 to 20 minutes after zero hour, Bn Cmdr cannot influence situation, but must depend on subordinates, after that runner and phone systems should be working — if not, attack is held up." Given Ormond's limited experience in his post, it is no condemnation to state that his report contained nothing brilliant or innovative. Indeed, his sole criticism was

reserved for poorly trained officers being assigned to the Battalion. "I have found that many officers on arrival from England know nothing about map reading or have a smattering that has in many cases proved worse than useless."[4]

Returning to the trenches on Tuesday, 14 November, the Tenth found little improvement in the situation. While engaged in the routine of shoring up parapets and bailing out dugouts, the Battalion patrolled vigorously and gained mastery over no man's land, enabling wiring parties to reinforce alarming weaknesses in the barbed-wire entanglements. The Germans were much quieter this time round, and during its four-day tour the unit suffered only three casualties. Two, unfortunately, were fatalities: Lieutenant Tom Baker, the scouting officer who had been with the Battalion since August, and Corporal Victor Galloway,[5] who had been recommended for bravery at the Somme.

There was no rest out of the line, either. Relieved on 18 November, the Tenth moved into divisional reserve at Estrée Cauchie, where it underwent intensive training.

The twenty-second was a typical day: "Physical Drill and Games — Musketry and Arm Drill — Squad Drill and Saluting — Bayonet Fighting — Platoon Drill — Lecture by M.O." The Battalion was also out-

Vimy Ridge, 9 April 1917: (above) Canadian troops advance to victory and (below) dig in atop the ridge

Courtesy National Archives of Canada/PA-1123, 1131

fitted with new gas masks, "Small Box Respirators," which were "fitted individually" and tested.

On the twenty-sixth, the unit marched up to Berthnoval, where it remained in Second Brigade support until 4 December, providing a steady stream of working parties which carried ammunition, constructed machine-gun emplacements, and upgraded the support-line trenches. The weather was miserable. Every day was cold, and fog had become a regular feature. There was often frost, which at least solidified the sagging trenches; when there was no frost, it usually rained. Some days, it both rained and snowed.[6]

While the Tenth trained and toiled, Colonel Ormond raged. The target of his wrath was Percy Guthrie, the one-time acting commander who had achieved minor-celebrity status in Canada and was using that status to promote the sobriquet "White Gurkhas" for the Tenth Battalion. Ormond hated the name and, unable to tolerate Guthrie's antics, sat down on 29 November to write him a scathing letter. "For some months past we have been deriving no little amusement from speeches printed in Canadian papers and credited rightly or wrongly to you," he wrote in reference to Guthrie's nickname for the Battalion. "It is most annoying to us all, and considering that you were only with the Bn. for thirty-two (32) days … we are sure you would not attempt to give the Bn. a name." Ormond also condemned Guthrie for publicly stating that the Tenth had vowed not to take prisoners. He pointed out that the claim was not only ridiculous, for the Battalion had captured Germans "on several occasions," but possibly dangerous for the two officers and twenty-five other ranks belonging to the Tenth who were in enemy hands at that time.[7]

More reinforcements arrived. During the first few days in December, a total of 142 new men came to the Fighting Tenth. Ten were Japanese-Canadians, the first of many who would serve in the Battalion. (The Tenth eventually was home to 25 per cent of the Japanese-Canadians who served in the Great War.[8] They were "all good soldiers," according to Private Walter Loudon, whose only complaint was that "they always shined their Buttons in the Trenches or out & Dan Ormond said if they could do it so could we!")[9] As a result of this infusion, the unit numbered thirty officers and 1094 other ranks. It was numerically stronger by Christmas 1916 than it had been since early May 1915, prior to Festubert.[10]

The Tenth's final tour of the trenches in 1916 lasted eight days. Relieving the 7th (1st British Columbia Regiment) Battalion on Monday, 4 December — in daylight, with no losses — it resumed the task of improving the water-logged defences. There was some excitement on Wednesday, the sixth, when a German sniper was detected in his own barbed wire. A salvo of trench-mortar shells flushed him out, "and he was shot down by one of our snipers." For the most part, the Germans laid low and offered no opposition to the

Battalion's patrols, which dominated no man's land. And they did not retaliate when the Canadians used their trench mortars to batter the enemy wire. Only four casualties were recorded, but one, Lance-Corporal Thomas Waring, died of his wounds.[11]

No losses were incurred during the daylight relief by the 15th (48th Highlanders of Canada) Battalion on Tuesday, 12 December. Six busy days in divisional reserve in Estrée Cauchie followed. In addition to squad drill and instruction in Lewis guns and grenades, the Tenth refitted "as far as clothing and equipment in stores permitted." On the eighteenth, the Battalion abandoned its billets here and moved to Divion, in Corps reserve, where it remained until the second half of January.[12]

The keynote of this period was intensive training. A week before Christmas, two officers and five NCOs assembled a party of 107 other ranks, all newcomers, and took them to Monchy-Breton for musketry training; a second party of 107 departed on the twenty-third on the same course. The rookies also received pointers in the use of grenades, while the unit's veterans alternated sports with more demanding pastimes: "physical drill, musketry, bayonet fighting and section and platoon drill." There were also ten-mile route marches accompanied by the Battalion's brass band, in pouring rain on the twenty-third and again three days later.[13]

Christmas provided a pleasant if brief diversion. Following church services on Monday morning, the twenty-fifth, the Battalion marched to the YMCA hut for a Christmas dinner attended by twenty-eight officers and 964 other ranks. An evening concert capped what the war diarist considered "a most enjoyable day." A second dinner was held on the twenty-eighth for the two officers and 130 other ranks who had missed the main celebration, most of them because of the musketry course at Monchy-Breton.[14]

As far as the weather was concerned, 1916 went out like a lion. Heavy rain on the twenty-ninth and thirtieth interrupted the training schedule, and the time was devoted to lectures and kit inspections instead. Sunday, the thirty-first, was a holiday during which a minor organizational change was instituted. "To day [sic] the New Establishment was put into force," reads the war diary, "the Grenade Section and Machine Gun Section have been transferred to Company Strengths. The officers commanding these sections also the sergeants of these sections remaining on Headquarters strength."[15]

The new year crept in quietly. Monday, 1 January, was another holiday for the Battalion, with sports in the afternoon and an evening concert in the YMCA hut. Major Eric MacDonald's DSO, awarded for his daring exploits in no man's land, was gazetted this day; it was the first of three DSOs the major would win before the end of hostilities. With such a pleasant and relaxing start to the year, no one could have guessed that 1917 would be the most demanding year of the entire war for the Fighting Tenth.[16]

With the holidays over, the Battalion resumed its rigorous training program on the second day of January, remaining hard at work, with only Sunday off, until the eighteenth. On two days, the twelfth and seventeenth, bad weather forced the cancellation of physical activities. These were replaced by lectures with a special emphasis on offensive operations, particularly company-formation attacks. Care was taken not to tire out the troops, who were encouraged to participate in a wide variety of sports.[17]

A return to the front lines was imminent. After an inspection by Colonel Ormond on 18 January, the men's kit and equipment were carefully inspected the following day, "preparatory to move," according to the war diary. On the twentieth, the Fighting Tenth left Divion for Fosse 10, a little group of houses on the Arras-Bethune road, where it occupied Second Brigade reserve positions for three days.

The First Division continued to hold the line north of the River Souchez, in the vicinity of Lens, an important coal-producing centre captured by the Germans in the early weeks of the war. On the afternoon of Wednesday, 24 January, the Tenth made its first appearance in the trenches since early December 1916, relieving the 7th (1st British Columbia Regiment) Battalion opposite Angres. The relief was completed without casualties.[18]

That this was a sensitive sector was indicated by a five-page scheme of defence issued by Battalion headquarters. "All positions will be held at all costs, no matter what the nature of the enemy attack," the document stated. "It must be remembered that this Battalion has never lost a trench and has never been raided." In urging the utmost vigilance by all ranks, the officers were assured that plenty of artillery was available — two brigades of 18-pounders, as well as several batteries of heavier-calibre guns — and told that they "should not hesitate to ask for it." The Tenth took over four lines of trenches, one in the firing line, two in support position, and one in reserve. It was defence in depth: two companies were responsible for the front-line and advanced-support trenches; one company held the main support line while the other remained in reserve.[19]

"Cold clear day," says the war diary. "Along our front enemy very quiet. Owing to weather conditions our patrols did not go outside our own wire." These comments, written on 24 January, were typical of the entire tour. The only casualties were three privates wounded during the unit's relief by British Columbia's 7th Battalion on the thirtieth.[20]

Even when things were relatively quiet, trench warfare held private terrors for young men who should have been home pursuing careers and raising families. Private Walter Loudon, who would turn eighteen on 30 January, vividly recalled this trip seventy years later. "Our trenches were only about thirty yards from the Germans in places," Loudon wrote. "I was on sentry duty looking around when a British officer passing said if you know what's good for yourself keep down as we had two men cut to pieces by Machine Gun fire in that spot."[21]

Coming out of the line, the Tenth was put to work. While billeted in brigade support in Bouilly-Grenay, just over a mile behind the lines, the Battalion furnished large working parties: 506 men were provided for this purpose on 31 January, and 520 on each of the first four days in February.[22]

Then it was back to the trenches. There were no casualties as the Tenth relieved the 7th Battalion during daylight hours on Monday, 5 February. However, the Germans were noticeably more aggressive than they had been earlier, and the unit endured several punishing bombardments. These resulted in retaliatory strikes by Canadian field guns and trench mortars. The weather was still cold and generally clear, although a couple of days were so misty that "observation [was] very indifferent." The Battalion made life miserable for enemy working parties, inflicting heavy casualties in clashes on the sixth and eighth. Alert sentries detected an enemy mine shaft under construction, and headquarters arranged a barrage during the afternoon of the ninth. The Canadian gunners scored a direct hit that demolished the German tunnel. Considering the activity on both sides, the Battalion could consider itself lucky to have suffered only two casualties during the tour.[23]

When it was relieved on 11 February, the Tenth returned to billets in Fosse 10. That day was clear and frosty, but it snowed on the twelfth, interrupting a scheduled bath parade. The baths, completed on the thirteenth, were necessary because the unit was to be inspected by the commander-in-chief of the BEF, Sir Douglas Haig. On the fourteenth, the Battalion marched to the nearby village of Hersin, where Field-Marshal Haig inspected the unit. The men shivered in the cold as they came under the dapper Scotsman's approving eye, but were back in their Fosse 10 billets by the time snowflurries arrived in the late afternoon.[24]

The Fighting Tenth returned to the front lines on Saturday, 17 February, again relieving the 7th Battalion near Angres. It was a somewhat more eventful tour, with the enemy's trench mortars as active as ever. The shelling was often ineffective, but one man was injured on the nineteenth; Private Alexander Morin, who had won the MM at the Somme, died of his wounds later that day. Just before dawn on the twenty-first, the Germans dropped nearly two dozen mortar shells on the Battalion's lines. "Many of these failed to explode," notes the war diary, "and the others did no damage." The dull, foggy weather resulted in "very poor" sniping and observation, as far as the unit was concerned.[25]

The tour was highlighted by the misadventures of a four-man patrol on Friday, 23 February. At 3:10 a.m., Corporal Robert Sharpe led Lance-Corporal Douglas Thomson — the younger brother of Major Alexander Thomson — and Privates Allan Sim and James Scott into no man's land. Within twenty-five minutes, the patrol was lost. Corporal Sharpe and his men crawled through a barbed-wire entanglement that looked familiar and slipped into a deep, solidly constructed trench which they presumed belonged to the Battalion. Proceeding along the trench for about ten yards, they encountered a pair of sentries. Unable to distinguish them, Private Scott called in a loud voice: "Hello."

"*Guten Morgen*," came the reply.

The four Canadians turned and raced back down the trench, scrambled over the parapet, and headed for the barbed wire. Oddly, the sentries did nothing, and the patrol escaped — for the time being.

Unfortunately, its luck soon ran out. After getting through the wire safely, Corporal Sharpe again lost direction. Taking Private Scott with him, he probed another entanglement, found a gap, and crawled through. The German sentries here were more alert and opened fire. Sharpe was killed and Scott was severely wounded in the left arm. Corporal Thomson and Private Sim rescued Scott, and the three survivors eventually reached the safety of their own lines.[26]

The tour ended that afternoon. After its relief by the 7th Battalion, the Tenth withdrew to Bouilly-Grenay, the brigade support position. The men were treated to a bath parade the next day, but then they went to work. On each of the succeeding four days, the Battalion provided working parties ranging in size from 412 to 500.[27]

The last day in February found the Fighting Tenth back in the trenches and looking for trouble. Shortly after midnight on Thursday, 1 March, it stirred up a hornet's nest by staging a simulated attack to gauge the enemy's reaction. While the Canadian artillery fired a barrage, smoke was released from six points along the Battalion's front. "The smoke was very effective and produced a large cloud which drifted over enemy lines, obscuring them from sight." After a lengthy delay, the Germans responded with a violent counter-barrage by their heavy artillery. Sixty-three 4.5-inch shells struck the Tenth's positions, but "no material damage was done," in the words of the war diarist. The next night several patrols were sent into no man's land, but the Germans refused to meet the challenge. "Apparently the enemy were very nervous," says the war diary, "and threw up a great many flares, also bombed his [own] wire several times during the night." Snipers on both sides took advantage of the fine, clear daylight hours and "were very active."[28]

The tour ended on Saturday, 3 March, when the Fighting Tenth handed over its trenches to a British unit, the 8th East Kents. It would be summer before the Battalion returned to the Lens sector. The Canadian Corps was being realigned, reduced to a four-mile front along the foot of Vimy Ridge, whose main crest would be the Canadian objective in the great spring offensive being prepared by the Allies. The First Division, responsible for the right, was in the process of being moved from its lines north of the River Souchez to its new sector, where the Fighting Tenth was now headed.

After spending the night at Fosse 10, on Sunday morning, 4 March, the Battalion set out for Houdain, seven and a half miles to the rear. It remained at Houdain until the eighth, in generally clear and cold and sometimes snowy conditions. The troops were trained in the use of the Lewis light machine-gun and hand grenades; they were also paid and enjoyed concerts by the regimental band. On the seventh, a reconnaissance party of five officers was sent up to the look over the Battalion's new front, and the next morning, the unit left Houdain. In spite of a heavy snowstorm, the Battalion made good time and by midafternoon was settling into billets in Ecoivres. It snowed again the next day, but it was raining on the tenth, when the Battalion marched out of Ecoivres, destined for the Second Brigade's support position, known as the Labyrinthe.[29]

It was aptly named. A testament to bloody fighting between the French and Germans over the previous two years, the Labyrinthe would later be described by Pierre Berton as a "city of the dead, a bewildering network of caves, tunnels, trenches, and dugouts, circulating and radiating in all directions. Here … French and Germans burrowing beneath the ground had blown each other up and fought hand to hand with knives and clubs. French equipment, human bones, wire, and scores of home-made bombs … lay everywhere. In the Aux Ruitz cave, it was said, there were so many dead that one tunnel had to be walled up."[30]

The Tenth's stay in the Labyrinthe was, thankfully, a short one. Three days later, on Wednesday, 14 March, the Battalion moved into the front lines. So narrow was its assigned sector that just one company took over the trenches held by the 8th (90th Winnipeg Rifles) Battalion. The unit's other three companies remained in close support. Sporadic shelling — a faint foretaste of things to come — greeted the Tenth, but the aerial activity in this area was of considerably more interest to the men in the trenches. Nearly every day, they witnessed dogfights in the sky overhead; one, on 17 March, involved so many aircraft on both sides that it was impossible to count them all. "Enemy planes were painted a great variety of colours," says the war diary, unwittingly noting the arrival of the celebrated Manfred von Richtofen, the famed "Red Baron," and his Flying Circus.[31]

Even with a single company in the line, the Fighting Tenth soon took command of no man's land, as was its practice. The first night in the line, on 14 - 15 March, patrols explored the entire frontage, which featured a series of huge mine craters, notably the Argyll Group, Victoire, and 500. The close proximity of the opposing lines was most unusual; in one place, no man's land was only thirty-five yards wide. The first night, a German listening post was discovered and dealt with, but no patrols were encountered until 19 March, when three Germans were detected creeping through their own wire. The Tenth promptly sent out a patrol, but the enemy retired behind a shower of grenades.[32]

Its first tour of the Vimy front had been notable in at least one respect: the Battalion had suffered not a single casualty by the time it was relieved on the afternoon of 20 March by Winnipeg's 8th Battalion. Billeted in Ecoivres, the Tenth enjoyed three quiet days, cleaning equipment, training, and attending evening band concerts in the town cinema. Aside from a heavy rain the first night, the weather was "bright and clear," indicating that spring was on its way.[33]

Improved weather notwithstanding, Colonel Ormond was in a foul mood, and it showed. His patience was tested by a visit from Lieutenant-Colonel William Nasmyth, an original member of the Tenth who had been wounded at Ypres. Then a major, Nasmyth had returned to Calgary to raise a reinforcement battalion, the 89th. This time his stay with his former unit was less than successful. Between 10 and 20 March, he spent only a few hours in the forward area, much to Ormond's evident disgust. "In view of the fact that he spent less than four hours forward with this unit," he wrote of Nasmyth to the brigadier, General Loomis, "I am not in a position to make any report on him."[34]

Even more pressing was the matter of supernumeraries. These were officers attached to a combat unit for the purpose of gaining experience, and Ormond was unhappy with the arrangement. "This Unit is at present carrying an unsatisfactory number of senior supernumerary officers," Ormond had complained a month earlier, to no avail. Now, in late March, the Tenth had "six supernumerary majors, none of whom I am willing to absorb other than as subalterns." The colonel's concern was for the morale of his junior officers. "It cannot have a stimulating effect to an Officer to be called upon to be in command over another Officer, of from one-twelfth to one-twenty-fourth of his own service at the front, when the officer over whom he has command carries a rank one or two grades higher than his own and the monetary considerations attached to the higher rank."[35]

Another complaint concerned the Japanese-Canadians who were joining the Fighting Tenth. On 19 March, a draft of forty other ranks arrived, and Ormond was displeased to see that twenty-two of

them were of Japanese descent. There were now thirty-three Japanese-Canadians with the Battalion, and Ormond simply did not want them. "The extra work entailed in handling these men is much more than should be expected from a Company Commander," he explained in a letter to Second Brigade headquarters. "From three months experience with 11 Japanese, I do not consider them to be satisfactory reinforcements and ask for them to be transferred."[36] His request was ignored.

There was much more activity and danger when the Fighting Tenth returned to the front-line trenches on Saturday, 24 March. Vimy Ridge was now under constant shelling by Canadian and British batteries, and the enemy's retaliation was violent. On the twenty-fifth, for example, the Germans fired "over a hundred shells at our work parties in the vicinity of Anniversaire and Vase Trenches." The next day, "the enemy artillery replied much more vigorously than ever before during our tour in this Sector," resulting in three casualties, the first of many the Tenth Battalion would suffer here.[37]

Colonel Ormond proposed a major raid during this tour. In a 24 March letter to Second Brigade headquarters, Ormond suggested sending out four parties, totalling seven officers and 150 other ranks, to destroy German wire and fortifications. In daylight, assisted by "a sufficient barrage [to] 'box in' the area penetrated," the raiders would "remain only 15 minutes in enemy trenches."[38] However, the colonel's proposal was turned down.

The 2nd (Eastern Ontario) Battalion relieved the Fighting Tenth at midday on 29 March. Leaving behind three officers and 91 other ranks "to carry on work of improvements, etc." in the reserve trenches, the Tenth settled into billets in Ecoivres. After cleaning up and resting, the Battalion moved to the training ground near Estrée Cauchie on the thirtieth.[39]

Here, in bright sunshine, the Fighting Tenth underwent its specialized training for the impending attack on Vimy Ridge. The troops were conducted over a replica of the battlefield, with tapes, flags, and signposts indicating German trenches, barbed-wire entanglements, machine-gun posts, and other strongpoints. Each man was told what to expect and where to expect it, what his objective was and how long it would take to get there. As far as Colonel Ormond was concerned, the main benefit of these full-dress rehearsals was that they gave the men a sense of the distances involved, "a hundred yards, or eighty yards, or a hundred and fifty yards. A hundred and fifty yards into the other fellow's country, it's quite a long distance, so that was the necessity of the tapes. On the other hand, it was pretty wearing on the troops, because we had to march for an hour and play around for a couple of hours, then march back [to Ecoivres]. In fact, they called off the last couple of days, because it was too wearing on the troops. Don't forget, if you

View from Vimy Ridge

march troops six or eight miles, 30 per cent of your shoes are going to be out of business. So you can't do too much of that."[40] After a day off to bathe on Sunday, 1 April, the Tenth went back to the practice fields on each of the next four days.

The emphasis was on manoeuvre by sections and platoons. This was one of the most important conclusions made by General Currie in his studies of the fighting in 1916. While it was vital that the artillery blast a path for the infantry, he maintained it was up to the infantry to utilize its own firepower and manoeuvre its way around enemy strongpoints. Platoons, which had a minimum strength of twenty-eight and a maximum of forty-four, were organized into four sections of equal strength: one each of riflemen, bombing specialists, rifle-grenadiers, and Lewis light machine-gun. The Lewis gun was the key: an air-cooled weapon weighing twenty-six pounds and fed by a forty-seven-shot drum magazine, it could be fired by a man standing or prone. The men were taught that defenders were to be pinned down by Lewis guns and rifle grenades, then outflanked by bombers and riflemen.

The change in tactics was just one of many taking place in the Canadian army as it adapted to the demands and complexities of modern war. As Professor Reginald Roy, a Canadian historian, points out, nowhere were the modifications more evident than those taking place at the battalion level:

As the war progressed certain special duties evolved at battalion headquarters. These included the Signals Section, commanded by a lieutenant with a sergeant understudy. Its responsibility was to maintain communication by the most expeditious method possible, be it telephone, visual wireless or runners. This section had an establishment of 53 signallers with a variable number of runners. The Intelligence Officer, a lieutenant, was responsible for the collection, collation and dissemination of tactical information. He was assisted by a staff of Scouts, Snipers and Observers. The Lewis Gun Officer, a lieutenant, was responsible for the technical training on that weapon, assisted by a sergeant. The Bombing and Works Officer was responsible for the training of all ranks of the battalion in the use of grenades and supervised all battalion construction, whether in the trenches or out of the line. He was assisted by the Pioneer Sergeant, his section of Pioneers and the Sanitary Corporal. This section also found stretcher bearers. The Gas Sergeant was responsible for gas training within the battalion and the maintenance of respirators.[41]

Before the Battalion went over the course at Estrée Cauchie, Colonel Ormond explained the operation in detail to all ranks. Under Second Brigade instructions issued on 26 March — Ormond later cited them as an example of General Loomis's thoroughness, declaring that "there was no more thorough brigade commander in the British army."[42] — the Fighting Tenth was named one of the brigade's three assault units. It would be on the left of the line, with the 7th (1st British Columbia Regiment) Battalion in the centre and the 5th (Western Cavalry) on the right. The brigade's assignments were designated on maps as the Black Line, the first objective, and the Red Line, which was the second and final objective. Each battalion was to attack in four waves, with the leading two responsible for the Black Line, the succeeding two for the Red Line. While the reserve 8th (90th Winnipeg Rifles) Battalion relieved the Second Brigade's three attacking formations, the First Brigade would pass through and press the First Division's attack to the Blue and Brown lines.[43]

The precision planning was unprecedented. Zero day and hour were as yet unknown, but for the first — and, as it turned out, only — time in the war, all four Canadian divisions would attack simultaneously. They were arrayed in numerical order from right to left, backed by a dazzling array of artillery which had already started a systematic bombardment of the ridge and its rear areas. The German defences were not the gunners' sole target; the Canadians were employing a new technique, counter-battery, which was designed to destroy as much of the enemy's artillery as possible and to disrupt the supply of front-line forces and the movement of reserves.

The Fighting Tenth's role exemplifies the detail of the plans. A Company, on the right, and D would form the first two waves, with C, on the right, and B in the other two. Twenty yards would separate the first two waves, which would be 100 yards ahead of the follow-up waves. The Battalion's first objective, the Black Line, encompassed the German forward defensive zone, a triple line of trenches anchored by Zwölfer-Stellung, within 750 yards of the Canadian front line. The second objective, the Red Line, included the enemy's intermediate defences, centered on Zwischen-Stellung, just below the crest of the ridge. All of this ground had to be captured according to a strict time-table: thirty-five minutes were allowed for the fall of the Black Line; after a forty-minute pause to reorganize, the Red Line was to be taken within twenty additional minutes. In other words, the Tenth was to complete its part in this epic battle in barely an hour and a half.[44]

Enormous quantities of material were being stockpiled. The Tenth was allocated 75,000 rounds of small-arms ammunition, 2000 Mills bombs, 500 rifle grenades, hundreds of Very lights, ground flares, and SOS rockets. In addition, they would have engineer-

Captain Alfred Trimmer, MC and bar
Courtesy National Archives of Canada/PA-149625

ing supplies: 250 shovels, 100 picks, 10,000 sandbags, 100 sheets of corrugated iron, 50 coils of barbed wire along with the pickets and stakes on which to mount them, and 50 pounds of 4- and 5-inch nails.[45]

The key to success was, as Colonel Ormond readily admitted, the artillery. In addition to the complex bombardment and counter-battery programme, the assault would be accompanied by an elaborate creeping barrage which would dictate the speed of the infantry's advance. "The guns were in good shape," Ormond later commented, "and we had more of them than we ever dreamed of. We had one 18-pounder to every two hundred yards with two rounds per gun per day [in 1915]; at Vimy, we had a gun to about every eighty yards, with a hundred and fifty to seven hundred rounds per gun, plus, superimposed on that, some 6-inch and one or two heavier guns. It's a different thing when you've got a flock of guns behind you to depend on." The technology was also improving. In addition to more and better guns and ammunition, the gunners had at their disposal the revolutionary 106 fuse, which allowed high-explosive shells to explode on contact with barbed wire, rather than high above or far below the ground, as in the past. "When we got the 106 fuse," Ormond recalled, "it would rip a chunk out ten feet wide, or twelve," in the wire.[46] Unfortunately, as with so much of the new weaponry introduced during the Great War, the 106 fuse was available in strictly limited quantities.

Despite more sophisticated technology, Ormond was under no illusions about the difficulties facing the

Fighting Tenth. The Battalion's front was only 480 yards, he later noted, "but only less than a hundred and twenty-five yards of that was passable, because the largest craters on the ridge were within our [sector]. So the only way to go was between these craters, and the Boche had wired them very, very heavily."[47]

It was the enterprising Captain Stanley Kent who surveyed the ground. On the night of 4 - 5 April, he crept into no man's land and reconnoitred the area between Victoire Crater and the Argyll Group, of which Craters 1, 2, and 3 lay within the Battalion's zone. Sixty yards separated Victoire and Argyll 1, Captain Kent reported. "The ground is fairly even, not having many shell holes, and if dry is good for advancing over." There was only a four-yard space between Argyll Craters 1 and 2, and the ground was badly pocked. "In my opinion troops can cross at this point in sections of fours, but conditions are bad." They were worse between Argyll Craters 2 and 3, which actually touched each other, effectively blocking any passage. And Kent warned against sending soldiers into the craters themselves, because "the inside walls … are almost upright and the soft soil affords poor foothold." The captain also noted the existence of a

battered trench formerly used by the French, which "offers a good jumping off point with good cover. There is old b[arbed] wire 5 yds in front — it is badly broken up but most of the iron stakes remain with strands of wire attached and if an advance was made at night it might hold up a few men temporarily but in daylight affords no obstacle."[48]

The situation was complicated by the limited observation of the German forward defences. Because of the enemy's aerial superiority, ground observation was the only way of determining the effect of the shelling that was in progress. Unfortunately, the Tenth's narrow frontage offered few vantage points. The Battalion's intelligence officer, Lieutenant Edward Milne, who had won the DCM and bar as a sergeant, warned of this problem in late March. Only two observation posts, he reported on the thirty-first, were of any use. The better one was on the western lip of 500 Crater, but he pointed out that it "would not be a good place to be in case of a heavy bombardment by either side. Victoire Crater also gives a short view of the enemy's front line but would be even a worse spot in a bombardment."[49]

This difficulty had not been resolved by the time the Battalion concluded its specialized attack training and returned to the front lines on Good Friday, 6 April. While two companies, A and B, remained in billets in Ecoivres, the other two took over the unit's forward, support, and reserve trenches. As Colonel Ormond later explained, he wished to keep "as few men as possible in the line" until the night before the assault.[50] It rained heavily that day, and on Saturday Ormond rotated his companies. He moved A and B into the trenches while C and D pulled back to Ecoivres, where they arrived in time to be shelled by the enemy's long-range artillery. Fortunately there were no casualties.

By now zero day had been set. Originally scheduled for Easter Sunday, 8 April, it had been postponed until the ninth. But there was still the nagging question of the state of the German barbed wire. The artillery's ground observers insisted that the entanglements opposite the Tenth were being cut as methodically and effectively as they were along the entire Corps front, but the Battalion's intelligence section was not so sure. The heavy bombardment was burying the wire, and the limited observation points made it impossible to say with certainty that it was actually cut.[51]

It was General Currie who, once again, saved the Fighting Tenth from disaster. According to Colonel Ormond, the divisional commander "personally" monitored the conflicting reports and finally proposed a raid to settle the matter once and for all.[52] Ormond, who had earlier suggested a raid but was turned down, readily agreed to the operation. The colonel placed the reliable Captain Kent in charge, and plans were quickly drawn up. Scheduled for 4:30 a.m. on 8

Walter Loudon

Courtesy W.A. Loudon

April, it would be carried out by three parties. One, from A Company, was composed of twenty-five other ranks under a supernumerary major, Alexander MacDonald. The other two parties, both thirty strong, were drawn from D Company and were under Major James Motherwell, another supernumerary, and Lieutenant Alfred Gibaut.

The raiders were to break into the German defences to a depth of 100 yards. To assist them, the artillery prepared a box barrage to isolate the area. The technique was straightforward, according to Colonel Ormond. "You made a box. You [selected] a hundred yards of trench and the artillery and trench mortars laid a barrage around that, in behind it, and along each side. Then, either after the men had started over on the raid or simultaneous with them, these [shells] would come down, then they'd dash in and grab up anything [the enemy] had and otherwise dispose of those who didn't come along quickly. But it was hit-and-run. A raid was never reinforced."[53]

This raid was successful, but far from easy. The alert Germans detected the raiding parties as they assembled in no man's land a few minutes before zero hour, raking them with heavy rifle fire spiced with hand grenades. Luckily for the raiders, an SOS signal brought but a "feeble" response from the enemy artillery, and no machine-guns joined the fusillade. One of the supernumeraries, Major MacDonald, a thirty-five-year old law student from Swift Current, was one of the first to be hit, dying of gunshot wounds seventy-five yards from the German wire at Victoire Crater. Corporal Robert Coates, showing fine initiative, took charge of the A Company survivors and led them through the wire and into the enemy trenches beyond. The two parties directly under Captain Kent's control were also caught by the enemy while working their way through the Argyll Group. The other supernumerary, Major Motherwell, "penetrat[ed] the enemy defences to a depth of 150 yards," thanks to the work of a pair of privates, Hugh Henry and John Dunbar. Together they attacked a group of nine Germans, killing four and capturing two others. Sergeant George Stone led a bombing party down a communication trench and destroyed four dugouts. A scout, Private Alexander Mackenzie, was wounded in the first few minutes, but remained in action until the end of the raid.[54]

The whole thing lasted less than an hour, but the toll was heavy, with five dead and thirteen wounded. Several of the latter were brought in by a former DCM-winner, Lance-Sergeant Frederick Shoesmith, who organized a rescue party in spite of the heavy fire sweeping no man's land. Captain Kent's heroic efforts earned him a bar to his MC, the second officer of the Tenth to gain that honour. Corporal Coates and Private Henry both won the DCM. The MM was awarded to Sergeant Stone and Private Mackenzie.

But more important than the recognition was the information gained. Besides pointing out that "too much care cannot be exercised in taking up assembly positions," the raid showed conclusively that the enemy's foremost defences had not been "seriously damaged by our bombardment" to date, and that the barbed-wire entanglements were virtually intact in several spots.[55]

The oversight was corrected that very afternoon. On General Currie's orders, the Tenth Battalion temporarily abandoned its forward trenches, in order to bring to bear the full weight of the divisional heavy artillery on the enemy positions. According to Colonel Ormond, Currie "turned everything onto that, and when we went over on the morning of the ninth, the wire was no obstacle. That was his own personal attention to that. We would have been ready to go over as it was; from what we could see, we thought we could go over it, because it was close to us. But he was right. The artillery went to it, and they did a first-class job."[56]

After dark on Sunday, the Tenth began to form up for the Monday-morning assault on Vimy Ridge. It was frigid, and the warming effects of a last-minute hot meal were short-lived. In the interests of security, no bayonets were fixed until the last moment before zero hour. The troops assembled soundlessly. "It must be impressed on all ranks," stated Colonel Ormond's handwritten orders, "that talking or smoking after the Battalion is in the Assembly Position will not only endanger the lives of several thousand men but would make the obtaining of all objectives more difficult, as the element of surprise is of paramount importance."[57]

Effectively using old trenches, shell holes, and the lips of the huge craters in no man's land, the Tenth took up its positions. By four o'clock in the morning, the move was completed, signalled by the code word "Kamloops" flashed to brigade headquarters. The temperature dropped steadily, imposing an added hardship on the soldiers. "Although socks were changed daily, they suffered a great deal," Ormond later wrote, attributing "the large percentage of deaths from wounds to the weather conditions prior to the attack." On the plus side, the colonel noted, "I am satisfied that the low-hanging clouds ... assisted in screening our assembly."[58] By zero hour, the weather had worsened with the arrival of a spring snowstorm.

To ensure the best possible co-operation, both with the artillery and with neighbouring infantry units, Colonel Ormond selected some of his best subordinates to serve as liaison officers. Captain Geoffrey Burbidge was assigned to Third Brigade headquarters, while B Company's commander, Captain David Black, was sent to Anvin with the heavy artillery. A newcomer to the Battalion, Lieutenant Frank Costello, went to the 7th (1st British Columbia Regiment) Battalion, on the right of the Tenth, while the ever-dependable Captain Kent joined the 15th (48th Highlanders of Canada) Battalion on the left.

Ormond also juggled his senior officers. On brigade orders, the second-in-command, Major Alexander Thomson, was left out of the battle and Major Walter Critchley designated to act in his place. Lieutenant Stanley Stewart took charge of B Company in Captain Black's absence. While A and C companies were led by their regular commanders, Majors Hugh Ferguson and Walt Sparling, respectively, D Company was placed in the hands of Major Alfred Dawson, a supernumerary since the middle of February. That Major Dawson would be given such a responsibility can only be regarded as a surprise, in view of Ormond's low opinion of him. "He lacks keenness and gives me to understand that he came to France because he was sent," the colonel complained in a letter to General Loomis. "From my observation of him I know him to be of a too highly strung and nervous temper[a]ment to ever be given the command of men in an engagement ... he lacks the stamina and attitude which are looked for and required in an officer."[59]

The formation adopted was that outlined in Second Brigade orders. The first two waves, twenty yards apart, consisted of Major Ferguson's A Company on the right, and Major Dawson's D Company on the left. Each wave consisted of a double line separated by a mopping-up party. When these waves went over the top, the third and fourth waves would follow at 100 yards' distance: Major Sparling and C Company was on the right, and Lieutenant Stewart, with B Company, on the left. The first wave formed up in no man's land; the second and third waves were in Bonnal Trench, the unit's foremost position, and the fourth was in nearby support trenches.

They would make a slow, steady advance up the long, gentle slope. The creeping barrage would move at the rate of 100 yards every three minutes and, outside of the forty-minute pause at the Black Line, there was to be no stopping. Colonel Ormond's orders stressed the need to keep going at all times: "Should the leading waves, at any stage of the attack, be faced with an obstacle such as wire or a 'hold up' by a Machine Gun, on no account are they or succeeding waves to mass on to it. Rather, the troops faced with the obstacle or 'hold up' will manoeuvre so as to overcome, or circumvent, the obstacle, exercising to the fullest possible extent the tactical resources and weapons at their command."[60]

The Battalion's combat strength was twenty-two officers and 741 other ranks. The troops were heavily encumbered, with each rifleman carrying sixty-five pounds of equipment. Bombers and rifle grenadiers packed seventy pounds, and Lewis gunners struggled under an eighty-eight pound load.[61] To steel the men's nerves, and to ward off the morning chill, each soldier was given a quarter-ounce ration of rum. Daniel Foley, a Scots-born private who had a fondness for the harsh-tasting liquor, pleaded with his sergeant for an extra ration. "Come on," he implored prophetically, "I promise you it'll be the last shot you'll ever give me." The sergeant refused.[62]

A few minutes before zero hour, a random German shell killed one man and wounded four others;[63] many more would fall before the day ended.

The Fighting Tenth stormed Vimy Ridge at 5:30 a.m. A bombardment of gargantuan proportions — 983 guns of all calibres were backing the Canadian Corps operation — lit the early-morning sky with an impressive pyrotechnical display that was only partially obscured by the sleet and snow. "It was spectacular, because it was just alive with shells," recalled twenty-nine-year-old Corporal Fred Maiden. "It was ghastly, because nothing could live in it. Tremendous bombardment. Just a sheet of flame."[64]

Several facts emerge from a study of this battle. The Tenth took its objectives on 9 April, but the cost was enormous. Certainly the price in blood would have been prohibitive without the artillery's outstanding contributions, both in the preliminary bombardment and in the creeping barrage. "Officers and Other Ranks taking part in the Raid on the morning of 8.4.17 could not recognise portions of the Enemy defences, when they entered them on the morning of 9.4.17," Colonel Ormond later wrote. "The Enemy wire on the morning of 8.4.17 was a most serious obstacle, but was almost entirely swept away by the 'Heavies.'" The work of the field artillery was, in Ormond's opinion, "most effective and made the capture of the Enemy position possible."[65]

Most of the Battalion's casualties were suffered in the first fifteen minutes of the assault. Enemy SOS signals in this sector fluttered into the sky a mere fifteen seconds after the attack began, and the opposition, primarily from machine-gunners and riflemen, was "very strong." Four men were killed and eight wounded by their own barrage, but the Battalion was not to be denied: at 5:47 a.m., the attackers overran Toff Weg, the main front-line trench, where sixty prisoners were rounded up.[66]

Without a pause, the Fighting Tenth forged on towards Zwölfer-Stellung, its Black Line objective. But the slippery slope was covered with khaki-clad corpses, including that of Sergeant Chester Pettit, who had won the MM at the Somme, and of Private Peter McPherson, who was killed "as he entered the enemy defences — No Man's Land was but 35 yards wide at this point," Colonel Ormond explained in a letter to Private McPherson's widow. "Your husband was a brave and good soldier who always performed his duty willingly and without hesitation."[67]

One of the first to fall was Private Daniel Foley, who had promised his sergeant a few minutes earlier that his request for another shot of rum would be his last. Private Foley did not even have the opportunity

The infantry's success was often predicted on the skill of the artillery, empoying weapons ranging from the trench mortar (above left, the resulting explosion) to the huge siege guns (above right).

Courtesy National Archives of Canada/PA-1655, 2372

to reflect on the irony of his words: a shell decapitated him as he climbed over the parapet. Also hit was Private Walter Loudon, the eighteen-year-old Calgarian who had seen his first action at the Somme, where he escaped injury. He was not so fortunate at Vimy. "I can remember getting spun around a couple of times," as shells burst nearby. He continued on to his objective, unaware that he had lost part of his right ear. It was an injury that ended his combat career.[68]*

Another seriously hurt man was Corporal Marvin Whyte, a twenty-one-year-old original member of the Battalion. Corporal Whyte, who had been promoted just the previous day, was hit by bullets in the head, chest, and leg, but he recovered and returned to the Tenth within a year.[70]

There were, by now, few officers left. A and D companies, forming the leading waves had between them only one unwounded officer, Captain Leo Carey, who took command of D Company when Major Dawson was wounded. However, A Company's Major Ferguson refused to leave the fight. Wounded once, then a second time, the major had to be half-carried by his runner, Private William Madge. Ferguson was later awarded the DSO, while Madge earned an MM. Other officers were equally stubborn. Lieutenant Charlie Stevenson, disregarding a bullet wound in the throat, led a bayonet charge which overran a machine-gun nest. He was awarded the MC, as was Lieutenant Walter Duncan, who was so badly hurt that he had to crawl on his hands and knees, yet stayed in front of his men.[71]

Some were simply unable to continue. Lieutenants Cecil Seddall and George Ross both sur-

vived, but never returned to active duty. Lieutenant Seddall, a twenty-six-year-old Irish-born Calgarian, had been commissioned barely four months before. Now, his shoulder smashed by a German bullet, he would soon be invalided home, accompanied by Lieutenant Ross. At twenty-two, Ross was, like Seddall, Irish-born and employed by the Canadian Bank of Commerce. Wounded in the left foot and leg, Ross returned to Calgary and took up farming, unlike Seddall, who went back to the bank.[72]

When officers went down, other ranks filled in admirably. Lance-Sergeant Frederick Shoesmith, who had organized the rescue party to bring in the wounded from the previous day's raid, took over his platoon and led it to the Black Line, even though he was soon wounded himself. Sergeant Shoesmith was awarded the MM.[73]

No one was more courageous than Private John Dunbar. This was the same Private Dunbar who had distinguished himself during Sunday's raid, when he and Private Hugh Henry had taken on nine Germans, killing four and capturing two. Now, with the officer and all NCOs casualties, Dunbar took over his platoon and led it in a wild charge. Dunbar killed nine Germans with his bayonet before he was fatally wounded. "He is a great loss to the service," mourned Colonel Ormond.[74] Surprisingly, Dunbar received no posthumous recognition of his brave deeds on Vimy Ridge.

Enemy resistance was inconsistent. The defenders, according to Ormond, "appeared to be one of two distinct types, one type which made up the Machine Gun Crews and Snipers, were the equal of any of the Enemy encountered by this Unit, and fought to the

---

* After recovering from his wound, Loudon instructed military training at Bexhill, England, as a sergeant with the 23rd Reserve Battalion. He returned to Calgary after the war, but left in 1922 in search of work. Loudon eventually arrived in Montreal, where he spent more than forty years with Bell Canada. He still lives in Montreal.[69]

"This war is too important to be left to military men." These memorable words were uttered in 1916 by the premier of France, Aristide Briand. They were heartily endorsed by the new British prime minister, David Lloyd George, who had come to power atop a shaky Liberal-Conservative coalition in December of that year. Lloyd George's arrival at 10 Downing Street signalled the start of a protracted personality clash which came close to costing the Allies the war.

As a senior cabinet minister, Lloyd George had quickly become disillusioned with the army's conduct of the war. He was also upset at the War Office's apparent reluctance to accept his sage advice. "I am the butcher's boy who leads the animals to the slaughter," he raged after his July 1916 appointment as secretary of state for war, succeeding the late Lord Kitchener. "When I have delivered the men my task in the war is over."

An advocate of "bringing Germany down by the process of knocking the props under her," Lloyd George favoured shifting the focus of the war away from the bloodsoaked Western Front and making the main British effort against Germany's chief allies, Austria-Hungary and Turkey. The Somme, which Lloyd George considered to be "a bloody and disastrous failure," seemed to lend urgency to the need to wrest control of the war away from the generals whose willingness to incur casualties was "running the country on the rocks."

One general in particular raised Lloyd George's ire. That was the BEF's commander-in-chief, Sir Douglas Haig. Lloyd George was appalled when King George promoted Haig to field-marshal in December; if he had had his way, the prime minister would have sacked Haig instead. "Haig does not care how many men he loses," Lloyd George fumed. "He just squanders the lives of these boys." He eventually acquired a psychopathic disliking for the commander-in-chief, and joked bitterly: "We could certainly beat the Germans if only we could get Haig to join them. The German armies would then be a pushover for us — with Haig leading them."

But Lloyd George lacked both the personal courage and the political clout necessary to get rid of Haig, who reciprocated the prime minister's enmity. "Lloyd George seems to be astute and cunning, with much energy and push," he commented after meeting the prime minister in January 1917, "but I should think shifty and unreliable." Later, the gentlemanly Haig would be more emphatic in his denunciation of Lloyd George. "It is, indeed, a calamity for the country to have such a man at the head of affairs in this time of great crisis. We can only try and make the best of him."

Haig and Joffre had already made their plans for 1917 by the time Lloyd George came to power. They had agreed that the BEF would shoulder the load and allow the French army to recover from Verdun. Following a joint offensive in the spring — one more step in "the wearing down battle," as Haig liked to call it — the British would mount the main effort in Flanders during the summer. But these preparations were upset when Joffre was given his marshal's baton and kicked upstairs as the French government's military advisor.

He was replaced as commander-in-chief by the young and ambitious General Robert Nivelle, whose actions and words — "Ils ne passeront pas" — had been so inspirational at Verdun.

Smooth-talking and charismatic, General Nivelle easily won Lloyd George's support for his own plans. These called for the French army to mount the primary offensive in early 1917, between the Oise and Somme rivers, while the BEF conducted large-scale diversionary operations. Nivelle said all the right things and Lloyd George was charmed by the Frenchman's confident rhetoric. "Our method has been tested — victory is certain," Nivelle declared. "The German army will run away; they only want to be off." Lloyd George was so impressed that he took the unusual step of placing the BEF, and Haig, under Nivelle, a temporary and unpopular arrangement that cost the prime minister the confidence of his soldiers.

The Nivelle offensive was doomed. Lax security warned the Germans, who withdrew along a wide front behind the newly constructed Hindenburg Line, a complex array of fortifications. Undaunted, Nivelle decided to attack anyway, despite Haig's pleas to reconsider the entire operation. In mid-April Nivelle hurled his armies at the strongest German positions, and watched in dismay as the French were slaughtered by the thousands. A week earlier the BEF had launched its diversion, highlighted by the Canadian capture of Vimy Ridge, a success which only heightened the bitter disappointment which accompanied Nivelle's failure.

No one was more disappointed than David Lloyd George. Years later, he angrily complained that "General Nivelle in December was a cool and competent planner. By April he had become a crazy plunger." In other words, he was just like Haig.

Nivelle was soon sacked, replaced in May by General Henri Pétain. But the demoralized French army was haunted by the spectre of mutiny among troops tired of being used as cannon-fodder. General Pétain eventually restored morale, but many months would pass before France was again able to carry out its share of the load.

In the meantime, it was left to the British to continue the war. By now the rift between British generals and politicians was so wide that it was irreparable. Prime Minister Lloyd George was more determined than ever to spare the lives of his soldiers, while Field-Marshal Haig remained convinced that attrition on the Western Front, where the main German forces were located, was the only way to win the war. Their views, along with their personalities, were incompatible, and relations could only get worse. It was a recipe for trouble.

last causing us many casualties." Notably, said the colonel, "none were taken prisoner. The other type were men over 40 years, and a very few under 22 years. These fought well until our men were in actual contact with them, they then threw up their hands and expected to be taken prisoners."[75]

Ormond was effusive in his praise of the Battalion's Lewis gunners. He called their performance "especially satisfactory," pointing out that in at least two cases, these light machine-guns — manned by Corporal George Burkett and Lance-Corporal Alexander Jackson, respectively — knocked out heavier German guns blocking the advance. Ormond also singled out Private Ernest Bowering, who, firing his Lewis gun from the hip, led his company's irresistible advance. When he ran out of ammunition, Private Bowering wielded his gun like a club and charged four Germans, "killing one of the enemy and causing the other three to surrender." Corporal Burkett and Private Bowering won MMs for their efforts.[76]

In sharp contrast to the Lewis guns was the contribution of the unit's Colt heavy machine-guns. Vimy Ridge marked the last time that the Tenth took the American-made weapons into combat. Two of them were carried as far as the Black Line, "but owing to their weight, and in the difficulty in taking them forward, they did not get into action in time to be of great use." After the battle, Ormond ordered the Colts returned to Ordnance, on the grounds "that they have not such great superiority over the Lewis Gun" and he was unable to justify "training the extra personnel to handle them."[77]

The Battalion swept onwards. At 6:08 a.m., the enemy's retaliatory barrage intensified, and an estimated 100 gas shells fell into no man's land. But it was too late for the embattled Bavarians defending the Zwölfer-Stellung. By ten past six, the Fighting Tenth had overrun the position.[78]

Among the first into the trench were the injured Major Ferguson and his runner, Private Madge.

Assisted by the private, Ferguson scribbled a hasty note on a card, then handed it to Madge who, braving shell and small-arms fire, hurried back down the slope to Battalion headquarters. This was located in a dugout in Saint-Aubin's Ditch, which ran at an angle behind the Canadian front line. As Colonel Ormond recalled, it had been a long, nerve-racking wait for news. "You see, you don't know anything about how things are going for twenty minutes. Anyone who thinks they can tell every two minutes, you're crazy. The person in command should go to sleep for from twenty to forty minutes after the kick-off, so that he won't bother the people who are doing the job."[79] The colonel had spoken to some of the walking wounded who passed his dugout, but Ferguson's card, timed 6:10 a.m., was his first concrete evidence that the attack had so far succeeded. Further confirmation came a few minutes later, when the first batch of prisoners — two officers and thirty other ranks — arrived at his dugout.[80]

At the Black Line, the Battalion consolidated its gains and prepared to press the assault. The creeping barrage had moved ahead 200 yards, where it became a standing barrage, a curtain of high explosive and shrapnel which protected the infantrymen during the prescribed forty-minute pause. The leading waves were disorganized and pitifully weak. An hour later, Major Ferguson could find only eighteen of his men from A Company. D Company was in better shape with Captain Carey estimating his strength at nine o'clock that morning at "about 75 all ranks." As before, the shortage of officers was more than offset by the initiative of senior NCOs. Sergeant Hugh McCullough, for example, "worked unceasingly," supervising the troops as they dug in and distributing supplies of bombs, small-arms ammunition, and water. "His work and example," Colonel Ormond later commented, "were of the highest order," and McCullough was awarded the MM.[81]

Meanwhile B and C companies prepared to renew

113

the assault. Both companies lost heavily moving up to the Black Line; by the time they had moved into position, C Company's Major Sparling was the only unwounded officer. (Among the dead was the acting commander of B Company, Lieutenant Stanley Stewart.) Word of this situation was rushed back to Battalion headquarters, and the acting second-in-command, Major Critchley, the polo-player from Cochrane, was dispatched to assist Sparling. Senior NCOs continued to compensate for the fallen officers. Company Sergeant-Major James "Mustang Pete" Watchman led B Company to the objective, while platoons were commanded by corporals like Fred Maiden, who had been so impressed with the accompanying barrage that morning. Corporal Hugh Caminer not only led his own platoon, but took over a second leaderless platoon, and brought both to the Red Line on schedule. Sergeant-Major Watchman and Corporal Caminer both won the DCM, while Corporal Maiden, a Manitoba farmer born in Africa, was awarded the MM.[82]

The advance to the Red Line went remarkably smoothly. B and C companies went over the top precisely according to timetable, at 6:45 a.m., and by 7:07 had overrun the Zwischen-Stellung. "Some of the garrison put up a strong resistance," Colonel Ormond noted, "and required vigorous treatment." Major Critchley, carrying a Lewis gun and yelling "like a Commanche Indian," caught up with the attackers in time to lead the final rush, while Major Sparling, a twenty-five-year-old farmer from Saskatchewan, tackled and disarmed a sniper. Both Critchley and Sparling won the DSO.[83]

The Battalion suffered only six more casualties in capturing its final objective. The low losses may be attributed in large part to the work of the artillery. Corporal Maiden, whose route took him past a railway cutting, marvelled at the destruction. "I don't think there was a piece of railroad more than two feet long left. The rest was all cut up in little pieces."[84] The weather also played a prominent part. Although it was now daylight, the wind was blowing sleet and snow directly into the faces of the Bavarian defenders, who could not pick out targets until the Canadians were practically on top of them. By then it was too late.

Many Germans were huddled in their deep dugouts as the Tenth passed overhead, and mopping-up parties had no trouble dealing with these often disillusioned defenders. Mills bombs proved to be most useful in "urging people to come out of dugouts," Colonel Ormond recalled. "Faced with a couple of Mills bombs bouncing down the steps, why, the Germans didn't like to stay there very long!"[85] This was a variation on the chilling practice that came to be known as "the Tenth Battalion solution." The unit's moppers-up began using flares to clear enemy dugouts, sometimes with horrifying results. In one

instance involving an underground aid station, the occupants ignored a summons to surrender, and the subsequent flare ignited a box of ammunition. "The wounded," commented an observer, "came running out on their stumps."[86]

While Zwischen-Stellung fell with startling swiftness, the task of rounding up prisoners and reorganizing the attacking companies took half an hour, and it was not until 7:37 a.m. that Major Critchley was able to find the time to scribble a hasty message to Colonel Ormond. "Things are going quite fine," he reported. "Retaliation very weak." The feeble German artillery fire was proof of the effective Canadian counter-battery programme, which knocked out a high proportion of the enemy's guns. The few shells that did come over landed, according to Ormond, "on the area between 140 and 270 yards behind our Front Line;" the Germans, he observed, seemed to be "shelling certain points as if from habit, or lack of imagination."[87]

As they had been throughout the battle, the unit's runners were magnificent. Private Leonard Rowley, having delivered a message, was returning to his company when he noticed that the mopping-up party had lost its sergeant. He "took charge of the party, and conducted the work with vigour." Similarly, Private Sidney Taylor directed another mopping-up operation, and later assisted in the consolidation of the objective. Signallers also did fine work, including Privates Richard Harrison and Joseph Milne, who laid telephone lines during the attack and repaired them under heavy fire. Private Milne, who followed the first two waves to the Black Line, accompanied the other two waves to the Red Line, and was one of the few members of the Tenth to be involved in the entire action.[88] Rowley and Taylor were later awarded MMs for their efforts, while Harrison and Milne won bars to the MMs they had earned the previous year.

For some, the capture of the Red Line did not necessarily mean the end of the fighting. Corporal Alfred Eakins, a Lewis gunner, was wounded early in the advance, but remained in action even after the fall of Zwischen-Stellung. On the right, the 7th Battalion from British Columbia was held up, and Corporal Eakins went to the rescue. "He caused many more casualties to the Enemy with his gun," and enabled the advance on that flank to continue. Only then did he accept Major Sparling's order to seek treatment for his wound. Eakins, too, was awarded the MM.[89]

Not until later did the Battalion's survivors realize what they had accomplished. While troops of the First Brigade passed through during the morning, carrying the attack to the Blue and Brown lines — the latter fell by early afternoon — a few members of the Fighting Tenth wandered up to the crest of the ridge. They were treated to an unforgettable sight, according to D Company's twenty-five-year-old sergeant-major, Chris Scriven, who had been wounded in the assault. "You could look right down for miles, into a beautiful,

Vickers heavy machine-gun
Courtesy National Archives of Canada/PA-635

I cannot hope to have command, or be associated with, Officers or men with a higher standard of Morale. I believe that the Morale was almost the equal of the Unit when it first came to France in February 1915. There are many reasons for this, some of which are: that the men had not been in an engagement for several months; a general feeling of optimism prevailed; no raid was carried out by the Battalion, until the occasion demanded it, and the men felt that they were being held back and prepared for a decisive engagement.[91]

But the cost had been dear. Vimy Ridge stands as one of the bloodiest battles in which the Fighting Tenth participated. Its losses on 9 April totalled 101 killed, 252 wounded and twenty-one missing, for an aggregate casualty list of 374, all ranks.[92]

Lewis light machine-gun
Courtesy Glenbow Museum, Calgary

fertile plain ahead of you — the Douai plain — and that's where we saw all the German army just moving out. It was the most magnificent sight you ever saw: horses rushing in, hooking up to the guns, tearing off across the fields to get out of there."[90]

Vimy Ridge had been a great victory. By nightfall on 9 April, the Canadians had captured all of the ridge, save for a feature known as the Pimple, at the far northern end, which held out until the twelfth. The Corps suffered 10,602 casualties in the process.

The Fighting Tenth had done its share, and more. The Battalion had kept to its timetable, despite unusually heavy losses among the officers; in both phases of the operation, it was reduced to just one unwounded officer. Such an achievement was a tribute to the unit's discipline and training, and its many decorations were well-merited. Officers were awarded four DSOs, one of which went to Colonel Ormond for his efforts in preparing the attack. As well, six MCs were awarded, including Captain Kent's bar, and those won by the medical officer, Captain Richard Kenny, and by Lieutenant D.W. Stephenson. Other ranks received five DCMs; four have been described in the narrative, and the other went to Sergeant Percy Legg. Including bars to the medals held by Privates Harrison and Milne, twenty-one MMs were also awarded. In addition to those already described, they were awarded to Sergeants Frederick Buddry, Frank Henry, and Harry Templeman; Corporal Edwin Martindale; Lance-Corporals James Corry and Thomas Markinson; and Privates George Adams and James Fisher.

Colonel Ormond's pride was evident when he later wrote:

The Battalion remained on the ridge until the middle of Monday afternoon. While they took note of their losses and counted their captures — sixty prisoners and four machine-guns[93] — the men munched on their hardtack biscuits and savoured the chocolate which had been provided from regimental funds. But no one was in the mood to celebrate. There were too many friends and comrades littering the slope behind them. "We tried to identify some of the boys," recalled one of the MM-winners, Corporal Fred Maiden, "to try to get their identity discs off them. But we couldn't do it. See, the boys were blown to pieces, lots of them."[94] Relieved by Winnipeg's 8th Battalion, the Tenth marched back to its original front lines. By seven o'clock that evening, the men had settled into these familiar surroundings, and were served a hot meal.

The Tenth remained here for two days. It was a quiet time, devoted to rest and recuperation. On Wednesday, 11 April, the Battalion moved up to the Red Line in the early evening. By now, it was snowing heavily, and the ridge was swept by a chill wind. The unit was a mere shadow of its former self; its trench strength on this date was sixteen officers and 372 other ranks.[95] On Friday, the thirteenth, the Battalion moved up to the Blue Line, relieving the 3rd (Toronto Regiment) Battalion. "The accommodation was very poor," the war diary complains, "and the weather remained unsettled throughout the day." Added

Colonel Ormond: "At this stage the men were very tired for lack of dry cover and interrupted rest."[96]

Their rest was interrupted again on Saturday, 14 April, when they took part in a modest advance on the eastern side of the ridge. The Little Black Devils of the 8th Battalion moved past Willerval that morning, and the Fighting Tenth offered close support, with two companies, A and D, moving into Farbus Wood. B and C companies dug in along the railway. There was no opposition, and the day passed uneventfully.

Sunday night, the Battalion was relieved and returned to its old positions in the Labyrinthe, in sunny but cold conditions. The weather deteriorated once again, with rain for the next few days, but the men's discomfort was somewhat eased on 18 April by a welcome bath parade followed by an issue of clean underwear. Two days later, the sun came out, and spirits soared with the rising temperatures. The Battalion marched back to billets in Mont Saint-Eloi, west of the ridge, for a pleasant week. The Battalion band performed a concert each night, and there was a regular agenda of sports, with footballs provided by regimental funds. "The weather conditions were all that could be desired, bright sunshine and Spring Conditions prevailing."[97]

But there were disturbing signs that this happy interlude was about to end. On the twenty-fourth and twenty-fifth, the Battalion trained intensively, practising offensive operations.[98]

In fact, major fighting loomed ahead. The main offensive in April 1917 was undertaken by the French army. Launched a week after Vimy Ridge, it was a dismal failure, leading to widespread mutinies in French regiments angered by futile attacks on impregnable positions. To divert attention from the French, Field-Marshal Haig renewed his own operations on a wide front astride the River Scarpe. The initial attack, on 23 April, achieved minimal results, and Haig turned his attention to the Oppy-Méricourt Line, behind which the Germans had retired following the loss of Vimy Ridge. The commander-in-chief desired the elimination of the Oppy-Méricourt Line before undertaking his main effort and the First Canadian Division was one of six divisions to take part in the preliminary action. Its objective was the Arleux Loop, flat, featureless terrain around the fortified villages of Arleux-en-Gohelle and Fresnoy-en-Gohelle, a mile east of Willerval.

The Canadian plan of attack underwent several changes. It was intended to scoop up both villages in one large operation but, in view of the powerful defences facing the Canadians, the offensive was divided into two separate stages at General Currie's insistence. It was originally envisaged as a joint effort by the First and Second brigades; the latter was to employ one battalion, the 8th, with the Fighting Tenth in support.[99] This was later expanded to a two-battalion operation, with the Tenth and 8th attacking

Germans captured at Arleux

Courtesy National Archives of Canada/PA-1307

The Tenth Battalion band, wiped out by a long-range shell at Mont Saint-Eloi, 1 May 1917.

Courtesy National Archives of Canada/PA-32

side-by-side,[100] and finally to a three-battalion frontage 2600 yards long, with the Tenth flanked by the 5th (Western Cavalry) Battalion on the left and the Little Black Devils on the right. British Columbia's 7th Battalion, and the 16th (Canadian Scottish), borrowed from the Third Brigade, were to be in support. A battalion of the Second Division was to provide protection for the brigade's exposed left flank during the attack.[101]

Time was of the essence. The creeping barrage would roll over the enemy's front-line defences in eight minutes; ten minutes were allotted for the capture of the village of Arleux. The attackers were warned to expect the strong counter-attacks that had been noticeably absent during the Vimy operation. Their orders stressed the need to dig in quickly. An outpost line was to be established immediately and protected by barbed wire and Lewis guns and active patrols. In addition, they were to construct strongpoints defended by Lewis guns and the eight Vickers heavy machine-guns — British-made, water-cooled, belt-fed, .303-calibre weapons — allocated to each battalion.[102]

Intelligence was spotty. "The enemy is at present reported to be holding the Objective with an ordinary trench garrison, but with an unusually large number of machine guns." Because Arleux had been used as a rest billet by the Germans, the plans warned that it "is certain to contain numerous deep dugouts," but there was not a hint that the attackers would be facing vast fields of virtually intact barbed wire, in spite of prolonged softening-up by the artillery.[103]*

Zero hour was set for 4:25 a.m. on Saturday, 28 April.[105]

Two days before the attack, the Tenth began its move towards the front lines. On the afternoon of the twenty-sixth, it advanced to Farbus Wood where it relieved the 2nd (Eastern Ontario) Battalion after dark. Remaining here until late the next night, the Battalion then marched up to its assembly positions for the assault, within 200 yards of the Arleux Loop. A shallow jumping-off trench had been dug in front of the Canadian lines, and the three attacking companies aligned themselves; B, under Captain David Black, occupied the centre, with Captain Geoff Burbidge and C Company on the right, and D, under Captain Wilfred Romeril on the left. Captain Alfred Trimmer, commanding A Company, remained in support immediately to the rear of the jumping-off trench. Since Colonel Ormond had been ordered to leave himself out of the battle, Major Alexander Thomson, the second-in-command, was in charge of the operation. He deployed fourteen officers and 625 other ranks,[106] virtually every veteran in the Battalion, knowing that a draft of 171 reinforcements had arrived earlier that night and was being held on Vimy Ridge, awaiting further developments.[107]

The Battalion suffered grievous losses during the difficult assembly. The weather was "dull and unsettled," according to the war diary,[108] and "hampered the movement of the troops," as Major Thomson later complained. Worse, German shell fire delayed the proceedings, and it was not until 3:25 a.m., one hour before zero, that Thomson was able to report that his Battalion was ready. Sadly the Tenth lost one of its finest officers when Captain Stanley Kent was seriously wounded while guiding the troops into the jumping-off line; the twenty-seven-year-old, English-born banker died the next day. Then, only half an hour

---

* This was part of a dispute involving General Currie, the divisional commander, and the Corps heavy artillery. The gunners were using Vimy Ridge as their main observation post, which Currie considered to be "too far away from the wire.... I find a tendency on the part of the gunners to consider that they are doing fairly well on the wire; infantry patrols do not agree with this contention, and the Infantry are the ones who must be satisfied."[104] Currie's concerns were subsequently shown to be valid, as was so often the case.

before the attack, a single shell hit the support company, killing eleven men, including A Company's thirty-three-year-old commander, Captain Trimmer, and Lieutenant Stanley Jackson, who had joined the Battalion just one week earlier. The impact of the loss of Captains Kent and Trimmer can scarcely be overstated, for both were two-time winners of the MC as well as first-rate leaders. Lieutenant Stanley Robertson hurried over from Battalion headquarters, but he, too, was fatally wounded minutes after the attack began.[109]

At 4:24 a.m. the bombardment opened, and one minute later the Fighting Tenth went over the top. B and C companies, in the centre and on the right, respectively, made rapid progress by finding wide gaps in the enemy's barbed wire. But there were problems on the left, where D Company found that the wire was virtually intact. Forced to cut through it by hand, a time-consuming process, Captain Romeril and his men came under heavy machine-gun fire, as well as the German counter-barrage, which opened three minutes into the assault.[110]

Casualties mounted rapidly in hard-hit D Company. With the exception of Lieutenant Frank Costello, every officer fell, including Captain Romeril, a twenty-nine-year-old financial agent from Montreal. Lieutenant Costello "held his Company together by his courage" and was later awarded the MC. He was ably assisted by senior NCOs who, as at Vimy, filled in admirably. In this case, it was four sergeants, David McAndie, Herbert Mortimer, David Murray, and Charles White, along with Corporal Michael Sullivan, who helped the young subaltern as he led D Company through the wire. These five won MMs for their efforts.[111]

After getting through the wire, the company struggled forward, fuelled by pure bravery. On the northwestern corner of the village were two machine-guns that had caused so much grief. Lance-Corporal Frank Rump took charge, pinning down the defenders with rifle grenades and Lewis-gun fire, while the post was outflanked. Private Frank McMackin was infuriated when his Lewis gun jammed, but he grabbed a rifle and kept up the covering fire. This enabled Corporal John Crane to get close enough to wipe out the Germans with well-aimed bombs. Their performance brought Corporal Crane and Private McMackin the MM.[112]

On the right, C Company encountered a similar situation. When the advance was checked by a machine-gun nest on the western edge of the village, Captain Burbidge — who would celebrate his twenty-seventh birthday in two weeks — and Private Michael Matson quickly outflanked and destroyed it. Their actions won Burbidge the MC, while an MM was later given to Private Matson.[113]

Overrunning the enemy's front-line defences, the Battalion swept into Arleux-en-Gohelle. The village had been reduced to rubble by the artillery, but the debris provided plenty of cover for the defenders. The Tenth encountered "considerable resistance from enemy infantry, also from snipers," and a short, vicious battle ensued. The Canadians fought from door to door, street by street, making use of their bayonets and rifle grenades. The Lewis gunners were, as before, invaluable, and three won MMs here. Private Roland Dewar was singled out for his effective work in pinning down the defenders so that bombers and riflemen could come to grips with them. Private Nathaniel Hunter was the only survivor of his Lewis-gun crew. Buried by a shell burst on the outskirts of Arleux, he recovered in time to join the battle in the village, carrying on "as though nothing had happened," in Major Thomson's admiring words. Private Ronald Young was not a Lewis gunner, but he picked up a weapon from a crew that had been wiped out and "used it to best advantage in fighting in the Village."[114]

The battle for Arleux was brief but bloody. The enemy's collapse came as a surprise, for the defenders were numerous. "It is the general opinion," Colonel Ormond later wrote, after interviewing surviving officers, "that if the enemy had made a determined resistance that there were not sufficient men" to capture Arleux. "All officers are satisfied that if we had been holding the village with the same number of men, that the enemy had, and were attacked by a force equal to that used by us, that we would have no difficulty in holding the village."[115]

Beyond Arleux there was some confusion. "When the first few men emerged from the village," Major Thomson reported, "they could see the enemy retreating very rapidly, but in such good formation (being more or less in waves), that our men, owing to the very bad light, were undecided as to whether some of the attacking force had crossed ahead of them. They did not hesitate long, but fired into them, apparently causing many casualties."[116] Particularly effective was the work of a Lewis gunner, Corporal Ernest Bowering, who manned his machine-gun alone after losing his crew on the way through the village. Corporal Bowering inflicted such heavy losses on the fleeing Germans that he was awarded the bar to the MM he had won at Vimy Ridge.

Reaching their objectives, the three assaulting companies dug in. Lewis gunners took up positions in a rough line of shell holes, and infantrymen went to work laying barbed wire. The Tenth's right flank was in touch with the 8th Battalion, but on the left, where the 5th Battalion had been slowed by an exposed flank, D Company took up a position a hundred yards short of its objective, forming a defensive flank.[117] Captain Romeril, who had ignored his injury and returned to action, reported to Major Thomson at 5:50 a.m. that his men had been "held up for few minutes after taking first trench but are going strong now."[118]

The Battalion's position was tenuous, to say the least, but it took some time for a clear picture to emerge. Not only was the situation on the left uncertain, but the rest of the line was weakly held. After hearing of the heavy losses among the officers, Lieutenant Edward Milne, the Battalion's intelligence officer, and Lieutenant Frederick Easterbrook, the signalling officer, hurried up to the front.

It was Lieutenant Milne, in a 6:40 a.m. message to Battalion headquarters, who noted the vulnerable left flank. "Seem to be very few men holding gained ground," he wrote. "Isolated men in front of us but cannot get in touch with our main body."[119] Lieutenant Easterbrook added his own warning at 7:20 a.m.: "Line is very thinly held here. Sniping and machine gun fire (enemy) heavy, and movement very dangerous. I have swung my left flank backwards a little to small sunken track. Am trying to connect with left flank [i.e., 5th Battalion]."[120] Even more pressing was a message from Captain Burbidge, commanding C Company, on the right. "Reinforcements needed," Burbidge urged. "Digging in 700 yards from Fresnoy. Must have artillery on Fresnoy and Fresnoy wood. No ammunition for Lewis Guns. Send reinforcements. Treat artillery as urgent. Being badly sniped from good many rifles."[121]

Major Thomson responded first by sending Major Walter Critchley up to the front lines, then went up to have a look himself at midmorning. On the right, he was alarmed to find "that there were only 2 Officers, and less than 100 Other Ranks, who got through and were in the front line, and of course, a support trench could not be considered with a handfull [sic] of men on such a long frontage. There was considerable shelling and heavy sniping." Worse, there was no artillery support. At zero plus 120 minutes, as scheduled, the Canadian and British batteries backing the assault ceased firing, "and when I was forward between 9.00 A.M. and 10.00 A.M., scarcely a shell was being fired by our Artillery."[122]

Braving the enemy fire, Thomson hurried back to his headquarters, where he contacted the brigadier, General Loomis. Within minutes of the appeal for artillery support, the guns came to life once more, and the major was pleased to see that "our artillery kept up a continuous steady fire, which kept down the sniping considerably." Loomis also committed a company of the 7th Battalion to shore up the Tenth's line after dusk. As well, Thomson sent up 120 of the reinforcements which had arrived the night before.[123]

This proved to be an eye-opening experience for the newcomers. "We went right from the railhead," recalled Private Ernie Lambert, "we hiked a distance, then they took us right into the line. And as a matter of fact, as some of us chaps were going in, some of the wounded were coming out." Private Lambert ended up in the sunken road on the left, with D Company. "I remember getting shot at by a sniper, and I remember a German lying on a stretcher here, hollering for a drink of water." It was not the worst of Lambert's introduction to war. At midnight, he was recruited by Major Critchley for a burial party, collecting identity discs and burying the dead. "That was pretty rough."[124]

Few if any tasks were as distasteful as burial detail. In addition to the identity discs, all personal effects were to be removed from the dead, and the location of each grave carefully recorded. Like almost everything else in the army, there were rules governing the disposal of bodies. A regulation grave was two feet wide and six-feet-six-inches long. "The bodies should be buried at least 3 to four feet deep. If the bodies cannot be removed or graves dug on the spot, the bodies shall be placed in shell holes or disused trenches, covered with quicklime and then with earth." Corpses which could not be removed were to be sprayed with "a solution of cresol (1/2 pint to one gallon)."[125]

Sergeant Frank Henry's body lay sprawled among the others awaiting burial. The NCO had died without knowing that he had won the MM at Vimy Ridge.

The Battalion braced for counter-attacks. One man single-handedly broke up one such effort before it could get started. Private John Seeley spotted the Germans assembling nearby for an attack, and calmly "he picked them off as they crossed a small ridge, accounting for quite a number," and completely disrupting the attempted attack. At eight-thirty that night, the Germans brought down a heavy barrage along the Battalion's line, but the Canadian artillery responded promptly, discouraging the prospective counter-attack. Although the Germans were seen collecting for a possible attack on the neighbouring 8th Battalion, no further operations materialized on the front of the Fighting Tenth.[126]

The Tenth was there to stay. Sunday, the twenty-ninth, proved to be relatively uneventful, although the enemy shelled the area "continuously," and a barrage in the late afternoon by both sides caused more than a little concern.[127]

On both days of the Arleux operation, the Battalion's runners were wonderful. Private Leonard Mallory was typical, making many trips between the front lines and Battalion headquarters, in broad daylight and under heavy fire. He continued "until he was completely exhausted, but insisted that he was quite able to carry on." Private Mallory won a bar to the MM he won at the Somme, and several other runners were also awarded that medal, including Privates Walter DeMarre, Hugh Henry — who had won the DCM at Vimy Ridge — Charlie Launder, Alfred McLatchie, and Leonard Melbourne. Privates Henry and Melbourne were twice buried by shell fire, but remained on duty in spite of apparent exhaustion.[128]

The Fighting Tenth was relieved on the night of 29 - 30 April. The 13th (Royal Highlanders of Canada)

Battalion took over the Tenth's line, although there were delays that Major Thomson blamed on the 13th. The relief was not completed until 4:45 a.m.[129] Nearly two months would pass before the Tenth saw another tour of front-line duty.

It was a weary unit that staggered back to the shelter of Vimy Ridge. In making its second successful major assault in less than three weeks, the Tenth paid a heavy price. The capture of Arleux, along with 179 prisoners and five machine-guns, cost the Battalion 304 casualties, including twelve officers.[130] Much praise was directed towards the medical officer, Captain Richard Kenny, who had won the MC at Vimy Ridge and who at Arleux abandoned his dugout dressing-station and treated the wounded in the open, "until he had personally attended to over 200 cases," each one being cleared to the nearest field ambulance "within half an hour of arrival."[131]

There were several aspects about Arleux with which Colonel Ormond was unhappy. Zero hour was, in his opinion, "too early. It was impossible to distinguish our men from the Enemy. It is freely stated that many enemy got away owing to the difficulty of being sure that the people seen were not ours." Ormond was even unhappier with the work of the artillery. The wire, he complained, "was cut but so much remained on stakes that it was an obstacle," while the main German trench "was not greatly damaged. It was still clear cut on [the] sides" when it was captured. And the creeping barrage, he noted, "was not intense enough, was disappointing as compared with barrage on 9th inst."[132]

Decorations were distributed with surprising stinginess. Three officers won MCs; besides those won by Captain Burbidge and Lieutenant Costello, B Company's Captain David Black also received the award. MMs went to twenty-three other ranks, including bars to Corporal Bowering and Private Mallory. In addition to those described, MMs were won by Sergeant James Shaw, Lance-Corporal Frederick Rowley; and Privates Percy Fairbank, George Fowlie, and James Sullivan. There were no DSOs or DCMs for the Tenth in this action.

At least the weather co-operated as the Fighting Tenth marched back to the Labyrinthe sector west of the ridge. It was warm and sunny, but the most memorable moment was a "wonderful" meal served soon after the Battalion arrived. "They had brought up hot mulligan [stew], and cigarettes and chocolate bars," recalled Private Ernie Lambert, the rookie whose first night in the line included burial duty. "I've never had anything like it, before or since."[133]

That afternoon, the Tenth moved further back, to billets in Mont Saint-Eloi, where tragedy waited.

It happened the very next morning. At 6 a.m. on Tuesday, 1 May, a single long-range shell — probably from a 13-inch naval gun mounted on a rail car — struck the château in which most of the Battalion was billeted. "That was our reveille on May the first," recalled a shaken Private Lambert, now in just his fourth day of service with the unit. "We got up, we got out, we lined up a human chain and we had to clear all this debris, you know."[134]

Some members of the Tenth were trapped upstairs, including Colonel Ormond and Major Critchley, whose rooms were across the hall from each other on an upper floor. After the explosion, Critchley opened his door and found that he could "look down to the basement." He and Ormond were both rescued, but not before they assisted in the rescue of Private Jack Moyes, who was bunked above them. "He was in by the roof," recalled Critchley, "that's what saved him, and he may have got a bit of chicken wire and made himself a hammock, he was in the hammock and he couldn't get out. We had to get a ladder to get him out."[135]

Within an hour, all casualties had been collected from the ruins, and the toll was shocking, indeed: fifty-three, including fifteen dead. The entire regimental band had been killed or injured, along with all but one member of the scout section. The Battalion orderly room was also destroyed in the blast, but all records were recovered.[136]

The destruction of the band was serious. In any military unit, a band plays an important role in the maintenance of morale, and the Tenth's was no exception ("Colonel Bogey's March" was the regimental song). Not only were its concerts well received, but the band also accompanied the Battalion on route marches. While marching is seldom a favourite occupation, any soldier will attest that the presence of the band and martial music makes the task much easier. Moreover, the bandsmen stored their instruments during combat and went into action, unarmed, as stretcher-bearers. They were universally admired for their willingness to rescue the wounded under fire.

It took half a year to effectively reconstitute the band, and in a less stalwart unit, the consequences could have been considerable. However, the Fighting Tenth recovered quickly from this blow. After spending one more day at Mont Saint-Eloi, with bath and pay parades, the Tenth marched to Estrée Cauchie on the morning of 3 May, remaining there for two days, near the site where it had trained so intensively for the Vimy Ridge operation. On 5 May, the unit took a leisurely four-hour march to Maisnil-les-Ruitz, where it would spend the rest of the month.[137]

Far from the sound of the guns, the Battalion's time at Ruitz was almost idyllic. The weather, for the most part, was beautiful. Aside from occasional thunderstorms, most days were bright and clear, and the lush, green countryside revived spirits worn ragged by trenches and mud, barbed wire and shell holes. The troops were kept busy with training and sports — chiefly baseball and football — and evening concerts and cinemas, all of which had a noticeably vivifying effect on the unit. A small number of reinforcements arrived during this period — nine officers and ninety-nine other ranks — and on 23 May, Major Thomson took over temporary command of the Battalion when Colonel Ormond was given two weeks' leave in England.[138]

There were also plenty of "brass hats" and "red tabs" in the area. These included the brigadier, General Loomis, who visited on 9 May and "was well pleased with the appearance of the Battalion." The Corps commander, General Byng, inspected the unit two days later and "commented on the steadiness of the Battalion." On the thirteenth, a Sunday, General Currie and the First Army's General Sir Henry Horne joined the Fighting Tenth for church service.[139] Afterwards, an admiring General Horne, aware that the Battalion had been twice over the top in April, losing nearly seven hundred casualties, asked Colonel Ormond: "How do you do it?"[140]

On Friday, 1 June, the Fighting Tenth returned to Mont Saint-Eloi, the scene of its nightmarish tragedy exactly one month earlier. It was a bright, clear day, and the thirteen-mile march from Ruitz was completed in less than seven hours. After a night in tents at Mont Saint-Eloi, the Battalion moved up to Neuville Saint-Vaast, at the western foot of Vimy Ridge, for a week in Second Brigade support. Its main task here was to provide working parties for the extensive entrenchments being constructed atop the ridge. The German air force greeted the Battalion by bombing its billets at least three times that week.[141]

June 1917 marked the departure of three of the Tenth's senior officers. Majors Thomson and Sparling both left to take command of their own battalions: Thomson took over the 4th (Central Ontario) Battalion, where he would die at the hands of a German sniper in November, and Sparling was assigned to the 1st (Western Ontario) Battalion. While the moves said much for the calibre of the Tenth's officers, it was clear that Colonel Ormond would be hard-pressed to replace the likes of Thomson and Sparling, not to mention the courageous captains, Stanley Kent and Alfred Trimmer, killed at Arleux.

When Major Thomson left on 2 June, he handed over temporary command of the Battalion to Major Critchley, who was also packing his bags. Soon after Colonel Ormond's return from leave, on the seventh, Critchley left the unit to join the Royal Flying Corps. As one of the Battalion's originals, Critchley, who had won the DSO at Vimy Ridge, held the distinction of being among the few officers, if not the only one, who had avoided injury although participating in every action. "I figured that I'd put about three years in the trenches," he later explained, "and I didn't think my luck was going to hang out very much longer, so I thought I'd go with the flying birds." However, the major regretted the decision. "I never made a bigger mistake in my life! As a matter of fact, my training wasn't finished when the armistice came."[142]

Thomson's departure was the most serious loss among the three majors, from the standpoint of the Battalion's efficiency, but Critchley's was probably the one felt most keenly by the unit. The twenty-five-year-old Critchley was a popular, hard-drinking officer who, much to Colonel Ormond's chagrin, rang up considerable debts which he charged to the Battalion. But he was "a helluva nice guy," according to Private Walter Loudon. "I don't think he was scared of anything."[143]

Another quiet period awaited the Tenth. On Saturday, 9 June, the unit went back to Mont Saint-Eloi, moving into billets at Winnipeg Huts. It spent the next week here, training, cleaning equipment, and enjoying concerts. More reinforcements arrived — forty other ranks, on 10 June — and on the fifteenth, a refreshed Colonel Ormond conducted a "thorough inspection" of the Battalion, including a smart march-past. The next day, after bathing parade, the unit returned to Vimy Ridge, relieving the 14th (Royal Montreal Regiment) Battalion. After dark on 18 June, the Tenth moved into brigade reserve along the railway line east of the ridge. During the next four days, all available manpower was devoted to improving the local defences. Although enemy shell fire was sporadic, two men were killed by a direct hit on a dugout on the nineteenth.[144]

On Friday, 22 June, the Fighting Tenth made its first front-line appearance since Arleux, nearly two months before. Moving into the trenches between Fresnoy-en-Gohelle and Méricourt, the Tenth relieved the 2nd and 4th Canadian Mounted Rifles. It was a dull day with showers at intervals, and there were, according to the war diary, "only two casualties, which resulted from [a] stray whizz bang shell."[145]

There were twelve more casualties, all due to shell fire, before the Battalion was relieved on 26 June. Most activity in the trenches took place at night, when working parties strove to upgrade the defences and patrols explored no man's land. While there were no incidents in these undertakings, a German bombardment on 24 June was a much different matter: a 5.9-inch shell struck a strongpoint, killing two soldiers and wounding two others. Two more men died the next day and one was wounded, during another barrage. The relief, carried out by the 15th (48th Highlanders of Canada) Battalion, was even costlier, with five casualties, including Lieutenant Henry Vickery, who was killed coming out of the line. And two more men were injured after the Battalion reached the brigade support position near Thélus, where it remained until the end of June. With Thélus as its base, the Tenth sent up large working parties to toil on the massive defences being prepared along Vimy Ridge, day and night. It was raining heavily on the thirtieth when the unit moved back to Neuville Saint-Vaast.[146]

Dominion Day was the highlight of the three-day stay here. The first of July was a bright, sunny Sunday, and the occasion was marked by the firing of "three salvoes" by the Canadian artillery, according to the war diary. It was the first time in the war that the Canadians had celebrated their national holiday; not coincidentally, the Corps was now commanded by a native Canadian, Lieutenant-General Sir Arthur Currie. He had succeeded General Byng the previous month, when the latter had been promoted to take command of the BEF's Third Army. Currie, in turn, was succeeded at First Division headquarters by silver-haired, sharp-tongued Archie Macdonell, one of the few professionals in the pre-war Canadian army.

The Fighting Tenth left Neuville Saint-Vaast on 4 July, moving into divisional reserve at Mont Saint-Eloi amid alternating sunshine and rain. The Battalion bathed by companies on a daily basis, while working parties were detailed for cleaning up the camp, Ottawa Huts. In addition to the ever-popular sports programme — D Company's team won the Battalion football competition — there was the usual training, including route marches, Lewis-gun instruction, company drill, and bayonet fighting. A musketry competition at La Motte rifle ranges was won by C Company. While the weather was unsettled, it did not spoil an impromptu inspection on 11 July by King George, who reviewed the Battalion during a route march on the Lens-Arras road. The next afternoon was spent in cleaning equipment and making preparations for a move on the thirteenth.[147]

The Tenth was about to depart for a new front. The Canadian Corps was being shifted north of the River Souchez for imminent operations against the important coal-mining centre of Lens. The Battalion marched out of Mont Saint-Eloi at 8:30 a.m. on Friday, 13 July, and a three-hour march in the sunshine took the troops to Cauchin Légal. It rained that night, and the following day, the unit moved into brigade support near Les Brébis, settling in just before midnight.[148]

The next night, the Battalion moved into the front lines. With a trench strength of thirty-two officers and 702 other ranks, it relieved elements of three British battalions, the 2nd and 14th Durham Light Infantry and 1st Shropshires. B and D companies held the forward trenches in this sector, near Loos, with A Company in support and C in reserve. The complicated relief was completed just before dawn on Monday, 16 July.[149]

It was an active sector. German artillery and machine-guns were busy all that first day, and the Battalion was fortunate to escape without loss. Subsequent days were different, however, with one man killed and another wounded on 17 July, five wounded on the eighteenth, one killed and five

injured on the nineteenth. On the night of 18 - 19 July, the Tenth side-stepped to the right, relieving the 5th (Western Cavalry) Battalion while the 15th (48th Highlanders of Canada) from Toronto took the Tenth's place. The manoeuvre, "hindered by the intense darkness and heavy rain," was not completed until after dawn on the nineteenth. Battalion scouts spent the rest of the day exploring the many "tunnels which honeycomb this sector, with a view to calculating the accommodation capacity for troops, and communication purposes." The losses continued to mount, even when the Tenth was relieved by the 7th (1st British Columbia Regiment) Battalion. During the relief, there were seven more casualties, including the only officer killed on this tour, Lieutenant William Bilsland. Moving back to Les Brébis, where it spent a single night, the Battalion was shelled, and four other ranks were wounded. Late on 22 July, the Fighting Tenth marched to new billets at Fosse 7 and Barlin, completing the move after midnight.[150]

Here, in divisional reserve, the Battalion prepared for the coming offensive. The Canadian Corps had been assigned the capture of Hill 70, overlooking the western suburbs of Lens, as a diversionary operation for the BEF's main offensive in 1917, scheduled to open at month's end in Flanders. On 24 July, "all ranks were given a general outline on intended operations." The next day, the unit marched seven miles to the taped course, where a practice attack was conducted, "the objectives and general formation and idea of attack being explained on the ground." On the twenty-sixth, the Battalion marched to Houchin to view a replica of the battlefield, and another lecture "covering the different stages of the attack" was given to all ranks.[151] Private Norman Eastman, who had joined the Tenth the previous month, recalled the elaborate preparations:

> They had set up a big model of Hill 70, and we all gathered around it, in a big ring around this set-up, you see, and we were all instructed by the officer in charge at that particular moment as to what our objective would be and the different things that we were to look for as we moved along. Great stress was laid on the fact that at no time must we run — never, ever run, because you'll run into our own barrage. We had to move along slowly; as our barrage lifted, then we were to move along. And they pointed out that there would be certain trees that we could use as landmarks.[152]

More practice and lectures followed, and by the time the Battalion returned to Les Brébis late on 29 July, every member of the unit was fully versed in the requirements of the coming operation. The only question no one could answer was its timing.[153]

As the month ended, an alarmingly negative note was sounded by Colonel Ormond. Having kept a close eye on the men who had recently reinforced the Fighting Tenth, Ormond was openly worried about them. "Drafts received by this Unit since April 9th, 1917, have been especially good in so far as physique is concerned, but up to the present have shown a lack of keenness and spirit," he wrote. "They do not perform work with the same keenness as men who enlist-ed at an earlier date, this causes one to wonder what their value will be as fighting men! This also applies to officers!!"[154]

The men would soon show that the colonel's concerns were unfounded; they were more than capable of upholding the Fighting Tenth's traditions.

Chapter Seven

VICTORIA CROSS HILL

(29 July - 19 October 1917)

Preparations for the Hill 70 operation culminated quickly. Moving back into Second Brigade support at Les Brébis on 29 July, the Tenth was addressed the following day by the brigadier, General Loomis, and the new divisional commander, General Macdonell, whose presence underlined the importance of the impending offensive. On the thirty-first, the Battalion went over the taped course for a final time "and carried out a practice attack in detail."[1]

An air of urgency was lent by the Germans, who shelled Les Brébis on each of the first three days in August. There were no casualties, fortunately, and on 4 August — the war's third anniversary — the Tenth returned to the trenches east of Loos. The Battalion took over from the 5th (Western Cavalry) Battalion, suffering a single casualty in the process. A and D companies held the front lines, with B and C in support.[2]

Its two days here gave the Fighting Tenth a last look at the terrain it would soon assault. Directly ahead stood Hill 70, its crest the Battalion's objective. A seemingly inconsequential rise, standing a mere fifteen feet above the Canadian forward lines, it offered a commanding view of the immediate vicinity. It was, remembered Private Norman Eastman, "a gentle slope. You were constantly going uphill, but there was nothing sharp, you know, nothing where you had to scramble."[3] This was a coal-mining area, and it was "chewed up," according to Lieutenant Hugh Pearson. "Oh, it was a miserable piece of country, really."[4] Both Private Eastman and Lieutenant Pearson would be wounded on the gentle slopes of Hill 70, along with a great many of their comrades.

While the Canadian artillery subjected the German defences to continuous shelling, there was relatively little retaliation by the enemy. Still, the Tenth suffered three casualties, including one fatality, before its relief during the early-morning hours of 7 August. Marching back to Les Brébis, it moved into tents at Fosse 2. Rain was falling when it arrived, and it continued to rain as the Battalion left for Hersin, in divisional reserve, on the ninth. That same day, the 577 eligible members of the unit began voting in the Alberta election, concluding on the twelfth.[5]*

The Battalion remained at Hersin until Monday, 13 August. By now, action was imminent. "Companies and Detachments carried on with completion of Battle Equipment and final preparations for the trenches." At nightfall, the unit marched out of Hersin, stopping at Les Brébis long enough to pick up a supply of grenades and forty-eight hours' rations. Then it moved into the front lines, relieving the 4th (Central Ontario) Battalion, completing the move without loss by half-past three in the morning on the fourteenth. The weather was near-perfect — "Bright and Clear," according to the war diary — as it would remain for the next few days, except for a light shower that afternoon. The Tenth, with a trench strength of twenty-two officers and 693 other ranks, held the line with D Company, while the other three companies were in close support.[6]

The same day, Colonel Ormond learned that the assault would go in the next morning. Zero hour was scheduled for 4:25 a.m., on Wednesday, 15 August.[7]

The battle plan was simple enough, although its execution would prove to be anything but easy for the Fighting Tenth. Two Canadian divisions, the First on the left and the Second on the right, were taking part in the assault, on a three-mile front. While the First stormed Hill 70, the Second's objective was the northern suburbs of Lens. The final objective was denoted as the Green Line, 1500 yards from the Canadian starting positions. The Second Brigade employed two battalions, the Fighting Tenth on the left, and the 5th (Western Cavalry); their goal was designated as the Blue Line, the German support line which ran across the top of Hill 70. The 7th (1st British Columbia Regiment) and 8th (90th Winnipeg Rifles) battalions would then leapfrog and carry the attack through the Red Line to the Green Line. Heavy counter-attacks were anticipated, and the artillery's preparations included ranging on the enemy's expected lines of approach.

---

* The election was won by the incumbent Liberals, under Premier Arthur Sifton, who would soon resign in favour of federal politics. A notable feature of the election was that it marked the first time women were allowed to vote in Canada and two women won seats in the Legislature. One of them was Roberta McAdams, a nurse serving overseas.

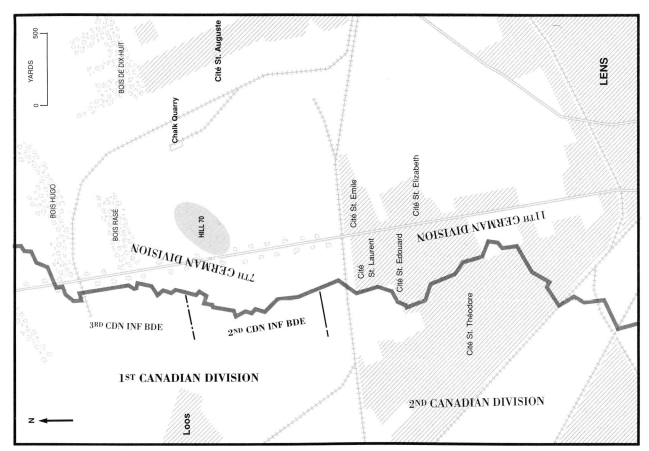

Hill 70: Canadian Corps Operations, 15-16 August 1917

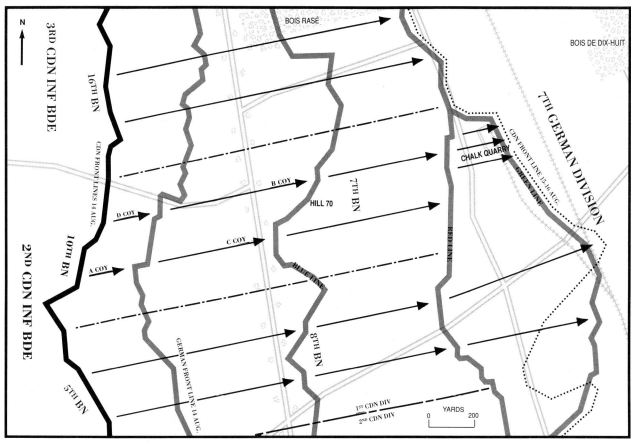

Hill 70: Tenth Battalion Operations, 15-16 August 1917

125

Private Harry Brown, VC

The long-awaited British offensive in Flanders opened on 31 July 1917. Lacking the resources to spread his efforts over a wide area, Field-Marshal Haig decided to mount a strong diversionary attack in a sensitive location, hoping to distract the Germans and confuse them about his intentions. The sector he selected for the diversion was in the vicinity of Lens, a coal-mining centre just north of Vimy Ridge. Responsibility for the project was given to the First Army, under General Sir Henry Horne, who handed it over to the Canadian Corps and its new commander, Lieutenant-General Sir Arthur Currie.

General Currie was one of the war's few success stories. In a war that ruined more reputations than it made, Currie emerged as one of the leading soldiers in the Allied armies. At six-foot-four, weighing 250 pounds and plagued by ill-fitting uniforms, Currie hardly looked like a dashing military leader. And his background was just as deceptive as his looks. A militia officer from British Columbia, the Ontario-born Currie had never been in action before going overseas in the fall of 1914 as a brigadier.

Within a year, he was a major-general commanding the first Division. The first non-regular officer to rise above the rank of brigadier-general in the BEF, Currie led the First Division with distinction; General Horne called it "the pride and wonder of the British Army." Currie had been largely responsible for the striking successes won by the Canadian Corps in the spring of 1917, for he had studied the 1916 campaigns, selecting the best of British and French tactics and adding a few of his own ideas. His recommendations stressed fire and movement, concentrated artillery fire on selected targets, surprise and, above all, exhaustive preparations. He concluded that "if the lessons of the War have been thoroughly mastered; if the Artillery preparation and support is good; if our Intelligence is properly appreciated; there is no position that cannot be wrested from the enemy by well-disciplined, well-trained and well-led troops attacking on a sound plan."

Currie and Horne disagreed about the Lens diversion. While the army commander favored a strike towards the railway line south of the city, Currie's view was that "it offered no serious threat" to the Germans, who "would soon see that it did not amount to much." Arguing "that if we were to fight at all we ought to be fighting for something worth having," Currie pointed to Hill 70, north of Lens. Possession of the hill would directly threaten the German grip on the city, said Currie, who predicted that they would fight hard to retain it. Horne disagreed and referred the dispute to Haig. The commander-in-chief sided with Currie, and the Canadians attacked Hill 70.

Delayed by rain, the operation did not take place until 15 August, but it proved to be an "entire and complete success," in Currie's words. "During the course of the next eight days the Boche launched against our newly won positions no less than 35 counterattacks. We identified no less than 69 German Battalions although we were employing not more than 24. Not only did we succeed in holding the Boche opposite us but he became so alarmed that he withdrew from the battle line of Ypres two divisions and put them in the line against us at Hill 70." While Canadian casualties, according to Currie, "were less than 8,000," the Germans lost "more than 30,000," and Haig later called it "one of the finest minor operations of the war."

While the Germans were not deceived by the Canadian attack — correctly deducing that the BEF did not have the resources for two major offensives and that the main effort was being made in Flanders — they nevertheless were forced to react to the threat. "The fighting at Lens cost us, once again, the expenditure of considerable numbers of troops who had to be replaced," wrote a German general, Hermann von Kuhl. "The whole previously worked out plan for relieving the fought-out troops in Flanders had been wrecked."

The Tenth began moving into its assembly positions at 12:30 a.m. on 15 August. Captain Leo Carey's D Company, which was holding the line, side-stepped to the left. A Company, under Captain Charlie Stevenson, now recovered from his neck wound suffered at Vimy Ridge, moved onto its right. These companies formed the two leading waves; their task was to take the enemy's forward trenches, then serve as moppers-up for the third and fourth waves. These consisted of Captain William "Tommy" Thompson's B Company and C Company under Captain Forrest

Ladd. B and C companies would carry the assault to the Blue Line, about five hundred yards away. Each company comprised four officers and 150 other ranks.[8]

There were difficulties and delays in moving into position. Beginning just before midnight, and continuing until two o'clock in the morning, the Germans shelled the area with gas and high explosives, causing five casualties in the Battalion. Two were wounded by shrapnel and three suffered the effects of gas poisoning. As well, the bombardment slowed the deployment. All companies were supposed to be ready by

Major Hercules Lefebvre, MC
Courtesy National Archives of Canada/PA-6857

one-thirty, but none met the deadline, and only B Company was ready by two o'clock. It was after three-thirty when the last company, C, reported that it was in place. A runner arrived at Battalion headquarters with this report at 4:03 a.m., enabling Colonel Ormond to dispatch the code-word "Aberdeen" to brigade headquarters, indicating that the Tenth was ready to go over the top.[9] Zero hour, 4:25 a.m., passed soundlessly. The barrage failed to materialize and officers nervously checked their watches, wondering what was wrong. (Their watches had been synchronized incorrectly.) Long seconds passed. Then, at 4:27, Tenth Battalion time, the guns opened fire. "This did not interfere with the attack in any way," Colonel Ormond later wrote. The officers blew their whistles and scrambled out of the shallow jumping-off trenches, following closely by the men of the Fighting Tenth, bayonets fixed.[10]

Going over the top, "it seemed to us as if every machine-gun in Creation opened up all at once," recalled Private Eastman. The enemy front was lit up with red SOS flares, and within four minutes of zero, the first German artillery shells were being fired, soon swelling into a heavy barrage. "After we got out of the forward trench," recalled Private Ernie Lambert, "I doubt if I got more than two hundred yards" before being hit by fragments from a shell burst. "It bashed the button on my tunic, my equipment got cut, and a piece went into [my arm], and a piece was left in my pocket, and my prayer book, it was scraped right along the top." The injury ended Private Lambert's war. A stretcher-bearer bandaged his arm and left him to crawl back to the farmhouse which was being used as the dressing station. The shell fragment also

carved a one-franc note in his pocket into four pieces. It was a treasured souvenir that he loved to show visitors to his home in Calgary for years afterwards.[11]

Canadian shell fire was also dangerous. Captain Carey, commanding D Company, reported that "the two platoons on the left moved up too close to the barrage and so suffered casualties."[12]

A and D companies swiftly overran the German forward trenches. In the process, A Company's Captain Stevenson was severely wounded, hit in the shoulder and neck. A month away from his thirty-fifth birthday, Stevenson, who had been wounded three times previously, stayed with his men until the gains had been consolidated. Then Colonel Ormond ordered the former Calgary carpenter to report to the medical officer, Captain Kenny.[13] An original who had come overseas as a sergeant, Stevenson would not return to action with the Battalion.

At 4:53 a.m., B and C companies leap-frogged the leading waves and pressed the assault towards the top of Hill 70. By now enemy resistance had stiffened and the machine-gun fire was devastating. Within minutes C Company had been reduced by half, including the officer commanding, Captain Ladd, who had a leg broken in two places and shrapnel in both thighs. Lieutenant Hugh Pearson, a twenty-nine-year-old land surveyor from Edmonton, assumed command of the company and led it to the objective. In the meantime, B Company was in even worse shape with two-thirds of its men casualties by the time it reached the Blue Line. However, the losses were more than offset by the inspiring leadership of Captain Thompson, a thirty-two-year-old Manitoba carpenter. "He was in

Private Tokutaro Iwamoto, MM, one of many Japanese-Canadians who served with the Tenth Battalion

Courtesy Don Graham

128

Private Ernie Crowe

Courtesy E.W. Crowe

time. Lance-Corporal Gordon Jones, seeing the advance momentarily held up by a machine-gun post, worked his way round its flank, and calmly wiped it out with a well-aimed Mills bomb. He was later awarded the DCM. Private Hugh Wright also out-flanked and bombed a machine-gun, capturing its crew, and Privates Paul Oleson and William Adamson performed similar feats. All three won MMs.[17]

By 6:12 a.m., the Blue Line had been conquered. British Columbia's 7th Battalion passed through soon afterwards, en route to its objectives on the Red and Green lines, while the Fighting Tenth counted its captures. These totalled 100 prisoners, including three officers, six machine-guns, and two *Grenatenwerfen* (grenade throwers).[18] Colonel Ormond was warned to keep close tabs on these trophies. "The 5th Bn have sent 2 pioneers to paint the name of their Bn on all trophies captured," wrote Ormond's liaison officer Lieutenant Harry Templeman, a little after eight o'clock that morning. "Expect we will have to watch they don't claim ours."[19]

every respect," Colonel Ormond later wrote, "the life of the attack."[14]

There were several notable feats of heroism. Corporal Nicholas Purmal, one of the Battalion's originals, spotted an enemy machine-gun being brought into action from a nearby dugout. Purmal rushed the gun as the Germans hurriedly set it up, and the Canadian won the deadly race. The enemy squeezed off a burst, wounding Purmal in the right arm, but the corporal seized the gun and knocked it back into the dugout. The crew of seven, including an officer, promptly surrendered, and the wounded NCO proudly led them back to Battalion headquarters. He appeared at Colonel Ormond's dugout at 5:27 a.m., providing the first indication that the attack was going well. Purmal won the DCM.[15]

Corporal Frederick Bond was no less determined. When his Lewis gun was put out of action by a German shell, he searched until he found another which had also been knocked out. He was able to salvage it and used it to capture an officer and sixteen other ranks. Corporal Bond won the MM, the first of a record sixty awarded to members of the Tenth Battalion in this battle.[16]

German machine-guns put up stubborn resistance, but their crews paid the ultimate price every

Lieutenant-General Sir Arthur Currie

Courtesy National Archives of Canada/C-4764

Major-General Archibald Macdonell
Courtesy National Archives of Canada/PA-42974

Thompson's company was severely understrength. At five in the afternoon, he reported "I have about 15 all ranks to each platoon so am very weak."[22]

Besides consolidating, there was also the tough task of collecting and caring for the dozens of wounded men scattered across the slope. It was a job that took up much of the rest of the day, amid terrible shell fire. Among the walking wounded was a member of C Company, Private Norman Eastman, who had been hit in the foot by shell fragments.

I was knocked end-over-end into a shell hole. And I couldn't feel my foot. I was a little afraid to look for fear it wasn't there! But, however, it was okay as it was still on, and I crawled out of the shell hole and, using my rifle as a [walking] stick, I went along until I caught up with some of the lads.

By this time, we'd reached our objective, this Blue Line, so-called. And a fellow by the name of Byran and another by the name of Currie came over to me. And they had to yell in my ear to ask questions, you know, the noise was just absolutely deafening. And so I pointed to this foot, you see, so they sat me down and we got the puttees [off]. The boot wouldn't come off, so they took a knife and slit down the boot, and as soon as they started down the boot, the blood came all over. I got my sock off, and they slapped a field dressing on it and bandaged it up, then wound my puttee around it.

I couldn't go any further forward, so they headed me back. I gave them my cigarettes and extra rations and Mills bombs and extra ammunition that we were all carrying, you see, and using my rifle [as a crutch], I started back.

On the way, Private Eastman met a wounded German officer, and they helped each other to the dressing station.[23]

Even more seriously hurt was Private Stuart Weir Stuart, Jr. A twenty-three-year-old bank clerk from Vegreville, Alberta, Stuart had been a sergeant in England but had reverted to private in order to join the Fighting Tenth in April. He had escaped injury at Vimy Ridge and Arleux, but his luck ran out at Hill 70. With bullet wounds in the head, left eye, and foot, Private Stuart was later declared medically unfit for further service and was back at his bank by the following April.[24]

The battle should have been over, as far as the Tenth was concerned, but this was not the case. The first indication of trouble came from Lieutenant Templeman, the liaison officer with the 5th Battalion. "8th Batt held up at Red Line," he informed Colonel Ormond at 8:12 a.m. "Have been to Green Line but had to come back and consolidate Red Line. Have been telephoning wanting a new barrage put up. Chalk Quarry appears to be the source of trouble. I

Mopping up was reported complete by 8:35 a.m,[20] but consolidation took a little longer due to a shortage of supplies. B and C companies both called for quantities of barbed wire and stakes, a need which D Company remedied before nine o'clock by sending forward fifteen rolls of wire and seventy-five stakes. Captain Thompson of B Company described the situation in a 10 a.m. message to Battalion headquarters:

We are in need of more barbed wire and screw stakes. Water should be sent up if possible. I have 1 1/2 dozen white Very lights and 1/2 dozen red. If possible send up another two dozen white and 1 doz. red Very lights.

My Company is consolidating seventy five yards in front of Blue line and connecting with C Coy on the right where they are consolidating in the old German trench. We are also connecting up with 16th Bn on the left.

The Hun is shelling the Blue line pretty hard at present with 4.1 & 5.9 shells. Have had several casualties since capturing my objective.[21]

think this is on the 7th Bn front so expect they are held up also."[25]

Lieutenant Templeman's information was, unfortunately, accurate. Both the 7th and 8th battalions carried the Red Line with no difficulty, but stalled at the Green Line, on the outskirts of Cité Saint-August directly north of Lens. The attackers ran into withering small-arms fire from the Chalk Quarry, a veritable fortress defended by at least 300 Germans and twenty machine-guns.[26] The 7th Battalion actually gained a toehold in the quarry, but was unable to hold on and had joined the 8th back on the Red Line by midmorning.

Colonel Ormond alerted all of his companies "to reequip and be ready to move forward to assist the 7th and 8th Bns." One platoon of C Company was eventually sent forward, followed by the rest of the company in the late afternoon.[27]

One more abortive attempt was made by the two battalions before dark. They were scheduled to attack at 6 p.m., but neither unit was able to make much of an effort, as C Company's Lieutenant Hugh Pearson reported. After the barrage opened, he wrote Colonel Ormond, "I waited for the 7th and 8th to go over, but could not find their officers and finally heard from a corporal that the 8th Bn were not going over and the 7th could not move without them." Pearson pulled back to the Tenth's position in the Blue Line at seven that evening, and awaited further orders.[28]

Acting on verbal instructions from the brigadier, General Loomis, (written orders didn't arrive until ten o'clock), Colonel Ormond sent A, B, and C companies to the Red Line to relieve the 7th Battalion at eight-thirty, while D held the Blue Line. Knowing that the Tenth was sadly depleted, Ormond sent his second-in-command, Major Hercules Lefebvre, to supervise the operation. Its trench strength after a day of fighting was seventeen officers and 316 other ranks. Major Lefebvre was later awarded the MC for his coolness in directing the difficult relief*, which was not completed until one-thirty the next morning, due to the enemy's intense shelling. C Company, or what was left of it, moved into the centre of the line, with A on the right and B on the left. As they were taking their places, they fired SOS flares on at least two occasions, bringing down artillery barrages on suspected German troop concentrations. Fortunately, the enemy made no effort to recapture Hill 70 that night, because the Second Brigade informed Battalion headquarters "to use great discretion in the use of artillery ammunition for a short time."[30]

Early the next morning, Colonel Ormond attended a conference at brigade headquarters. General Loomis had decided that the Green Line must be taken, and the Fighting Tenth, along with the 5th Battalion, would attack at 4 p.m., hoping that the daylight assault would catch the enemy by surprise. Ormond agreed, but added a wrinkle of his own. To ensure surprise, he dispensed with the customary preliminary bombardment; the gunners could save their ammunition for the creeping barrage that would shield his riflemen. But the colonel was under no illusions about the task facing the Battalion, knowing the three front-line companies were woefully weak. Captain Thompson, who was placed in command of the attack, had only seven officers and 120 other ranks with whom to carry the Chalk Quarry, where the full-strength 7th Battalion had come to grief.[31]

Their position was precarious. Late in the morning of 16 August, Lieutenant Harry Templeman reconnoitered the Red Line and filed a situation report with Colonel Ormond. Templeman was satisfied with the efforts made to improve the defences, but was concerned about B Company, on the left of the line. There were only three officers and thirty-eight other ranks left, and they were having a difficult time working on the trench due to intense machine-gun and sniper fire. This was being directed with startling accuracy from the enemy's vantage points in the Chalk Quarry. To make matters worse, there were also shortages of small-arms ammunition and water. But the soldiers' spirits remained high. "All the men," Templeman reported, "appear to be fairly cheery in the circumstances."[32]

During the hot afternoon, the Battalion made its final preparations for the attack on the Chalk Quarry. The intense shelling and shooting gradually subsided, and a deceptive quiet settled over the battlefield. Colonel Ormond, interviewed half a century afterwards, never forgot the moments leading up to the four o'clock zero hour and the barrage that suddenly exploded over Hill 70. "It was just out of a blue sky," he recalled. "There was not a shot fired for some time before on our front, and then we had the finest barrage I've ever seen come down ahead of us. Then we went in."[33]

Twenty-one minutes later, the Fighting Tenth had taken the Chalk Quarry.[34] But those twenty-one minutes involved fighting of unrivalled ferocity and bravery of breathtaking proportions.

On the left, B Company, with the heroic Captain Thompson at its head, followed the barrage closely. Within eighty yards of the quarry, the riflemen and two teams of Lewis gunners manned shell holes and engaged the defenders in a vicious shootout. "In less than two minutes they had obtained superiority of fire

---

* A Montreal native who had joined the Battalion as a subaltern in July 1915, Major Lefebvre had not been one of Colonel Rattray's favourites. "His actions when under shell fire," Rattray complained in July 1916, "ha[ve] been such that it renders it impossible to retain him as an officer. His influence on the men under him, in case of an attack, would be detrimental to bravery and efficiency. He should be sent back to Canada as 'unlikely to become an efficient soldier.' "[29]

and drove the enemy from his positions." As the Germans fled, they were cut down by the charging Canadians. One Lewis-gun team, Privates Ewart Bateman and Harry Baxter, inflicted terrible casualties, even though they lost their tripod. As they hurried after the retreating enemy, Private Baxter threw himself on the ground and allowed Private Bateman to use him as a human tripod. Both men were awarded the MM.[35]* A proud Captain Thompson, who won the DSO for his part in this battle, later wrote: "We went through them like a dose of salts." But B Company was reduced to two officers and twenty other ranks.[36]

One of the wounded was a young man from Cochrane, northwest of Calgary. Seventeen-year-old Ernie Crowe had been unscathed in his baptism of fire at Vimy Ridge as well as the previous day's assault here. But he was only half-way to the Chalk Quarry when, "zing! I felt something hit my arm." A bullet had struck him in the right forearm, "and coming out, it exploded and smashed the whole elbow." Private Crowe jumped into a shell hole filled with muddy water. Cutting off his equipment and bleeding profusely, he then crawled and staggered to join his comrades in the quarry.[37]

Meanwhile, in the middle, C Company was enjoying a startling success. Lieutenant Pearson, the Edmontonian who would be wounded three times this day en route to an MC, led his men towards a trench seventy-five yards from the edge of the quarry. They overran it in a few minutes, but not before witnessing an unusual sight. Private George Moir recalled that two of the machine-guns in this trench were manned by marksmen who were chained to the weapons. One of these guns had accounted for "about ten of our men," Private Moir remembered, "and the officer wouldn't let us kill him when we got there, either." The German surrendered as soon as the Canadians began to surround his post, and many others did likewise.[38] "So many prisoners were taken that the situation became very serious for a short time as they outnumbered the attacking party."[39] Unable to spare anyone to guard these shell-shocked Germans, Lieutenant Pearson sent them to the rear unescorted. "I think the boys behind us thought the Germans were attacking them," the subaltern recalled with a chuckle, "but it was German prisoners going back!"[40]

Private Masumi Mitsui, seeing a Lewis-gun crew wiped out, grabbed the gun and put it back into action, inflicting heavy losses on the enemy troops fleeing to the supposed security of the quarry. Private Mitsui, one of the Japanese-Canadians for whom Colonel Ormond had so little regard, won the MM.[41]**

There were problems on the right. The neighbouring 5th Battalion was making slow progress in the face of fierce enemy fire, and this in turn exposed the flank of the Tenth's A Company. Worse, the acting company commander, a subaltern named Alexander Gleam — one of the newcomers who had worried Colonel Ormond before the battle — panicked. With two hundred yards still to go before reaching the quarry, Lieutenant Gleam's hesitation might have been disastrous had it not been for quick thinking on the part of another lieutenant, Norman MacEachern, who took charge of the situation. His first decision was to ignore the enfilade fire and proceed with the assault. Had Lieutenant MacEachern formed a defensive flank as Gleam wanted, Ormond later wrote, "there would not have been sufficient men left to carry the objective." Catching up to the barrage, the men of A Company rushed from shell hole to shell hole, giving each other covering fire. In one of these holes were two men from the 8th Battalion and one from the 7th, who had been cut off during the previous night's failed attack; they now joined the Fighting Tenth.[43]

The battle for the Chalk Quarry was brief but bloody. Honeycombed with dugouts carved out of the chalky soil, this position could have been virtually impregnable with more determined defenders. Fortunately for the Tenth, this was not the case; the Germans huddled in these dugouts surrendered rather easily. They were no match for the likes of Company Sergeant-Major Tom Carter, who led several bombing attacks, then organized a party and guided it through a hail of bullets to replenish the supply of grenades. Sergeant-Major Carter was later awarded the DCM for his efforts. Another DCM-winner, Lance-Corporal Gordon Jones, who had bombed a machine-gun post the day before, singlehandedly captured thirty of the enemy, sending them to the rear under the guard of some lightly wounded men. A Japanese-Canadian, Private Tokutaro Iwamoto, won the MM when he added twenty prisoners to the Battalion's take. One of them was a signals sergeant who was carrying a code book, which Private Iwamoto turned over to Lieutenant MacEachern. In another dugout were seven stretcher-bearers and a medical officer

---

* Bateman and Baxter survived Hill 70, but died within a month of each other later in the year. Baxter was killed at Passchendaele, and Bateman died in mid-December of wounds suffered in late November.

** Mitsui, a Japanese-born resident of British Columbia, ended the war as a sergeant. Returning to Canada after the conflict, he was active in the Canadian Legion and led a successful effort, in 1931, to amend B.C.'s Election Act to give Japanese-Canadian veterans the right to vote. He endured, with thousands of other Japanese-Canadians and their families, the humiliation of internment during World War II. It was doubly degrading for Mitsui, in view of his distinguished record with the Tenth Battalion in World War I on behalf of his adopted country. Mitsui's successful poultry farm near Port Coquitlam was confiscated and his family lost all their possessions. Before he was taken to the internment camp, an angry Mitsui threw his medals at the feet of the inducting officer and shouted, "What good are these?" The bitterness of that moment remained with Sergeant Mitsui until his death in Hamilton in 1987, at the ripe old age of 100.[42]

Wreckage of German trench captured at Hill 70, August 1917

who "rendered very valuable assistance in caring for our wounded."[44]

It was one thing to capture the quarry; holding it was something entirely different. Within minutes, the Fighting Tenth was attempting to consolidate its hard-won gains, and a trench was hastily dug on the far side of the quarry. "It was a good place to dig in," Private Moir recalled of the chalky soil.[45] Several posts, most of them manned by the surviving Lewis-gun crews, were established at key points across the Battalion's frontage. These were supposed to be strictly defensive measures, but this was not the case at a post occupied by five riflemen — Privates Frederick Roberts, James Aitken, Lemuel McCallum, James Ballantyne, and Ernest Beer — who were subjected to intense fire from three enemy machine-guns. So accurate and deadly was the marksmanship of these Canadians that the Germans withdrew the guns to a safer location. All five privates were awarded MMs for their spirited fight.[46]

Then came the counter-attacks. The Germans brought down a devastating barrage at 4:43 p.m. "They just threw everything at us," remembered the thrice-wounded Lieutenant Pearson.[47] Shortly after five o'clock the enemy could be seen assembling for an assault on the quarry and within minutes, the Canadian artillery responded to the Battalion's SOS flares with a pinpoint bombardment. "The enemy dispersed in confusion," celebrated Colonel Ormond, who never forgot the magnificent work of the gunners who laboured so hard to assist the Fighting Tenth at the Chalk Quarry. "The artillery support was all that could be desired. They were wonderful."[48]

Time and again the Germans attacked, but Canadian shrapnel and high-explosive shells repeatedly wrought havoc among their grey-clad ranks. When the artillery failed to stop them, the enemy recoiled in the face of concentrated small-arms fire. "I just forget how many counter-attacks the Germans made to try and drive us out of there," commented

The Chalk Quarry, Hill 70

Private Moir, "but not one of them drove us out. And they suffered severe casualties. The machine-guns, you know, really mowed them down," and he, like Colonel Ormond, rated the work of the artillery as "wonderful," although Canadian shells sometimes fell among the Tenth. Moir remembered the one German who made it through this gauntlet of fire. He "tumbled in just beside me, you know, he was badly wounded, and he pulled out a picture from his pocket — his wife and two of her family — and he showed it to me. And he practically died then, you know."[49]

Despite the intensity of the counter-attacks and the accompanying shell fire, the Fighting Tenth held on. Much of the credit for the feat was later attributed to Captain Thompson, who seemed to be everywhere, encouraging and exhorting the troops to do their best. "The splendid example and determination shown by this officer," Colonel Ormond contended, "was almost solely responsible for the holding of this position." But others shared the captain's fiery spirit. Lieutenant Pearson stubbornly refused to be evacuated in spite of his three wounds, and one of his platoon commanders, Lieutenant Frank Fane, a future member of Parliament, was so badly injured that he had to be propped up in the trench in order to fire his rifle. Lieutenant Fane, too, refused to leave, although he was later wounded a second time, and was rewarded with an MC.

Their determination was contagious. Sergeant Dougall Maxwell was buried by a shell burst, but after digging himself out merely joked about "the severe shaking up which he received." Sergeant Maxwell won the DCM, as did Private Henry Smith, whose Lewis-gun team was wiped out not once but twice. Although he was wounded, Private Smith stayed at his post, raking the advancing enemy with his light machine-gun. Private Herbert Hazlewood, manning another Lewis gun, was wounded and his Number Two killed; when his gun was smashed, Private Hazlewood picked up a rifle and continued the fight, a display which earned him an MM.[50]

Battles around the isolated outposts were no less remarkable. Private Thomas Fidgett and four others manned a bombing post which was subjected to repeated counter-attacks. "Two of his men were wounded, but he along with the remaining two successfully beat off several enemy counter attacks, on one occasion with the bayonet." His companions were inclined to abandon the post, but when Private Fidgett vehemently disagreed, they changed their minds and stayed to fight to the bitter end. Fidgett won the DCM for his stubborn bravery.[51]

A DCM was also awarded to Lance-Sergeant John Wennevold, one of the originals. As a corporal, Jack Wennevold had been seriously wounded at the Second Battle of Ypres, and after his recovery served as an instructor in England. Dissatisfied with the easy life, the carpenter from Kenyon, Minnesota, rejoined the Fighting Tenth in combat. Now posted to the extreme

right flank, which was still exposed due to the 5th Battalion's difficulties, Sergeant Wennevold and the small party with him were soon under attack. Wennevold held on, but he was the only survivor, and Lieutenant MacEachern rounded up another party and placed it with the sergeant. Again the post was attacked, and again Wennevold was the only one still standing when the Germans fell back. Once more, MacEachern gathered a party and led it to Wennevold's battered, blood-stained post. A third counter-attack ensued, and for a third time Wennevold was the only one to emerge unscathed. Finally, MacEachern and five other ranks joined the tough sergeant and held it for the rest of the night. A Wetaskiwin grain dealer who was six weeks shy of his twenty-third birthday, MacEachern won the DSO for his efforts.[52]

No one performed more selflessly and fearlessly than the Battalion's reliable runners. That the Fighting Tenth was able to stand its ground in the face of overwhelming numbers was due largely to the brilliant work of the Canadian field artillery. However, the gunners could have done little without the critical information delivered by the runners, who had to be employed whenever the telephone lines were cut — which was often, despite the work of signallers such as Private Joseph Milne. He laid new lines and repaired old ones under heavy fire, and was later awarded the second bar to his MM, the only member of the Tenth to gain that distinction.

To deliver their messages, runners had to cross ground that was exposed to the full force of the enemy's small-arms and shell fire. Private Charles Cracknell, wounded in the wrist during the assault on the quarry, braved enemy shells and bullets to deliver news of a counter-attack on the right, where Canadian shells were missing the mark. He arrived in time to enable the gunners to adjust the range and crush the enemy thrust. Only after he was certain that his report had been received did Cracknell depart for treatment of his wound, and won the DCM as a result. Private Arthur Fisher not only carried an important message but brought back the receipt issued by headquarters, even though he suffered wounds in both legs. Private Percy Stewart was hobbled by a twisted knee but still delivered an urgent message. Privates Fisher and Stewart were both awarded MMs.[53]

Most famous of all was Private Harry Brown. Nineteen years of age, a native of Ganonoque, Ontario, Private Brown was handed a message calling for urgent artillery support to repel a counter-attack. A duplicate was given to a fellow runner, who set off with Brown across the bullet and shell-swept slope. The other messenger was killed; Brown's arm was nearly severed by a shell fragment, and his right thigh was riddled with shrapnel. Ignoring the injuries, the profusely bleeding Brown staggered into D'Company's headquarters, in a dugout behind the

Red Line. Corporal Charlie Launder witnessed Brown's arrival. "I remember that boy coming down, his arm was shattered, just hanging. And he fell down — it was a shaft down, I should say, about twenty feet down. And his arm was hanging."[54] Before losing consciousness, Brown gave his crumpled, blood-soaked note to an officer, gasping, "Important message."[55]

Brown arrived with not a moment to spare. The Canadian barrage was brought down in the nick of time, and one more enemy attack was ruined. But it was too late for Brown. Dying of his wounds a short time later in the dressing station, he was buried in the Noeux-les-Mines Communal Cemetery near Bethune. "This man displayed courage and self control seldom witnessed," wrote Colonel Ormond. "His devotion to duty was of the highest possible degree imaginable, his action undoubtedly saved the loss of the position, at least temporarily, and saved many casualties to our troops."[56]

Harry Brown was subsequently awarded the Victoria Cross, the Empire's highest award for bravery in battle. It was the first of two VCs won by members of the Fighting Tenth.

But the desperate battle in the quarry was almost over. At eight-thirty that evening, Colonel Ormond appealed to Second Brigade headquarters for reinforcement, and General Loomis responded by authorizing the 4th (Central Ontario) Battalion, which was under his jurisdiction, to relieve the Tenth. At 9:10 a.m., a company of the 4th Battalion began crossing the original Canadian front line and relieving the front-line companies. The manoeuvre was finally completed around two-thirty on Friday morning, 17 August. Ormond commented that it "was carried out in a most efficient and splendid manner."[57]

Before departing, the Battalion evacuated its wounded. German prisoners were employed as stretcher-bearers, and the dozens of injured men were carried from the quarry. Among them was Private Ernie Crowe, the seventeen-year-old from Cochrane whose elbow had been shattered by a bullet. By now, he was severely weakened by loss of blood; "my arm was twice as big as the other one by then, it all swelled up, and blood and dripped and soaked right

September 1917: General Currie presents ribbons to Tenth Battalion officers and other ranks decorated for bravery at Vimy Ridge and Arleux

Courtesy National Archives of Canada/PA-1873

135

down into my uniform pants, tunic, and everything else." Crowe's war had ended.[58*]

The bone-weary survivors withdrew to the Blue Line. However, a few members of the unit stayed behind to ensure that all of the Battalion's wounded were evacuated and treated. One of these was Private Grant Knapp, who won the MM after making "two trips of over one mile each with water for the severely wounded men. He also reconnoitred the forward area by daylight, locating wounded who were in shell holes and trenches. Although repeatedly sniped at, he continued to work regardless of his personal safety."[60]

With everyone accounted for, the Tenth Battalion moved out of the battle zone. Relieved on the morning of Saturday, 18 August, by another company of Ontario's 4th Battalion, the Tenth trudged to the rear, first to Les Brébis, then to divisional reserve at Barlin. But the Germans gave the Battalion a less-than-fond farewell, subjecting its line of march "to a heavy gas bombardment" that compelled everyone to don box respirators. Sergeant Davis Forbes, another original, realized that his men could not see sufficiently well to make their way through the wire and shell holes in the early-morning darkness, so he removed the face covering from his respirator and ordered the men "to take hold of bayonet scabbards to keep in touch ... and in this way led his platoon through the gas without casualty." Sergeant Forbes won the DCM.[61]

Still, the gas took its toll. It was here that most of the Battalion's three dozen gas casualties were suffered, including Private Norman Ridge, an Irishman from Shaunavon, Saskatchewan, who had joined the Battalion just after Vimy Ridge. Private Ridge, who was five days away from his twenty-third birthday, survived the gassing, but the effects rendered him incapable of further military service.[62]

Hill 70 was one of the most outstanding performances in the Battalion's history. "It was a good show," declared Colonel Ormond.[63] He added the bar to his DSO for his strong leadership in this battle, which netted the Tenth twenty-six machine-guns and 225 prisoners, as well as an unprecedented yield of decorations. Foremost, of course, was Private Brown's VC. The Battalion's officers won three DSOs and seven MCs; in addition to the three mentioned in the narrative, MCs were awarded to the adjutant, Captain Jack Miller, and to Lieutenants Herbert Andrews, Lewis Balfe, and Frederick Easterbrook. Nine DCMs were awarded to other ranks, along with sixty MMs which included the second bar won by Private Joseph Milne. Besides the nineteen already described, MMs were won by Sergeants Robert Burns, Charles Darwin, Cornelius Hood, James McCallum, and James Smart; Lance-Sergeant Edward Arnold; Corporals Andrew Elliott, William Keith, Robert McGregor, and Maurice Oldenburg; Lance-Corporals John Evans, William L'Hirondelle, and David Hampton; and Privates Dalton Bell, Edward Bowers-Taylor, James Burbridge, Frank Corrall, Norval Curtis, Alfred Daum, William Dyson, Charles Foss, James Fowler, Robert Gibson, William Gibson, George Golics, James Gray, Daniel Heinrichs (posthumous), Harry Henry, Gus Holliday, Frederick Knight, Donald Kyle, Charles Lee, John Lynch, Wilfred Malkinson, David McGregor, Donald McLean, Kenneth McPhee, William Moore, Frank Morrison, Robert Sutherland, and Harry Wilson.

At Hill 70, the Fighting Tenth gained the distinction of winning more medals than any other Canadian combat unit acquired in any single action in the course of the Great War.[64]

There is a sad irony in Hill 70. It represents what was possibly the Tenth Battalion's finest moment on the battlefield, as well as its "only black mark."[65] The central figure in this tragedy was Sergeant William Alexander, an English-born original who became one of twenty-five Canadian soldiers executed during the Great War.

This is a little known but sorry story. The total number of executions in the BEF was 346, most of them for desertion or cowardice, a handful for murder. Besides the twenty-five Canadians, five New Zealanders were also shot, but no Australians suffered that fate. While Canada and New Zealand bowed to British military justice by placing their overseas forces under the jurisdiction of Britain's Army Act, which governed crime and punishment in the British army, Australia did not. The execution of Australians during the South African War had outraged the nation, and its government insisted that no death sentence be carried out until it had been confirmed by the governor-general, a technicality which spared Australian soldiers the anguish of killing their comrades.

Canadian troops were not so fortunate. Firing squads were assembled for twenty-two men court-martialled for desertion and for one man convicted of cowardice; the remaining two were executed for murder. All but three of the executions occurred in infantry battalions; only two units lost more than one man in this manner, the 22nd (French-Canadian) Battalion, five, and Ontario's 3rd Battalion, two. No

* Crowe spent several months recuperating in England and was sent to Canada in mid-1918 on the hospital ship *Llandovery Castle*, which was sunk by a German submarine on its return trip to England. Back in Cochrane, Crowe helped found the local branch of the Great War Veterans Association, now the Royal Canadian Legion. He spent twenty years with Alberta Government Telephones, then moved to the West Coast until his retirement in 1965. He resided in Calgary until his death in early 1990.[59]

Installation of poison-gas projectors near Lens, September 1917
Courtesy National Archives of Canada/PA-1867

Canadian officers were shot, but the Tenth's Sergeant Alexander was the only condemned man above the rank of private.

William Alexander's career had been undistinguished. He was born in London on 18 September 1880. His heavily tattooed forearms gave evidence of the eight years he spent in the British army (60th King's Royal Rifles) before emigrating to Canada. A rubber worker, the diminutive (five-foot-six, 135 pounds) Alexander was managing an automobile tire company in Calgary when the war broke out. He enlisted on 26 August 1914, was sent to Valcartier, and became a member of the Tenth Battalion on 24 September. By virtue of his military experience, he was named one of eight colour-sergeants (forerunner of the company sergeant-major) but reverted to sergeant when the Battalion was reorganized on a four-company basis. There was nothing remarkable about his war record. He was twice promoted to acting company sergeant-major, but both times went back to sergeant "at own request," according to his personnel file. Alexander performed "exceedingly well"[66] at Mount Sorrel in June 1916. After that battle, perhaps as a reward, he was promoted to company quartermaster-sergeant. Hospitalized for various ailments in late 1916, he rejoined the Battalion in time for Vimy Ridge but was back in hospital within two weeks with an inflamed knee. He rejoined the unit on 11 August 1917.

Four days later, the Fighting Tenth went into action at Hill 70. With the heavy losses in the initial assault on 15 August, he was sent into the front lines the next day as a platoon sergeant in D Company. Alexander's assignment was to lead 14 Platoon in support of the three companies attacking the infamous Chalk Quarry. But, at zero hour, he was nowhere to be found, and the platoon had to be led by a corporal.[67]

Where was Alexander? After being given a direct order by his company sergeant-major to lead 14 Platoon, Alexander disappeared for two days. Discovered in the village of Les Brébis, where the Battalion had been billeted before the battle, the sergeant claimed that he had been "knocked down by a shell," but could offer no marks or other signs of injury. When he admitted "that he had not gone sick nor reported to any superior officer," he was placed under arrest. The formal charge against him read: "When on active service — Desertion, in that he, in the Field on 16-8-17, when acting as Platoon Sergeant of No. 14 Platoon, during active operations, absented himself without leave from his platoon and remained absent until 18-8-17."[68]

Alexander was tried on 26 September, eight days after his thirty-seventh birthday. The records for this, like all Canadian courts martial in the Great War, no longer exist and it is difficult to say exactly what happened. According to the *Manual for Military Law*, a field general court martial comprised not less than three officers, the president preferably holding the rank of major or higher; it is not known who presided over Alexander's. "A judge-advocate could be appointed to assist them," notes historian Anthony Babington, "but this very rarely happened."[69] The prosecution was customarily handled by the adjutant, in this case, Captain Jack Miller.

"It can be confidently asserted that no man suffered the extreme penalty except after a fair trial and after due consideration had been given to all extenuating circumstances." So wrote the chief of Canada's general staff, Major-General James MacBrien, in a post-war report on the Canadian executions. In cases such as Alexander's, where a death sentence was possible, "special provision was made to ensure that the accused was afforded the utmost assistance in his defence and every possible latitude was allowed him at his trial." MacBrien contended that the man was provided with "the best legal assistance available — a professional barrister or solicitor where possible — unless the accused himself elected to have as 'next friend' a person of his own choosing."[70]

Sergeant Alexander was convicted of desertion and sentenced to die in front of a firing squad. All that is known about the verdict is that it was unanimous, for that was the only way a death sentence could be passed. States a summary of the proceedings:

> There is no record of the reports and recommendations which were made in this case as to the carrying out of the death sentence. It is certain, however, that the responsible position held by this n.c.o. would cause his display of cowardice to have an especially grave effect as an example to the men under him, and this would doubtless be a material factor in deciding his fate even though his previous record had been good.[71]

137

Even so, Alexander's fate was far from final. All death sentences in the BEF were forwarded to the commander-in-chief, Field-Marshal Sir Douglas Haig, for confirmation. And, because only an estimated 10 per cent were confirmed,[72] the sergeant still had a very good chance, at this point, of escaping the firing squad. En route to GHQ, the details of the case would be studied "from a legal point of view, by the special officers dealing with court-martial work at divisional, corps and army headquarters, and finally, before they were laid before the Commander-in-Chief they were the subject of most critical review by the Judge Advocate General — the highest legal authority in France."[73]

In making his decision, Field-Marshal Haig considered not only the legality of the conviction but reports from Alexander's relevant commanding officers, Colonel Ormond, General Loomis at brigade headquarters, the divisional commander, General Macdonell, General Currie, and the First Army's General Horne. Each offered his assessment of the sergeant's personal and combat records, and whether the crime "was committed deliberately with a view to avoiding duty in the trenches or other dangerous duty, such as taking part in a pending attack." The reporting officers also ventured opinions on the Battalion's "state of discipline, generally," and whether desertion and/or cowardice were "so prevalent as to justify an example being made."[74]

The report that carried the most weight, naturally, was Colonel Ormond's, because he was closest both to the Battalion and to Alexander. Ormond sealed the sergeant's fate. "I have known this N.C.O. since August 1914, and the best that I can say for his work is that it has always been indifferent, with the exception of the period from 1st to 16th-6-16, during the fighting in the Ypres Salient [i.e., Mount Sorrel] when he behaved remarkably well." Ormond noted Alexander's refusal to accept promotion to company sergeant-major, which indicated to the colonel that he lacked the "will power to make himself do duty in the trenches." His report concluded: "I regret to have to say that it is my opinion that he deliberately endeavored to avoid the particular service in the charge against him."[75]

Ormond clearly felt that he had a problem that had to be nipped in the bud. Alexander's actions had not been the only blight on the Battalion's brilliant performance at Hill 70; there was also the matter of Lieutenant Alexander Gleam, whose panic could have caused disaster in the attack on the quarry. Gleam, who was court-martialled four days before Alexander, faced two charges of conduct to the prejudice of good order and military discipline and two of neglecting to obey orders. He was convicted, dismissed from His Majesty's service, and sent back to Canada. It might even be argued that Gleam's behaviour was potentially far more serious than Alexander's had been. Gleam,

after all, had led a company in the attack, while Alexander's platoon was merely in support (although Gleam at least showed up, which is more than can be said for the sergeant). In any event, two similar cases in the same operation was too much for coincidence, and Ormond was evidently determined to do something about it.

His superiors agreed with him, for Field-Marshal Haig subsequently confirmed the death sentence. As General MacBrien pointed out in his post-war report, "where a death sentence for desertion or cowardice was inflicted when a man's past record had been good it is safe to say that the offence was of a particularly flagrant character or the particular crime had become so prevalent in the unit that further leniency would have had possibly a grave effect."[76] So William Alexander, who had left a comfortable home in Calgary to volunteer his services for the glory of the British Empire, whose modest record contained only one black mark (he forfeited his field allowance and part of his pay during a six-week stay in hospital in late 1916), was to be sacrificed in the name of a disciplinary problem which probably did not even exist, except in the perception of the officer commanding his Battalion.

The last three weeks of his life must have been agonizing. Since only "not guilty" verdicts were announced at the conclusion of courts martial, Alexander knew that he had been convicted; what he did not know was his fate, death or imprisonment. Held in confinement, he waited anxiously for news, day after interminable day. The death sentence was confirmed on 15 October, but two more days passed before Alexander was informed. The messenger was one of his officers who came to his cell at six o'clock in the evening of 17 October, twelve hours before the scheduled execution.

The grim event took place at 6:10 a.m. on Thursday, 18 October, in a secluded spot outside Houdain. When Sergeant Alexander arrived, in handcuffs, the firing party was already there, an officer and fourteen other ranks selected from all four battalions in the Second Brigade, standing five paces away with their backs to the prisoner. While the attending medical officer blindfolded Alexander's blue eyes with a three-cornered bandage, military policemen tied him, in the recommended fashion, "with ropes or strap to tree or post stuck in the ground, or fastened in a chair which itself should be secured to some fixed object." Finally, the medical officer pinned "a small paper disc" to Alexander's tunic over his heart, for a target.[77]

All was ready. The officer in charge of the firing party, using hand signals, turned his men to face Alexander. The fourteen riflemen were in two ranks; the front knelt. Each man drew a bead on the piece of paper pinned to the sergeant's tunic, each man hoping that he was holding the one rifle that had been loaded

Liévin, on the western outskirts of Lens

Courtesy National Archives of Canada/PA-1971

with a blank round. Then the officer gave the single spoken command in this terrible ceremony: "Fire!"[78]

And Company Quartermaster-Sergeant William Alexander, regimental number 20726, died.*

After the medical officer certified that Alexander was dead (had he not been killed instantaneously, the officer commanding the firing party would have had to "complete the sentence" with his revolver), the body was unbound and removed for burial in a grave prepared by a party from the Tenth Battalion. The headstone of this unfortunate man can be seen today in the Barlin Communal Cemetery Extension.

One act remained to be played in the tragedy of William Alexander, and it involved his family. His brother, and next-of-kin, A.M. Alexander of Winnipeg, did not receive official notification of William's death, due to a mix-up in addresses at the Militia Department. He did get "a nice letter" from a captain in the Tenth "saying that he had been killed in action," as well as a message from William "saying if I ever got that letter he would have gone under." In the absence of official notice, Alexander sought confirmation from local militia officials. It was only then, in

the second half of December 1917, that he learned the horrifying truth. His anguish is painfully apparent in his letter of reply:

This is the first official notice we have received of my brother's death, and an awful death at that. Some people will have a merry Xmas, and some will have a sad one, for their loved ones, who had given all they had to give to fight for their King and country, and under the circumstances fallen in battle. But my lot was even worse than that, to be shot like a spy and a traitor to his country, that was the lot for my brother. Even in death, he is still my brother and his noble spirit will live forever with me even in death, and his death was awful to be shot like a dog. I hope he is in peace on the Lord's side....

Now first of all, he had kept his rank and more too, so that shows his character had been all right up to his sentence, he has served 33 months in the firing line without a grumble in his letter[s], and looked forward to coming back. I can hardly believe, that for the first offence of deser-

---

* Sergeant Alexander may well have been the subject of a desperate, last-minute mercy mission by Canon Frederick Scott, the First Division's beloved chaplain. Scott recounted the episode in a dramatic chapter of his book, *The Great War as I Saw It*. Unfortunately, aside from two clues, Scott's account is so vague — deliberately mentioning no names or places — that it is impossible to say with certainty that it relates to Alexander. One hint is the location of the chapter in the book which, if chronologically correct, places the event in October 1917. There were two Canadian executions that month, but only Alexander was a member of the first contingent, the second hint provided by Scott.

The divisional chaplain spent all night driving back and forth in a bid to avert the execution. He travelled twice to army headquarters and once to the division's headquarters, but his efforts were fruitless. The execution was the only one he witnessed, and it profoundly shocked him: "I have seen many ghastly sights and hideous forms of death. I have heard heart-rending tales of what men have suffered, but nothing ever brought home to me so deeply, and with such cutting force, the hideous nature of war and the iron hand of discipline, as did that lonely death on this misty hillside in the early morning."[79]

139

tion, that they were justified in passing that sentence. I can hardly believe that ... because for such an offence in my opinion [it] would have been severe enough had they reduced him to the ranks, or given him imprisonment, as long as nobody suffered through his offence. To shoot a man for desertion after his service there, and other places, is going beyond the limit.... May the Lord have mercy on the man who judged him if he was wrong.[80]

The public remained largely ignorant. In mid-November, the Calgary *Daily Herald* published Alexander's name in a list of battle casualties. The brief article noted that Alexander "frequently wrote to friends in Calgary, telling of his exceptional luck."

The fighting in and around Lens continued until 25 August. While the Canadian Corps gained its initial objective, Hill 70, on the very first day, it had to continue the offensive in order to mislead the enemy about British intentions and divert attention from the main attack under way at that time in Flanders. However, the Fighting Tenth played no further part in the fighting for Lens.

After spending a day at Barlin, the unit moved on 19 August to Brunay, where it was joined by a draft of ninety-eight reinforcements. The weather was perfect, and on the twenty-first, General Macdonell inspected the Battalion, afterwards congratulating "all ranks for their splendid work" at Hill 70. Following a restful stay at Brunay, the Tenth marched to Caucourt, seven and a half miles away. Its sojourn in Caucourt was pleasant enough, with some drill and plenty of sports to keep the troops fighting-fit. Another draft of ninety-eight reinforcements arrived here, making good half of the Tenth's battle losses.[81]

Monday, 27 August, was a memorable occasion. It was overcast, with rain later in the day, but poor weather conditions failed to dampen a visit from the commander-in-chief, Field-Marshal Haig. The four battalions of the Second Brigade were assembled in a field outside of Caucourt, and General Loomis looked them over and "complimented the Brigade on its smart appearance."[82] Then Haig inspected the troops, who left a strong impression. "The experience and training of the past year have done wonders for the Canadians," he wrote in his diary that night. "Their morale is now very high, and though they have been opposed by the flower of the German Army (Guards, etc.) they feel that they can beat the Germans every time."[83]

This quiet time ended all too soon. On Monday, 3 September, the Tenth moved out of Caucourt, returning to its previous billets in Barlin. Two more weeks were to pass before it returned to the front-line trenches and, in the meantime, the unit re-equipped, received more replacements, and trained. Sports, as

usual, figured prominently, and one day, the 4th (Central Ontario) Battalion — commanded by the Tenth's former major, Alexander Thomson — was soundly trounced in baseball and football games.

On the sixth, the troops started on the first step towards the front lines, relieving the 52nd (Ontario) Battalion at Noulette Huts, in brigade reserve. Here, in addition to its training and sports activities, the Tenth provided working parties for the construction of a new camp at nearby Marqueffles Farm. Fifty more other ranks joined the Battalion, along with three new officers; the Fighting Tenth was, slowly but surely, being restored to its normal high level of combat proficiency.[84]

On Thursday, 13 September, the Battalion moved closer still to the front. Taking over the brigade support position at Liévin, on the western outskirts of Lens, the Tenth spent the next four days raising work parties, watching the many dogfights in the sky above, and dodging the occasional long-range shell.[85]

Its first front-line appearance in a month occurred on Monday, 17 September. Relieving the 5th (Western Cavalry) Battalion that evening, the Tenth found the Germans in a vicious mood. Tuesday passed quietly, but Wednesday was much different, featuring a furious battle for Alpaca Trench. This had been partially captured in August, and Canadians and Germans were separated by a hastily constructed block. After dark on 19 September, the enemy, emerging from the ruins of a nearby building, launched a surprise attack on Alpaca Trench, which was being held by eleven members of B Company. Within moments, every defender was a casualty — one dead, the rest wounded — but reinforcements rushed to the scene and drove off the attackers. The Germans tried once more an hour later, again with no success.[86]

They renewed the battle on Thursday night with the first of three attacks mounted at 9:15 p.m. It was repelled with three casualties to the Fighting Tenth; a second attempt, at 10 p.m., was driven back without loss. At one o'clock in the morning, another German party stormed Alpaca Trench, wrecking the block and inflicting seven casualties. In view of these repeated attacks, Colonel Ormond decided that the disadvantageous position was not worth holding and, pulling the Battalion beyond hand-grenade range, ordered a new block built out of the debris of the many wrecked buildings in the area. This was completed by daybreak. The five battles at the block in Alpaca Trench had cost B Company twenty-one dead or wounded.[87]

That night the Tenth was relieved by the 8th (90th Winnipeg Rifles) Battalion. Moving to Noulette Huts, in brigade reserve, the unit enjoyed several busy days. In addition to the unceasing training and inspections, working parties were sent into the trenches each night to work on the local defences. On 25 September, the Tenth relieved the 5th Battalion in brigade support at Liévin, where working parties buried telephone cable, carried trench-mortar bombs into the front lines, and dug support-line trenches. On the twenty-eighth, there were three casualties, including one killed.[88]

The Battalion's last appearance in the front lines in this sector came on Wednesday, 3 October. After relieving British Columbia's 7th Battalion, the unit mounted a small operation intended to capture a prisoner. Just before seven o'clock on the evening of 4 October, Captain Charles Costigan and four other ranks slipped into no man's land and laid an ambush, hoping to catch an unwary enemy. But there were no German patrols this night, and Captain Costigan's party returned empty-handed four hours later. In the meantime, the Battalion's lines were heavily bombarded, resulting in twenty-one casualties: one of the five men killed was Private William Adamson, who had won the MM at Hill 70. Because "the attitude of the Enemy is one of extreme alertness," Colonel Ormond cancelled further efforts to take prisoners.[89]

The tour ended on the night of 6 - 7 October, when Ontario's 4th Battalion took over the line, and the Fighting Tenth moved back to Nessian Huts near Marqueffles Farm. A further move to the rear was made the following day, when the unit marched to Gouy Servins, where those eligible voted in the Saskatchewan election.*

The weather turned wet and cold, minimizing the amount of training which could be carried out, but the men were able to bathe and were issued a change of underclothing. There were also more inspections and lectures.[90]

While the veterans had by now become accustomed to this lifestyle, both in and out of the trenches, it never failed to amaze and appall the newcomers. The trenches, particularly in sectors such as this where the ground was relatively firm, were vastly superior to the primitive entrenchments constructed in the first couple of years of the war. Deep enough to enable a man to walk about, they could be relatively comfortable if the rats and lice were not too numerous and if the mud did not overflow the duckboards, or wooden sidewalks, which were laid along the bottom. The dugouts that honeycombed the walls of the trenches ranged in size from one-man "funk holes" to rooms with electric lighting and wooden bunk-beds, but few men managed to have more than a fitful sleep because of the "water dripping on you and rats running over your face."[91]

Even where conditions were reasonably good, the trenches were far from pleasant. Not only was it easy to get lost in the maze of multiple defence lines and the communication trenches which connected them, but the smell was perpetually bad, due to the proximity of rotting corpses and carcasses. Even when they had been properly buried, the bodies of men and horses were constantly being unearthed by barrages.

As well, sanitation left a lot to be desired. "We had latrines in the trenches," recalled Private Tom Ross, "a few sandbags hiding you and a deep hole with a piece of board for a seat."[92] Fresh water was in short supply, and personal hygiene suffered as a consequence. Because water was strictly rationed, there was little available for luxuries like washing and shaving. It was not uncommon to see soldiers shave with leftover tea, and everyone had to wait until they came out of the line before enjoying a hot shower. Often showers were a week or ten days, and sometimes as much as a month apart.

Discomfort was a way of life for these men. "There's three things," said Private Ernie Crowe, the seventeen-year-old whose war service started at Vimy Ridge and ended at Hill 70 when a sniper's bullet smashed his right elbow, "that I still remember: the rain, the mud, and the lice. Lousy, you know, we were all lousy as pet coons." In reserve, he recalled, "we'd sit up in the sun, turn our underwear inside out, and get a stick with creosote on it — you know, that hot tar stuff? — and smear all the seams in your underwear." But the lice always returned as soon as the men went back into the trenches. There was no relief even when freshly laundered uniforms were periodically issued. "Well, in the laundry, they didn't kill the lice, they just stunned them for a while, and as soon as you warmed up that uniform, you were just as lousy as ever!"[93]

Food, as always, was a major concern. Rations were brought up each night, first by supply wagon to a predetermined location, then by carrying parties that delivered the food in sandbags. These were later used for repairing trenches and dugouts. "We got MacConachie stew that came in a round can about two inches deep, and pork and beans," recalled another Tenth Battalion veteran, Private Jack Moyes. "Once in a while you'd get little cold steaks or pork chops, and bacon, but never any eggs.... You got sugar, dry sugar, and tea, but no coffee. I don't believe I ever saw coffee in the trenches.... The jam came in one-pound cans, plum and apple was the favorite." Another staple was bully, or corned, beef and hardtack biscuits. "Bully Beef's good," Private Moyes remarked, " I don't mind Bully.... I've ate many a hardtack, I liked it, too! It was a biscuit about three inches by six, they were oblong, and [when] you were hungry, they were good. They were just like brown bread and harder than hell." Hardtack, he declared, had other uses. "We'd make picture frames out of it and take pictures out of magazines and paste it on the back of the hardtack."[94]

It was possible to supplement this less-than-appetizing menu when the Battalion moved into reserve. Every village had an estaminet, where the troops could purchase a hot meal. Eggs and chips were a

---

* The election was won by the Liberals, under Premier William Martin.

favourite, along with weak beer or strong coffee, although the latter did not meet with everyone's approval, according to Private Moyes: "That damn coffee the French made was rotten."[95] Prices were often exorbitant, and for privates earning $1.10 per day, visits to the local estaminet had to be kept to a minimum. The Salvation Army and the Young Men's Christian Association (YMCA) set up concessions in the rear areas. Their prices were much more reasonable, earning for both organizations the eternal gratitude of the soldiers who patronized them.

There were other temptations in these villages. As one veteran of the Fighting Tenth recalled, "the French girls were most obliging. Of course, the officers made out better than the men." Close to the battle zone, the selection was less than tantalizing, as Private Moyes later commented: "Only fat girls and middle-aged women." Brothels proliferated, particularly in the larger cities like Boulogne, Calais, and, naturally, Paris. These were popular among Canadian soldiers, and this popularity was reflected in an alarmingly high rate of venereal disease.[96]

Mail was vitally important, for most soldiers it was their one link with what they considered to be reality. In the trenches, each man could fill out a postcard containing a check list of questions such as, "I received your letter," "I am fine & in good health," "Why haven't you written?" These were carried out by runners and mailed without charge, but letters could not be mailed until the Battalion moved out of the front lines. The YMCA provided free stationery, which further endeared that organization to the troops.

Incoming letters and parcels arrived regularly, even in the trenches. "Our mail came up every night with the ration wagons," recalled Private Tom Ross. Parcels containing clothing or food were highly valued, although they were sometimes rather humorous. "One fellow in our bunch got a parcel from Canada," Private Ross later wrote, "& it contained, of all things, 2 cans of Bully Beef, 3 rolls of toilet paper and one box of 10 cigarettes. Bully Beef was everywhere, lots of it in the trenches. He was pretty mad but the toilet paper came in handy at the time as he had diorhea [sic]." The postal service was reasonably good; while the travelling time from Canada was about three weeks, London newspapers could be read in the trenches a day or two after they were published.[97] But English news was small comfort to men who were thousands of miles away from home.

On 12 October, the Battalion moved to Houdain to prepare for what was, ostensibly, its next offensive operation. Detailed planning to enable the Canadian Corps to capture Lens had been under way for some time. While the Hill 70 attack had been a success in terms of its diversionary intent, it had not forced the enemy to abandon Lens. Unwilling to mount a direct attack on the rubble-filled city, General Currie selected Sallaumines Hill, on the southern outskirts, as the objective for his next operation. Its capture would give the Canadians complete command of Lens.

But events elsewhere interceded. In Flanders, the great British offensive had bogged down in unprecedented conditions of rain and mud. Attacking out of the Ypres salient in a northeasterly direction, the BEF had by now set its sights, not on the breakthrough envisaged by planners at GHQ, but on the long, low ridge named for the ruined village which sat on the crest: Passchendaele. This was, so far as Field-Marshal Haig was concerned, the minimal requirement to allow him to call off operations for the winter. When attacks on 9 and 12 October led by the Australians and New Zealanders failed to dislodge the Germans, Haig, his job on the line, called in the Canadian Corps to finish the job. General Currie protested, but to no avail, and when he received his written orders on the thirteenth, the Corps began withdrawing from the Lens sector.

The Fighting Tenth was among the last units to leave the area. On Friday, 19 October, the day after the execution of Sergeant Alexander, the Battalion marched out of Houdain on the way to one of its worst experiences of the war.

Chapter Eight

"A USELESS WASTE OF LIFE"

(19 October 1917 - 1 August 1918)

The fighting in Flanders had been under way since 31 July, when two armies of the BEF attacked in a northeasterly direction out of the Ypres salient. The primary objective was the scarcely perceptible rise of Passchendaele Ridge. Field-Marshal Haig, having staked his reputation on the outcome of this campaign, foresaw a long and bitter struggle, but cherished the thought of reaching the ridge, then unleashing his cavalry divisions on the flat Belgian plain that lay beyond. The potential for a major success was undeniably there; even a modest advance in this strategic sector would cause serious problems for the enemy. However, Haig's designs were destined to be thwarted, not by the Germans, but by the weather. Instead of being a decisive victory, Passchendaele became synonymous with futility, slaughter, suffering, and, above all, mud.

It rained on the first day of the offensive, and continued to do so throughout much of August. Coming on the heels of a two-week long preliminary bombardment, in which millions of artillery shells had been pumped into this small corner of Belgium, the precipitation had a disastrous effect. In addition to wrecking German defences, the shelling destroyed the delicate drainage system, and the low-lying area soon turned into a vast soupy swamp. Men, horses, and guns disappeared forever into the slime. Stretcher cases which normally required two bearers now needed as many as sixteen to undertake the tiring trek to the nearest dressing station. They slogged through hip-deep mud around and through shell holes, filled with icy water and bloated corpses. Troops moving up to launch new attacks were often exhausted by zero hour. Advances of a few hundred yards under heavy artillery and machine-gun fire — the latter coming from concrete bunkers called "pillboxes" and organized in a checker-board pattern — required superhuman efforts.

The weather improved in September and, when the ground hardened in the hot sunshine, the British enjoyed considerable success. New tactics were employed: each assault was strictly limited in scope, and the infantry dug in under the protection of their artillery to minimize the impact of the inevitable counter-attacks. In this manner, the BEF battled its way to the foot of Passchendaele Ridge.

And then, in early October, it started to rain again. The effect was even more serious than in August, because lower temperatures lengthened the time it took for the ground to dry between showers. The British position was arguably worse than it had been before the offensive had begun; they were now directly under the enemy's guns, which had a perfect view of the BEF's lines of communication. After disappointing failures on 9 and 12 October, Field-Marshal Haig called on the Canadian Corps to capture the ridge and salvage the campaign.

The Canadians did it. In the face of conditions which defy description, the Corps staged a series of limited but powerful attacks on 26 and 30 October and on 6 November, when the village of Passchendaele, on the crest of the ridge, finally fell. The operation stands as a tribute to Canadian military efficiency and to General Currie's sound leadership and organizational abilities. No one admired the Corps commander more than the Fighting Tenth's own Colonel Ormond, who considered the preparations for Passchendaele to be Currie's "outstanding work that he ever did." Recalled Ormond: "When we went in, we had no maps. The people ahead of us didn't have the staff. Currie, he had everything right. He had the staff, he had the maps — he had them made. So he knew what he was doing."[1]

To secure these hard-won gains, Currie planned a final operation on 10 November. The objective was the highest point on the ridge, Hill 52, half a mile north of Passchendaele village. And the Fighting Tenth was the unit that would take it.

After departing the Lens sector on 19 October, the Battalion arrived in Flanders on the twenty-second. The weather was dull and cloudy, with occasional rain, but during its two-week stay at Le Nieppe, the Tenth underwent a steady programme of rigorous training. A typical day's work is described in the war diary:

Training was carried on from 7.00 A.M. to 12.00 Noon, with usual interval for breakfast, and consisted of Dress and Interior Economy, Platoon in Attack on Strong Points, Reading of Trench Orders, and Lecture on Wiring and Entanglements and Engineering. Company Bombers carried on with instruction under Battalion Grenade Officer, Lewis Gunners, Signal

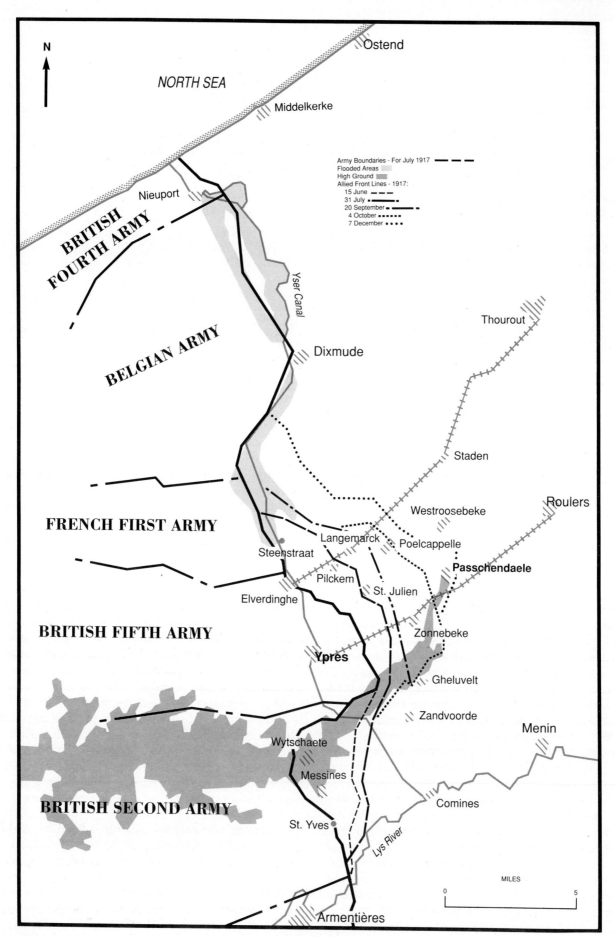

N

NORTH SEA

Ostend

Middelkerke

Army Boundaries - For July 1917
Flooded Areas
High Ground
Allied Front Lines - 1917:
   15 June
   31 July
   20 September
   4 October
   7 December

BRITISH FOURTH ARMY

Nieuport

BELGIAN ARMY

Yser Canal

Dixmude

Thourout

Staden

FRENCH FIRST ARMY

Westroosebeke

Roulers

Langemarck

Poelcappelle

Steenstraat

Passchendaele

Pilckem

St. Julien

Elverdinghe

BRITISH FIFTH ARMY

Zonnebeke

Ypres

Gheluvelt

Zandvoorde

Menin

Wytschaete

Messines

BRITISH SECOND ARMY

Comines

St. Yves

Lys River

MILES
0   5

Armentières

Flanders 1917

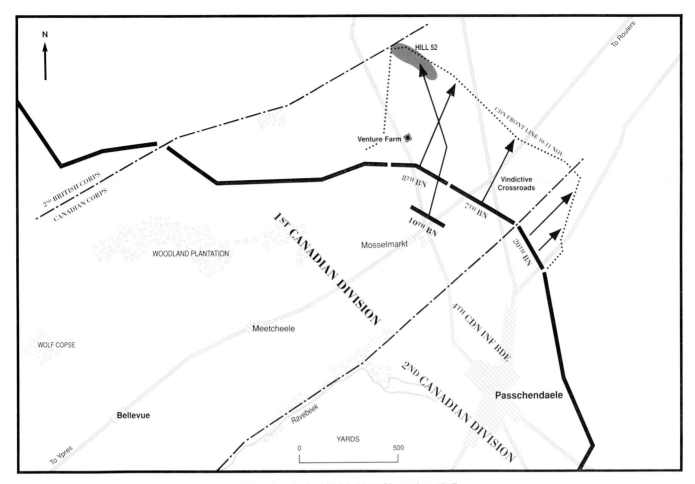

Passchendaele: Hill 52, 10-11 November 1917

Section, Scouts carried on with instruction under respective Instructors.

On 25 October, one officer per company was sent to Poperinghe to view a model of Passchendaele Ridge.[2]

Two notable visitors inspected the Battalion during this time. On 22 October, the former governor-general, the Duke of Connaught, reviewed the entire Second Brigade, capped by a march-past in column of fours. Six days later, General Currie attended a church parade with the brigade's officers, then presented decorations to recent winners. Currie also gave a short talk which members of the Fighting Tenth long remembered. "He told us what a fine body of men we were, and all the rest of it, and he'd volunteered to take Passchendaele," recalled Private William Curtis. It was "a terrible speech," in Private George Moir's opinion. "He told us the Australians had tried to take it, and the British tried to take it, and now they've called on the Canadians. And he says, 'You'll have to take it before you ever get out of there!' "[3]*

By early November, there were signs that the Tenth would not be at Le Nieppe for long. On the second and third, the Battalion carried out practice attacks, emphasizing "Strong Points and open warfare." On the fourth, it left its billets and marched to Erlingham Station, where it boarded trains for Brandhoek. Disembarking, the unit was billeted at nearby Derby Camp for three days of routine activities which included "cleaning up the camp and surroundings and making conditions as comfortable as possible for all ranks," as well as checking and inspecting equipment needed for the coming operation.[5]

On Wednesday, 7 November, the Fighting Tenth moved into the Ypres salient. The few originals were familiar with the place-names from their first tour here in April 1915: Ypres, Saint-Jean, Wieltje, Saint-Julien. Only Ypres was remotely recognizable, although it was almost entirely in ruins; the other villages had ceased to exist, except for signs that marked their locations. Indeed, the salient had become a monument to death: a grey-brown sea of mud pocked by craters as far as the eye could see, without a single

---

* Currie's actual words were recorded by Fred McKenzie, a Canadian war correspondent. "The Commander-in-Chief has called on us to do a big job," Currie told his troops. "It has got to be done.... I promise you that you will not be called upon to advance — as you never will be — until everything has been done to clear the way for you. After that it is up to you, and I leave it to you with confidence." The Corps commander received "cheer after cheer" in response, according to McKenzie.[4]

Mired in mud, the BEF's Flanders offensive was also plagued by controversy arising from the ongoing personality clash between Prime Minister David Lloyd George and Field-Marshal Sir Douglas Haig. The prime minister had opposed the proposed campaign, even before it was launched. He contended that it would merely follow the pattern established at the Somme: "Brilliant preliminary successes followed by weeks of desperate and sanguinary struggles, leading to nothing except perhaps the driving of the enemy back a few miles — beyond that nothing to show except a ghastly casualty list." Lloyd George, who preferred to fight almost anywhere other than on the Western Front, favoured British backing for the Italians against Austria-Hungary. The advantage of fighting the enemy in Italy rather than in France and Belgium was, he said, "if we fought them in France we should be doing it at the expense of our own troops, whereas in Italy we can use the enormous reserves of the Italians." Lloyd George, it seems, was prepared to fight to the last Italian.

Not surprisingly, Field-Marshal Haig rejected these arguments. In a 5 June memorandum, he claimed "that if our resources are concentrated in France to the fullest possible extent, the British Armies are capable of and can be relied on to effect great results this summer — results which will make final victory more assured and which may even bring it within reach this year." Haig remained convinced that the war could not be won unless and until the main German forces, which were located on the Western Front, were defeated.

Two days after this memo, Haig mounted a preliminary operation to the Flanders offensive. The capture of Messines Ridge on 7 June was one of the most impressive victories of the entire war, and reinforced Haig's conviction that the BEF was capable of beating the Germans in 1917, with or without help from the mutinous French army. With Messines Ridge in his possession, Haig had secured the flank necessary for his campaign in Flanders, further north.

Prime Minister Lloyd George was undeterred in his efforts to scuttle Haig's Flanders venture. In mid-June, he attempted to convince his war cabinet to withhold its approval of the field-marshal's plans, and he almost succeeded. The climax came on 19 June, when Haig appeared before the cabinet to explain his intentions; the field-marshal, who had trouble talking to laymen about military matters, fared poorly in the face of Lloyd George's eloquent arguments against the Flanders offensive and favouring support for the Italians instead.

"It was a regular lawyer's effort," Haig fumed afterwards, "to make black appear white!" Fortunately for the field-marshal, the Admiralty dropped a bombshell on the proceedings by declaring that Britain was being strangled by unrestricted submarine warfare. Begun by the Germans in February 1917, it was a key reason for the April entry of the United States into the war, and the Admiralty considered it imperative to capture the U-boat bases on the Belgian coast.

The war cabinet wavered. Swayed by Lloyd George's oratorical brilliance, but unwilling to contradict the Empire's leading soldier, the cabinet vacillated for more than a month. It was not until 25 July, with the two-week preliminary bombardment already under way, that Haig finally received reluctant permission to proceed with his attack in Flanders.

It was the greatest bombardment to that time. Between 17 and 30 July, the British fired 4.3 million shells of various calibres into this small corner of Belgium, inflicting incredible damage not only to the German front-line defences but to the landscape as well, by destroying the delicate drainage system in this low-lying area.

The BEF, led by General Sir Hubert Gough's Fifth Army and supported by the Second Army of General Sir Herbert Plumer, attacked at 3:50 a.m. on 31 July, and had made modest gains along a fifteen-mile front when it started to rain during the afternoon. A gentle rainfall at first, it quickly turned into a torrential downpour, turning Flanders into an immense pool of evil-smelling mud. Unable to drain properly, the water collected in millions of shell holes and in the shallow valleys that separated the many low ridges and hills in the battle zone. Disappointed, Haig finally halted his campaign on 4 August and waited for the weather to improve.

It was a similar story for the rest of the month. The weather improved, the British attacked, and it started raining again: the pattern repeated itself each time the struggling offensive resumed, on 10, 16, and 22 August. Toward the end of the month, growing impatient with the lack of progress, Haig paused to reorganize and resupply his two attacking armies, and put the Second Army's General Plumer in over-all command. Plumer took his time instituting new tactics; each future attack would be deliberately limited, in order to keep the infantry within the range of their own artillery as a safeguard against the enemy's counter-attacks.

The weather improved in September, and the BEF enjoyed considerable success. The ground was dry and hard in the hot sunshine when Plumer's troops attacked on the twentieth and the Germans reeled under the pounding, which was repeated on 26 September and 4 October. Advances brought the British to the foot of Passchendaele Ridge. Beyond lay the flat Belgian plain, where Haig hoped to unleash his beloved cavalry divisions to play havoc with the enemy lines of communications. The BEF was on the brink of the great victory which Haig had been so confident he could achieve.

Then the rains returned. Attacks on 9 and 12 October failed in the face of steadfast resistance and the steady downpour which turned the battlefield into swampland. But Haig was unwilling to concede defeat. His armies, directly under the enemy's guns, were now in an arguably worse position than they had been before the offensive began. The field-marshal did not have to be told that, thanks to the optimistic forecasts which had raised unrealistic expectations, his job was on the line. At the very least, Haig had to have Passchendaele Ridge, in order to give his forces a sound position in which to spend the winter.

To save both his campaign and his career, Haig called on the Canadian Corps to take Passchendaele.

---

living tree to interrupt the sombre landscape, which seemed perpetually shrouded in bleak, overcast skies.

Due to limited accommodations, the Battalion was split in halves. Two companies, A and B, spent the night in what was left of Ypres, while C and D companies moved into tents near Saint-Jean. It was very late by the time the shivering soldiers drifted into a fitful sleep. The Germans marked the return of the Fighting Tenth to the scene of its trial by fire more than two years earlier, dropping several bombs in the vicinity during an overnight air raid. Although there were no casualties,[6] the effect on nerves was noticeable, as Lieutenant Hugh Pearson, recently recovered from his injuries at Hill 70, recalled. "The ground was just wet, and cold, and soggy. I was given a tent. And one of these German planes flew over at night, and all our machine-guns opened up, and of course the German artillery came right back and just pounded hell [out of us]. And I remember I was cold and wet and lying with a ground sheet and a blanket, and I began to shiver and shake — I suppose I was scared to death, too, you see. Gosh, that was a miserable night."[7]

It would get worse — much worse. The next day, the Tenth reunited and moved to a nearby camp, relieving the 7th (1st British Columbia Regiment) Battalion, which in turn moved deeper into the salient. It rained heavily during the afternoon and evening of the eighth, and German aircraft returned to attack an observation balloon tethered in the area. The Battalion's Lewis gunners assisted the anti-aircraft guns in driving away the enemy planes. They came back the following day to bomb the camp, "but did no apparent damage."[8]

Misery set in swiftly amid the desolation. "There was nothing there but shell holes," Private William Curtis remarked in an interview half a century after the war. "I was buried there that night, as a matter of fact, up to my neck in mud and sand and chalk." Private Curtis went on to describe the incident in detail:

We had nothing to do but do the best we could to get out of sight and keep ourselves as protected as we could. So we cleaned out what was in the crater, or the shell hole, dug a little bit of a ledge all round it, so we could sit down, found some old galvanized iron laying around, sheets of galvanized metal, and made a roof out of it, and established ourselves for the night.

A dud shell from the enemy came over and dropped in the crater behind us, and in dropping in it did not explode. But it did disturb the earth between the two craters, and we got all the water that was in the other one, and the whole thing caved in, and there was two or three of us buried to our neck. We had one whale of a time getting out of that, but we got out.

And we stayed there for the whole day, and moved up to Passchendaele the second night.[9]

That was Friday, 9 November. During the afternoon, the Battalion moved into Second Brigade reserve, and Colonel Ormond set up his headquarters in a battered pillbox at Bellevue, on a spur projecting from the ridge.[10] The move was completed in the early evening, without loss, but it was tough going. Each man had been issued 170 rounds of small-arms ammunition, forty-eight hours' rations, and two water bottles. Ormond was satisfied that "at no time was any great want felt, except in cases where men were buried by shell fire and lost rations, water and some equipment. There were an unusually large number of such cases."[11]

It was a hazardous approach. There were few usable roads and paths, and these were prime targets for the German artillery, as the Fighting Tenth quickly discovered. Following a plank road into the heart of the salient, the troops had to negotiate a precarious passageway of duckboards, eight-foot sections of wooden sidewalk laid across the mud and shell holes. The duckboards were just wide enough for a single man, so all traffic was one-way, and it was to be expected that some soldiers fell off.

One of these was Private Curtis, who had already been buried up to his neck in mud and water the previous night. He recalled with wry humour that when an officer stopped to lend him a hand to crawl back onto the duckboard — causing the men behind to bunch up, a dangerous situation in these circumstances — someone muttered, "Leave the son-of-a-gun there!" Private Bill "Scotty" Murray saw his sergeant, a big Englishman named Edward Arnold who had won the MM at Hill 70, slip into a shell hole filled with slimy, icy water — and something worse. "Aye," cried Sergeant Arnold as he floundered in the muck, "another couple of blokes down here!" It was impossible to tell whether they were Canadian or German, and since Arnold had no desire to get close enough to identify them, his mates hauled him back onto the duckboard.[12]

The attack was scheduled for 6:05 a.m., Saturday, 10 November. The Second Brigade planned to deploy two battalions, British Columbia's 7th, and the 8th from Winnipeg, with the 5th (Western Cavalry) in support and the Fighting Tenth in reserve. The main objective was Hill 52, a half-mile north of Passchendaele. Its possession was a "tremendous necessity," according to Colonel Ormond, because it offered "our people observation clear through to Bruges, you see." To take it, the 7th Battalion, on the right, would have to overcome the enemy defences at Vindictive Crossroads. On the left, the 8th faced Venture Farm, a heavily defended strongpoint. But there was, at this time, no intention to involve the Tenth in the battle. "We'd been more times over the top [in 1917] than any other unit in the Canadian Corps," Ormond later related. "And it wasn't intended that we should go into the Passchendaele show at all."[13]

The colonel, however, took no chances. "This Unit will be equipped as if they were actually going to make the initial assault," read his orders of 8 November, "and will be prepared to make an attack from a flank or do any other work that may be required."[14] Ormond's preparations would pay dividends, for the coming battle would prove to be as demanding as any in which the Fighting Tenth participated.

The Battalion's combat strength on the night of 9 November was twenty-two officers and 631 other ranks. At 9:20 p.m., when runners from each company arrived at Colonel Ormond's headquarters to synchronize watches for the next morning's assault, the Germans unleashed a violent bombardment of the area. The colonel's crowded pillbox took three direct hits. There were nine casualties, including four dead; one of those killed was the regimental sergeant-major, James "Mustang Pete" Watchman. And this was just the beginning. "The bombardment continued without cessation for 19 hours," Ormond reported, and the pillbox took several more hits. It "cracked, but did not collapse" — a commentary on German craftsmanship. The enemy also used gas shells three times during the night, and to make matters even worse, the weather was, according to the colonel, "most inclement."[15]

While the Tenth huddled in mud and misery in reserve, the Second Brigade's attack was launched on schedule. At 6:05 a.m., 126 18-pounders, 42 4.5-inch howitzers, and 67 larger-calibre guns opened fire, an impressive array of artillery to support a two-battalion assault. The infantrymen went over the top in a thick mist which soon turned to heavy rain; it rained so hard that some of the attackers had to crawl to their objectives. Major David Philpot, commanding British Columbia's 7th Battalion, on the right, reported that the rain fell all day, "making the whole terrain and system of trenches into one vast mud-hole and calling for the utmost limits of human endurance to carry on."[16]

Major Philpot's battalion overran Vindictive Crossroads, ably supported on its own right flank by the 20th (Central Ontario) Battalion, while the 8th Battalion captured Venture Farm, including four field guns. But there was trouble further to the left, where a timely counter-attack checked the advance of the British 1st Division. The British difficulties exposed the 8th Battalion's flank to severe enfilade fire, and the Little Black Devils, unable to continue their attack towards Hill 52, formed a defensive flank to return the fire.

At his headquarters at Bellevue, Colonel Ormond was unaware of these problems until the middle of the afternoon. Communications were continually cut during the enemy's prolonged bombardment, forcing the Battalion's signallers into the open to make repairs on severed telephone lines. The work of these men ensured that, as the colonel reported later, "connection was not lost for more than 20 to 25 minutes at a time." While the phone was out, the runners braved shell fire and mud to carry messages back and forth, but it was not until three o'clock in the afternoon that Ormond had his first intimation that all was not going well with the attack on Hill 52. At that time, he wrote, "the S.O.S. went up on both flanks of the Brigade and reports were received to the effect that the enemy were counter-attacking." Shortly afterwards, he was warned by the brigadier, General Loomis, to be prepared to reinforce the 7th and 8th battalions. The colonel promptly dispatched Lieutenant Charles

Brigadier-General Dan Ormond, CMG, DSO

FitzRoy to the headquarters of the 5th Battalion's Lieutenant-Colonel Paul Tudor, to find out what was going on. Lieutenant Fitzroy reported that the situation was "bad," and that the entire 5th Battalion had already been committed to the foundering attack.[17]

Ormond acted quickly. On his own initiative, he sent Major William Bingham and A Company to join Lieutenant Fitzroy at 5th Battalion headquarters. Major Bingham led the company through the mud and craters, but on reaching his destination was informed that there was a crisis on the left. The major was instructed to report to the 8th Battalion's Lieutenant-Colonel John Prower.[18]

By now, it was around five o'clock, and A Company had already suffered twenty-eight casualties. The rain had eased slightly, but the mud was truly horrendous, as a young Scottish-born private, Bill Walkinshaw, later attested. "The front line — there was no front line, just little shell holes, pockets in this mud. You never saw such mud, you never will see such mud."[19] Major Bingham led his troops into the 8th Battalion's supposed position, but could find no sign of Colonel Prower. A corporal, however, directed the men of the Fighting Tenth to the vicinity of Venture Farm, to shore up the Winnipeg unit's exposed flank.[20]

At this point, a terrible misunderstanding occurred. Major Bingham knew that he was merely reinforcing the 8th, but the Little Black Devils believed that they were being relieved. Bingham argued the point to no avail, and watched with dismay as the mud-caked survivors of the 8th pulled out and slogged to the rear, leaving A Company to hold an entire battalion's frontage. Undaunted, the major deployed his men in a dangerously thin line, linking up with the 7th Battalion to the right. But Bingham surely realized that it would be impossible to hold this position in the face of a counter-attack.[21]

Fortunately, Colonel Ormond came to the rescue. At six o'clock, having received no further information, he impatiently set out for Colonel Tudor's 5th Battalion headquarters. Along the way, he met men of the 8th, "who informed me that they had been relieved by the 10th Battalion." This was news to Ormond, of course, but he was sympathetic. "Their condition was pitiable, the shelling was very heavy," he later wrote. The 5th Battalion, he learned from Tudor, had been sent to the left of Venture Farm and to the support of the 7th, and the 8th's Colonel Prower arrived within minutes to add further details. As Ormond pieced together this information, an alarming picture took shape: A Company could be crushed unless help was sent, and fast. The three colonels considered their options, and Ormond agreed to take over the brigade's entire front line; the 7th Battalion would support his right flank, while the 5th backed up his centre and left. "This arrangement," the colonel wrote, "was arrived at after careful consideration of the posi-

tion and the state of the men, and at that time appeared to be what the G.O.C. [General Loomis] would have ordered if he had been present." Around six-thirty, Ormond ordered his remaining three companies into the front lines as soon as possible.[22]

It was a decisive move, and Ormond displayed admirable initiative in making it, but years later he expressed regrets. The left flank, far from being a danger point, offered what he considered to be a golden opportunity to roll up the enemy defences for a considerable distance. "Had we been lucky, we could've attacked to our flank," he remarked. "We were ready to do that, but when we had to go ahead and take the line, it spoiled a very good operation; it would've been a striking event. We were disappointed about that. We had an open flank of about twenty-five hundred to three thousand yards. We could have got right in behind them."[23] Instead, the Battalion was shoring up the front lines, trying to make good the day's gains.

Digging was a near-impossibility. The mud was "fantastic," according to Private George Moir, and a fellow private, William Curtis, readily agreed. "We

Passchendaele: (below) aerial photograph of water-filled shell holes and (above) ground-level view of the sodden battlefield.
Courtesy National Archives of Canada/PA-2165, RG9 III C3, volume 4091

were trying to dig. As fast as we dug one shovelful of mud out, two rolled in." A Lewis gunner, Private Scotty Murray, never forgot the frustration of working in the slime. "We dug holes, and you had a bully-beef tin to keep the water out — you had to keep throwing water out all the time. I was busy — you know how big a bully-beef tin is? — slipping water out, slipping water out, and when I finished I laid it up here, and old Heinie shot it out of my hand. That's the God's truth."[24]

Darkness, thankfully, was settling over the battle-field, but it would prove to be an eventful evening for the Fighting Tenth. Around seven-thirty, Captain Jack Mitchell, the twenty-one-year-old Winnipegger who commanded C Company, slipped and stumbled to Battalion headquarters. Captain Mitchell, who had originally come to the Tenth in the summer of 1915 as a lieutenant, had just rejoined the Battalion after spending much of 1917 attached to Second Brigade headquarters. Now, meeting Colonel Ormond, he had two complaints: not only was he dissatisfied with his line, but it was being shelled by the Canadian heavy artillery. While a runner was dispatched to call off the guns, Ormond went with Mitchell to have a look at the Battalion's positions.[25]

The colonel received a shock. He had been under the mistaken impression that Hill 52 had fallen earlier in the day, but as he slopped through the mud he "saw at once" that his front line was well short of the objective.[26]

Ormond immediately organized an attack. He instructed all three of the newly arrived companies, B, C, and D, to advance their line to include Hill 52, about 200 yards to the north. With the Canadian heavy artillery still dropping, according to the colonel, "about 4 shells per minute" into the Tenth's defences, no one objected to the move.[27]

It was completely impromptu but it worked, mainly because it took the enemy by surprise. As one Lewis gunner, Private Bob Alderman, recalled, the Germans' fire was not nearly as heavy as might have been expected. "The opposition seemed to come from way back of their lines, rather than from the front, I thought. That is, by machine-gun fire and mortars and whiz-bangs, and so forth, of that nature, you see." Of German soldiers, there were few. "I only saw a couple," said Private Alderman, whose experience was shared by others such as Private George Moir, who flatly declared that "I never seen a German at Passchendaele." It was a slow advance in the mud, but it did have certain advantages, as far as Private Samuel Hemphill was concerned. "It was soupy, you see, and it was really muddy, and when [the Germans] shelled us while we were making the attack, these shells were dropping in the mud and not exploding. It was just so muddy. There's no doubt about it, the mud kept us from having a lot more casualties."[28]

Colonel Ormond was never prouder of his men.

The Battalion, he recalled, "was the last one to be used in the Passchendaele salient by the Canadians, and we took Hill 52."[29] The higher ground was not only more secure, it was easier to work in. "We were able, then, to dig a nice trench in straight gravel," Private Curtis recalled. "Got out of the mud; a little higher, I guess."[30]

To hold its front of 1250 yards, the Fighting Tenth deployed all four companies in the line, each with three platoons forward and one in support. "Patrolling was not extensively carried out during the night," Colonel Ormond reported, because "we were satisfied with numerous posts pushed forward in shell-holes. The men were very tired but dug well."[31]

Having placed the Battalion in the best position possible under the circumstances, the colonel returned to his headquarters at Bellevue. When he got there, he was startled to find orders from General Loomis cancelling the relief that had just been carried out. However, the 8th Battalion's Colonel Prower had already gone back to brigade headquarters "to acquaint the G.O.C. of the situation." Since the brigadier's orders were obviously out-dated, "no other action was taken," Ormond later wrote.[32]

The night of 10 - 11 November was long and tiring. Having driven a deep salient into enemy territory, the Fighting Tenth was now paying the price for its success. "We were being shelled on three sides," complained Private Moir. "That was the whole trouble." Private Curtis added: "It was every man for himself, the gun fire was so heavy. They hammered the day-lights out of us."[33]

Casualties mounted steadily throughout the night. Private Moir was one of the injured, hit in the knee as he lay huddled in a shell hole. "We got up to the top of the hill there," he remembered, "and I'm sure it was one of our shells that got me."[34] A Lewis gunner, Private Bob Alderman, was also hurt. "I got wounded by a whiz-bang dropping in front of my little billet that I was trying to dig in and put a [piece] of machine-gun through my leg. That's what really wounded me, was bits of the machine-gun going through my legs."[35] Neither Moir nor Alderman returned to action.

Another injured man was a newcomer to the Battalion. Twenty-one year-old Private Thomas Rattray never forgot his brief stint in combat:

We used to take turns as observer in an O.P. [observation post] just above the trench. I was lucky it was my turn. All my chums were killed down in that muddy trench. We did not know what hit us. I was the only survivor, though I did receive chest and leg wounds. Six men carried me out, walking up to their knees in mud, lugging me out.

Some old German dugouts in the reserve line were used for the wounded. An officer was killed while trying to put a tourniquet on me. I layed [sic] there a long time before the stretcher-bearer party had arrived. The mud oozed over me.

I noticed how full the dugouts were of wounded men. A lot of men died right in the dugouts. There wasn't enough room for myself and some others, so we had to lay outside. That was luck, because I was among the first to be put in those horse drawn ambulances.

Private Rattray survived, but his war was over.[36]

As Rattray's experience indicates, Passchendaele was a nightmare for stretcher-bearers. One of these was Private Bill Walkinshaw, a twenty-three-year-old Scot who had joined the unit the previous April.

This famous photograph, which carries the caption "Jolly Canadian", exemplifies the post-Passchendaele spirit of the Fighting Tenth.
Courtesy National Archives of Canada/PA-3678

That was my worst experience. We went up that line, up that night, and through mud, shell holes, and shelling up to a forward dugout, which had been reversed and taken over from the Germans — the front line was just a short [way] ahead of that. Then we were detailed to carry back — and there were a lot of them — wounded.

Quite a few of the stretcher-bearers never did get back, because that road was continuously under shell fire, and it was raining, and I saw several stretchers and their bearers fall into these mud holes. You'd see men drowned on that road even.

Well, that was my worst experience in the war, carrying — and I'm not a very big man —

carrying men on my shoulders. We had to carry them for a mile back.[37]

Whether a stretcher-bearer, or a wounded man being carried to the rear, no one who followed the plank road ever forgot it. "There was nothing but dead," observed Private George Moir, his shattered knee bound in blood-stained dressings, "dead horses and dead everything on that road." Lieutenant Hugh Pearson, who had been so unnerved by the enemy air raid before the battle, was no happier to be in charge of a stretcher detail. "Boy, that was a miserable few days," he recalled. "A shell hole full of water — you didn't know whether you were going to step on a piece of mud or a dead mule or what it was going to be, under the water."[38]

Colonel Ormond appreciated his men's plight. Although in later years he believed that Passchendaele's reputation as a horror show "has probably been exaggerated," he noted that "it wasn't a Sunday afternoon at the beach," either. "It was tough going, but we'd been in there for three years, pretty near, and this was just another job. It was hard on the men, it was tiring. It was heavy going, there was no question about that, so that even sandbags were a heavy thing to carry." Ormond recalled that one man's greatcoat, after he came out of the line, "weighed forty-seven pounds, with the water and the mud."[39]

Despite the mud, there were few instances of weapons jamming in action. This was due to improvised precautions, as the colonel reported: "Small loose semi-water proof sacks were used over muzzles of rifles and found to be the best protection and absolutely indispensible [sic]. They were slipped over the bayonet and shot through when necessity demanded without damage to the rifle. Old socks were used on the breech and gave good satisfaction." Lewis guns were also protected, "carried wrapped in the ordinary ground sheet, which this Unit accepts as the best way to carry a gun in action under the conditions that prevailed. The result was that not a single gun was out of action on account of dirt."* In the course of the fighting, three Lewis guns were knocked out by shell fire, and another was damaged, but the latter was repaired with parts from the wrecked weapons.[41]

The rest of the night was marked by sporadic shelling. When the Germans tried to organize a counter-attack, the darkness proved to be an insurmountable obstacle. Mired in the mud and attempting to scale the slight heights of the ridge, the enemy now faced the same problems the Canadians had dealt with earlier. And the Fighting Tenth was eager to capitalize on those problems: when the Germans were heard assembling on the Canadian right flank, they "were scattered by Lewis Gun and rifle fire."[42]

---

* The Tenth's success in this regard contrasts sharply with the problems experienced by the 5th and 8th battalions. "The Rifles became choked with mud and useless," reported Colonel Tudor of the 5th, while the 8th's Colonel Prower noted that his troops found it "most difficult to keep rifles and Lewis Guns clean."[40]

At dawn on Sunday, 11 November — who could have guessed that the war would be over in precisely one year? — the Battalion made a slight adjustment of its front. At Colonel Ormond's direction, the right-hand companies advanced over the crest of the ridge, a manoeuvre which gave the Tenth "command of the whole slope on our right front."[43]

It resulted in several determined efforts by the Germans to dislodge the infuriating Canadians. The first attempt was made around seven-thirty that morning, when a group of twenty-five of the enemy advanced in extended order. The Germans were allowed to approach to within fifty yards of the Battalion's front line, before they were pinned down by small-arms fire. Lieutenant Jack Clark and a handful of other ranks took advantage of the enemy's momentary confusion to slip around their flank. When Lieutenant Clark attacked, the Germans were routed. Several were killed and one was captured; the rest fled, dragging their wounded with them.

Another counter-attack later Sunday morning was stopped by small-arms and artillery fire before it could get properly started. Then, around eleven o'clock, German troops were observed collecting by twos and threes to the north and east. "The artillery was turned on with splendid results," wrote Colonel Ormond, "and our Lewis Guns on the Left flank did most gratifying execution on the enemy who bolted."[44]

More troublesome was the work of German air-craft and artillery. Colonel Ormond was mystified by the performance of British fighters in the air, noting that they seemed to be "very much harrassed by the enemy." On the other hand, he pointed out that German "planes were very active, flew very low," but were driven off by the Battalion's Lewis guns. The Germans also made extensive use of poison-gas shells, one of which made a direct hit on the pulverized pill-box which served as Ormond's headquarters. Private Jesse Webb was wounded by the shell burst, and later died; Ormond reported that "it was most difficult to keep his respirator in place. It is not known if he died from gas or his wounds." Several members of the Battalion developed gas blisters within ninety-six hours, "but not more than 6 cases of lung and throat cases have appeared."[45]

The Tenth's position gradually improved as the day progressed. The main concern was the left flank, where the British 1st Division had failed to keep pace with the previous day's advance. But the plucky British persisted on Sunday, and by noon had closed the gap considerably, although, as Colonel Ormond noted, "200 to 300 yards separated our posts." Later, the colonel summoned assistance from the 5th Battalion, which sent a party to reinforce vulnerable Venture Farm.[46]

There was also a problem on the right, but this did not become apparent until late in the afternoon. When Ormond learned that his right flank was not in touch with the neighbouring 20th (Central Ontario) Battalion, he ordered a platoon under Lieutenant Norman Henderson to fill the hole. Lieutenant Henderson, a thirty-five-year-old Manitoban who had been shot through the thigh but refused to go to the rear for treatment, posted his platoon as instructed. However, it was evident that even "this disposition was not satisfactory," in Ormond's opinion.[47]

The effort to further improve it cost the Fighting Tenth one of its outstanding officers. Colonel Ormond dispatched Captain Charles Costigan to report to Major W.R. Bertram, the officer commanding the 20th Battalion, and arrange a suitable junction between the two units. Captain Costigan, accompanied by Private William Beggs, carried out his assignment, but on the return trip he ignored Private Beggs's advice to keep close to the Canadian front line. Working their way through no man's land, they ran into a German patrol. In the fire fight that followed, Costigan and Beggs became separated. Beggs escaped, and was afterwards awarded the DCM, but the captain was not so fortunate. Costigan was listed as missing in action, but it was later determined that he had been killed.[48]

The Battalion grieved at the loss of Charles Telford Costigan. Nicknamed "Pat," the English-born, thirty-seven-year-old Costigan had been one of the unit's originals, going to England as its paymaster. As a divisional field cashier, he had rejoined the Fighting Tenth at Ypres, locking his pay chest and serving as a combat officer when the Battalion was cut to pieces in the attack on Kitcheners Wood. Afterwards, Costigan had distinguished himself in trench raids, being recommended for a Victoria Cross and winning the DSO and MC. Wounded at both Festubert and Vimy Ridge, he had also served as the Second Brigade's grenade officer and commanded a trench-mortar battery for much of 1916 and 1917 before rejoining the Tenth

Railway station, Bouilly-Grenay
Courtesy National Archives of Canada/PA-2114

153

prior to Passchendaele. Now the man described by Lord Beaverbrook as "a medium-sized officer of the most charming manners"[49] lay dead in the Flanders mud.

It was dark by the time Private Beggs was able to get back to the Battalion, and he found its relief was under way. The 52nd and 58th battalions, both from Ontario, were taking over the Tenth's front, and completed the move by eight o'clock Sunday night. Exhausted, soaked, and shivering, the troops of the Tenth marched to the rear, following the flimsy duckboards and then the battered plank road. The Germans bade farewell to the Battalion by staging an air raid on its transport lines near Ypres. Enemy bombs killed one man and wounded four others; eight horses also died.[50]

The Fighting Tenth spent the night near Wieltje, at C Camp, "where the conditions were very bad," as Colonel Ormond complained, and shell fire "was more or less trying."[51] On Monday morning, 12 November, the Battalion left the Ypres salient for the last time. Marching to Ypres, the unit boarded trains for Brandhoek, taking up billets in Derby Camp by early afternoon. Its ordeal at Passchendaele was finally over.[52]

In fact, the Flanders offensive had ended, too. With Passchendaele firmly in British hands, Field-Marshal Haig called off further operations, and the Canadian Corps was ordered to return to the Lens-Arras sector for the winter. The Fighting Tenth, which had not been expected to participate in the attack, was the last battalion in the entire BEF to be committed to action in the Flanders campaign.

No military campaign in history has generated the kind of controversy that Passchendaele brought about. Even today, the very word strikes sensitive nerves in the ongoing debate over its merits. His many political opponents used the mud-plagued battle to bludgeon Sir Douglas Haig's reputation after the war, but Colonel Ormond was not among the field-marshal's detractors. "It would appear that Haig had not received as full information as he should have, or he wouldn't have kept on going," Ormond later commented. "On the other hand, it was a gamble, and an unlucky one. And the weather was against them. Had they had ordinary luck, they'd have got the Channel ports, they'd have got through to Antwerp, in the summer of '17." In any case, he observed, Passchendaele served its purpose in this terrible war of attrition. "You've seen heavyweight boxers going at it, giving each other everything they can, and they stand up to each other. And it's whoever can stand it longest that wins, or has a lucky stroke and gets the other fellow out. Well, the same way with a war of attrition."[53]

The Tenth Battalion in training, April 1918

Courtesy National Archives of Canada/PA-2624, 2625

154

Few, if any, of his men felt the same way. Most would have agreed with the weary stretcher-bearer, Private Bill Walkinshaw, who summed up Passchendaele succinctly and bitterly: "It was a useless waste of life."[54]

Colonel Ormond was more concerned about the lack of recognition for members of the Battalion. The Fighting Tenth took Hill 52 despite horrific battlefield conditions and considerable confusion but few of the men received medals. "The Unit had no opportunity to execute any brilliant moves," Ormond later wrote, "but many Officers and other ranks performed most gallant acts in connection with saving of lives of men who were buried by shell fire, and caring for wounded." He singled out Major William Bingham, who "showed exceptional initiative in executing the pushing forward of our line on the left flank and in supervising the formation of a Front Line"; Major George Ferguson, a supernumerary; Lieutenant Norman Henderson, who had remained in action despite a serious wound; and the medical officer, Captain Allen McNair, who "worked for 54 hours unceasingly." However, the only officer decorated was C Company's heroic Captain Jack Mitchell, who was awarded the MC. Other ranks did somewhat better, winning one DCM (Private William Beggs) and eighteen MMs, including bars to medals won at Hill 70 by Sergeant William Keith and Private Charles Lee. The remaining MMs were awarded to Sergeant James Parry; Corporal E.R. Hughes; Lance-Corporal Richard Chandler (148157); and Privates James Atkinson, George Brown, Robert Catte, Thomas Campbell, Richard Chandler (22558), Charles Haydon, Frank Honey, Alexander McInnes, George McLanders, Joseph Mitchell, Jack O'Hearne, John Smith, and Frederick Tuffnell.

Perhaps the best thing that can be said about Passchendaele was that, as far as the Tenth Battalion was concerned, the casualties were remarkably light. The final toll came to 154: 33 dead, 104 wounded, and 17 missing.[55] Considering the battlefield conditions and the heavy shell fire which the Battalion had to endure, it was an unusually short casualty list. But, as always, many brave men had fallen, including Captain Costigan and RSM Watchman, and three MM-winners, Corporals Edward Flynn and Edwin Martindale and Private Harry Baxter.

The very day that the Fighting Tenth went into action at Passchendaele, the Battalion made the front page of the Calgary *Daily Herald*. Or, to be precise, a former member of the unit did so. His name was Omar Macklem, a man of rather unsavoury character who joined the Tenth on 26 October 1915. As a private, "his letters home contained such prodigious lies that on one occasion the battalion was paraded and his letter read out to his comrades." A thirty-one-year-old Ontarian, Private Macklem was something of an

expert at crown and anchor, the outlawed game of chance that was so popular among the soldiers.

Macklem's story got even more interesting after his departure from the Battalion on 8 January 1916.[56] Posted to a Canadian army base as a munitions worker, he was eventually wounded. His face terribly disfigured, Macklem convalesced in England. By the time he had recovered, he had charmed and schemed his way into high social circles in London and was rubbing elbows with the titled elite. "He was the most wonderful actor of our time," recalled one hoodwinked nobleman. "Everybody believed him and received him."

He was, indeed, a prodigious liar. Macklem not only claimed to be a colonel, but convinced his wealthy friends that he had won both the DCM and Croix de Guerre. He repeated these lies so often and so convincingly that Canadian Military Headquarters in London confirmed them when discreet inquiries were made about his credibility. This set the stage for his biggest lie, that he had invented "a fool-proof hand grenade" and sold it to the War Office for $100,000. Spinning his web of deceit, Macklem ingratiated himself with some of the richest people in London, charming them out of substantial funds in support of a variety of nefarious projects that were supposed to aid the war effort but actually padded his bank accounts.

One of his victims was Vicountess Mastland. "I gave Macklem letters of introduction", she later explained, "believing his story of the invention of the grenade fuse was true, after inquiries at Canadian headquarters, where I was told that he was genuine. I prefer to leave subsequent events to speak for themselves."

Macklem's success proved to be his undoing. He became the subject of much interest, which led to newspaper articles about his alleged accomplishments. These stories eventually reached the Fighting Tenth. Knowing of his questionable character, and wishing to dissociate itself from him, the Battalion filed protests with the appropriate authorities. Embarrassed, Canadian Military Headquarters discharged Macklem and shipped him home as soon as possible. Lieutenant-General Sir Richard Turner, who commanded the Canadian forces in the United Kingdom, explained that Macklem's extraordinary behaviour was undoubtedly due to his war injury, which was practically the only thing about the man that was genuine. But General Turner was unable to explain the laxity of his subordinates who inadvertently aided and abetted Macklem's intrigues. Bemused officials at the Canadian War Records Office in London, when questioned by reporters about Macklem, merely referred to him as "the fake colonel."

For a while, Macklem managed to stay one step ahead of his reputation. After his return to Canada, his stature was such that he was selected to head a

Officers of the Fighting Tenth, April 1918.
Top row (l-r): Lieut. Frederick Noland, Lieut. Benjamin Skinner, Capt. Ralph Harrison (padre), unidentified French officer, Lieut. William Hamilton, Lieut. Frank Rump, Lieut. Gerald Flinn, Lieut. George Guthrie, Lieut. William Oliver, Lieut. Douglas Thomson, Lieut. Charles FitzRoy, Lieut. St. Clair Fisher, Lieut. Norman MacEachern, Lieut. Frederick Rowley, Lieut. William Hedges, RSM Jack Nuttall.
Middle row: Lieut. Ralph Feurt, Lieut. Gordon Graham, Capt. Frank Costello, Capt. Hugh Pearson, Capt. Leo Carey, Maj. William Bingham, Maj. Eric MacDonald, Lt-Col. Dan Ormond, Capt. Jack Mitchell, Maj. Hugh Ferguson, Capt. Edward Milne, Capt. Allen McNair (medical officer), Capt. Thomas Fawcett (paymaster), Lieut. Herbert Andrews.
Bottom row: Lieut. Bertram Godden, Lieut. Bernard McDaniel, Lieut. David McAndie, Lieut. Robert Donald, Lieut. Ernest Vose, Lieut. Thomas Dale, Lieut. Sidney Grimble, Lieut. David Teviotdale, Lieut. Jack Clark, Lieut. Herbert Booth.

British government mission involved in top-secret negotiations with the United States. Talks were under way in Detroit when London belatedly realized that Macklem was a phoney. He was hastily replaced.

Returning to Toronto, he enjoyed a carefree lifestyle, profligately spending on himself and his friends the money which he had acquired by such devious means in England. Acquaintances noted that before he volunteered to go overseas, Macklem had been virtually penniless.[57] Following the war, he moved to Montreal, where his mailing address was the American Commercial Association.

After leaving the Ypres salient, the Fighting Tenth licked its wounds at Derby Camp for two days. The weather remained dull and cold, and the troops "devot[ed] most of their time to cleaning up." The sun was shining when the Battalion departed on Wednesday, 14 November, boarding buses at Brandhoek for Lesart-Merville, where it spent the night before moving on to Fouquereuil. There, on the sixteenth, the men were treated to a luxurious shower and an issue of fresh, clean clothing. At pay parade that afternoon, all ranks received fifty francs as "additional Christmas Pay." Then the Battalion moved to the vicinity of Lens, settling into billets at Vancouver Camp near Château de la Haie during the afternoon of 18 November. Just a week had passed since it had pulled out of the front lines at Passchendaele.[58]

Its stay at Vancouver Camp was brief and activities strictly routine: cleaning equipment, repainting helmets, medical inspections, and bath parades, as well as the usual training. For the riflemen, this included instruction in "Bayonet Fighting." As usual, the Lewis gunners and signallers underwent separate instruction.[59]

Then, on Thursday, 22 November, the Battalion moved into the trenches. The weather was wet and cold as the Fighting Tenth relieved the 4th (Central Ontario) Battalion in the front lines opposite Lens. The 4th was grieving over the loss of its commanding officer, Lieutenant-Colonel Alexander Thomson, who had been killed by a sniper three days before. The Tenth shared in the 4th's grief, because the thirty-year-old native of Scotland had spent two years with the western unit, rising from lieutenant to major and winning the DSO and MC, before departing in June for his new command.

Thomson's death seemed to accentuate the grey bleakness of this neighbourhood, so close to the scene of the Battalion's triumph in mid-August. A and D companies took over the forward trenches, before switching with B and C in the support position four days later. This tour, which featured the first snowfall of winter, was marked by a couple of minor episodes. On 25 November, Canadian engineers supervised the firing of 600 gas drums* into Lens. As a precautionary measure, the men of the Tenth were required to wear their gas masks for several hours. The next day, a German patrol was detected in no man's land, but it was dispersed by a few well-aimed grenades. The enemy artillery became noticeably more active on the

---

* The drum employed by the British consisted of a thirty-one-pound cylinder filled with thirty pounds of poison gas, fired by a Livens projector. Similar to a mortar, the Livens projector was a tube up to four feet long which was buried in the ground up to its muzzle. They were placed at a forty-five-degree angle, in batteries of twenty-five. Fitted with percussion fuses, the drums had a range of one mile.

last day of November, when the tour ended. Relieved by British Columbia's 7th Battalion, the Tenth filed quickly and quietly out of its trenches and marched to the rear, gratefully noting that it had not suffered a single casualty.[60]

A quiet week awaited the Battalion. In brigade support at Liévin, the Tenth provided large working parties on a daily basis, building new trenches and improving existing fortifications. Long-range shelling by the Germans "did no apparent damage," according to the war diary.[61]

On 8 December, a frosty Saturday, the Fighting Tenth made its final front-line appearance of 1917. Taking over from the 7th Battalion during the evening without incident, the Tenth spent three days in the trenches, and for the second tour in a row escaped unscathed. When it was relieved by the 15th (48th Highlanders of Canada) Battalion on the evening of 11 December, the unit marched by column of fours to Vancouver Camp.[62]

Voting in the federal election highlighted its stay here. While the civilian vote in Canada took place on 17 December, the soldiers on active service cast their ballots earlier. The men of the Fighting Tenth exercised their right to vote on Friday, 14 December, with polling booths opening at 9 a.m. and closing at 5 p.m. There was much interest in the election, not only because the main issue was conscription, but because Major Lee Redman, who had been one of the Battalion's originals until he was wounded at Kitcheners Wood, was running as a candidate in Calgary East.[63] Redman, his left arm shattered, had pledged to "support the Union Government in the prosecution of the war, and devote my time, attention and ability to furthering the legitimate objects of soldiers." He won a ringing endorsement from that controversial Calgary newspaperman, Bob Edwards, who wrote: "In him the boys will have a sympathetic friend to whom they can always turn freely, frankly and as soldier to soldier, with no B.S. in the offing."[64]*

Winter arrived in earnest on 16 December with a heavy snowfall, and it was still snowing when the Tenth vacated Vancouver Camp for Noulette Huts, a two-hour march away. After a day of lectures and training, the Battalion moved into huts at nearby Houdain, where it spent its third Christmas in France, the fourth since leaving Canada. While the days alternated between sunshine and sleet, it was consistently cold, and "several stoves etc. were placed in huts and billets to add to the comfort of the men."[66]

An unusual Christmas celebration was planned. Each company staged its own dinner: D on Christmas Eve, B on Christmas Day, C on Boxing Day, and A on 27 December. Colonel Ormond attended each gathering and during his speech to the troops read the "personally written" greetings from the commander-in-chief, Sir Douglas Haig, "wishing all ranks the compliments of The Season." The unusual arrangement was, in Ormond's opinion, "one of the most successful ever held since this unit has been on active service."[67]

Christmas interrupted a rigorous training schedule, which resumed on the twenty-seventh. The last day in December was typical, according to the war diary:

> Training was carried out from 6.30 A.M. to 3.00 P.M. consisting of: Dress and Interior Economy under supervision of Company Officers. Route March by Companies. Specialist Officers delivered $1/2$ hour lectures on the following subjects: Sanitation, Bombing, Lewis Guns and Scouting. Special instruction classes on grenades were held under supervision of the Battalion Bombing Officer. Signallers, Lewis Gunners and Scouts carried out training under their respective commanders.[68]

New Year's Day brought another brief interruption. On this chilly holiday Tuesday, the only scheduled activity was pay parade, and the first day of 1918 was capped by a brass-band concert put on by the artillery at nearby Brunay.[69]

It was back to training on 2 January. There were, however, a few pleasant diversions. Colonel Ormond lectured all ranks on the Battalion's history, and there was a bath parade on the fourth, followed on the fifth by a soccer game with the 2nd Canadian Field Ambulance. (The game was won by the Fighting Tenth by a 5-1 score.)

On Monday, 7 January, the Battalion moved via light railway to St. Lawrence Camp near Château de la Haie, where musketry was added to the programme. Each company went to the rifle range and "fired 5 rounds application at 100–200–300 yards and 10 rounds rapid at 200 yards." On the fourteenth, General Currie came to visit the Battalion.[70]

The Corps commander was a deeply troubled man. Just three days earlier, he had learned of a proposal that would, if carried out, radically alter the organization of Canada's fighting forces. Canadian Military Headquarters in London advocated the reduction of each of the four combat divisions from twelve to nine battalions, as already implemented in British divisions. Unlike the British, who were getting desperate for manpower and broke up 141 battalions

---

* More than 90 per cent of the soldier's vote went to Prime Minister Sir Robert Borden's Union government, a coalition of Conservatives and Liberals, which won a convincing victory and implemented conscription in early 1918. Major Redman, who had returned to his law practice after recovering from his wounds in 1916, won his seat in the House of Commons by the second-largest majority in Alberta. When the Commons reconvened in February 1918, Redman was given the honour of moving the address in reply to the Speech from the Throne. The major responded with what the Ottawa *Journal* called an "unusually able" oration.[65]

in order to provide reinforcements for the remaining units, the Canadian plan was to take its surplus battalions and, with the Fifth Division which was in England, form a small field army of six divisions, in two corps. Currie vigorously opposed the reorganization, arguing that it would impair rather than improve Canadian military efficiency.

By early February, his view had prevailed: not only was the Canadian Corps kept intact, but the persuasive Currie actually convinced the authorities to add 100 trained men to the establishment of every Canadian battalion. Colonel Ormond, in whom Currie confided, fully supported the Corps commander on this issue. "Currie had the strength and the foresight to buck that to the limit," he recalled half a century later. "You see, that would have put your overhead out of all proportion to the number of troops. You'd have increased your headquarters; you've got no more efficiency." This was a purely political manoeuvre, and Ormond resisted efforts by Currie's opponents to enlist his endorsement for the proposed reorganization. "Oh, I had people other than Currie approach me, putting forward the idea of having six divisions and suggesting that I would get a brigade right away. Well, I wasn't interested a bit, compared with finishing the war and doing it efficiently."[71]

By the middle of January 1918, more than a month had passed since the Fighting Tenth had occupied the front-line trenches, and a return appearance was imminent. On 18 January, the Battalion made its move towards the front by shifting to Braquemont, settling into billets in time to avoid a chilling afternoon rainstorm. Two days later, it moved again, this time to Bouilly-Grenay for three days. Then it shifted to Mazingarbe, closer still to the front lines.[72]

During the evening of Saturday, 26 January, the Fighting Tenth made its first tour of the trenches in 1918. Relieving the 7th Battalion near Loos, the Tenth found itself in familiar surroundings; the sector included Hill 70, the scene of its brilliant battle the previous summer. This was a relatively quiet front, and for the third tour in a row, the Battalion suffered not a single casualty. Thursday, 31 January, typified the experience: "The situation was very quiet throughout the day, except for enemy artillery which fired a number of rounds into our Support trenches and into Loos, no damage being done. Our artillery fired into the enemy Front and Support positions at intervals during the day." That night, the 16th (Canadian Scottish) Battalion relieved the Fighting Tenth, which moved to billets in Fosse 10 on the Arras-Bethune road.[73]

The Battalion spent a week at Fosse 10, in weather which was generally clear and cool. There were bath and pay parades, and the ever-present training stressed manoeuvres by platoons. As well, much time was devoted to what the war diary calls "general smartening up drill." On 7 February, the Battalion divided into halves for rifle practice on the ranges at Braquemont and Hersin. That night, the reconstituted regimental band staged a concert at the cinema hut at Sains-en-Gohelle. "The concert was a great success," notes the war diary, merely hinting at the emotions that must have been present, as the strains of "Colonel Bogey's March" brought back memories of the awful day in May when the band had been wiped out.[74]

It had taken months to rebuild. Within three weeks of the disaster, Colonel Ormond had apparently made arrangements to acquire the twenty-five-man band belonging to the 254th Battalion, based in England.[75] But this deal had fallen through, and the colonel had entered into long, tiresome negotiations with divisional and Corps headquarters and with the authorities in London. That these talks were less than satisfying was revealed by a note written to Lieutenant-Colonel William Armstrong, the veteran from Calgary who at that time commanded the 9th Reserve Battalion at Bramshott. "We have a chance to get a band," Ormond confided in September, "but they want us to pay the sgt. $55.00 per month over his pay — and enter into a great old agreement that would tie my estate up forever."[76]

Instead, he chose to reconstruct the band by awaiting the return of its injured musicians, bringing in new men to replace the dead, and equipping it with second-hand instruments. "I cannot afford at the present time to purchase a complete set of new instruments," he wrote, "and my efforts to get same through the Canadian Authorities have been without success."[77] The band's performance indicated that his patient efforts had paid handsome dividends.

While the Battalion was at Fosse 10, there was a foreshadowing of the colonel's future. On 5 February, Ormond left to take temporary command of the Second Brigade, and Major Eric MacDonald looked after the Battalion. Ormond returned three days later, but he was clearly being evaluated for promotion.

The same day that Colonel Ormond returned from brigade headquarters, 8 February, the Fighting Tenth moved into the forward area in the Cité Saint-Emile sector, halfway between Lens and Hill 70. The relief of the 1st (Western Ontario) Battalion in the trenches near Bouilly-Grenay proved tragic. An officer in the advance party was wounded and two other ranks were killed by enemy shell fire, the first losses suffered by the Battalion since its departure from Passchendaele nearly two months before.[78]

There was plenty of hard work to be done. "Every available man was employed on work parties, wiring the forward area, digging and improving trenches and reclaiming the old unused dug-outs," reads the war diary. "The parties commenced at 6.00 P.M. and worked until the early hours of the morning." German shelling was sporadic, but a random shell burst on 16 February claimed the life of one man.[79]

158

The following night, the Fighting Tenth returned to the front lines in Cité Saint-Emile, a suburb of Lens. Fine, clear weather conditions gave way to cold, steady rain, which was a blessing in disguise, as it minimized enemy aerial and artillery activity. As a result, the Battalion again recorded no losses during its front-line tour, although its previous stint in support had cost four casualties, three of them fatal.[80]

Relieved by the 14th (Royal Montreal Regiment) Battalion on the evening of 24 February, the Tenth moved into divisional reserve at Bouilly-Grenay, 2000 yards behind the front lines. Here everyone was given a hot shower and a clean change of underwear, followed by pay parade and kit inspection. Then it was back to rigorous training, including extensive work on the musketry ranges. On Friday, 1 March, the Battalion staged a practice attack with tanks, and that night Colonel Ormond hosted the tank officers at dinner at his headquarters at Château Bouilly-Grenay.[81]

Ormond had been a tank enthusiast since first seeing them in 1916. The tank was a weapon with enormous potential, as demonstrated at Cambrai in November 1917,* but the colonel was only too aware of the severe limitations of these thirty-ton mechanical monsters. "The greatest advantage the infantry got out of them was the crushing the wire," he later commented, "to put the wire so that the infantry could pass over it. The principal reason the infantry wasn't keen on them — they were so easily stalled, and they were so slow, and they drew fire." Limited communications contributed to the difficulty of effectively employing tanks in battle, as Ormond pointed out: "for the infantry to guide them it was a case of getting up behind them and tapping on them and getting somebody to do something. And they were quite noisy, about the same as a bulldozer, the same noise."[82]

On Monday, 4 March, the Fighting Tenth abandoned its billets at Bouilly-Grenay. The Battalion moved into brigade reserve behind Hill 70, relieving Ontario's 1st Battalion, which was commanded by Walt Sparling, who had formerly served with the Tenth. As usual, working parties were detailed nightly. "The work consisted of Wiring and strengthening defences, deepening and improving trenches etc." These activities were hampered by the enemy's liberal use of gas shells, which remained a minor but annoying problem when the Battalion took over the front lines on 10 March. "The night was very dark and made the move rather difficult," says the war diary, but the relief was completed without loss.[83]

A night raid highlighted this tour. Planned and organized by Major MacDonald, who conducted a dar-

ing daylight reconnaissance in no man's land, the raid itself was led by Lieutenant Hugh Pearson on the night of 12 March. Lieutenant Pearson took into action forty other ranks drawn from B, C, and D companies, organizing them into four parties, each under a lieutenant: Frederick Noland, Frank Rump, Jack Clark, and Victor Evans.

The raiders were treated to a hot meal at Battalion headquarters in the early evening, then each party filed into the trenches and, guided by a scout, took up positions in no man's land after dark. There, they waited for the barrage scheduled for 9 p.m. Each man carried his rifle and bayonet, a bandolier of small-arms ammunition, and eight Mills bombs or rifle grenades. The raiders also carried seven ten-pound "Mobile Charges" for demolishing dugouts. Except for identity discs, they wore no identification; distinguishing patches were removed from jackets, and officers were ordered to collect "pay books, letters etc. containing information about the owner."[84]

The barrage opened precisely on time. "The usual display of flares went up from the enemy lines," Lieutenant Pearson later reported, "but they seemed to be sent up from some distance behind the front line. Enemy machine guns were very active for the first minute but our trench mortars and 'heavies' effectively silenced them." Then the raiders, running at a crouch, dashed through the gaps cut in the enemy wire and disappeared from Pearson's view in the smoke and darkness.[85]

They enjoyed mixed results. Lieutenant Evans's party had no success whatever. "They had encountered gas," recounted Pearson, "or what they thought was gas and put on their masks, and then apparently became confused and failing to get into the enemy trench, returned" within six minutes. On the other hand, Lieutenant Rump's raiders had a field day. Rump, the first man into the trench, barged into a dugout, where he and Private John Robertson shot two Germans, killing one and wounding the other, who was brought back as a prisoner. Then, using explosives, Rump and Private Walter Holley destroyed five dugouts before retiring.[86]

The whole operation was over by 9:35 p.m. The cost was five wounded, including Lieutenant Clark, who stayed in action despite two wounds in his neck; several others showed the effects of gas poisoning two days later.[87] Major MacDonald and Lieutenants Rump and Clark won the MC as a result of the raid, and the DCM was awarded to Private Michael Kosko for helping the injured Clark keep his party intact, then carrying a wounded comrade on his back for 250 yards.

---

* The British Third Army, under the former Canadian Corps commander, General Sir Julian Byng, staged a large-scale attack near Cambrai using several hundred tanks. The attackers achieved complete surprise, because the tanks enabled them to dispense with the customary preliminary bombardment to destroy the German barbed wire. However, the results were not particularly impressive. The British failed to capture key features such as Bourlon Wood, and the Germans recaptured most of the lost ground in violent counter-attacks at the end of the month.

MMs were given to Privates Robertson and Holley, who were so helpful to Rump. But Colonel Ormond was somewhat disappointed in the outcome, which he blamed on the Germans. "The lack of greater success," he wrote, "was due to the lack of resistance by the enemy, who was holding his line very lightly, and very few of his men could be found."[88]

There were other instances of bravery by members of the Battalion during this tour. Lieutenant Charles FitzRoy, the unit's intelligence officer, went on several daylight missions into no man's land. On one of them, Lieutenant FitzRoy and two other ranks slipped over their parapet, worked their way through the barbed-wire entanglements, entered the German trench opposite, then followed it for sixty yards. The trio was challenged by a sentry, who was shot by FitzRoy, before the Canadians scrambled back to the safety of their own lines. FitzRoy won the MC for this performance. The DCM was awarded to Private Lloyd Graham, who encountered an enemy sniping post during a daytime patrol. As he examined the sniping plate — a piece of armour plating with a viewing slit — a rifle was thrust through it, right in Private Graham's face. "He immediately seized the rifle [and] tore it from the German. He jumped over the parapet and killed this German. He threw a bomb at another fleeing German and killed him." Later the same day, Graham helped to wipe out an enemy observation post in no man's land.[89]

The rest of the tour was comparatively uneventful, and the only other casualties occurred during the relief by the 2nd (Eastern Ontario) Battalion on 20 March, when two other ranks were injured by shell fire. Relieved by midnight, the Fighting Tenth marched to Fosse 10, where the next two days were "spent in cleaning up and making billets as comfortable as possible for the men." As well, there was the usual regimen of bath and pay parades, before resuming a comprehensive training programme on 23 March.[90]

Under normal circumstances, the Battalion would have remained at Fosse 10 for several days. But the situation on the Western Front was far from normal, although no one in the Tenth realized it yet.

The BEF was facing its gravest crisis of the entire war. Over-extended and undermanned, thanks to well-intentioned but damaging political interference, the British armies in France had borne the brunt of a massive German offensive launched on 21 March. The long-expected attack fell on a fifty-mile sector held by the BEF's Third and Fifth armies, but what was not anticipated was the extent of the success enjoyed by the Germans, who plunged twenty-five miles in six days and crushed the Fifth Army in the process. Two days passed before the British high command recognized the magnitude of the crisis.

For the Fighting Tenth, the first hint of trouble came during the afternoon of Saturday, 23 March. B Company had been sent to the rifle range at Marqueffles Farm, but was recalled when Colonel Ormond received "an urgent movement order" from the Second Brigade. By 5:20 p.m., the Battalion had assembled on the main road and marched in the bright sunshine for Château de la Haie, where it was accommodated at St. Lawrence Camp.[91]

Sunday, 24 March, passed quietly. Following divine services in the morning, the men spent the afternoon engaged in games of soccer and baseball, taking advantage of the continuing fine weather. Training resumed the following day, but 26 March brought a reminder of the grave situation. During the early-morning hours, the Battalion was instructed to stand to arms "and be ready to move at one hour's notice after 5.30 AM." The day's training schedule was cancelled, and the officers ensured that the entire unit was battle-ready. Throughout the day, orders were issued and countermanded.[92]

The reason for the confusion was that the Canadian Corps was being broken up to bolster the beleaguered British line. The First Canadian Division had been assigned to the British XVII Corps, in the Third Army. The division's marching orders directed it to the Arras-Cambrai road, just south of Vimy.

The Fighting Tenth formed up at 7:45 a.m. on Wednesday, 27 March.[93] By now, the rumour mill had done its work, and everyone was aware of the crisis facing the BEF. This knowledge was reflected in the men's attitude. According to Colonel Ormond, this was one of only two occasions in the entire war in which he witnessed troops who were genuinely anxious to fight, the first time being the night of 22 April 1915, the Battalion's baptism by fire.[94]

At eight o'clock Wednesday morning, the Tenth hit the road. Its first destination was Village Camp, near Ecoivres, a two-hour march in "cold and damp" weather. An even more gruelling march awaited the Battalion that night. Receiving orders to make for the Third Army's sector, the Tenth assembled on the parade ground at 11:30 p.m., and set out shortly after midnight. Originally destined for Couin, where it arrived at eight o'clock Thursday morning, the Battalion was next ordered to Saint-Leger. It rained during the afternoon, after the unit settled into its billets in Saint-Leger, but the Battalion was then instructed to move on to Thieves, where it was to "be ready to embuss at 9.00 PM." This order, however, was cancelled, and the Tenth spent the night at Thieves. The unit moved again on Friday, marching first to Berneville, then to Warlus, where it spent the next week.

Each day, between 5:30 a.m. and 7:30 p.m., part of the Battalion stood-to, ready to move at five minutes' notice. The rest of the men devoted time to training, sports, working parties, bath and pay parades, and concerts by the regimental band.[95]

This routine ended on Friday, 5 April, when the Fighting Tenth was sent into the divisional support position at the Ronville Caves. The relief of the 16th (Canadian Scottish) Battalion was completed in pouring rain at 1:15 a.m. on the sixth. Later in the day, Major MacDonald led a party of officers to reconnoitre the brigade support line about Telegram Hill, astride the Arras-Cambrai road. The next night, the Tenth moved in, taking over from four British battalions. To man this line, the Battalion organized its transport and quarter-master's sections into a combat unit three platoons strong, under Lieutenants Herbert Andrews, George Guthrie, and David McAndie. "It was designed that this Unit should man a position and defend it at all costs, in the event of the enemy attacking and breaking through the flanks." The measure indicates the perceived gravity of the situation at this time.[96]

In fact, the worst was already over, although this would be obvious only to historians enjoying the benefit of hindsight. The first German offensive, in Picardy, ended on 5 April, and a new attack was launched in Flanders on the ninth. Like its predecessor, this offensive enjoyed considerable success at first; among the landmarks to fall to the enemy was Passchendaele Ridge, captured at such cost and with so much difficulty by the Canadian Corps just a few months earlier. Also like its predecessor, this offensive eventually ran out of steam and, in desperation, the Germans launched two others between late May and late July against the French. Skilfully directed by the newly appointed supreme commander, Ferdinand Foch, the Allies parried each thrust. (The French general always considered the Fighting Tenth's night attack at Ypres in 1915 to be one of the highlights of the whole war.) The cumulative effect of these operations wore down the German army and it became obvious that the advances which looked so impressive on maps had merely extended the length of line which it now had to defend. However, months would pass before anyone realized that the pendulum had swung in the Allies' favour, and the intervening period was most worrisome.

The Canadian Corps took no direct part in this prolonged fighting. Indeed, when all four divisions were removed from General Currie's jurisdiction and his headquarters placed in reserve in late March, the Corps ceased to exist at all for a short time. Currie protested vehemently, and successfully, that the Canadians fought better together rather than dispersed among British corps. By 8 April, Currie's three divisions — the Second Division remained with the British until the beginning of July — were holding a 16,000-yard front, which included the vital Vimy Ridge. By the middle of the month, this frontage had been widened to an incredible 29,000 yards, however, the Germans never seriously tested the weak Canadian line. It was the only major sector held by the BEF that was not attacked by the enemy in 1918,

and Colonel Ormond argued, with justification, that the reputation of the Canadians had a lot to do with it. "The Boche was quite aware of who was holding it," the colonel maintained, "and he deliberately stayed away."[97]

Ormond's beloved Battalion moved into the front lines on Thursday, 11 April. No one regretted leaving the vicinity of the Arras-Cambrai road, which had proved to be a hot spot. The area was heavily shelled, causing a number of casualties — eight resulting from high explosives and shrapnel, and twelve due to gas — in just three days. During the evening of the eleventh, the Fighting Tenth relieved the 44th (New Brunswick) and 50th (Calgary) battalions astride the Blangy-Gavrelle road, south of Vimy Ridge. The relief was reported complete at 1:30 a.m. on the twelfth.[98]

The first day in the trenches was pleasant enough. The weather was fine and clear, and the enemy was quiet, enabling the Battalion to send out working parties to make improvements to the local defences. These included the construction of a Lewis-gun post.[99]

The next day, the Fighting Tenth introduced itself to the defenders on the other side of no man's land. The Battalion's snipers claimed five hits during 13 April, and several patrols slipped into the German trench and caused havoc. The first patrol went out at 9:15 a.m., and encountered an enemy post a short distance along the trench. In the ensuing battle, the post was destroyed and three Germans were killed. The second patrol, six other ranks under Lieutenant William Hamilton, leapt into the trench and engaged in a short, sharp fire-fight. At 9:40 a.m., a third patrol entered the trench at another point, and Corporal John Porter killed two Germans with a grenade. Then, in the early afternoon, Lieutenants Frank Rump and Charles FitzRoy, who had distinguished themselves in similar activities the previous month, led four snipers through the enemy wire. Destroying a post in the trench, the snipers did deadly work among the grey-clad reinforcements rushing to the scene of the intrusion. After a brief battle, this patrol withdrew safely. In fact, not a man was hurt in any of these daring forays. Lieutenant FitzRoy won the bar to his MC as a result of this operation.[100]

Aside from occasional shell fire, the next few days were rather uneventful. Still, there were casualties, including thirty-six-year-old Lieutenant Norman Henderson, who was killed by a German shell while supervising the distribution of water rations near Battalion headquarters on 14 April. The Tenth was treated to the spectacle of a major air battle three days later, when "a flight of our machines attacked a number of enemy planes which were endeavouring to fly over our Line, and were successful in forcing one down, and driving the others back to their own Lines." That night, the unit was relieved by the 8th Battalion's Little Black Devils from Winnipeg. The

Tenth's casualties for the six-day tour totalled two dead and one wounded.[101]

Moved back to billets in brigade reserve at Roclincourt, the Battalion enjoyed a well-deserved rest. The weather was generally cool, and it snowed at least once. Every man was given a hot bath and a change of clothing, and all equipment was checked and cleaned. As well, a limited amount of training was undertaken, but the emphasis was on relaxation. There were, sadly, reminders that the war was close at hand. On 20 April, a shell burst killed Sergeant Alfred McLatchie, who as a private had won the MM at Vimy Ridge.[102]

The next day, the Fighting Tenth moved to safer quarters in Corps reserve, near Anzin and Saint-Aubin. The week's stay here was restful, with a full agenda of training activities and inspections by General Currie and the brigadier, General Loomis. On the afternoon of 25 April, "Cinematograph pictures were taken of the Battalion in the 'March Past.' Photographs were also taken of all Officers of the Battalion and all N.C.O.s of the Battalion with decorations." Not many of the men in these pictures would still be alive within a few months.[103]

More important matters than photographs were soon at hand. On Saturday evening, 27 April, Colonel Ormond led the Fighting Tenth down the Anzin-Arras road, eventually relieving the 1st (Western Ontario) Battalion in the Fampoux sector, on the north bank of the River Scarpe. It was cloudy and cool, and the Battalion took advantage of the dreary conditions to patrol intensively. Enemy shelling was fairly heavy and, on the first night in the trenches, two members of a ration party were hit by shell fragments. However, a measure of revenge was exacted on Wednesday, 1 May, when considerable movement was detected in and behind the enemy lines. "The artillery were notified," says the war diary, "and harassing fire was increased at various points."[104]

That night the Tenth shifted into the support position, after being relieved by the 7th Battalion from British Columbia. It was somewhat quieter here, although there was plenty of aerial activity and long-range shell fire injured two men on 3 May.[105] One was Corporal Marvin Whyte, only recently returned to duty after being wounded at Vimy Ridge. His thigh torn open, Corporal Whyte, who was one of the unit's originals, was soon sent home as medically unfit.[106]

Tragedy occurred here, as the result of a misunderstanding at a listening post. One of the most demanding tasks in trench warfare was the manning of these posts; their purpose was to warn of any attempt by the enemy to cross no man's land. A newcomer to the Battalion, Private Stan Carr, remembered them another way. " 'Sacrifice posts,' they called a lot of them, because you went out there with the idea that if the Germans moved, you didn't come away. You opened [fire with] your gun and the boys

behind you got the warning, and the Germans walked over you." The twenty-seven-year-old Calgarian admitted that the assignment never failed to terrify him. "Anybody that wasn't scared," he later commented, "there was something wrong with him."[107]

It may well be that the two members of the Battalion who manned the listening post near the river were scared, too, which would explain the ensuing confusion. During the early-morning hours of 4 May, their post was approached by three British Highlanders who had escaped from the Germans after being captured some time before. Mistaking the shadowy figures of the Highlanders for the enemy, the defenders threw a grenade, giving the alarm to the Vickers heavy machine-gun covering their position. In the darkness and confusion, both men in the listening post were killed by Canadian bullets, and one of the Highlanders was wounded. The error was soon discovered and the shooting ceased. The three Britishers were escorted to Battalion headquarters and then to brigade, where they were able to give useful information about the enemy's rear areas.[108]

The same day, the Fighting Tenth was relieved by elements of the British 46th Brigade. As it was replaced in the trenches, each company moved independently to the nearby light-railway line, and rode the rails back to Moreuil. It was a short stay, however. After a bath parade and a change of clothing on 5 May, the Tenth moved twelve miles away, to Liencourt, the following day. It was a fine, clear Monday, and the Battalion was inspected on the march by Generals Currie and Loomis.[109]

The Tenth remained at Liencourt for nearly three weeks. Like the rest of the Canadian Corps, the Battalion was to prepare for coming operations with a solid grounding in an unfamiliar concept: open warfare. These tactics stressed mobility and manoeuvrability, and co-operation with tanks and aircraft; much time was spent on the nearby rifle ranges honing the men's musketry skills. Evident progress was made, according to the war diary. "The weather being very fine, and the men having benefited considerably from their rest," reads a typical entry, on 9 May, "it was considered that this was one of the best day's training ever put in by the Battalion."[110]

As usual, the training was complemented by sports, and the Fighting Tenth proved to be as adept on the sports field as it was on the battlefield. The Battalion baseball team won all eight games played in May, and the soccer team did nearly as well, losing the brigade championship in a hard-fought struggle with the 7th Battalion's team. The highlight of the month took place on 18 May, when the Second Brigade staged a military circus, as the war diary describes:

The Brigade Circus, organized by a Committee composed of representatives of the Battalions in the 2nd Canadian Infantry Brigade, was held this afternoon. This consisted of a number of Athletic and Equestrian Contests, Base-Ball Foot-Ball Games, and a Grand Circus Parade, in all of which the 10th C[anadian] I[nfantry] Battalion was well represented, and was the first Military Circus held in France.

A number of the Officers of Corps, Divisional and Brigade Staffs, including the Commanders, attended, and expressed their pleasure at the Performance. Nurses from the 2nd, 3rd, and 4th Casualty Clearing Stations were among those present, and evidently enjoyed the Spectacle. The various Units of the Brigade paraded en masse, and altogether the Brigade Circus was conceded to be a great success.

Afterwards, a dance was held at brigade headquarters, with the nurses and officers from the four battalions attending, "and a pleasant evening was spent."[111]

The party atmosphere nearly landed the Battalion in serious trouble. The same night, in the nearby town of Fervent, military police scuffled with men belonging to the Tenth. The culprits evidently escaped the red-hatted policemen, but the incident prompted a stern letter of rebuke from Second Brigade headquarters the following day. Referring to "some disturbance" in Fervent, the letter warned that the town "would be placed out of bounds to troops should this happen again."[112]

The episode was quickly forgotten amid the tumult of a significant change involving the Tenth. Late on Thursday, 23 May, came word that "Dangerous Dan" Ormond was being promoted to command the Ninth Brigade. The thirty-two-year-old colonel departed the following afternoon, with what must have been an emotional farewell. The warm words of the war diarist were well merited:

This Officer was one of the original 10th Battalion Officers, and took over command of the Unit from Lieut-Col. J.G. Rattray, D.S.O. during the operations on the Somme, in September, 1916. The success of this Battalion in all the operations in which it took part, under his command, was very marked, and in a large measure due to the wonderful ability for organization and capacity for detail, possessed by this Officer. The Officers and men alike, of the 10th C.I. Battalion, recognizing his ability as a Commander, found no training too arduous, and no task too hard to carry out.

The loyalty of all ranks was well shown by the large number who called on him before he went away to say goodbye, and offer their best wishes for his continued success in his new Command.[113]

Ormond had made an indelible impression on the Battalion. He had served in it and led it with distinc-

tion, and he ranks as the most dominant personality in the unit's history.

Command of the Fighting Tenth devolved on Major MacDonald. The Nova Scotia native had served with the Battalion since the summer of 1915, and had already won the DSO and MC, en route to becoming the unit's most decorated officer. At twenty-five, Eric Whidden MacDonald was now the youngest battalion commander in the Canadian Corps.[114]

Major MacDonald's first task was to lead his new command to another billeting area. On the morning of 25 May, the Tenth set out for Caucourt, twelve miles away, marching fifty minutes and resting for ten minutes each hour. Along the way, the Battalion passed the approving eyes of the divisional commander, General Macdonell.

Following a six-hour march, the men reached Caucourt in the early afternoon, and spent the rest of the day settling down in their new surroundings. Ahead lay several days of training and sports, with added wrinkles designed to maintain everyone's interest. The officers formed a soccer team and challenged each of the companies, losing 6 - 0 to A Company, 4 - 0 to B, and 1 - 0 to C, before holding D to a scoreless draw. Training was spiced up by competitions such as stripping and reassembling the Lewis gun, with cash prizes offered for the best times. The winner was D Company's Private Ernest Holmes, with a time of four minutes and twelve seconds.[115]

An incident in early June illustrates Major MacDonald's forceful personality. On the second, the Battalion moved to new billets in Ecoivres, eight miles from Caucourt, and the officers' quarters were, in MacDonald's words, "so crowded as to be altogether disagreeable." Several officers chose to sleep under the stars rather than remain indoors in such discomfort, and MacDonald appealed to the town major, an officer named Joyce, for better housing. Joyce was unsympathetic, and a shouting match ensued; shortly afterwards, the town major filed a complaint at Second Brigade headquarters, claiming that MacDonald had "insulted" and "abused" him with "violent" and "profane" language. MacDonald sheepishly admitted that a "very petty" matter had escalated out of hand. "Probably had I been a little more tactful and had he been a little less negative in his attitude, the required results which I had hoped for could have been obtained."[116]

Aside from this episode, June passed pleasantly and quickly. It was generally hot and sunny, with occasional showers to cool things off. On 8 June, a familiar face rejoined the unit: Major Phil Walker, who was attached to D Company as a supernumerary. The same day, the Battalion won the brigade musketry competition at the Morieul rifle ranges. On the eleventh, thirty-two other ranks arrived as reinforcements; two-thirds of them were conscripts, the first to join the Fighting Tenth.

The Battalion marched fourteen miles to somewhat better housing in La Thieuloye on 16 June, and more than half of the unit was assigned to a large working party — eighteen officers and 500 other ranks — upgrading the trenches near Arras for three days. There was also a brief but irritating problem with sickness; a platoon of B Company had to be quarantined for chickenpox on 20 June, and four days later the whole of C Company was placed in quarantine for influenza. On 28 June, Lieutenant-Colonel Canon Frederick Scott, the First Division's chaplain, gave a talk. "His subject was 'My Leave to Rome,' " says the war diary. "The Canon's talks are always popular with the boys, and although attendance was voluntary, the Field was crowded, and everyone thoroughly enjoyed themselves."[117]

The following day, the Battalion tallied its decorations. Throughout the morning, all other ranks paraded to the orderly room "for the purpose of having an entry made in their Paybook, showing the date and authority of the award." To date, 266 all ranks had been decorated, including Private Harry Brown's Victoria Cross.[118] These numbers would swell substantially during the next few months.

Sports assumed added importance in June 1918. The entire Canadian Corps was gearing up for a spectacular day of sporting events scheduled for 1 July, Dominion Day, and the Fighting Tenth prepared to do its part. On 9 June, it dominated the Second Brigade sports day at Saint-Aubin, and did well in the divisional sports meet at Tinques on the seventeenth. The unit's baseball team, after losing for the first time earlier in the month, could not recover its poise and lost the divisional semi-final to Ontario's 1st Battalion. But the lacrosse team defeated another Ontario outfit, the 2nd Battalion, 13 - 7. Captain Jack Mitchell won the half-mile run and placed third in the mile, while Sergeant Leonard Melbourne won the 440-yard dash. Lieutenant Edward Watling came second in the 220-yard dash, and Private Ephraim Harber placed third in the high-jumping competition.[119]

The Corps sports meet on Dominion Day was a dazzling success. Prominent guests included the former governor-general of Canada, the Duke of Connaught, and the Canadian prime minister, Sir Robert Borden. The preparations at Tinques were impressive, as the Fighting Tenth's war diary observes:

The Quarter-mile Track, neatly roped off, was in good condition. Two large Grand Stands were erected on opposite sides of the track and Forms built up all the way round, as well as several Band Stands at various points close to the Arena. A large Arch was built at the entrance to the grounds from the Arras-St. Pol road, supplemented by several others leading to the Main Grand Stand where seats were reserved for visitors, Nurses, and Officers, close to the finishing point. The Arches and Stands were tastefully decorated with Flags and Bunting, and the Grounds presented a gala appearance.

Inside the Arena were the stands for Boxing and Wrestling, and the necessary equipment for some of the other Events, including Tilting the Bucket, Obstacle Race, and Pillow Fighting....

The various events brought out the pick of Canadian athletes in France, and considering everything, they showed remarkable form.

The First Division won the trophy put up by the Corps commander, General Currie, and the Fighting Tenth contributed to the triumph when its fleet-footed Captain Mitchell won the half-mile run, "one of the best contested events of the day."[120]

Then the Battalion returned to its rigorous training programme. This included "instruction in Lewis Gun, Bombing, Musketry, First Aid, and Map Reading."[121] By now, the men were lean, hard, tanned, and at the peak of physical fitness, qualities that would help some of them survive the trying times that lay ahead.

The Fighting Tenth went into the front lines in mid-July, for the first time in ten weeks. On 13 July, Major MacDonald went ahead to survey the Battalion's assigned sector, while the rest of the unit made final preparations before setting out at 9:30 p.m. Marching into the support position near Arras, the Battalion relieved the 2nd London Regiment, prior to moving into the trenches two nights later. Here they took over from the 16th London Regiment and a portion of the 5th (Western Cavalry) Battalion. It was raining heavily, and the relief was not completed until 2:50 a.m. on 16 July. The rain stopped around nine o'clock that morning, "and the day turned very hot," according to the war diarist.

While the forward positions were subjected to routine shelling, it was a different story in the Battalion's transport lines, near Anzin. "The enemy bombarded one of our Observation Balloons commencing about 7.00 P.M. this evening, with high explosive shells. A piece of one shell landed in one of our huts in our Transport Lines, burying itself in the ground. Examination showed it to be of fairly large calibre, evidently about nine inch. Several men in the hut had a narrow escape from being badly wounded, but the only damage was to the roof and floor of the hut."[122]

The next night, Lieutenant Frank Rump set out with a patrol to probe the enemy lines. Accompanied by six other ranks, Lieutenant Rump slipped through the German outpost line and entered a series of dugouts. These were unoccupied, except for the last one, where three sleepy Germans resided. Rump engaged in what the war diary calls "an exciting struggle," since the doorway was only big enough to permit one man at a time to enter. Corporal Arthur Barlow and Private William Beggs came to his rescue, and all the Germans were killed. However, the noise alerted other Germans, who came running. Rump's patrol narrowly escaped and returned to the Battalion's trench without loss. The lieutenant won the bar to his MC and Corporal Barlow was awarded the MM.[123]

The same day, 17 July, the Fighting Tenth was warned to expect an enemy attack. Unusual movement had been detected behind the German lines, and there was a perceptible increase in shelling. Added to this was the testimony of an escaped French prisoner who reported that the Germans were planning an offensive on the eighteenth, between Albert and Arras. "Instructions were issued that special watchfulness was to be maintained, and all precautions taken to avoid surprise." The following morning, the Canadian artillery brought down a tremendous barrage along the enemy front, but no attack materialized.[124]

However, the Battalion did not lower its guard. Intensive patrolling was carried out for the next few days and compiled detailed information that would soon be put to good use. During the evening of 22 July, the Fighting Tenth was relieved by the 7th (1st British Columbia Regiment) Battalion and moved into the brigade support position.[125] The Germans were undoubtedly glad to see the departure of the troublesome Tenth, but the Battalion still had one more nasty surprise in store for them.

On Friday, 26 July, the Fighting Tenth took part in a large-scale raid with the neighbouring 5th (Western Cavalry) Battalion. The previous night, the five officers and 142 other ranks — many of them about to see action for the first time and "very keen," according to the war diary — proceeded to their assembly positions, under the direction of the supernumerary, Major Phil Walker. The force divided into five parties, each under a lieutenant: Sidney Grimble, Tom Carter, William Oliver, Renwick Anderson, and Gordon Graham. The main effort was to be undertaken by the 5th Battalion; the Tenth's role was to protect the former unit's flank.[126]

Zero hour was 9 p.m. on the twenty-sixth. A minute later, the barrage burst overhead and the raid was underway. The 5th Battalion had a difficult time; although it gained much useful information about the enemy defences and brought back seven prisoners, it suffered unduly heavy casualties in the process. The Tenth, however, executed its part flawlessly. Each of the covering parties slipped through gaps in the German wire and took up positions along the nearest trench, where they could intercept reinforcements rushing to deal with the 5th Battalion's raiders. No Germans were seen, and by 10:05 p.m., the operation was over, with only one casualty, Private Peter Parker, who was slightly wounded.* Before departing, Lieutenant Grimble's party destroyed two dugouts and brought back a "postcard and addressed envelope" for identification purposes.[128]

Although it was relatively uneventful, half a dozen decorations arose from the raid. Lieutenant Grimble won the MC, and Corporal Arthur Barlow added the bar to the MM he won just a short time before. Typically modest about the medals, Barlow, in a post-war interview commented, "They sent mine up with the rations, and I happened to be around when they handed 'em [out]."[129] The other MM-winners were Sergeant William Ritchie, Corporal Thomas Greenwood, and Privates Herbert Connor and Harry Webb.

Meanwhile, the Battalion was informed that it would soon be returning to the trenches. In order to give the men a bath, the 5th Battalion relieved the Fighting Tenth on the evening of 28 July in the brigade support line. On the way back to Arras, working parties were detailed to assist Canadian engineers in burying cable in the Second Brigade's forward area. These parties, after completing their nocturnal tasks, rejoined the Battalion in Arras, where during the twenty-ninth "each man had a hot bath and received clean underclothing. In addition, Tunics and Trousers were disinfected." That night, the Tenth marched into the front lines, taking over from British Columbia's 7th Battalion. The relief was completed without incident around midnight.[130]

It was destined to be a short tour, highlighted by the appearance of a young German deserter who had to be rescued from the barbed-wire entanglement. During the evening of 31 July, the Tenth was relieved by the 13th London Regiment and marched back to Arras, where it boarded a train on the light railway for Lattre Saint-Quentin. It was already daylight when the train reached its destination, at five o'clock on the morning of 1 August. Three hours later, a hot breakfast was served, and then the troops were allowed to sleep for the rest of the morning. They were awakened at noon, and the companies fell in at three o'clock and marched to Ambrines, arriving two and a half hours later. This was just the first in a series of rapid, tiring, and bewildering moves that were part of the war's greatest secret operation.[131]

---

* There were actually two, counting an inexperienced lance-corporal, Sydney Hampson, who was winged by a Canadian sentry the previous night when he failed to respond to a challenge.[127]

Chapter Nine

"PURE BLOODY MURDER"

(1 August - 28 September 1918)

The Battalion spent the first three days of August in Ambrines, with routine activities filling the time, according to the war diary. "Clothes and equipment were brushed, brasses and buttons polished; Shortages of Battle equipment were checked, and indents submitted." During the morning of Saturday, 3 August, verbal orders were received by the acting Battalion commander, Major William Bingham. Bingham was filling in for Eric MacDonald, a lieutenant-colonel since late July and now enjoying ten days' special leave in Paris when Bingham learned that the Battalion was to be prepared to move at short notice.[1]

The move took place that night. Reveille was sounded at 12:45 a.m. on Sunday and breakfast was served fifteen minutes later, while the men were still rubbing the sleep from their eyes. At 4:40 a.m., the Battalion set out on foot for Ligny Saint-Florchel, where a train was waiting. Marching into the village at seven o'clock Sunday morning, the troops were allowed to patronize a temporary counter set up by the YMCA "with their usual promptitude," and "practically all the men of the Unit were able to get a drink of hot tea, and purchase some biscuits or chocolate."[2] The train pulled out of the station at 8:10 a.m., but no one, not even the officers, knew where they were headed.[3]

The train took the Tenth to the French coast, through Saint-Pol, Montreuil, Etaples, and Abbeville, before arriving at Senarpont at five-thirty in the afternoon. Prior to this, there had been just one stop, when the train pulled onto a siding allowing the soldiers to stretch their legs and munch on their rations, which were washed down with hot tea. Detraining at Senarpont, the men marched to a nearby field for a short rest.

Around eight o'clock Sunday evening, they fell in again and started on a long march. Halting for tea at nine, the Battalion marched all through the night.[4] "Even the officers were cursing, from fatigue and the length of time," recalled Private Stan Carr of Calgary.[5] At four o'clock Monday morning, 5 August, the footsore Fighting Tenth reached Lincheux. "After getting settled in billets," says the war diary, "everyone went to bed, the fatigue of the train journey and the all night march being very great, especially as the dress was full marching order."[6]

It rained most of the day, but few paid much attention. Breakfast was served at noon, and the rest of Monday was "spent in getting washed, shaved, and cleaned up after the long trip."[7]

But the journey was not yet over. Late on Tuesday afternoon, 6 August, the Battalion fell in, and at five-thirty marched for Campeen-Amienois, an hour away. Colonel MacDonald, refreshed by his leave in Paris, rejoined the unit here, and supervised the boarding of buses. At nine that evening, the bus column departed for Amiens, which was reached at one-thirty Wednesday morning. After getting off the buses, the Battalion marched to its billets, "old artillery dugouts and 'bivvies' " near Gentelles.[8]

Although nobody knew what was up, it became clear to everyone that something very big was in the works. The roads were terribly congested, and progress was slow. To Private Carr, the young Calgarian, it seemed that every few minutes they "had to fall out to let tanks, motor lorries, guns, everything, move up."[9] This vast array of weaponry and manpower must have brought to mind the admonition which had been pasted in each man's pay book: KEEP YOUR MOUTH SHUT. It was well after dawn on 7 August when these tired troops finally laid their stiff and sore bodies to rest in their cramped quarters.

The mystery was cleared up later that day. Amiens lay eighty miles straight north of Paris, and it was here that the Allied supreme commander, Marshal Foch, intended to deliver the first big blow of 1918 against the enemy. It would be a surprise attack involving French, British, Australian, and Canadian forces, all supported by hundreds of tanks and thousands of guns. This sector was weakly fortified compared to other parts of the Western Front, and marked the enemy's farthest advance during the spring offensive. The attack was to be spearheaded by the Canadian and Australian corps, supported on the left by the British III Corps — all of which comprised the Fourth Army — and on the right by the French First Army.

Three Canadian divisions would lead the way, with the First Division in the centre. Each of the First's three brigades was assigned a successive objective. The Third Brigade, on a three-battalion front, would take the Green Line, and three battalions of the

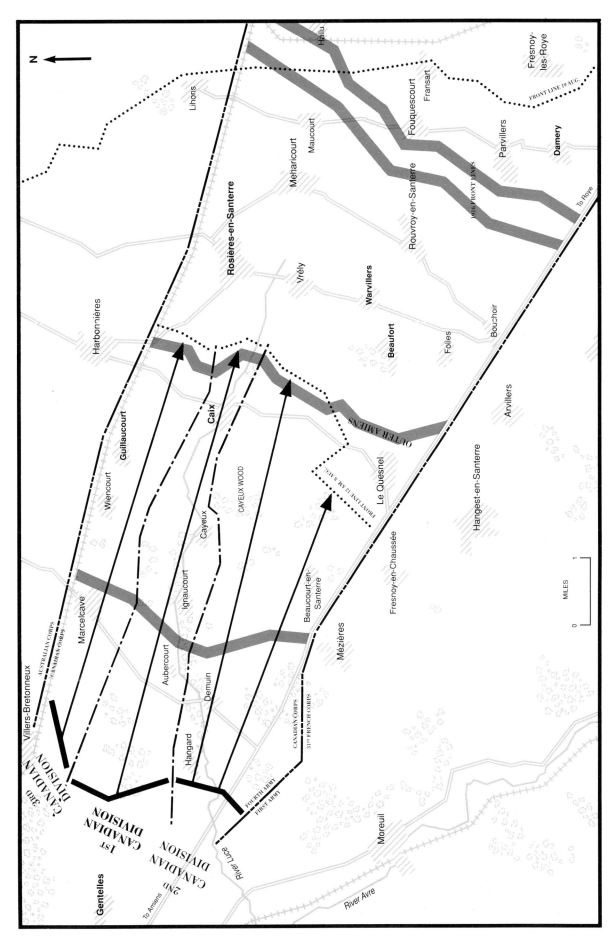

Amiens, 8 August 1917

167

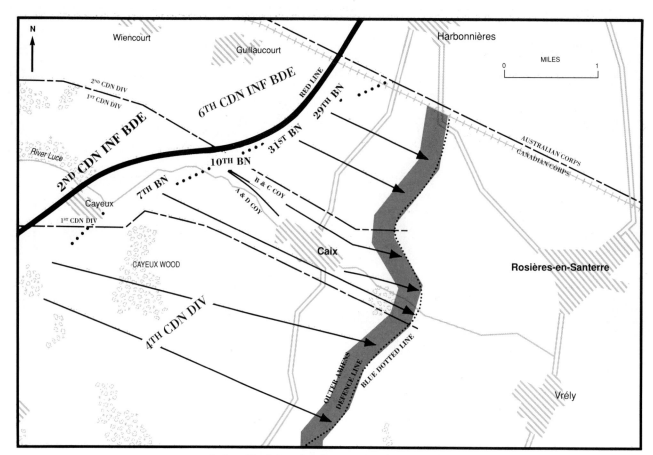

Amiens: Tenth Battalion Operations, 8 August 1917

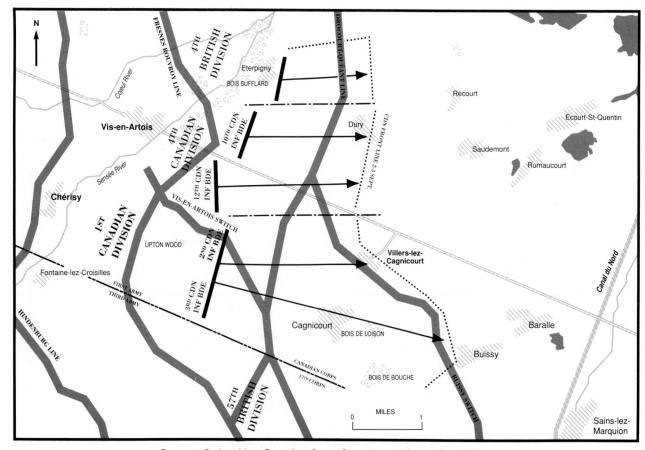

Drocourt-Quéant Line: Canadian Corps Operations, 2 September 1918

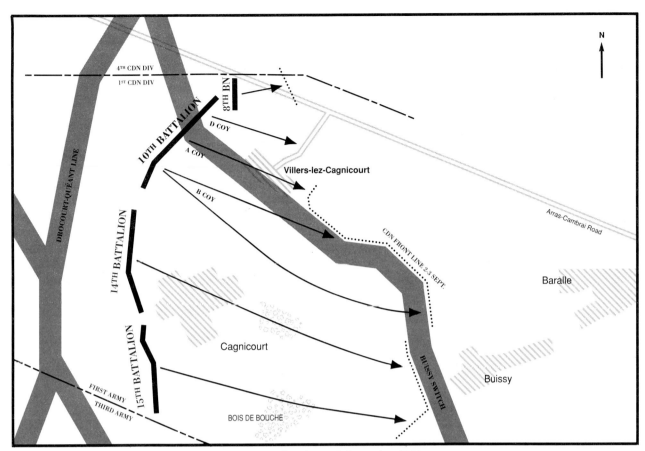

Villers-lez-Cagnicourt, 2 September 1918

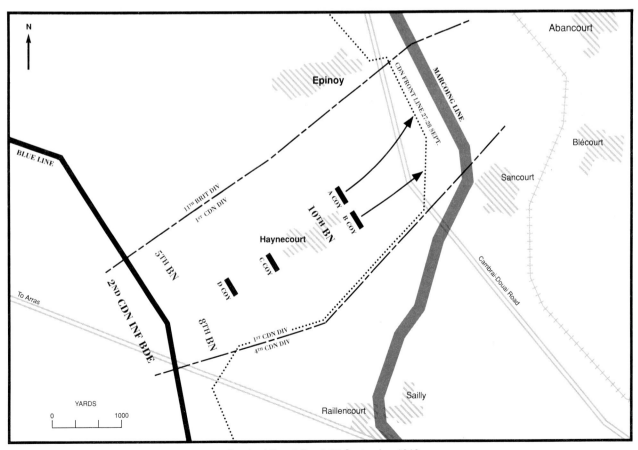

Cambrai-Douai Road, 27 September 1918

Canal du Nord, 27 September 1918

170

Lieutenant-Colonel Eric MacDonald, DSO, MC

Courtesy Calgary Highlanders

First Brigade would then leap-frog and capture the intermediate Red Line. The final objective, designated on Corps maps as the Blue Dotted Line, was the responsibility of the Second Brigade. Because the division's frontage narrowed due to the meandering River Luce on its right, there was room for only two battalions. The brigadier, General Loomis, chose to employ the Fighting Tenth, with the 7th (1st British Columbia Regiment) Battalion on its right.[10]

It was an ambitious plan. The Blue Dotted Line lay 14,000 yards from the Canadian front lines — a distance of about eight miles. The creeping barrage that would accompany the assault would be maintained by field batteries leap-frogging at regular intervals. There would be no preliminary bombardment, for two reasons. One was that the 106 fuse, introduced in early 1917, was now available in substantial quantities. The 106 fuse ensured consistent wire-cutting by causing shells to explode on contact; previously, they would detonate either high above the wire or far below the ground, which required a deluge of shells for a prolonged period to make sure that gaps were cut for the infantry at zero hour. The second reason to dispense with preliminary bombardment was the presence of tanks — 324 Mark V heavy tanks and 96 Medium Mark A "Whippets." With a road speed of 4.6 miles per hour, the Mark V weighed more than thirty tons and carried a crew of seven who manned six machine-guns (the so-called "female" tank) or four machine-guns and two light guns (the "male" version). The Whippet's top speed was 8.3 miles per hour, but it was equipped only with light machine-guns. The Mark Vs would lead the attack, crushing barbed-wire entanglements and smashing strongpoints, while the Whippets would go into action with the Cavalry Corps during the exploitation phase of the battle.

Fourteen Mark Vs were assigned to the Second Brigade; eight men from the Fighting Tenth and six from the 7th Battalion were detailed to ride in the tanks. Each man's duty was "to keep his Battalion or Company in sight and to inform the Tank Commander of any signals from the Infantry to the Tank, and also to inform him if the Tank is getting too far ahead of the Infantry to which it is allocated." Three of these heavy tanks were given to the Tenth to aid its drive towards the final objective, the Blue Dotted Line.[11]

The attack was scheduled for 4:20 a.m. on Thursday, 8 August.

Colonel MacDonald received this information Wednesday morning.[12] "That afternoon," Private Carr recalled, "we pulled into a woods off the side of the road, and the colonel, MacDonald, took us out in companies in the middle of a field" and explained the battle plan in full detail. This was MacDonald's first action as Battalion commander, and he made certain that every man in the unit knew precisely what he was supposed to do, and how, where, and when to do it. MacDonald, who turned twenty-six on 20 July,

endeared himself to the Fighting Tenth. Captain Hugh Pearson called the colonel "a great soldier."[13]

Wednesday evening, the Battalion moved up to its assembly position, occupying shallow trenches behind the First Brigade by one-thirty Thursday morning, three hours before zero. It was a clear night, but a ground mist was beginning to gather in the valley of the Luce. A few of the hardier souls in the outfit managed a quick snooze, but most of the men were too anxious or nervous, or both, to sleep. At 4 a.m., the Battalion stood-to and, eight minutes later, the tanks began to rumble past, their noise masked by low-flying aircraft.[14]

At 4:20 a.m., the world seemed to explode. The barrage overhead lit up the dark sky. "You could've read a newspaper whichever way you looked — reflection from the gun fire," recalled Private William Curtis, who professed amazement at the amount of artillery assembled for this operation. 'We had to step over the wheels of the guns, between the hubs, to get forward." More than an hour passed before the Tenth was required to advance, so the men were allowed to have breakfast. Private Carr and his fellow Lewis-gunner, Private William Thompson, treated themselves to café au lait and a piece of leftover ham, which they fried.[15]

It was soon evident that the attack was going well. While Private Carr and his mates ate their improvised meal, wounded Highlanders from the Third Brigade began to pass by, on their way to dressing stations. Their morale was sky-high, knowing that the Germans had been completely surprised and were being soundly trounced. "They're away, laddie, they're away," one injured kiltie shouted to Carr.[16]

"It was foggy, quite foggy," according to Carr,[17] when Colonel MacDonald ordered his companies to fall in, around five-thirty. At 6:20 a.m., the Fighting Tenth started forward. Spread out in artillery formation, B, on the right, and C companies led the advance, with A and D in support. Pack horses and mules carried the Battalion's Lewis guns, along with additional supplies of small-arms ammunition and water.[18] Each man carried 250 rounds, gas mask, water bottle, iron rations of corned beef and biscuits, entrenching tool, two Mills bombs, and two sandbags.[19]

At first progress was slow. According to Colonel MacDonald, "there was a very heavy ground mist and a considerable amount of low-lying smoke which made it very difficult to keep direction and touch."[20] However, the fog had "started to break" as the Battalion moved into the battle zone, as Private Carr remembered:

We crossed no man's land — just a ploughed field with pieces of wire and equipment sticking out of it. You didn't know you were crossing trenches. And, in no time at all, we were right out in a nice, pleasant countryside, the scene we'd always talked about and dreamed of. It turned out more-or-less a picnic.

That was the best plan that was ever pulled off, and if "Old Guts and Gaiters" planned it — excuse me, I mean General Currie — if he planned it, he did a masterful piece of work.[21]

The Battalion maintained a steady if leisurely pace through the morning. "During this phase," Colonel MacDonald later wrote, "no special attempt was made to hurry, the men being given plenty of opportunity to rest."[22]

Enemy shell fire was little more than annoying. The Third Brigade's initial assault had overrun a large number of German batteries, and most of these guns, observed Private William Curtis, "still had the muzzle covers on. We just went straight through, and so many of them guns had never been used." The Fighting Tenth also passed large numbers of German prisoners, disconsolately heading for the rear, often without an escort. "They just came along, you know, and you just motioned them back," said Private Carr. "One German said, 'Americans.' And, of course, [we] told him in no polite language that it was the so-and-so Canadians!"[23]

The Battalion's line of advance took it through the valley of the Luce. The Luce itself was no obstacle — "Why they called it a river, I don't know," wondered Private Carr,[24] and anyone who has seen this small stream would wonder the same thing — but the valley was "flanked by a number of tree-clad ravines that gave the defender every advantage."[25] By midmorning, resistance was more noticeable. The First Brigade, which had passed through the Third around eight-thirty, had its hands full with near-fanatical opposition from machine-gunners in these woods. At ten-thirty, the Fighting Tenth suffered its first casualties of the day here, when machine-gun fire raked B Company, wounding Lieutenant Ernest Vose and several other ranks.[26]

It is impossible to say precisely when the Tenth opened its phase of the attack. According to the war diary, the Battalion reached its jumping-off point "about 11.00 A.M.," while Colonel MacDonald's report places the time "about 11.30 AM;" the history of the 3rd (Toronto Regiment) Battalion states that the Tenth leap-frogged "at 12:15."[27]

Regardless of when it started, two things are clear about the Tenth's attack. One is that it went ahead without artillery support. The 2nd Field Artillery Brigade, which was supposed to provide mobile support for the First Division, was unable to keep up with the infantry's rapid advance, and it was not until the late afternoon that its batteries were able to cover the Canadian front line in this sector.[28] In an attempt to provide some assistance, some guns fired at extreme range, only to have their shells land among the men of the Tenth. Among the several casualties inflicted in this manner was B Company's commander, Captain Edward Milne, who ignored his wounds and was later awarded the MC for his outstanding leadership qualities.

The second fact is that the Tenth's left flank was in the air. There was no sign of the 31st (Alberta) Battalion, which was supposed to move from the Red Line alongside its fellow Albertans of the Tenth.*

Captain Jack Mitchell, the fleet-footed commander of C Company, decided not to wait and, with his colonel's approval, advanced on schedule with the rest of the Battalion.[29] Considering that C Company had to move a mile and a half to its objective, it was a risk, but clearly one that was acceptable.

C Company was magnificent this day. At least twice, its advance was checked by German machine-guns hidden in the woods on the open left flank, and Captain Mitchell unhesitatingly committed his troops to the area, although it meant crossing into the zone of neighbouring units. Mitchell would later be awarded the bar to his MC for displaying "exceptional leadership," and two of his subalterns won MCs here. Lieutenant William Oliver detached a section of his platoon to outflank an enemy position, while he led a frontal assault. The manoeuvre resulted in the cap-

The church at Caix, August 1918
Courtesy National Archives of Canada/PA-2952

---

* Although it contained men from all parts of Canada, the Tenth now drew its reinforcements primarily from Alberta, as it had been doing for some time. For the first part of the war, the Battalion had also drawn men from Manitoba, reflecting the duality of its origins. But, as the war went on, Manitoba had trouble providing manpower for all the units which had been formed in that province; as a result, one Manitoba battalion, the 44th, had to be transferred to the New Brunswick reinforcement depot in mid-1918. The Tenth drew its reinforcements from the Alberta Regiment Depot, which was created in March 1917 and reorganized in April 1918.

The apparent failure of the Flanders campaign led to renewed skirmishing between Prime Minister Lloyd George and Field-Marshal Haig. On 12 November 1917, the day Haig halted the offensive for the winter, Lloyd George publicly denounced the military conduct of the war. "We have won great victories," he sarcastically told a Paris luncheon. "When I look at the appalling casualty lists I sometimes wish it had not been necessary to win so many." Passchendaele, as the Flanders offensive is popularly remembered, cost the BEF 244,897 casualties, slightly less than the best estimate of German losses.

But, while the prime minister had lost confidence in his commander-in-chief, he failed to follow the obvious course and replace Haig. Lloyd George later explained that there were no clear choices as a successor. Instead, he actively sought to thwart Haig's plans to pursue a war of attrition on the Western Front, and in so doing came dangerously close to losing the war.

His first opportunity came even before the Flanders fighting had ended. On 28 October, the Italians were routed at Caporetto by German divisions brought in from the Eastern Front. Russia, racked by revolution,was all but out of the war by now, although it would be March before the shaky Bolshevik regime signed an armistice with Germany. After dispatching British troops to Italy, Lloyd George engineered the establishment of the Supreme War Council. Manned by the political leaders of Britain, France, Italy and United States, along with their chief military advisors, the war council was a blatant attempt to limit Haig's influence while at the same time promoting Lloyd George's preference for a more vigorous effort in the Middle East.

But the prime minister was just getting started. Late in 1917, he cleaned house at the BEF's General Headquarters, removing several of Haig's top officers, including the intelligence chief, General Charteris. Early in the new year, he dismissed the field-marshal's main ally in London, Sir William Robertson, the chief of the Imperial General Staff.

Lloyd George was infuriated by Haig's stated intention to renew the campaign in Flanders at the earliest possible moment in 1918. It would do nothing more, he felt, than "throw away another 200,000 or 300,000 men." He attempted to strip the BEF of its offensive capability by restricting reinforcements and agreeing to a French request to widen the British share of the Western Front by 20 per cent. While three-quarters of a million British troops languished in the hot sun in the Middle East, BEF units in France and Belgium faced the prospect of being 40 per cent understrength by the end of March 1918. With 100,000 fewer combat troops than a year earlier, the BEF was also forced into a demoralizing reorganization when its forty-seven British divisions were reduced from twelve to nine battalions each; 141 battalions were divided to provide reinforcements for the battalions that remained unchanged.

While all this was going on, the Germans were preparing to attack. Aware of the millions of fresh American troops en route to France, the German high command decided to take the forces freed by Russia's imminent demise and employ them in a series of massive offensives on the Western Front, a last desperate bid to win the war. And there was no doubt in the enemy's mind about the objective: "We must beat the British," declared General Erich Ludendorff, the *de facto* commander-in-chief.

The Germans almost succeeded. Thanks to the interference of Prime Minister Lloyd George, the BEF was undermanned, overextended, and demoralized. The Germans were also exceedingly lucky in that the weather was unusually dry, a sharp contrast to the exceptionally wet conditions which prevailed during the British offensives in the second half of 1917. In addition, the attackers were often masked by thick morning mists. Attacking on 21 March, the Germans crushed the BEF's Fifth Army and battered the neighbouring Third Army. For a few days it appeared that the British would be driven back to the coast while the French fell back to protect Paris. However, while the enemy made huge advances and inflicted heavy losses, they captured not a single site of strategic importance. The Allied front bent but refused to break under the relentless attacks. One product of the crisis was the appointment of a supreme commander, the French general, Ferdinand Foch, whose duty was to co-ordinate the efforts of the Allied armies on the Western Front.

In the meantime, the beleaguered BEF bore the brunt of the furious fighting. By 5 April, the first German offensive had been stopped, at the cost of 178,000 British casualties. "We are paying in blood," remarked Haig's former intelligence chief, General Charteris, "for the follies of professional politicians."

Unfortunately, the crisis was not quite over. On 9 April, the anniversary of the Canadian conquest of Vimy Ridge, the Germans struck again, this time in Flanders. Once again, the weather co-operated with the enemy, who had the added good fortune to strike a sector defended by low-quality Portuguese troops who hijacked British bicycles at gunpoint in their haste to flee. Passchendaele Ridge, won with such sacrifice by Canada the previous fall, was given up without a fight as the British retired to stronger positions. Luckily for the Allies, the Germans were unable to sustain the momentum, as had been the case in their first offensive, and were stopped by the end of April.

Forty days of defensive fighting had cost the BEF 239,793 casualties, almost as many as it had lost the previous year in its 105-day offensive in Flanders amid horrendous battle conditions.

The Germans, desperate for a breakthrough, turned their attention to the French. Attacking on 27 May in Champagne, the enemy offensive followed the now-familiar pattern: early success, lost momentum, and eventual failure. The attacks were renewed on 9 June and 15 July, with similar results.

Now that it was clear that the Germans had shot their bolt, the Allies prepared to revert to the offensive. Foch, the supreme commander, and Haig, the British commander-in-chief, were in complete agreement, but Haig's political masters were not so sure. Indeed, there was high-level opposition in London to any major attacks in 1918. As late as 25 July, a draft military policy suggested limited operations for the rest of the year, with "the main offensive campaign" scheduled for 1 July 1919. Haig was baffled by the document. "Words! words! words!" he scribbled on his copy. "Lots of words! and little else." Ignoring his political adversaries, Haig, with Foch's encouragement and co-operation, planned a major offensive.

The sector he selected was near the crucial rail centre of Amiens, not far from the Somme in northern France. It was here that the Germans had achieved their deepest penetration during the spring offensives, and the defences were very weak. The Australian Corps was responsible for much of the line, and Haig agreed to augment General Sir Henry Rawlinson's Fourth Army with another elite formation, the Canadian Corps.

The Canadians posed a problem thanks to their reputation as storm troops. "Whenever the Germans found the Canadian Corps coming into the line," Prime Minister Lloyd George later wrote, "they prepared for the worst." The Corps was holding the line around Vimy Ridge, fifty miles north of Amiens, and any move would signal to the enemy the imminence of an offensive. To ensure secrecy, an elaborate deception plan was prepared, in which Canadian units — two infantry battalions with casualty clearing stations and wireless sections — were sent to Flanders. It was, according to the eminent British historian, John Terraine, a wartime "technological 'first' — the first use of a wireless deception plan...." The rest of the Corps was shifted by truck, train, and on foot to Amiens. In the interests of security, no one below brigade level was informed of the coming operation until a few days before 8 August, its scheduled start.

The deception was a mixed success; although noting the Canadian Corps' departure from the vicinity of Vimy, the Germans were not convinced that it was really headed for Flanders. But at least they had no idea of its actual destination, and there is no question that the strenuous efforts to ensure secrecy paid enormous dividends. When the British attacked at Amiens, supported by the largest number of tanks to be employed in a single operation in the whole war, it was a complete surprise to the enemy. The Canadians advanced eight miles in a single day, and the Australians went seven, prompting a depressed General Ludendorff to describe 8 August as "the black day of the German Army in the history of the war."

It was also the beginning of the end.

ture of sixty Germans and five machine-guns. Similarly, Lieutenant Charles Watt deployed his platoon under heavy fire, outflanked the enemy, and captured a pair of machine-guns "in a remarkably short time."[30]

Among the Battalion's objectives was the ancient village of Caix, which stood on the Luce. While B and C companies skirted the little community and advanced towards the Blue Dotted Line, A and D attacked Caix. Its sixteenth-century church towering over quiet, narrow, winding, high-walled lanes, Caix might have been a tough nut to crack if the Germans had decided to defend it. This was not the case — Private Samuel Hemphill recalled that there was "just the odd sniper" in the village[31] — and A and D companies quickly cleared the place. Its possession permitted British Columbia's 7th Battalion, which had been advancing on the far bank of the Luce, to cross the little river and cover the Tenth's right flank on the final objective.[32]

The Battalion reached the Blue Dotted Line at 1:15 p.m.* It was the first unit in the entire Canadian Corps to get to the objective on 8 August, and its final advance was highlighted by several instances of outstanding bravery. The Blue Dotted Line coincided with the Amiens Defence Line, constructed by the British and captured by the Germans earlier in 1918. Besides the stout trenches and dugouts contained therein, the German defenders utilized nearby sunken roads in a desperate bid to stop the Tenth. Lieutenant Oliver, the MC-winner, led a patrol into action, routing a party of Germans and capturing several, along with a machine-gun. One of Oliver's men won the DCM during this advance. Corporal Thomas Greenwood, who had won the MM in July, carried a captured machine-gun into action, storming a sunken road and killing several Germans; ten others surrendered to him. In another sunken road, Private Gordon Van Valkenburg, who had taken command of his section when the NCO was hit, led his men on a shooting spree, mopping up a number of dugouts and wiping out a machine-gun post. Private Van Valkenburg accounted for twenty-three prisoners during this romp, and was awarded the DCM for his efforts.[33]

There were two other DCM-winners here. Corporal Edward Hume, although hobbled by a shrapnel wound in the left hip, had refused to be evacuated for treatment. When his platoon was pinned down by enemy fire just short of the final objective, he skilfully led his section around the flank. Storming the strongpoint, Corporal Hume killed the five-man crew of the machine-gun and captured thirty more Germans in a nearby dugout.[34] Not far away, another strongpoint manned by fifty enemy soldiers and two machine-guns briefly stalled the Battalion's advance. Lance-Corporal William Cooper led eight of his men in a wild frontal assault covered by the fire of a single Lewis gun. Corporal Cooper took the position without losing a man.[35]

In taking its objectives so quickly, the Fighting Tenth had had precious little help. The three Mark V tanks which had been placed at its disposal were, to be blunt, useless. MacDonald sent one to aid C Company on the exposed left, but it failed to report to Captain Mitchell, "owing either to shortage of petrol or engine trouble." The other two tanks he intended to use against Caix; it was fortunate that there was negligible resistance in the village, because neither tank put in an appearance, "and nothing has since been heard from them. It is not known whether they were put out of action or got lost earlier in the attack."

The colonel was equally critical of the artillery, which not only left his men without any significant support but also caused losses — "40% of the entire casualties" suffered by the Battalion were due to shortshooting. MacDonald was not happy, either, with the slow progress of the 29th (Vancouver) and 31st (Alberta) battalions on the left, sourly observing that Captain Mitchell and C Company "had already cleared the way for them." He was also enraged by the actions of two unidentified officers of the support battalion, the 8th's Little Black Devils, from Mitchell's hometown of Winnipeg. These officers had tried to tell Mitchell that he was lost and suggested a change in direction. He ignored their mistaken advice, but MacDonald fumed that if he had listened to them, "serious results would probably have ensued."[36]

As the Tenth dug in along the Blue Dotted Line during the early afternoon of 8 August, the men were treated to a grand sight. "We could see the Germans, a disorganized mob, going over the hills, running," commented a jubilant Private Carr, his breakfast of fried ham and café au lait now only a pleasant memory.[37]

For a while, the Battalion's position was precarious: it was on the objective, but both flanks were in the air. At three o'clock the 7th Battalion finally came up on the right, but A Company's Captain David McAndie had already taken steps to shore up that worrisome sector by leading two of his platoons from Caix and posting them on the right. This move, in addition to the "great dash" which he had displayed in capturing Caix, earned Captain McAndie the MC, to go with the DCM and MM he had won as a sergeant.[38]

The left flank was an even bigger concern. The 29th and 31st battalions did not arrive there until after six o'clock that evening, and did so only because the Tenth's acting second-in-command, twenty-seven-year-old Major William Bingham — filling in for the absent Major Hugh Ferguson — personally went back to lead them into their proper places. While Major Bingham's "coolness and judgment" were recognized with the MC, it could not alter the fact that an important opportunity had been lost by the delay of these units. A thousand yards to the northeast lay the village of Rosières-en-Santerre, and Colonel MacDonald believed that if the 29th and 31st battalions had been less tardy, "Rosières would have been captured with very little opposition, and very few casualties." As it was, the village would not fall until the next day, and at heavy loss to the attackers.

In the meantime, while he awaited the arrival of these units, MacDonald appealed to the cavalry to press forward. Nearby, there were three British brigadiers to whom the colonel addressed his requests, but without success. "The Cavalry," he wrote later, with evident disgust, "at no time went ahead of, or through, us, although we tried on several occasions to point out where they could, or might, do very valuable work." By five o'clock in the afternoon, the chance to take Rosières faded, as the Germans rushed up

---

* This is according to Colonel MacDonald's report; the war diary says it was fifteen minutes later.

German barbed wire, Drocourt-Quéant Line

Courtesy National Archives of Canada/PA-3280

reinforcements, by trucks and on foot, to shore up the disintegrating front. By eight-thirty that night, the opportunity for an easy success was gone.[39]

Colonel MacDonald had no time to lament opportunities lost by other units; he was much too busy making sure that the Fighting Tenth held onto its own impressive gains. He immediately established an outpost line, and battle patrols were sent out to keep touch with the enemy. There were several vicious clashes, but in each instance the Germans were routed with considerable loss. "Our own casualties in this work," the colonel noted happily, "were negligible." A subaltern in A Company won the MC during one of these excursions. Lieutenant Edward Watling led a patrol which stumbled onto a German supply dump 300 yards beyond the Blue Dotted Line. Although he was outnumbered, Lieutenant Watling attacked at once, and routed the defenders. He and his patrol captured sixteen of the enemy, along with several horses and "a large quantity of stores and ammunition."[40]

A use was finally found for the cavalry, too. With the enemy massing in the vicinity of Rosières, a counter-attack seemed imminent, and the colonel called for help. While the horsemen refused to chase the Germans, they did respond to MacDonald's call for assistance, sending thirty machine-guns, and 200 troopers who were distributed across the Battalion's vulnerable left and rear. The reinforcement boosted the Tenth's complement of machine-guns to sixty-five,

and MacDonald "felt confident" that the Battalion "could repulse, without any difficulty, any attack that could be launched against us."[41]

His men shared that confidence. In the front line, gripping his Lewis gun, Private Carr waited for the enemy to make a move. "We had eight hundred yards' field of fire," he recalled, "and we were hoping he would make a counter-attack." There was no attack, but Carr had an unusual experience to relate to his grandchildren. That night, after the 31st Battalion came up on the left, Carr had a pleasant chat with a Calgarian in that unit. When Carr returned to Calgary after the war, he met this stranger again: he was his future brother-in-law![42]

As the sun set on Thursday, 8 August, everyone realized that it had been a great day. The Canadian Corps had plunged an incredible eight miles into enemy territory, unprecedented from the Allied point of view. And the Fighting Tenth had played a key role in the process by being the first Canadian unit to reach the final objective. The Battalion had captured 300 prisoners, eighty machine-guns, seven wagons and twenty-one horses, along with "large quantities of Stores, Bombs, Small Arm and Artillery Ammunition which it is impossible to tabulate." The cost had been unusually light. Eight other ranks had been killed, while two officers — B Company's Captain Milne* and Lieutenant Vose — and sixty-six other ranks were wounded.[43]

---

* Tragically, the thirty-year-old Milne was killed while on leave after recovering from his injuries. En route to visit relatives in County Galway, Ireland, the captain had the misfortune to be on board the mail steamer *Leinster* when it was torpedoed in the Irish Sea on 10 October 1918. He was among the 450 people who perished in the disaster. As a sergeant, Milne had been the only member of the fighting Tenth to twice win the DCM.

If there is such a thing as an "easy victory," Amiens surely falls into that category. The Tenth's operation was less an attack than a route march under fire. As the relatively light casualties indicate, resistance was, for the most part, isolated and half-hearted.

Morale was never higher than it was on the evening of the eighth. In a letter home, a twenty-six-year-old Calgary banker, Corporal James van der Water, applauded the victory as "a walk over. Our casualties were light and his were heavy in prisoners and killed."[44] Private Samuel Hemphill, a twenty-one-year-old Edmonton meatpacker who had been with the Battalion since the summer of 1916, never forgot the way he felt. "We got quite a thrill for the simple reason that we'd gone so far. You know, when you'd been to Ypres and you'd been around the Somme, when you got two hundred yards or a hundred yards, you thought you'd made a wonderful advance. But here, we'd gone *miles*. It was unbelievable." The little Lewis gunner, Private Scotty Murray — who, like Private Hemphill, won the MM here — remembered Amiens another way: "It was a long way to carry a machine-gun."[45]

The Fighting Tenth remained on alert all night long, patrolling vigorously to preclude the possibility of a surprise attack. The preparations were aided by the tireless efforts of Lieutenant Harry Templeman, who had won the MM as a sergeant at Vimy Ridge. Now, "in the face of the greatest danger" and with "utter disregard for his personal safety," Lieutenant Templeman supervised the shipment and distribution of ammunition and bombs "to the most advanced positions with the result that at no time did the forward troops lack supplies of ammunition." Templeman was later awarded the MC, the seventh won by an officer of the Battalion in this battle.[46]

Fortunately, the supplies which he had provided were not immediately needed. The only sign of the Germans during the night of 8-9 August was a deserter who slipped across no man's land with what the war diary calls "some interesting information, which proved to be of value, as to the position, distribution, and morale of the German Forces opposite our positions."[47]

The weather on Friday, 9 August, was much like the previous day, with a thick morning mist giving way to hot sunshine. It began, recalled Private Carr, with an unusual but welcome breakfast. "They'd issued us canned pork and beans, the first we'd ever seen — American issue, I believe. We got a whole can to a man." A few German shells fell to the rear, narrowly missing Battalion headquarters, but the front line was unscathed. The troops were treated to the spectacle of renewed attacks by other Canadian units. Due to the uncertainty of communications, not to mention the distances involved in Thursday's

advance, the Canadian offensive efforts on Friday were disjointed and often lacked proper artillery support, although overall results, with gains of up to four miles, were impressive enough. Private Carr and his comrades watched as his future brother-in-law and the rest of the neighbouring 31st (Alberta) Battalion attacked Rosières in the early afternoon. "Why, the 31st's whistles blew, and they started up the slope," Carr recalled. "But the 31st went up the way they did in manoeuvres — five men run ahead and open fire, and the other five run a little ahead of them and drop. We watched the 31st go up. They'd run and drop, run and drop. As they started to get half-way up the slope, some of them would get up and some wouldn't." It was costly, but the 31st prevailed, and soon a steady stream of prisoners passed by. Private Hemphill noticed that "they had on brand-new uniforms, they had never been dirtied. And they were just young fellows, just young men. Some of them would only be around sixteen, seventeen years old. They'd just been rushed up to the line."[48]

The Fighting Tenth was given a brief break later in the day. During the afternoon, the Battalion was withdrawn to rest and reorganize, but in the evening it was ordered to return to the front-line area. The Tenth set out at nine o'clock for Beaufort, about three miles southeast of Caix.[49] Its route took the unit past some grisly scenes, evidence of grim fighting over the previous two days. "The Germans were piled in heaps, like manure in a farmer's field," Private Carr marvelled, "and within a few days, when a breeze came, it wasn't eau de cologne!"[50] The Battalion reached Beaufort around midnight and, after being served tea, everyone went to sleep. The officers and most of the men billeted in dugouts and shelters in the wood bordering the village, while Colonel MacDonald established his headquarters "in a farm house vacated by the Hun earlier in the day."[51]

While the Canadian Corps continued the battle across its front, the Fighting Tenth spent nearly a week at Beaufort. Three miles behind the lines, it was a relatively quiet location, with sporadic long-range shelling and furious dogfights in the sky above serving as reminders of the bloodshed so close at hand. The Battalion was ready to move at a moment's notice, but found time in the hot sunshine for some sports and a little training, as well as cold showers in a captured German bath facility in nearby Warvillers.[52]

It might have been termed idyllic, had it not been for a tragic incident on Thursday, 15 August. Around nine o'clock that morning, several German 6-inch shells landed among the Battalion's billets, including one that exploded within fifty yards of headquarters. By the time the smoke and dust had cleared, seven members of the Fighting Tenth lay dead and fifty-three were wounded.[53] The dead included A Company's Captain David McAndie, the brave thirty-one-year-old Saskatchewan farmer who had won the MC, DCM, and MM. Among the injured was Private Carr, who was hit in the foot by shell fragments. "I just staggered out of there, hobbled out of there," he recalled. "One of these men helped me bandage my foot, and that was the war for me."[54]

In a matter of moments, the Tenth had suffered nearly as many casualties as it had incurred during its remarkable advance through Caix one week earlier. And, to add insult to injury, it was determined that the losses were due primarily to bad luck. "As the [enemy] fire passed through the Battalion Area and continued to the south for a considerable distance," says the war diary, it was obvious that the Germans were merely "carrying out a harassing 'shoot' with no particular target."[55]

The opportunity to exact revenge soon presented itself. The very next day, the Battalion was alerted for front-line duty. During midafternoon on 16 August, the Fighting Tenth marched out of Beaufort, halting briefly at Le Quesnoy-en-Santerre. Dinner was served near the site of the present-day Canadian war memorial before moving into the front lines after dark. In relieving the 58th (Central Ontario) Battalion, the Tenth was brushing elbows with its former commanding officer; the 58th belonged to the Ninth Brigade, under Brigadier-General Dan Ormond. The relief, in front of the village of Damery on the right end of the Canadian Corps sector, was completed by three o'clock the next morning.[56]

By now, circumstances had changed. Large-scale operations had ceased on 11 August on the Canadian front, and a series of minor attacks and raids had been staged in order to straighten out the line and to keep the enemy off balance. The Corps was about to be shifted away from Amiens and back to more familiar territory near Arras, where it would resume the offensive before the end of the month. The Battalion discovered that the Germans were still in a belligerent mood, answering Canadian barrages with their own bombardments, and sending out patrols to meet the Canadians crossing no man's land. Within a few hours of taking over from the 58th Battalion, the Tenth lost an NCO, who was killed by German shell fire, and several other ranks who were "badly wounded."[57]

Monday, 19 August was a hectic day. In the first of two raids, Lieutenant Leonard Rowley, the Battalion scout officer, led Lieutenant Thomas Dale and twenty-five other ranks on a mission "to investigate the enemy's Front Line." Slipping into no man's land at four-thirty in the morning, Lieutenant Rowley's raiders entered the nearest German trench just after dawn. They subdued a pair of sentries, then nabbed a third prisoner in a dugout. The Canadians followed the trench for fifty yards before the alarm sounded and large numbers of enemy troops swarmed into the area. Heavy firing broke out and in the "brisk fight" which ensued, Rowley was wounded in the face and

chest by a German grenade. When the raiders ran out of bombs, they withdrew, under the cover of a Lewis gun manned by Private Henry Smith. A DCM-winner at Hill 70, Smith inflicted considerable losses on the Germans who tried to pursue the party across no man's land. Lieutenant Dale coolly directed the withdrawal until he was seriously wounded. Private Harry Webb used the officer's revolver to drive off an enemy party, then carried Dale to safety. The Canadians took with them three prisoners and two machine-guns, along with detailed information about the enemy's positions. Lieutenant Rowley won the bar to his MC, while Lieutenant Dale was awarded the MC; Private Webb won the DCM (to go with the MM he had won on 26 July) and Private Smith was given the MM.[58]

Another raid took place that afternoon. In broad daylight, Lieutenant F. St. Clair Fisher led a patrol into no man's land and again the Canadians caught the enemy napping. Shooting and bombing their way along the parapet of the German trench, Lieutenant Fisher and his men inflicted heavy losses before returning safely to their own lines. "At one point, one of the enemy, evidently braver than his fellows, attempted to hold the party up with a pistol. He was killed with a bomb, when it was discovered that his weapon was an empty flare gun."[59] Lieutenant Fisher was awarded the MC, the last of eleven won by officers of the Fighting Tenth during the Amiens operations.

The harvest of decorations was the richest since Hill 70. For his strong leadership, Colonel MacDonald was awarded the bar to his DSO. In addition to the eleven officers who won MCs, five other ranks were given DCMs. Thirty-seven MMs were awarded, including the bar to Sergeant Charles White, who had won the MM at Arleux. The other MM-winners were: Corporals Harvie Currie, Sidney Hatherby, Reuben Kilmer, Arthur Pinder, Frank Ringrose, Louis Smith, William Southward, and Thomas Steadman; Lance-Corporals Charles Broadbent, William Foley, William Forbes, Henry Jervis (posthumous), George Marcellus, Norman Thompson, and Robert Wilson;

Canadian engineers bridging the dry bed of the Canal du Nord
Courtesy National Archives of Canada/PA-3287

Villers-lez-Cagnicourt
Courtesy National Archives of Canada/PA-4364

Privates Norman Armstrong, Austin Eide, Donald Finlayson, Samuel Hemphill, James Jones, Thomas Laverson, Percy Main, George Martin, Alexander McDonald, Hugh McDonald, William "Scotty" Murray, Thompson Reside, William Rimmer, Samuel Simms, Chesley Smith, Henry Smith DCM, Robert Smith, William Tait, William Thompson, Ernest Topp, George Trute.

Pride in these awards was tempered by sadness at the deaths of other medal-holders. Chief among these was the twenty-nine-year-old Calgarian, Lance-Corporal Joseph Milne, the only member of the Fighting Tenth to win the MM three times, who died of wounds on 1 September. Also killed here were Corporal Gordon Jones, who had won the DCM at Vimy Ridge, and Sergeant William Ritchie and Private Herbert Connor, both of whom had won MMs on the 26 July raid, just before the Battalion moved to the Amiens sector.

After dark on 21 August, the Battalion began its departure. Relieved by the French 173rd Regiment, the Tenth filed out of its trenches and marched back to Beaufort. It was three o'clock in the morning on 22 August when it reached its billets, and after breakfast was served, everyone crawled off to sleep. That afternoon, the companies paraded to Warvillers for another cold shower and a change of underwear, before setting out for Guillaucourt, two miles north of Caix. Arriving around midnight, the Battalion spent the twenty-third resting and cleaning equipment. There was long-range shelling in the area, but no damage was done. In the evening, the regimental band staged a concert "which was very much appreciated by a large crowd from the various Companies, of both Officers and men," according to the war diary.

Afterwards, the Battalion marched out of Guillaucourt at two in the morning on 24 August, arriving at Gentelles Wood at six-thirty. "The day was spent in resting, by all ranks, after the night march."

The pattern was repeated that night. Leaving Gentelles at ten o'clock, the Tenth marched for seven hours, to Salouel, where the band delighted soldiers and residents alike with another concert in the town square. During the evening of the twenty-fifth, the Battalion made the two-hour march to Bacouel, where it boarded a train for Arras.[60]

It was a tiring, thirteen-hour journey. The train pulled out of Bacouel at 12:40 a.m. on 26 August and reached Savy-Berlette at 1:45 p.m. Detraining, the Battalion had dinner in an adjacent field. Then it set out, by bus and on foot, for Saint-Catherines, on the other side of Arras. A change was most noticeable, as the war diary points out: "During the last trip in the line in front of Arras, movement through the town had to be made after nightfall, whereas today the Battalion marched through the city, headed by the band, during the afternoon. The billets in St. Catherines were not shelled, and our own Heavy Artillery were all arranging to move forward, the enemy having been driven out of range of their guns."[61]

East of Arras, the Canadian Corps had launched a major new offensive earlier in the day. It was one of a series of powerful blows by the British and French armies aimed at the Hindenburg Line, the enemy's last line of defence on the Western Front. The Canadians, attacking the northern end of the Hindenburg Line, faced a daunting array of defensive positions in front of Cambrai, a key railhead that was the main objective. The defences included the Fresnes-Rouvroy and Drocourt-Quéant lines blocking the way to the Canal du Nord which, in turn, stood directly in front of Cambrai.

Throughout the vicinity, for a distance of more than twenty miles, the Germans had converted every village and hamlet into fortresses connected by mazes of trenches, dugouts, concrete bunkers, machine-gun nests, and vast quantities of rusty barbed wire. They then took advantage of excellent fields of fire across long, gentle, treeless slopes. Three days of hard fighting carried the Canadians to within striking distance of the imposing Drocourt-Quéant, or D-Q, Line, where the Fighting Tenth would go into action for the second time in less than a month, and where its second Victoria Cross would be won.

After a one-day stay in Saint-Catherines, the Tenth moved into Arras proper, occupying Schramm Barracks late in the evening of 27 August. The next day, Arras was subjected to long-range shelling; unfortunately, the only shell that fell anywhere near Schramm Barracks killed one member of the Battalion and injured two others. That night, the unit marched out of Arras and followed the Arras-Cambrai road to the vicinity of Vis-en-Artois, where it occupied the Second Brigade's support position. The move was completed during the early-morning hours of 29 August.[62]

The Germans were left reeling in the wake of Amiens. The *de facto* commander-in-chief, General Ludendorff, was so disillusioned by the remarkable success of the British offensive that he concluded, "The war must be ended."

The course of action for the Allies was no less obvious. "Tout le monde à la bataille!" cried the supreme commander, Ferdinand Foch, who was rewarded with promotion to marshal of France.

For the time being, the BEF shouldered the main load. When the Fourth Army came up against the old Somme battlefields, Field-Marshal Haig widened the offensive, bringing the Third Army into action on 21 and 23 August, and the First Army on the twenty-sixth. The British were facing the strongest parts of the massive Hindenburg Line, Siegfried-Stellung and Wotan-Stellung, the latter known by the BEF as the Drocourt-Quéant Line. The Canadian Corps, shifted from Amiens to Arras, led the First Army's drive on the D-Q Line, which culminated in a shattering breakthrough on 2 September. The blow forced the Germans to relinquish virtually all the ground that they had captured at such great cost earlier in the year, and gave Kaiser Wilhelm a nervous breakdown. "Now we have lost the war!" Wilhelm wailed when he heard of the loss of the D-Q Line. "Poor Fatherland!"

Further punishing blows against the German army lay ahead. On 12 September, American troops went into action on a large scale for the first time, when the U.S. First Army attacked at Saint-Mihiel. During the same week there were more attacks by the British Third and Fourth armies as they closed on the main defences along the Hindenburg Line.

These moves set the stage for a series of powerful, co-ordinated, and widely separated attacks during the last week in September. These operations were designed, Marshal Foch later explained, to "prevent [the enemy] from bringing up units in proper form, capable of waging a well ordered battle, and from assembling artillery and infantry in defensive position of any considerable extent and prepared in advance — in short, prevent him from conducting any battle on a large scale, even a defensive on." The first of these operations was a Franco-American attack between Reims and Verdun on 26 September, followed the next day by the BEF's First (led by the Canadian Corps) and Third armies against Cambrai. There was an Anglo-Belgian attack in Flanders on 28 September, and on the twenty-ninth the British Fourth and French First armies attacked Saint-Quentin, the heart of the Hindenburg Line.

The BEF breached and outflanked the Hindenburg Line in hard fighting, and the results were startling. On 3 October, Field-Marshal Paul von Hindenburg, Ludendorff's superior, told the German government to make "an immediate offer of peace to the enemy." Hindenburg bluntly stated that it was now impossible to win the war and that "the only right course is to give up the fight, in order to spare useless sacrifices for the German people and their allies."

Not surprisingly, it was an active sector. The Battalion's positions were routinely shelled, but initially there was "no serious damage." That changed on 30 August, when the Germans blasted these trenches with gas and high-explosive shells, causing four casualties. However, the Canadian artillery was even busier, firing enormous barrages designed to cut the wire along the D-Q Line. The Germans were understandably nervous, and each night the sky was filled with their red and orange SOS flares. Other Canadian preparations for an attack were noted by the war diarist: "The roads continue crowded with transport of every kind; in addition, some Tanks and Armoured Cars were seen."[63]

An assault was clearly imminent, but the Fighting Tenth was kept in the dark until almost the last minute. On Sunday, 1 September, the Battalion vacated Vis-en-Artois for Chérisy, a mile to the southwest. Colonel MacDonald and his fellow officers waited patiently, expectantly, all day long, "but no move order

was received."[64] It finally arrived during the night: the attack on the D-Q Line would be made on Monday morning. The First Division, striking south of the Arras-Cambrai road, would operate on a two-brigade front, with the Second on the left and the Third on the right. The 7th (1st British Columbia Regiment) Battalion would lead the Second Brigade over the top at 5:20 a.m. At the Red Line, about a thousand yards into the enemy position, the Fighting Tenth, accompanied by the 8th (90th Winnipeg Rifles) Battalion on its left, would pass through at 8 a.m. Together they would carry the attack to the D-Q Line's main support position, the Buissy Switch Line, which was centered on the heavily defended village of Villers-lez-Cagnicourt.

Artillery support would be minimal for the Tenth. The Battalion's sector lay on the edge of an innovative plan to exploit the expected breach in the D-Q Line by means of a flying column of cavalry and armoured cars which would race down the Arras-Cambrai road and seize the bridges over the Canal du Nord. In order to ensure that the column's progress would not be impeded by shell holes, the barrage was to be lifted on a 1000-yard front astride the road; this would take effect at eight o'clock, just as the Tenth was going into action. To compensate the Battalion for the reduction in firepower, four heavy tanks were assigned to it.

Considering the time and resources the enemy devoted to this position, the Canadian Corps crushed the D-Q Line with surprising ease. Backed by the full power of the Corps artillery and bolstered by British batteries of field and heavy guns, the infantry of the First and Fourth divisions swiftly overran the network of fortifications, killing and capturing large numbers of defenders. But the exploitation phase of the fight proved to be disappointing. As soon as the barrage lifted on either side of the Arras-Cambrai road, German batteries firing over open sights and massed machine-guns came into play. Gunfire stopped the armoured cars before they could get started and endangered the formations on both flanks, including the Fighting Tenth.

The Battalion was in trouble within minutes of jumping off. Colonel MacDonald deployed three companies in the attack: A, under Lieutenant Norman MacEachern was in the centre, with Major Leo Carey and B Company on the right and Major Phil Walker's D on the left. In the first forty-five minutes, all four tanks were knocked out, but this was no surprise to MacDonald. He had been unimpressed with their performance at Amiens, the biggest tank attack of the war, and noted that in this battle "their organization did not seem to be as good as might have been wished for."* But the loss of the of the tanks, coupled with the interruption in the barrage, meant that the infantrymen of the Fighting Tenth were on their own.[66]

Its flank exposed by the failed armoured-car thrust along the road to the left, and raked by devastating machine-gun fire from the Buissy Switch Line in front, the Battalion's attack quickly stalled. As soon as he realized what was happening, Colonel MacDonald left his headquarters dugout and hurried forward to investigate. Surveying the situation, he decided that there was nothing to be done about the exposed left flank — which he later described as "a source of considerable worry and annoyance" — but he did offer a solution to the problem of renewing the assault. Seeing that the enemy's fire "made a normal frontal advance impossible," MacDonald unhesitatingly threw out the timetable and ordered his companies to use the tactics which they had so effectively employed on other occasions. These included moving

Corporal (later Sergeant) Wilfred Malkinson, DCM, MM
Courtesy Glenbow Archives, Calgary

by sections; covering each other and taking advantage of whatever protection was offered by physical features; and outflanking the enemy wherever possible. The colonel was pleased to see that it worked. "In this manner," he later wrote, "a slow and steady, although perhaps not brilliant attack was made, and the advance continued."[67]

Nevertheless, a hard and bloody battle lay ahead. MacDonald praised the Germans, calling them "exceptionally good troops.... They fought bitterly until the end in almost every instance, and in many cases were killed rather than captured. Moreover, they were in considerable force and greatly out-numbered our attacking companies."[68]

Bravery was the byword this day. Early in the fighting, an enemy strongpoint blocked the advance. Four bombers, acting on their own initiative, attacked it, braving a devastating hail of machine-gun bullets and shells fired over open sights by a battery of German field guns. Privates George LaDuke, Peter Mattison, Joseph Hughes, and Richard Clark miraculously emerged unscathed and knocked out the troublesome position. In addition to killing seven of the enemy, they captured thirty others, along with ten machine-guns. The four privates were later awarded

---

* The colonel's lack of confidence in the tanks was shared by his men, as illustrated by the experience of Private Scotty Murray, the little Lewis gunner who had won the MM at Amiens. Private Murray and his Number 2, Private Johnny Upton, spotted a tank lumbering into action and decided to keep close to it. Within a hundred yards, they had changed their minds — the tank was drawing so much fire that it was not safe to be anywhere near it. "This is no place for us, Johnny," Murray shouted over the din, and they scrambled in search of a safer location.[65]

DCMs, the first of eleven won here, a total rivalled only by Hill 70.

Similar feats of heroism were taking place elsewhere as the Fighting Tenth worked its way through the maze of defences. Private Thomas Flynn won a DCM when his platoon was held up by a German machine-gun post. Under the cover of a Lewis gun, Private Flynn crawled forward alone and attacked the enemy, killing two and capturing the machine-gun. Private William Holmes was also awarded the DCM when he single-handedly took on a sunken road full of Germans. Using his Lewis gun to deadly effect, Private Holmes pinned down the defenders and enabled his platoon to rout them. Sixty-one prisoners resulted from his action.

Typically, the Fighting Tenth enjoyed outstanding leadership, not only from officers but from other ranks, too. In the course of the attack, all three company commanders were wounded: A Company's Lieutenant MacEachern took bullets in the right arm and left thigh, B's Major Carey was hit in the chest by a bullet, and Major Walker of D Company suffered a smashed nose. Carey and Walker went down early, but the twenty-three-year-old MacEachern stayed in action long enough to win a bar to the DSO he had won at Hill 70. Continually braving intense fire, he led his company past one strongpoint after another, personally reconnoitring before leading his men into each assault. Lieutenant Gordon Graham, a twenty-nine-year-old store manager from Saskatoon, took Carey's place at the head of B Company, leading it to the final objective. At one point, he used a Lewis gun to tangle with a German field gun, which he captured after its crew fled. Lieutenant Graham was awarded the DSO for his efforts. Lieutenants Tom Carter and

Lance-Corporal Joseph Milne, MM and two bars
Courtesy National Archives of Canada/PA-2622

Charles Watt led their platoon through heavy fire to capture seventy-five prisoners by the end of the day; Lieutenant Carter won the MC, while Lieutenant Watt was given a bar to the MC he picked up at Amiens.

Where no officers were available, other ranks took up the slack. Lance-Sergeant Arthur Underwood stepped to the head of his platoon and led it through furious fire. Pinned down by a strongpoint, Sergeant Underwood calmly reconnoitred the position, planned his attack, then led it to success. Similarly Sergeant Wilfred Malkinson, who had won the MM at Hill 70, took over his platoon when the officer fell. Under Sergeant Malkinson's direction, the platoon stormed and captured a German strongpoint holding up the advance on the left flank. Both Malkinson and Underwood were awarded the DCM.

The key to the operation was Villers-lez-Cagnicourt, which Colonel MacDonald called, with reason, "a fortress." Later, after it had fallen, the troops appreciated the accuracy of the description. "What struck me," recalled one of the Battalion's veterans, "was that nearly all the houses facing our lines — wasn't too big a village — were all thick concrete walls."[69] As the morning gave way to afternoon, the Fighting Tenth battled its way closer and closer to it. On the left, D Company had a particularly difficult time. Now commanded by Lieutenant Jack Clark, this company found its approach blocked by a sunken road filled with German troops. Lieutenant Clark took the position, capturing sixty-one prisoners and thirteen machine-guns, then led his men into a fortified factory on the northern outskirts of Villers-lez-Cagnicourt. The factory held out until four in the afternoon but, when it finally fell, it netted D Company another twelve prisoners and eight machine guns.[70]

The village continued to resist the Battalion's best efforts to capture it and, by late afternoon, the prospects for success looked grim. But Colonel MacDonald refused to accept the possibility of failure. "It's got to be taken, at all costs," he insisted, "at all costs."[71]

Making amends for the first day at Amiens, the artillery came to the aid of the Fighting Tenth. After lifting off according to plan at eight o'clock that morning, the Canadian field gunners had taken several hours to resume the barrage that had proven so effective in the early going. It took even longer to re-establish the superiority of their fire over the stubborn enemy. This had been done by the time Colonel MacDonald contacted the brigadier, General Loomis, and arranged a barrage to aid the beleaguered Battalion.

The attack on Villers-lez-Cagnicourt went in at 6 p.m. The combination of Canadian high-explosive shells and glinting bayonets proved overwhelming. A and B companies outflanked the village on either side, and the end came within a matter of minutes.

Surrounded by the Fighting Tenth, the defenders had the unsavory choice of staying in their positions and being obliterated by shells, or running the gauntlet of rifle and machine-gun fire. In fact, few fled. The Germans "fought to the last," recalled Lieutenant Joseph Sproston, one of only two subalterns in B Company to emerge unscathed this day. "I never saw so many Germans dead as there was around that place — thousands of them."[72]

Others who witnessed the scene agreed with Sproston's recollection. "I never saw so many dead," said another Tenth Battalion veteran. "They were just caught like rats in a trap."[73]

The capture of Villers-lez-Cagnicourt gave the Tenth the upper hand, but the battle was far from over. More furious fighting lay ahead, in the course of which the Battalion won its second Victoria Cross. Sergeant Arthur George Knight, a thirty-two-year-old, English-born carpenter from Regina, had been a member of the Tenth since 1915. As a corporal, he had been awarded the Belgian Croix de Guerre in November 1917, for his efforts at Passchendaele. Now on this dull September day in 1918, the sergeant with the mischievous smile went on a rampage, according to the *London Gazette's* account of his actions:

[A]fter an unsuccessful attack, Sgt. Knight led a bombing section forward, under heavy fire of all descriptions, and engaged the enemy at close quarters. Seeing that his party continued to be held up, he dashed forward alone, bayoneting several of the enemy machine-gunners and trench mortar crews, and forcing the remainder to retire in confusion. He then brought forward a Lewis gun and directed his fire on the retreating enemy, inflicting many casualties.

In the subsequent advance of his platoon in pursuit, Sgt. Knight saw a party of about thirty of the enemy go into a deep tunnel which led off the trench. He again dashed forward alone, and, having killed one Officer and two N.C.O's. captured twenty other ranks. Subsequently he routed, singlehanded, another enemy party which was opposing the advance of his platoon.

On each occasion he displayed the greatest valour under fire at very close range, and by his example of courage, gallantry and initiative was a wonderful inspiration to all.[74]

Sergeant Knight's heroism paved the way to victory for the Fighting Tenth, but, like Harry Brown at Hill 70, he did not live to see the fruits of his bravery. Knight was wounded by a shell burst later in the day, and died without knowing that he had won the VC. It had seemed possible that he would recover, as he lingered for several days. As late as 8 September, Captain Jack Mitchell wrote Knight's parents in Surrey, England, that "we all hope he will be well and in England soon." But three days later Captain Mitchell wrote again: "It is impossible to say how sorry we all are to hear of your son's death or to express to you our sympathy. The news cast a gloom over the whole company, as we had all such hopes for his recovery and safe return to England. I am quite sure we will never forget the day your son was wounded. You will, I am sure, take great comfort and pride from the fact that your son has been recommended for the Victoria Cross."[75] Knight was buried in the cemetery at nearby Hendecourt-lez-Cagnicourt; Knight Crescent in Regina commemorates his heroism.

The VC was the highlight of many instances of bravery on 2 September. Lance-Corporal Alexander Culgin spotted Germans attempting to extricate a field gun, and rushed forward through daunting fire. With his Lewis gun, he killed the team of horses and captured the gun and crew. Later, when his Lewis gun was smashed in his hands, Corporal Culgin salvaged enemy bombs and killed six Germans with them. A fellow lance-corporal put on a similar display of courage. After the Germans had been routed from a sunken road, Harry Wilson pursued them with his Lewis gun, inflicting heavy losses at close range and precluding any opportunity by the enemy to rally. Although twice wounded, Private McLeod Fenwick led a party of bombers along a trench, enabling his platoon to take the position. In the process, Private Fenwick and his mates freed a British tank officer and four crewmen who had been captured by the Germans. Culgin, Wilson, and Fenwick all won the DCM.

Two officers played a vital role in the final advance. The Battalion's second-in-command, Major William Bingham, and C Company's Captain Herbert Andrews pushed forward on Colonel MacDonald's orders. Major Bingham manned a captured 77-millimetre field gun and used it to blast a group of stubborn defenders, then he and Captain Andrews led the tired, bloodied survivors of the Battalion to the final objective, the Buissy Switch Line. Both Bingham and Andrews won bars to the MCs they had won at Amiens and Hill 70, respectively.

As the men of the Fighting Tenth shot and bombed their way through the German trenches and dugouts, the enemy reluctantly acknowledged defeat in the fading light. "We could see them," recalled Private Scotty Murray. "They would turn around and fire a few at you, you know, but they would keep on a-going, they kept a-going."[76] The Battalion attempted to give chase, but, as Private Samuel Hemphill related, the long, gentle slope, devoid of cover, was completely commanded by the Germans on the far side of the Canal du Nord. As Private Hemphill and his mates advanced, the enemy "opened up with anti-tank guns and everything else at us," he remembered. "We could see the canal, but we weren't anywhere near it, although there was quite a sloping hill. Now, he was

Corporal (Acting Sergeant) Arthur Knight, VC, and (inset) his Victoria Cross, now in possession of the Glenbow Museum in Calgary.

giving us quite a bit of barrage there on the face of the hill, and we had to back up and entrench ourselves for the night back there." Hemphill, the twenty-one-year-old Edmontonian, was wounded in the knee soon afterwards, and did not rejoin the unit until three weeks before the war ended.[77]

Digging in along the Buissy Switch Line, the men of the Fighting Tenth could take satisfaction in a job well done. Sergeant James van der Water, the young bank clerk from Calgary, captured the mood of the moment when he wrote of the battle in a letter home:

> ... Fritz had his best troops against us and very strong positions. Nevertheless, we had our objective to make, and we not only made it, but we passed it. Our casualties were very heavy and some of the best have gone, but fortunately a large percentage were only wounded. It was very comforting that there were ten times as many German dead as ours, besides the thousands of prisoners we took. We absolutely fought him to a finish and beat him at every turn. It was grand to be in it.[78]

Besides capturing Villers-lez-Cagincourt and the Buissy Switch Line, the Fighting Tenth had rounded up the astonishing total of twenty-two guns,[79] along with 150 machine-guns and 700 prisoners — more men than the Battalion had taken into action.[80]

The cost had been high. The Tenth's losses on 2 September totalled eleven officers and 245 other ranks.[81*] However, as Sergeant van der Water noted in his letter to Calgary, the casualties included a very high percentage of wounded — nearly 85 per cent — and because most of them were clean bullet wounds, as opposed to the grotesque injuries inflicted by artillery shells, the majority of these men recovered and returned to the Battalion.

But good men were giving their lives. Corporal William Cooper, who won the DCM at Amiens, won the MM here posthumously, as did Private Charles Millar. Lance-Sergeant David Hampton and Private Tokutaro Iwamoto won MMs at Hill 70, and Lance-Corporal Robert Smith and Private Austin Eide had been awarded MMs at Amiens; all were killed in action in and around Villers-lez-Cagnicourt.

Some of the best officers in the unit were also casualties. Two lieutenants died of their wounds — Douglas Thomson, who had just come back from leave two weeks before, and David Milne, a thirty-year-old Calgary police detective who won the MC posthumously. Three company commanders, Majors Carey and Walker and Lieutenant MacEachern, the DSO winner, were wounded, along with half-a-dozen other

lieutenants, including St. Clair Fisher, William Oliver, and Edward Watling, who had all won MCs at Amiens; William Webb, who had joined the Battalion on 14 August; William Edwards, the goalkeeper on the unit's soccer team; and Ralph Feurt. But the Fighting Tenth, in spite of losing leaders of such quality, was able to prevail over a still numerous, well-equipped, and near-fanatical enemy in positions of great strength. The Battalion's success speaks volumes for the spirit and determination of the surviving officers and other ranks.

The Battalion's performance was richly rewarded. Three DSOs were won by officers, including Colonel MacDonald, who added the second bar to that decoration, the only member of the unit to gain that distinction. Six MCs were handed out; besides the five mentioned above, Lieutenant David Teviotdale received the MC for his part in the battle for Villers-lez-Cagnicourt. Eleven other ranks were awarded DCMs, and thirty-seven more won MMs, including bars to Corporals Frank Ringrose, Louis Smith, and Thomas Steadman, who had won MMs at Amiens, and to Private Rennie Paget, who picked up his original medal at the Somme. The other MM-winners were Sergeants John Campbell, William Gilchrist, Cliff Malcolm, Baset Riseley, Leslie Wallace, and Benjamin Whiteley; Corporals William Cooper DCM (posthumous), Arthur Kendall, John Porter, and Leslie Tate; Lance-Corporals John Hutchinson and Arthur Maxwell; Privates George Brooks, Thomas Connor, Frank Depeau, Frank Enderton, Peter Greig, Cecil Hewitt, John Hescott, William Humphreys, Walter Holcombe, Percy Johnson, Urban Jones, Alfred Maggs, John McKenzie, John McPhail, Charles Millar (posthumous), Gardiner Newton, Thomas Simpson, William Stevenson, James Turnbull, Harry Turvey, and Aylmer Williams.

The next day the Battalion moved up to the Canal du Nord. It was part of a general advance by the Canadian Corps, completed amid cloudy, cool, and occasionally wet conditions which reflected the enemy's dampened spirits. In sharp contrast to the previous evening when the Germans prevented such an advance, there was virtually no opposition to the unit's move to the canal bank. The Tenth started forward at eleven-thirty Tuesday morning, 3 September, and the troops spent the rest of the day digging in. There was no attempt to force a crossing. General Currie had already decided the defences were too strong to tackle without a properly prepared, set-piece assault.[83]

The Fighting Tenth was relieved Tuesday night on the canal line by British Columbia's 7th Battalion. Marching to Chérisy, the Tenth boarded buses for

---

* Colonel MacDonald's operational report gives a slightly lower aggregate, 233.[82]

Simencourt, west of Arras, where it enjoyed, according to the war diary, "the first real night's rest possible for some time" on 4 - 5 September. During its rainy, two-week stay in Simencourt, the Battalion undertook a comprehensive programme of training and sports, weather permitting. The troops also enjoyed concerts by the regimental band, attended pay and bath parades — the hot shower on 6 September was the first in more than a month — and checked and cleaned their equipment. Reinforcements (196 other ranks) arrived as well.

The Battalion also bade farewell to two prominent officers. Major William Bingham was bothered by an old head wound and had to be hospitalized on 13 September, six days after his twenty-eighth birthday. While Major Bingham later returned to the unit, this was not the case with the chaplain, Captain Ralph Harrison, a thirty-eight-year-old Anglican minister well-known in southern Alberta before the war. Captain Harrison was replaced on the fourteenth by Captain Francis Frost,[84] who had been twice-wounded as a stretcher-bearer with the 28th (Northwest) Battalion, winning the DCM at the Somme. After recovering from his injuries, Frost was appointed an honourary captain and chaplain in the summer of 1917, and was based first at Shorncliffe and then in Seaford, England, before returning to France in August 1918. His assignment to the Fighting Tenth was his first with a combat unit.[85]

It was raining on the morning of Friday, 20 September, when the Battalion left Simencourt. Marching to Wanquetin, the troops took a train to Boyelles — "a long and tedious journey," in the words of the war diary — and then marched through a rainstorm to their new billets in Mercatel.[86]

Here the Battalion prepared for its part in the next round of offensive operations. Another draft of thirty-four other ranks joined the unit, boosting its strength to 689, including twenty-nine officers.[87] After having three earlier inspections called off by bad weather, the Corps commander, General Currie, paid a visit on 25 September. Accompanied by the acting brigadier, Lieutenant-Colonel William Gilson, Currie discussed with Colonel MacDonald plans for what the war diary calls "the coming hostilities."[88]

General Currie had come up with a brilliant plan to force a crossing of the Canal du Nord. He intended to assault with two divisions — the First on the left, and the Fourth on the right — on a 4000-yard front between Sains-lez-Marquion and Moeuvres, quickly fanning out to a 9700-yard front on the far side of the canal. There would be no preliminary bombardment, but the barrage accompanying the infantry would overwhelm the defenders and knock out much of their artillery in the first few minutes of the attack. If all went well, the Canadians would capture Cambrai, the enemy's main railhead in this area, and seal the fate of the Hindenburg Line.

The canal, which was only partly completed, was "no obstacle as a canal," according to Corps intelligence reports. Sixty-four feet wide, it contained no water in the Canadian sector; its bottom was at ground level, with banks built up on either side, but these were "not obstacles of importance to infantry." Beyond the canal lay a series of defensive positions which appeared to be relatively weak but were protected by enormous fields of rusted barbed wire, much of it concealed by brush. Intelligence warned, however, that "the area between these systems is dotted with old excavations, dugouts, and shelters, any of which might be utilized for M.G. [machine-gun] defence."[89]

As at Amiens, the Fighting Tenth would be committed during the final phase of the assault. Elements of the First and Third Brigades would lead the First Division across the canal, through the Red Line to the Green Line, where the Second Brigade would come into action. The 7th Battalion from British Columbia would drive to the Blue Line, midway between the Bourlon-Sauchy-Lestrée railway and Haynecourt. The 5th (Western Cavalry) and 8th (90th Winnipeg Rifles) battalions would leap-frog and capture Haynecourt, and then the Tenth would continue the attack to the Brown Line, across the Cambrai-Douai road. If possible, the Battalion was to go as far as it could get beyond the Brown Line.

During the evening of Wednesday, 25 September, the Fighting Tenth moved into billets at Cagnicourt, about a mile south of Villers-lez-Cagnicourt. The weather was clear and cool as the Battalion made its final preparations. "The day was spent in resting the Battalion and issuing Stores for the coming offensive."[90]

The attack on the Canal du Nord began at 5:20 a.m., on Friday, 27 September. The barrage that accompanied the operation was devastatingly effective, according to B Company's Lieutenant Joseph Sproston. "What I particularly noted, which happened on several occasions, was the wonderful work that the artillery did, both in the creeping barrage and laying the barrage down before we jumped. On several occasions, they were completely demoralized — running, the Germans were. And when we moved forward, it was the marvellous work of the counter battery and the creeping barrage — that was a wonderful assistance, and saved thousands of lives for the infantry."[91]

For a while, the operation went like clockwork. On the right, the Fourth Division captured the crucial heights at Bourlon, but found its right flank exposed when the neighbouring British forces failed to get forward. The Fourth could make little headway beyond Bourlon, which was to have considerable consequences for the Fighting Tenth later in the day. The First Division, ably aided by the British 11th Division on its left, swiftly carried its objectives. In the early afternoon, the 7th Battalion joined the attack, taking the Blue Line by two o'clock. The 5th and 8th battalions passed through and captured Haynecourt, paving the way for the Fighting Tenth to play its part.

It was a cloudy, cool, windy day. After the attack began, the Tenth, numbering twenty officers and 580 other ranks for combat,[92] moved from Cagnicourt to its assembly positions behind the 5th Battalion. Colonel MacDonald, his second-in-command, Major Hugh Ferguson, Captain Hugh Pearson, the adjutant, and the four company commanders were on horseback. It was a difficult move, Colonel MacDonald later reported, "owing to the congestion of the traffic on the roads and the fact that no cross country paths had been sufficiently well opened up to allow the Units to move by them."[93]

Among those in the advance that fateful morning was a private named Tommy Ireland. A rancher in the foothills west of Calgary, the thirty-year-old English-born Ireland had tried three times to enlist, but had been rejected on account of his poor eyesight. Finally accepted in the fall of 1917, he went to England for three months' training at Bramshott, joining the 9th Reserve Battalion, which provided reinforcements for the four Alberta battalions in the field.* Equipped with eyeglasses, Private Ireland became a Second-Class shot, and he had to admit that he felt "a certain amount of exhilaration" as he marched with the Fighting Tenth on the morning of 27 September toward his first, and last, taste of warfare.[95]

There was a slight delay getting across the canal. This was due, not to enemy action, but to an 18-pounder field gun that had been on its way forward; it had fallen over, blocking the bridge. The infantry filed past, and "with more or less irregular halts caused by various reasons," the Fighting Tenth caught up to the 5th Battalion around two in the afternoon. Colonel MacDonald — on foot now, along with the other officers who had been mounted — deployed his companies: B on the right and C on the left, with D in support and A in reserve. MacDonald noted "some hesitancy on the part of the 5th Battalion to continue the advance," which he attributed to concern for the right flank. This was exposed to heavy artillery and small-arms fire, resulting from the inability of the Fourth Division to get past Bourlon. However, the 5th went into action around three-thirty and quickly captured Haynecourt.[96]

Two hours later, the Fighting Tenth joined the attack. Passing through the 5th Battalion along a sunken road east of Haynecourt, its advance "was made under great difficulties," according to Colonel MacDonald. "It was quite obvious that the Right Flank was very much exposed. It was not known how far forward the 4th Division had been able to proceed and large numbers of the enemy could be seen very distinctly moving about on our Right Flank." Casualties mounted steadily under the enfilade fire of "several well placed Batteries of Machine Guns and Field Guns."[97]

One of the first to fall was the adjutant, Captain Pearson, a land surveyor from Edmonton. Interviewed years afterwards, Pearson admitted that, simply because he was the adjutant, "I had the funny idea that I was safe for the rest of the war." It was a mistaken assumption, he ruefully admitted. "We were lying there, and dammit all, this machine-gun fire was coming over the hill — indirect fire — and it got me right through the flesh of one of my legs, you see. It was nothing but a slight wound — I mean, it was only a clean hole — but the colonel insisted that I go back, and he got my batman up — he was Japanese, incidentally — and we started back." On the way to the rear, Pearson was hit again, this time by shrapnel in both legs from an overhead shell burst. "This little Jap got me into a hole which was actually a German latrine, and when I came out of it, I smelled like nothing on earth!" With his batman's aid, the foul-smelling, twenty-nine-year-old captain was eventually evacuated to a dressing station, but his war was over.[98]

B and C companies braved the deadly enfilade fire and moved smartly across the generally flat, treeless ground towards the Cambrai-Douai road. "Two very thick and very wide belts of wire were crossed," wrote Colonel MacDonald. "This was a task of considerable difficulty owing to the fact that the wire had to be cut by hand, and while this was being done practically no cover was available for the men." Two platoons pressed ahead to a secondary road two hundred yards beyond this point, which marked the Battalion's deepest penetration into enemy territory.[99]

With darkness falling, MacDonald called "a temporary halt in order to ascertain the conditions of the flanks, the strength of the enemy, his method of holding the ground in front and the best manner of breaking down his resistance, and to once more re-adjust the distribution of the Battalion." The enemy's fire, he noted, "was very heavy and from close range," primarily from machine-guns "in carefully selected positions protected by very heavy belts of wire." Both "flanks were badly exposed, the Right Flank being at least one mile and [a] half in the air and the Left Flank

---

* Private Ireland was welcomed to Bramshott by Brigadier-General J.G. Rattray, who had formerly commanded the Fighting Tenth. General Rattray gave Ireland and the other newcomers a stirring speech:

> Look, men. We're going to work you hard. We've got to train you hard. You've got to work hard at this training and absorb as much of it as you can. You're going to reinforce the men of the four big battalions from Alberta — I can't tell you where you're going, which one — some will go to the Tenth, some will go to the 31st, some to the 49th, and some to the 50th. But I want to impress this upon you. You are going to take the places of men who have made traditions and seeded them with their blood. Never do anything that will bring discredit upon your battalion. Please remember that.[94]

about a mile." MacDonald was pleased to have the help of two companies of the 5th Battalion and a battery of Vickers heavy machine-guns, "making the position reasonably secure" against counter-attack.[100]

While the right flank remained a source of concern throughout the night and the following day, the left was shored up by the arrival of British troops. MacDonald sent Captain Tommy Thompson to look for units of the 11th Division that were supposed to cover the Fighting Tenth's left. Captain Thompson, a thirty-three-year-old carpenter from Manitoba who had won the DSO at Hill 70, dodged enemy bullets and shells to find the British falling back from the village of Epinoy, due north of Haynecourt, and his appeals to move forward fell on deaf ears. A dejected Thompson returned to MacDonald, who angrily sent him back with instructions to be more insistent. This time, the captain was successful, and "after some persuasion led them forward through Epinoy and established a line protecting our Left Flank on the outskirts of the village and joining up with our Left Flank Company," MacDonald later wrote. Thompson's efforts earned him the MC.[101]

With darkness descending and his situation uncertain, MacDonald resorted to the measure that had worked so well at Amiens, dispatching battle patrols to keep in close touch with the enemy as a precaution against surprise attacks. The divisional commander, General Macdonell, was most impressed, saying that these patrols displayed "great dash" in carrying out their assignments.[102] One patrol, under Lieutenant William Hedges, ran into a party of sixty Germans on the Cambrai-Douai road. Lieutenant Hedges and his men routed the enemy, killing several and capturing eight. Hedges won the MC but the award was posthumous, for the subaltern was killed soon afterwards.[103]

The Germans on this front were a match for the Canadians in skill and daring. During the advance earlier in the day, the Fighting Tenth had overrun a battery of enemy field guns, which were promptly marked in chalk: CAPTURED BY 10TH BATTALION. Not for long, as Private Scotty Murray recalled: "Old Heinie swiped them from us again!" Under the cover of darkness, the Germans boldly hitched the guns to horse-drawn limbers and hauled them away. "We could hear them," remembered one of Murray's comrades, "but we didn't know whether it was our transport or what it was, you see. But, by God, they came and got these guns out and got away with them."[104] The incident illustrates not only the calibre of the enemy facing the Fighting Tenth, but also the extent to which the Battalion's position was exposed.

Colonel MacDonald was busy all night long, too. Reconnoitring, the enemy positions proved to be protected by so many machine-guns and so much barbed wire that the colonel concluded it was "not practicable" to renew the attack in the morning as planned.

MacDonald informed the Second Brigade that, in his opinion, "the advance should be temporarily delayed until better preparations could be made, as it was quite obvious that any further attempts to force our way forward in the face of the opposition that had been encountered was not a wise policy and would result in a great wastage of man power."[105]

His wise advice was ignored. At daylight on Saturday, 28 September, MacDonald received orders to renew the offensive at 8:45 a.m., when a barrage would be provided. The colonel received this news, he later wrote, "with some surprise," in view of his recommendation to postpone further operations. Worse, he was horrified to see that "the proposed creeping barrage ... coincide[d] with the line which the Battalion was holding." MacDonald realized that he had to act quickly to avert a disaster. Since it was obviously impossible to change the barrage plan at such short notice, he issued orders to his front-line companies to withdraw a safe distance. The retirement, predictably, drew heavy fire and cost the Battalion, in MacDonald's view, "at least 50 unnecessary casualties."[106]

His men were no less disillusioned. Sergeant Marshall Neal, a dark-haired, handsome, twenty-two-year-old from Calgary, recalled that his platoon fell back under intense fire, losing men at every step. "And, lo and behold, after we had gotten back — and I was the last man to leave — what did I see but the troops advancing again back to the position they left! That's administration for you."[107] The MM won by Sergeant Neal was small compensation for the resulting heartbreak.

Confusion reigned supreme. The barrage which had already caused so much grief for the Fighting Tenth came down fifteen minutes late, and, in Colonel MacDonald's words, it "was of such a feeble nature that for our purposes it was practically useless."[108]

The consequences for the Battalion were tragic. The artillery, low on ammunition after supporting a number of attacks already that morning, was experiencing great difficulty in meeting all the demands for its services. Without significant help from the gunners, either in cutting gaps in the barbed wire or suppressing the enemy's machine-gun fire, the infantrymen were slaughtered. "There was the odd gap here and there in the wire which, I would say, three or four men abreast could go through," Sergeant Neal later testified. "I would imagine they would be about, oh, ten to fifteen yards apart, not much more. Of course, they were set there for that purpose, where they could concentrate their fire. And, naturally, you would run to the opening of any field of barbed wire in front of you, and that's where we suffered very heavy casualties."[109]

The topography of the area was also against them. The Fighting Tenth was attacking down a shallow valley, and the high ground on either side was outside of the First Division's jurisdiction. Unfortunately, neither the British 11th Division on the left nor the Fourth Canadian Division on the right, which attacked at 6 a.m., had taken these critical positions. In fact, it was not until late that night that any troops of the Fourth Division closed on the Cambrai-Douai road, and by then it was far too late to help the Fighting Tenth.

For Tommy Ireland, the short-sighted rancher who had just joined the Battalion, this was an unforgettable morning. While he was waiting for the signal to go over the top, a shell exploded nearby, showering him with shrapnel. The chunks of metal hitting his helmet "sounded like nothing so much as throwing a handful of gravel against a plate-glass window."[110]

Then his officer gave a brief speech to the troops huddled around him. "Now, there's a bad barbed-wire entanglement out in front there, and it's been partly cut. As you go over, extend to the left, and anybody who can't see a way through, flop. For Christ's sake, don't get bunched up." The officer paused and glanced at his watch. "All right, fellows," he muttered, "let's go."[111]

The Battalion was engulfed in a maelstrom of German bullets and shells. Sergeant Neal and Private Ireland were both badly wounded within the first few yards, and many of their buddies were hit, too. If anyone symbolized the futility of this bloody Saturday morning, it was the brave Winnipegger, Captain Jack Mitchell of C Company. His men were soon pinned down, but Captain Mitchell crawled ahead, desperately searching for a way through the wire. He was wounded: once, twice, thrice. The last wound proved to be fatal. Twenty-two-year-old John Broughton Mitchell, who had won the MC and bar since joining the Fighting Tenth as a lieutenant in July 1915, died without finding the passage he was seeking.

A lot of brave men perished with him. They included Lieutenant Charles FitzRoy, who had won the MC and bar earlier in the year; Sergeants David Murray (MM, Arleux), Arthur Pinder, who was awarded a posthumous bar to the MM he had won at Amiens, and Jack Wennevold, the American who had been grievously wounded at Second Ypres and returned to win the DCM at Hill 70; Corporal Harry Wilson, winner of the DCM at the D-Q Line and the MM at Hill 70; Lance-Corporal Charles Broadbent (MM, Amiens); Privates John Hescott (MM, D-Q Line), Cecil Hewitt (MM, D-Q Line), John Lynch (MM, Hill 70), Samuel Simms (MM, Amiens), Ernest Topp (MM, Amiens), and James Turnbull (MM, D-Q Line).

The one-sided struggle went on for two hours. Again and again, the men pressed the attack with characteristic determination and bravery, but they made little headway in the face of overwhelming odds. They were attacking in daylight, with no natural cover, in the face of appalling frontal and flanking fire, with no appreciable artillery support or assistance

from neighboring infantry formations, which were encountering similar difficulties. By the time Colonel MacDonald was able to call off the operation, the Fighting Tenth had merely regained the line it had been forced to abandon that morning under the threat of a Canadian bombardment. "This attack was worse than useless," the colonel later charged, "and resulted in approximately 100 casualties which could have been avoided had the recommendations already forwarded been carried into effect."[112]

Among those present that grim day in late September was the much admired Montrealer, Honorary Lieutenant-Colonel Frederick Scott, the First Division's chaplain. The fifty-seven-year-old Anglican canon had been at Ypres in April 1915 when the Tenth made its first attack, and now found himself in the combat zone during one of the Battalion's last actions. He recalled the episode on 28 September: "The 10th Battalion had established themselves partly in a ditch along the Cambrai road not far from Epinoy, and partly in outposts behind the German wire. The country was undulating, and in places afforded an extensive view of the forward area. German machine gun emplacements were in all directions, and our men suffered very severely." Making his way up to the Tenth's outpost line, he witnessed a remarkable feat of bravery by an unidentified soldier who crawled up to an enemy machine-gun post. "It was very exciting watching the plucky fellow approach the place of danger with the intention of bombing it," Scott later wrote. "Unfortunately just as he had reached the side of the trench the Germans must have become aware of his presence, for they opened fire, and he had to crawl back again as fast as he could."[113]

The Battalion's own chaplain also had a memorable day. Captain Francis Frost, who had been with the unit for only two weeks, was tireless in his efforts to rescue the wounded and relieve their suffering to the best of his ability. The injured private, Tommy Ireland, recalled that Captain Frost "had completed the cutting of a barbed-wire entanglement and picked up the broken pieces and thrown them aside so that the stretcher parties could get through to the wounded men, of whom I was one. Then he had erected a little shelter with boards and sheets of tin and anything he could find, and he was down at the first-aid post, making tea for the wounded men that were brought in."[114] However, Captain Frost sacrificed his health in the process; his nerves later deteriorated steadily, and he had to be hospitalized in November.[115]

With darkness, the redoubtable divisional chaplain, Colonel Scott, set out with a stretcher-bearer party to recover wounded men still exposed to German fire. Scott described the experience this way: "With my cane I managed to lead the party through a gap in the wire. I came to a poor fellow who had been lying there since the previous night with a smashed arm and leg. He was in great pain, but the men got him in safely, and the next time I saw him was in a Toronto hospital where he was walking with a wooden leg, and his arm in a sling."[116]

Returning to the Battalion's foremost positions, Scott crawled to an outpost manned by a handful of other ranks. "Where are your officers?" he inquired in a whisper.

"They are all gone."

"Who is in command?"

"A Lance Corporal."[117]*

After holding its tenuous position throughout the twenty-eighth, the Battalion was pulled out of the line. Relieved that night by the Little Black Devils of the 8th Battalion, the weary, bloodied Tenth moved a thousand yards back, to the vicinity of Haynecourt. Although it moved again on each of the next three nights, the Battalion played no further part in the furious fighting that continued until 2 October north of Cambrai. At last, on the evening of the second, the Tenth withdrew west of the Canal du Nord, occupying positions northwest of Buissy.[119]

The Fighting Tenth had been severely affected by the shambles on the Cambrai-Douai road, but could take considerable pride in its heroic effort, as reflected in the many decorations which came out of the battle. Besides Captain Tommy Thompson and the late Lieutenant William Hedges, Captains Bernard McDaniel and Allen McNair, the medical officer, and Lieutenants Robert Donald and Benjamin Skinner were awarded MCs. Seven other ranks won DCMs, including Sergeants Charles Jeeves and Samuel Leebody; Corporal Thomas Bradley; Lance-Corporal Arthur Burnell; and Privates John Collins and Norval Curtis MM. The thirty-eight MMs later awarded included nine bars, which went to Sergeants Harvie

Currie (who had won the MM at Amiens), Percy Fairbank (Arleux), Arthur Kendall (D-Q Line), Arthur Pinder (Amiens), and Leslie Wallace (D-Q Line); Lance-Sergeant Reuben Kilmer (Amiens); Corporal Maurice Oldenburg (Hill 70); Lance-Corporal Paul Oleson (Hill 70); and Private George Brooks (D-Q Line). Other MM-winners here included Sergeants Marshall Neal, John Seeley, Arthur Underwood DCM, and Richard Waller; Corporals Albert Harvey, George Leslie, and Frederick Murray; Lance-Corporals Roy Armstrong, William Smith, Vay Stephenson, Frank Weldon, and Robert Wood; Privates Luke Brown, Robert Coates DCM, William Dunn, Allan Ferguson, David Gillespie, Edward McDonald, Joe McNaughton, Charles Michie, Arthur Norris, Harold Riker, Frank Robbins, Elmer Smith, William Smith, Gordon Van Valkenburg DCM, Lawrence Vincent (posthumous), George Wigglesworth, and W. Wiskar.

But while medals were a gratifying recognition, they could not replace the good men who had been killed and wounded. Lieutenant Joseph Sproston of B Company later admitted that he was completely unnerved by this experience. His company had gone into action, he recalled, with 112 all ranks, and came out with only twenty-three. Sproston went to see Colonel MacDonald. "Sir, I've had it. I can't take no more," he told his commanding officer. "This isn't war, it's murder. It's just pure bloody murder."[120]

The young subaltern's distress was understandable. The battles of 27 and 28 September had cost the Fighting Tenth fifteen officers and 287 other ranks,[121] three-quarters of the officers and half of the other ranks who had crossed the canal. It was the Battalion's highest casualty count since Hill 70.

No one knew it, of course, but the Fighting Tenth had fought its last big battle.

---

* Canon Scott remained in the vicinity, and was wounded by a shell burst the following day, taking shrapnel in both legs. The Tenth's chaplain, Captain Frost, organized a stretcher party of four German prisoners to carry Scott to the rear. The beloved Scott was evacuated to England, where he recovered from his injuries.[118]

Chapter Ten

HOMECOMING

(29 September 1918 - 23 April 1919)

The Battalion was given little opportunity to lick its wounds in the wake of the tragic events on the Cambrai-Douai road. Within a few days, it returned to action and demonstrated its remarkable resiliency by performing as well as ever.

The intervening time was put to good use. Amid generally cloudy and cool conditions, the Tenth rested and reorganized and reinforcements arrived once again. These totalled 112 other ranks, along with fifteen officers, including Lieutenants Edward Watling and Ralph Feurt, who had been wounded at the D-Q Line. The second-in-command, Major Hugh Ferguson, departed to take a course at Aldershot, England, and was replaced by the popular Major Phil Walker, now recovered from the wounds he had suffered at the D-Q Line. All four companies had new commanding officers. Lieutenant Benjamin Skinner was given A Company, while Captain Herbert Andrews took B; C went to Lieutenant Charles Watt, and Captain James Dawson commanded D.

On 5 October, the Fighting Tenth was ordered to be ready to move forward and the next day each of the four companies moved independently to Recourt, relieving a British battalion, the Somerset Light Infantry. C and D companies held the front line, while A and B companies took over the support position. The weather was dull and cold, giving way to rain on the seventh. German shells also fell that morning, when as many as thirty small-calibre shells bracketed Battalion headquarters without casualties.[1]

The Battalion's latest assignment was part of a temporary arrangement. While the Canadian Corps was preparing for its final attack on Cambrai, which fell on 9 October, the First Division was transferred north of the River Sensée, where the Drocourt-Quéant Line remained intact. The Canadian division, as part of the British XXII Corps, committed two brigades, the First and Third, to the battle to smash these defences, which were breached by 11 October. The Second Brigade then joined the division's drive eastwards to the Canal de la Sensée.

The full operational plans were revealed on Tuesday, 8 October, when Colonel MacDonald and Major Walker attended an afternoon conference at Second Brigade headquarters. The new brigadier, R.P. Clark, presided.* The Fighting Tenth was to play a key role in the advance to the canal, but MacDonald would not be at the Battalion's head. Immediately after the conference concluded, he left for well-earned leave in England; Walker took over as acting commander and Captain Tommy Thompson served as second-in-command.[2]

The Tenth received its warning order on Friday, 11 October, and soon afterwards Captain James Dawson led D Company to the south bank of the River Sensée near Hamel. The rest of the Battalion marched to the neighbourhood of Lake Lecluse that evening, under the cover of a cold, wet mist. Its combat strength was twenty-seven officers and 482 other ranks, the fewest number of men the unit took into battle during the entire war. The three assaulting companies, A, B, and C, were in position by three o'clock Saturday morning, and Major Walker summoned their commanders to a conference in the pillbox which served as his headquarters. The Battalion, he explained, was to break through three heavily wired trenches and take the village of Arleux. "Although this was outside the Brigade Area," Walker later wrote of Arleux, "its capture was necessary in order to protect our right flank."[3]

The attack went in at 6 a.m. It was misty and drizzling rain when the Fighting Tenth went over the top, advancing behind a barrage which crept at the rate of 100 yards every three minutes. B Company, in the middle, and C on the left, encountered little resistance and quickly took their objectives.[4]

On the right, A Company had more difficulty in capturing Arleux. The town was heavily defended by machine-gun posts, skilfully manned by crews who fought to the last. Lieutenant Edward Watling, who had so recently rejoined the Battalion, attacked and captured the crew of one machine-gun nest, then was wounded while leading an attack on another position. Lieutenant Watling received the bar to the MC he had

---

* General Clark succeeded General Loomis, who had been promoted to command the Third Division, replacing Major-General Louis Lipsett, who departed to a divisional command in the British army in mid-September.

won at Amiens. Another subaltern, Lieutenant Arthur Nicolle, waded a stream in order to outflank and knock out a machine-gun nest. Despite these and other efforts, Arleux continued to hold out, and the company commander, Lieutenant Benjamin Skinner, sent word to Major Walker around nine o'clock that he would need artillery support to overcome the defenders. The Canadian field guns responded with the efficiency the infantry had come to expect, and the subsequent bombardment enabled Lieutenant Skinner to lead A Company in its final assault on Arleux at eleven. Under Skinner's skilful leadership — he afterwards added the bar to the MC he had won two weeks earlier — the company cleared the village within the hour. At noon, Major Walker reported to Second Brigade headquarters that the Battalion's objectives had been taken. As the Germans retired to the far side of the Canal de la Sensée, they blew up the bridges behind them, the explosions announcing their admission of defeat.[5]

The cost of this successful operation was, happily, modest. Three other ranks were killed, and fifteen were wounded. Two officers — Lieutenant Watling and a fellow subaltern, Noel Farrow, a twenty-six-year-old Calgary druggist who had joined the Battalion on 2 October — were injured. Six prisoners were taken, "and a number of the enemy killed." The

Tenth dug in along the canal, directed by Lieutenant Harry Templeman, who risked his life a number of times when placing his men in position and later bringing up supplies of bombs and small-arms ammunition. For this, Lieutenant Templeman won the bar to the MC he had won at Amiens.[6]

Drizzle turned to downpour that night as the Battalion was relieved by elements of the British 56th Division and moved back to the trenches captured the previous day in the vicinity of Arleux. Here the Tenth spent Sunday; the Battalion occupied the brigade's support position near Estrées on Monday, 14 October. Two days later, it returned to the canal, relieving the 5th (Western Cavalry) Battalion along the west bank. A and D companies held the front lines, with B and C in support. The relief, carried out in a driving rainstorm, was completed in a mere thirty-five minutes.[7]

The beginning of the end of the Great War was at hand. While the Fighting Tenth was taking over the entrenchments along the Canal de la Sensée, the Germans were evacuating theirs, here and elsewhere along the Western Front. The Canadian attack at Cambrai had unhinged the Hindenburg Line, which had also been breached by British and Australian forces farther south. Having lost their last major line of resistance, and feeling the cumulative effects of

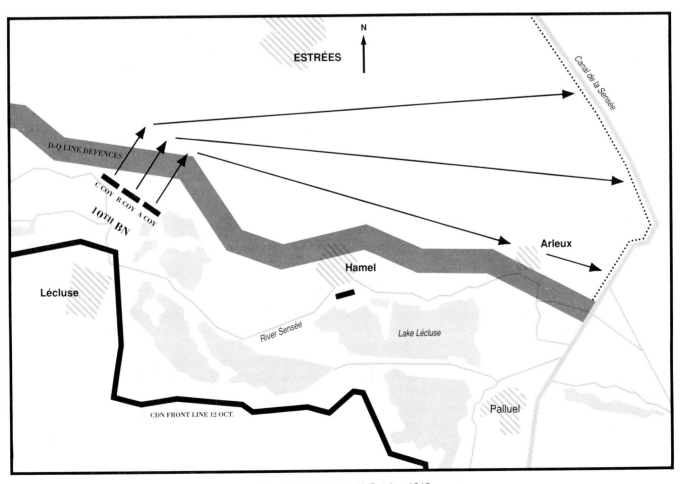

Canal de la Sensée, 12 October 1918

four years of attrition warfare, the Germans began a widespread, if reluctant, retirement.

The Canadian Corps became aware of the withdrawal early on Thursday, 17 October. A morning barrage fired by the First Division's artillery drew no response from the enemy, and the chase was on.

At one o'clock that afternoon, Major Walker was told by the brigadier, General Clark, to send "strong fighting patrols" across the canal "at once." Walker directed A and D companies to advance towards Roucourt, three miles to the east, "if we can get that far, without serious resistance." B and C companies were to support and protect the flanks, keeping in touch with the 8th (90th Winnipeg Rifles) Battalion on the right and with the First Brigade units on the left.[8]

Crossing the canal on temporary foot bridges built by the engineers, the Fighting Tenth made rapid progress. When Major Walker crossed later in the afternoon, he found that A and C companies were already on the road linking Cambrai and Douai. Although there was no sign of the formations on either flank, Walker, evidently exhilarated by the easy success, ordered the advance to continue to Roucourt.

That village was unoccupied by the enemy, and A, C, and D companies pushed through and beyond it by late afternoon. Walker, holding B Company in reserve southeast of Roucourt, set up his headquarters in a nearby château and waited for flanking formations to catch up. The 8th Battalion moved up on the right a short time later, but the 2nd (Eastern Ontario) Battalion on the left was still back at the Cambrai-Douai road, so Walker covered his exposed flank with four Vickers heavy machine-guns. Water and rations were brought up during the early evening, despite difficulties in getting them across the canal. "This was doubly important," the major later wrote of these supplies, "in view of the hard day's work which the troops had performed."[9]

Friday, 18 October, was another demanding day. Patrols pushed forward the previous evening revealed that the next large town, Lewarde, was virtually undefended. When Major Walker passed this report to brigade headquarters, he was ordered to resume the advance. Walker, in turn, issued instructions to B and C companies to lead the way, with D in support and A in reserve. They were to move in a northeasterly direction, towards Lewarde, Masny, Ecaillon, and

---

The war ended in anticlimactic fashion. With the fall of the Hindenburg Line, the Germans had lost their last complete line of fortifications and, with it, their only hope to prolong the fighting. Flushed with success, the Allies intended to give the crumbling German army no chance to recover. "We have got the enemy down, in fact, he is a beaten Army," a triumphant Field-Marshal Haig wrote on 10 October, "and my plan is to go on hitting him as hard as we possibly can, until he begs for mercy."

The Germans had already put out peace feelers. On 5 October, an armistice proposal was submitted, via neutral Switzerland, to U.S. President Woodrow Wilson. It was an obvious ploy to divide the Allies; President Wilson's Fourteen Points, a list of conditions for ending the war, had dismayed both the British and the French, and the Germans considered the American leader to be the weak link in the Allied chain. However, the German proposal was rejected, and desultory fighting continued on the Western Front.

Shattered and capable only of mustering rear-guard actions, the German army started a widespread withdrawal in front of the BEF on 9 October, the day the Canadian Corps captured the vital rail head at Cambrai. It was resumed on an even bigger scale on the seventeenth, and the Allied armies gave chase. But even at this late date and under these circumstances, there were few leaders who believed that the war was winding down; most expected it would take another year of campaigning to crush Germany.

In fact, however, the end was fast approaching. Its armies defeated and retreating, Germany was stricken by civil strife, including food riots, and faced the very real possibility of revolution. There was talk that Kaiser Wilhelm would abdicate.

On 8 November, a delegation of German representatives visited Marshal Foch in his private train parked in the forest at Compiegne. The Germans hoped to negotiate an armistice, but Foch was not interested in negotiations. "Do you ask for an armistice?" he gruffly inquired of his guests. "If you do, I can inform you of the conditions subject to which it can be obtained." The Germans were appalled by the conditions, which were intended to strip their nation of its capacity ever to wage war again. Their protests made no impression on Foch, and in the early-morning hours of 11 November they reluctantly signed the document. The armistice took effect at 11 a.m. that day.

The Kaiser had already abdicated and was on his way by train to the neutral Netherlands.

The Great War was over.

General Sir Herbert Plumer takes the salute from troops of the First Canadian Division, Cologne, 13 December 1918

Bruille-lez-Marchienne, "or as far as they can, depending on the resistance encountered."[10]

Zero hour was set for 4 a.m., but B Company got off to an early start, hitting the road at three-thirty. Under Captain Herbert Andrews, the company swooped down on Lewarde while it was still dark and, by dawn, the town had been consolidated. In the process, Captain Andrews and his command captured forty-eight demoralized Germans and three machine-guns.[11]

More patrols were sent out. Major Walker employed a platoon of cyclists placed at his disposal, while the acting second-in-command, Captain Thompson, reconnoitred on his own. The captain found no sign of the enemy in Masny, and B and C companies sped ahead to occupy the town, while patrols pressed ahead to assess Ecaillon. Until now, the only hindrance to the advance had been a heavy haze which hung over the area for most of the day, but beyond Ecaillon, "considerable enemy Machine Gun and occasional shelling was met." B and C companies entered Ecaillon, and dug in for the night on the town's eastern outskirts. While Major Walker established his headquarters in Masny, in a house behind the town's cathedral, scouts explored in the direction of Bruille-lez-Marchienne.[12]

At nine o'clock Saturday morning, the 16th (Canadian Scottish) Battalion passed through Ecaillon, and the Fighting Tenth — along with the rest of the Second Brigade — passed into divisional reserve. With A Company in Masny and B, C, and D companies in Ecaillon, "as much opportunity as possible was given to the men to rest," reported Major Walker.[13]

They had earned the respite. In the past two days, the Battalion had advanced 16,000 yards — nearly nine miles — liberating the towns and villages of Gouelzin, Roucourt, Lewarde, Masny, and Ecaillon. The Tenth captured fifty-four prisoners and three machine-guns, at the cost of three men "slightly wounded" — the unit's last casualties of the war. Major Walker was justifiably pleased with these operations. "I consider the excellent showing in this advance, and the light casualties, were due to the skill and initiative of the Officers and the great determination and energy with which all other ranks carried out their orders, in spite of the very heavy calls made on their strength and endurance. The spirit of the men was most excellent and they ably seconded their Officers in getting forward."[14] Walker's skilful handling of the Battalion brought him the DSO, the last of eighteen won by the unit.

So far as the Fighting Tenth was concerned, the war was over. On Monday, 21 October, Major Walker moved his headquarters and A Company from Masny, reuniting the Battalion at Ecaillon, where it remained until the end of hostilities. The same day, the major met with the four company commanders to work out a syllabus for training. Weather permitting, training was conducted each day, with the routine interrupted by sporting events, concerts, and welcome bath parades. In late October and early November, forty-nine other ranks arrived as reinforcements, and on 9 November, Major William Bingham rejoined the Battalion after his recuperation in England. The twenty-eight-year-old Major Bingham assumed acting command of the unit when Major Walker went on leave the next day.[15]

Several noteworthy inspections took place in this period. The most significant occurred on 24 October, "when the Prince of Wales [the future King Edward VIII], accompanied by several Senior Officers, paid an informal visit to Battalion Headquarters. A few minutes chat with the Senior Officers of the Battalion, an

Inspection of the Guard, and the visit was over."* On 1 November, the brigadier, General Clark, inspected the Fighting Tenth and "complimented the Battalion on the smart appearance." A scheduled inspection by the Corps commander, General Currie, on 6 November was cancelled due to inclement weather, but General Macdonell, the divisional commander, arrived on 11 November to inspect the Second Brigade, afterwards declaring "that the 10th Canadian Infantry Battalion was the finest he had inspected this date."[17]

By then, the news everyone was anxiously awaiting had been delivered. It came in the form of a wire from First Division headquarters which arrived at the Tenth's headquarters at 8:05 a.m.:

Hostilities will cease at 11.00 hours** on 11 November. Troops will stand fast on the line reached at that hour which will be reported to Corps Headquarters. Defensive precautions will be maintained. There will be no intercourse of any description with the enemy. Further instructions follow.[18]

Private Samuel Hemphill, who had just returned to duty after being wounded at Villers-lez-Cagnicourt, never forgot his feelings when told of the armistice. "I'm telling you," the former Edmonton meatpacker recalled, "it was quite a relief for a lot of us." The troops expressed their relief in a somewhat surprising breach of discipline, according to Private Hemphill. "Each of us had our rifles, and you should've heard the firing that went on. Everybody was firing those rifles off — it's a wonder somebody didn't get killed."[19]

Lieutenant Joseph Sproston, who had been so unnerved by the slaughter on the Cambrai-Douai road in late September, was on his way back to the Battalion that memorable day, after two weeks' leave in England. Along with two other lieutenants, Tom Carter and Percy Lockhart, Sproston had hitch-hiked a ride on the back of a truck bringing up supplies. Within a mile of Ecaillon, Sproston and his fellow subalterns were startled by the sudden outbreak of shooting. Attracting the driver's attention, Sproston wondered whether a big battle was in progress. "Didn't you know, sir?" the smiling driver responded.

"No, what is it?"

"The armistice has been signed."

"By God," Sproston growled, "that's the best news I've heard."[20]

Amid the elation, more than a few must have paused to reflect on the many brave men who had done so much to bring about the final victory but were not there to witness it. Only 114 of the Battalion's originals were still on the unit's strength on 11 November 1918.[21] From its formation in September 1914 until the conclusion of the conflict, 5390, all ranks, had served with the Fighting Tenth*** — the lowest total among the First Division's battalions, which averaged 5941 in total strength during the war.[23] Its losses totalled 4581, or nearly 85 per cent, including fifty-five officers and 1260 other ranks who were killed in action or died of wounds.[24]

The Battalion had come a long way since those chaotic days at Camp Valcartier. The Fighting Tenth, which General Currie had not wanted in his Second Brigade, had acquired a reputation unexcelled in the Canadian Corps. The Tenth was an elite unit, one of the few battalions to participate in a major way in every large-scale Canadian action during the war.

"Our misfortune or our glory," remarked the former commanding officer, Dan Ormond, "was that we were trusted and leaned upon by every commander under whom we served"[25] — a fact reflected in its high casualty count. Resolute in offence, steadfast in defence, the Battalion ended the war with 537 decorations, honours, and awards,[26] notably two Victoria Crosses, eighteen DSOs (including three bars and one second bar), sixty-four MCs (including thirteen bars), sixty-five DCMs (including one clasp), and 289 MMs (including twenty-one bars and one second bar).

Dan Ormond later attributed the success of the Fighting Tenth to its "high morale," which he contended "was a never-ceasing wonder to the higher command." The reason, however, did not become apparent to him until some time after the war:

Pondering the matter, it became obvious to me that we had never lost the initial morale of the winter of 1914 - 1915. The morale of the junior ranks was so high that they carried the seniors along with them. That was the case during the whole existence of the Battalion.

It was the keenness of the juniors that got us into the 1st Division on Salisbury Plains [sic].

During our time in France everyone was permanently scared, and there were times when we were also very tired and extremely fed up. But, when warning for the line came along, whether for a tour or an attack, with regrets and reluctance, everyone sprang to it, and the nearer to the job we approached the farther the regrets and reluctance [were] left behind, so that by the time we arrived on the job everyone was cheerful. Soldier language and jokes were in the air, each had a sense of sat-

---

* An officer of the Fighting Tenth once shared a shower with the Prince. "You know," the unidentified officer commented in later years, "he looked just like any other man, without his clothes on!"[16]

** The British army, including the Canadian Corps, had adopted the twenty-four-hour clock on 1 October. For the sake of consistency, however, the twelve-hour clock has been used throughout this narrative, save for quotations containing the new standard.

*** This figure, which was provided by the Tenth Battalion Association after the war, conflicts with the numbers compiled by the Department of Militia and Defence in the spring of 1920; the latter gives 6242 as the total taken on strength by the Tenth Battalion.[22]

isfaction and realized that he would not have been anywhere else....

In November 1918 after the Armistice, General Currie said to me, "The Tenth Battalion was the only unit in the corps that could go into a show, come out, reorganize and within three days be as good as before the action."

In my mind higher praise cannot be earned by any fighting troops.

After April 1915 we never lost anything that we ever held, and never failed to do anything that was asked of us, and on many occasions did more than the job assigned to us.[27]

The importance of morale cannot be overstated; without it, a military formation cannot function effectively, but only the very best units can maintain it for a prolonged period in the face of sustained fighting and heavy casualties. That the Tenth did so attests to the calibre of all ranks who served in the Battalion.

Passchendaele was a prime example. Eric MacDonald, then a major, offered the opinion that success in that struggle had been due "almost entirely to the high state of morale of the troops who took part in the operations, and also to the fact that they were confident of their ability to overcome obstacles and difficulties as they might arise."[28]

Leadership was an important factor, and the quality of officers and NCOs was consistently high. The Tenth produced two brigadier-generals (Colonels J.G. Rattray and Dan Ormond), and at least seven of its officers went on to command other battalions (Majors Percy Guthrie, James Lightfoot, William Nasmyth, Walt Sparling, and Alexander Thomson, Captain Charles Robinson, and Lieutenant William Lowry).

"We never tolerated bullies in our outfit," recalled the grizzled sergeant-major, Chris Scriven, whose war ended with a wound at Vimy Ridge. "If I ran across a sergeant or a non-commissioned officer with any tendency of bullying in him, he was cooled down. I wouldn't even take it from an officer. I tangled with one officer over that, and I surprised him by quoting some military law, and he never repeated it. But we were always very, very fortunate. We always seemed to get a damned good type of man that seemed to be able to mould himself into the situation and the position he found himself in."[29]

Discipline was uniformly high, but it was tempered by common sense. The Tenth had its share of courts martial, and, as illustrated by the execution of Sergeant William Alexander, the punishment could be severe, if not extreme. There were other instances when leniency was desirable, as Private Charles Pettengill proved. Private Pettengill was sentenced to nine months' imprisonment with hard labour after injuring another member of the Battalion in a fight. Several months later, in September 1917, Colonel Ormond recommended that the balance of the sentence be rescinded because "he is a most excellent man in the trenches. He lacks the amount of self-control while out of the trenches that is desirable," but Ormond was confident that he could rectify that shortcoming. Pettengill repaid the colonel by winning the DCM.[30]

The result was a feeling of intense pride. Interviewed on the war's fiftieth anniversary, Joseph Sproston was asked to recall what he had done. "What the Tenth did," he gently corrected the interviewer, "I

The Tenth Battalion band in Germany, 17 December 1918

The Canadian army's contribution to victory in the Great War can only be described as extraordinary. From a nation with a population of under 8 million, the army enlisted 619,636 men and women; total fatalities were 59,544. In the course of four years, Canadian soldiers acquired a reputation as first-class fighters. They routinely succeeded where others failed, in a war synonymous with futile slaughter. General Currie later wrote of the exploits of the Canadian Army Corps: "In no battle did the Corps ever fail to take its objective; nor did it lose an inch of ground, once that ground was consolidated; and in the 51 months that it had been in the field the Canadian Corps has never lost a single gun. I think that one cannot be accused of immodesty in claiming that the record is somewhat unique in the history of the world's campaigns."

This record had been achieved on bloody battlefields in France and Flanders: at Ypres in 1915; through the horrors of the Somme in 1916 and the impressive string of victories in 1917; at Vimy Ridge; at Hill 70, and Passchendaele; and, finally, in the war's last hundred days. It may be said that the British Expeditionary Force won the war for the Allies by defeating the cream of the German army and breaching its most powerful defenses during the summer and fall of 1918, but it was the Canadian Corps that led the BEF to victory.

The Corps, Currie noted, "in that short period met and defeated decisively over 50 German divisions, i.e., approximately one-quarter of the total German forces on the Western Front. Elements of 17 additional divisions were also encountered and crushed.... No force of equal size ever accomplished so much in a similar period of time during the war, or any other war." By drawing inordinate numbers of enemy forces, including elite machine-gun units, to their front, the Canadians enabled the rest of the BEF to break through the Hindenburg Line; its loss to the Germans proved to be a decisive blow, psychologically and militarily.

But the cost to Canada was dear. "You cannot meet and defeat in battle one-quarter of the German Army without suffering casualties," Currie later explained, and the losses were heartbreaking. Between 8 August and 11 November, 1918, 45,830 Canadians were killed, wounded, or captured; this was more than one-fifth of Canada's casualties on the Western Front during the entire war.

was part of the Tenth." Similarly, Tommy Ireland, who was wounded the first time he went into action with the Battalion, at the Canal du Nord, was fiercely proud of his association with the Fighting Tenth. "Naturally, we think there isn't another like it."[31]

The war was over, but there was still work to be done. Two Canadian divisions, the First and Second, were selected to join the Second Army, the British army of occupation in Germany. This decision meant the Fighting Tenth would soon be standing on enemy soil.

Preparations for the march to Germany were undertaken immediately. On 13 November, the day Colonel MacDonald returned from leave, the Battalion marched to Denain, nine and a half miles away. The first frost of winter had appeared during the previous night, but the day was bright and sunny. The fourteenth saw another move, this time eleven miles to Onnaing, and the following day to Hornu, where arrangements were finalized. The troops were paid and given showers, and the rest of their time was devoted to cleaning their equipment and resting. The intention was to present the best possible appearance to the German population.[32]

The 250-mile march to Germany began at 7:20 a.m. on Monday, 18 November, one week after the Armistice. It was a chilly morning, with a thick ground mist that restricted visibility, and things improved little, alternating between snowflurries and light rain for the rest of the day. A five-mile march brought the Battalion to Masnuy-Saint-Pierre, where it settled into billets early in the afternoon. Another short move, this time conducted in heavy fog the next afternoon, took the Tenth to Soignies.[33]

On 21 November, the Battalion formed the Second Brigade's advanced guard. Moving out of Soignies at 9 a.m., a full day's marching ended in Nivelles, where the citizens "turned out en masse to meet the Battalion on its arrival." The weather remained clear and cold on the twenty-second, as the troops cleaned their equipment and rested. When the march resumed on 23 November, A Company was detached to advance to a specified outpost line through the villages of Genappe, Quatre-Bras, and Frasnes-lez-Gosselies. The rest of the Battalion moved from Nivelles to Hautain Laval, where the troops received "extra Christmas Pay." The next day's move, to Gembloux, brought the Battalion closer to the historic battlefield of Waterloo. While the unit remained at Gembloux on the twenty-sixth, ten of its officers participated in an automobile tour of Waterloo organized by the brigadier, General Clark.[34]

It was dull, cold, and misty when the Fighting Tenth left Gembloux on 27 November. Setting out at 7:30 a.m., it reached Petit Waret by four o'clock in the afternoon. The next morning, the Battalion marched

Triumphant homecoming: the Fighting Tenth returns to Calgary, 23 April 1919

to nearby Andenne, an hour away, remaining there until the thirtieth; due to supply difficulties, no rations arrived, and the march scheduled for 29 November had been cancelled. An eight-hour march to Les Avins on the last day of the month saw a repeat of the ration problem, forcing the cancellation of 1 December's planned advance.[35]

Movement resumed on the second day of December, in clear but cold conditions. The nine-hour march to My was demanding. The Fighting Tenth was now in the Ardennes, a hilly and heavily wooded region in eastern Belgium, where scarcity of rations combined with hard marching took their toll on the troops. "We were doing sixteen and seventeen kilometres a day," recalled Lieutenant Joseph Sproston, "and I know in my company, B Company, we had 38 per cent casualties. [The men] just couldn't take it." Lieutenant Sproston laid the blame, unfairly, at the feet of the Corps commander. General Currie, he insisted, was "forcing the issue, to get into Cologne, to [have] the Canadian Corps be the first troops in there."[36]

If that was Currie's intention, it was no race, because supply difficulties again delayed the march. After spending 3 December at My, the Battalion hit the road again on the fourth. It was raining heavily when the troops left My at 8:30 a.m., and everyone was soaked to the skin by the time the unit reached its billets in Trois-Points late in the afternoon. Another lengthy march followed on the fifth, taking the Battalion to Neuville and Burtonville.[37]

On Friday, 6 December, the Fighting Tenth crossed into Germany. It was a dull, cold day, as the Battalion's forty-two officers and 719 other ranks[38] left the vicinity of Neuville, at eight o'clock in the morning. Two and a half hours later, the unit's leading elements passed the German border at Petit Thier, under the watchful eye of the approving General Currie. That afternoon, the Battalion occupied billets in Meyerode, where it spent its first night on enemy soil.[39]

The Tenth's destination was, as Lieutenant Sproston indicated, Cologne. Here, on the River Rhine, the First Division was to cross and established a bridgehead, under the terms of the Armistice; the Second Division did likewise at Bonn. The Battalion's route, in a more or less northerly direction, lay in terrain which was both rough and picturesque, particularly as it got closer to the Rhine. "Pine woods, high hills, and neat little villages, looking like illustrations from some old copy of *Grimm's Fairy Tales*, were pleasant to the eye, even if the up and down-hill marching was [hard] on the feet."[40] Silent, sullen civilians watched from windows or the roadside as the khaki-clad victors marched past, but the reception was not as hostile as many expected.

"In some of the places that we were billeted at, we were treated very good by the German people," recalled twenty-one-year-old Private Samuel Hemphill, who, like most of his comrades, was longing to return home. "Other places, of course — you couldn't blame them — they were very arrogant about us being there."[41]

The Fighting Tenth left Meyerode for Hunningen on Saturday, 7 December, with subsequent overnight stops in Hellenthal, Mechernich, and Lommersum, before reaching Meschenisch in a driving downpour on the eleventh. Aside from pay parade and boot inspection, no specific tasks were assigned the troops here. "Men occupied their spare time," says the war diary, "in cleaning their equipment and clothing." The Battalion's final advance was to be made on Friday, 13 December, when it would, at last, cross the Rhine.[42]

It was raining heavily when the Tenth proudly marched across Cologne's New Bridge, where the Second Army's General Sir Herbert Plumer took the salute that morning. The men were in full marching order, with fixed bayonets, ten yards separating each company.[43] The Battalion crossed the Rhine behind a wool-bunting Union Jack which had been issued to all units that did not have their own colours.[44]*

Massive crowds of civilians lined the route. According to one member of the Fighting Tenth, "our officers had to teach them good manners by knocking off their hats in the mud."[46] More astute was the observation of C Company's commander, Captain Wilfred Romeril. A chill ran through the thirty-year-old Montrealer, and it was not just because of the cold, wet conditions, as he noted that a very large percentage of the watching civilians consisted of wide-eyed young boys. "Twenty years from now," Captain Romeril remarked, "you watch."[47]

Passing through fabled Cologne, the Battalion headed for nearby Wahn, where it settled into billets for the night. The next morning, the Tenth took up its position in the bridgehead, moving to the village of Volberg, four hours away, in cold, wet weather. The Battalion remained here until 2 January 1919 — in the meantime marking its fifth Christmas overseas.[48]

Christmas Day was clear and cold, one of the few days on which it did not rain or snow.[49] The kindness of some German civilians did much to make it a happy Christmas for certain members of the Battalion. Private Samuel Hemphill was billeted in a small hotel in neighbouring Hoffungsthal, fifteen miles from Cologne, and each night he was invited to dine with the family, an older couple with three children. A son who was a well-cared-for prisoner in England was the

---

* While the Tenth had no colours during the war, it was authorized, in 1917, to have a battle flag. This red flag, which featured a white circle with the unit's division-brigade shoulder patch on it, was basically a headquarters marker. It is not known whether the Tenth used such a battle flag.[45]

Major Hugh Ferguson, DSO

Sergeant David Tomlinson, who ended the
war as a lieutenant and an MBE and went
on to command The Calgary Highlanders.
Courtesy Calgary Highlanders

Brigadier-General Harold McDonald
Courtesy National Archives of Canada/PA-7485

Reunions of the Tenth Battalion were staged on an annual basis from 1920. A smiling Major Hugh Ferguson, DSO, (above left) attended the
1938 reunion. At Calgary City Hall in 1951, those taking part in the wreath-laying ceremony (front row, below) included, from left to right,
Major Mark Tennant and Lieutenant-Colonel H.T.R. Gregg of The Calgary Highlanders, Mayor Don McKay, Major-General Dan Ormond, and
Marshall Neal, president of the Tenth Battalion Association, as well as Laura Boyle, the widow of Colonel Boyle, who was killed at Ypres in
April 1915.

Courtesy Calgary Highlanders

probable reason for their amiable attitude, but it was no less appreciated by the homesick Hemphill. On Christmas, he recalled, they went out to chop down a tree, and later, after dinner, the young meatpacker from Edmonton joined the family in a jovial celebration, taking turns singing carols in German and English. "We had a really nice Christmas there, really. These people were very good to us." Private Scotty Murray, who was also staying in Hoffungsthal, fondly remembered being billeted in the home of an elderly woman. She "had a cow, and every night before we went to bed, that old lady came through and gave us a drink of hot milk." However, it was Jack Nuttall, the regimental sergeant-major, who gave Murray his most vivid memory of Christmas 1918. The RSM got "lit up," in Murray's words, and when his liquor was cut off, he fired his revolver, putting a bullet through the ceiling.[50]

The year ended happily. During the morning of the thirty-first, a cold, wet Tuesday, the Battalion was lectured by the divisional commander, General Macdonell, in Volberg's theatre. Afterwards, A and B companies held their annual dinners in the same building. The day was capped by a show staged by the Fighting Tenth's newly formed concert party, the Beavers.[51]

After enjoying a quiet New Year's Day, the Battalion was warned to make another move. Its destination was the Second Brigade's outpost line near Marialinden. At 9:30 a.m., on 2 January, the Fighting Tenth boarded a train for Overath, and a short march enabled A and D companies to relieve the 5th (Western Cavalry) Battalion's outpost elements by four-thirty in the afternoon.[52]

"Nothing of importance happened during the day." This is a standard entry in the war diary for the five days spent here. The weather was still cold, but there was no precipitation.[53]

The Battalion's time in Germany was fast approaching its end. The two Canadian divisions in the British bridgehead about Bonn and Cologne were being readied to return to Belgium, where the Canadian Corps would be reunited for demobilization and the long-awaited return home. On 6 January, the Fighting Tenth received its orders; after being relieved by the British 122nd Brigade, the Battalion was to move first to Overath, then to Hoffungsthal, where it would prepare for the trip to Belgium.[54] These moves were carried out according to plan.[55]

There were no regrets about leaving Germany. It had not been an unpleasant stay, although the British military governor of Cologne briefly banned the rowdy Canadians from the city, until General Currie angrily intervened. There were plenty of distractions, and the German people, as noted above, proved to be surprisingly friendly, considering the circumstances. Some were much friendlier than others. As one member of the Fighting Tenth remarked: "Some of those German frauleins are pretty husky maidens!"[56]

The Battalion boarded the train for Belgium at three o'clock on Thursday morning, 9 January. Its strength on that date was forty-one officers and 659 other ranks.[57] The overnight ride on the rails ended at six-thirty Friday morning at Huy, midway between Liége and Namur, but, even then, the journey was not quite over. After breakfast, the companies fell in for a six-hour march to their billets in Villers-les-Bouillet, which would be the unit's home until it was demobilized.[58]

Demobilization proved to be a long, involved process. Naturally, the Canadians were anxious to return home as quickly as possible, but they were not alone. There were millions of equally impatient Allied soldiers from other countries who needed transportation but, unfortunately, there was a limit to harbour facilities and suitable shipping.

The original plan was to return the Canadian divisions in the order that they had arrived overseas, which would have meant that the First Division would lead the way back across the Atlantic. But the brief occupation of Germany disrupted that plan, because it left the Third Division closest to the coast when demobilization began. Thus, the Third departed first, via England, and the First Division went next. Unfortunately, there were long delays — resulting from, among other things, British labour disputes which tied up the ports — and the First did not begin its departure from Belgium in earnest until mid-March. For the Fighting Tenth, the first sign of demobilization came on 25 January, when nine officers, including Major Walker and Captain Romeril, were sent to England as supernumeraries. Another month would pass before any other members of the Battalion followed.[59]

In the meantime, the main task was to keep everyone as busy as possible. There were the usual pay and bath parades, medical and dental inspections, and a light training programme. The Beavers staged concerts, and officers gave lectures on topics such as "Belgium and Her Problems" and "When We Go Home." A busy sports schedule was also arranged. It was highlighted by inter-battalion competitions which included soccer and long-distance road races and the Tenth was edged by British Columbia's 7th Battalion in both events.[60]

Most important of all in maintaining morale was the education offered under the auspices of the Khaki University of Canada. A surprisingly complete educational syllabus was prepared for the Fighting Tenth, with qualified officers and other ranks acting as instructors. The object was to prepare the men to return to new or better vocations. Captain Philip Dykes, the new chaplain, and Private Harry L. Brown ran the English classes; Lieutenant Herbert Booth taught French; Lieutenant William Oliver and Private

Depositing the new Colours of the Tenth Battalion, 26 April 1953: (above) The Calgary Highlanders lead the parade to Knox United Church where (below) the dedication service took place.

Courtesy Glenbow Archives, Calgary/NA-2864-1223a, c

Joseph Hoffman were the arithmetic instructors; bookkeeping was taught by Sergeant Ernest Craven; shorthand was the specialty of Lieutenant Thomas Nevin; Private Albert Phillips offered his expertise in advertising and publicity; Private Maurice Houldsworth taught mechanics; and the medical officer, Captain Allen McNair, instructed the physiology class.[61]

There were victory celebrations, too. On Thursday, 23 January, fifteen of the Battalion's officers travelled to Liége for a victory ball. Less than two weeks later, on Tuesday, 4 February, Major Hugh Ferguson, the second-in-command, led a contingent of the Fighting Tenth through the streets of Liége as part of an enormous, glittering victory parade. A proud Colonel MacDonald stood among the many thousands of exultant spectators. "The troops were met with a great reception from the civil population who lined the route," says the war diary, "and were highly complimented on their splendid turn out." More praise came their way on the nineteenth, when General Sir Henry Rawlinson, commanding the Fourth Army, inspected the Second Brigade. "The Battalion was complimented on its splendid appearance."[62]

Throughout this trying time, while the men awaited their turn to cross the Atlantic and get on with their lives, the Battalion's discipline proved to be as unshakable in peacetime as it had been during the war. There were minor instances of discontent in other units of the Corps, and rioting by non-combat Canadian troops in the United Kingdom, but there was no hint of trouble in the Fighting Tenth. Enforcing discipline in the wake of a war is always more challenging than maintaining during hostilities, but the Battalion's officers were more than equal to the task. The weather was little help — it rained almost every day in February 1919 — but the many physical and educational activities kept everyone's minds off the disappointing delays that seemed to be endless.

There were encouraging signs that demobilization was imminent. The first of these came on 15 February, when all ranks were required to fill out what the war diary terms "Demobilization Questionnaires in connection with the Department of Soldiers Civil Re-Establishment in Canada." This was the start of a confusing array of paperwork with which each soldier had to deal before being sent home. Later in the month, the Battalion began handing over its horses to the Belgian government, but the best news came on the twenty-third, when thirty-six other ranks departed for England, the first step on the journey to Canada. They were followed two days later by another twenty-two other ranks, and on the last day of the month by Lieutenant Ernest Vose and two other

ranks. The end was finally in sight.[63]

Once it was under way, demobilization proceeded swiftly, although not quickly enough to satisfy everyone. By 16 March, the Fighting Tenth was in Witley, in southern England, where all ranks completed their paperwork. Each man filled out fourteen documents, two in duplicate and two in triplicate, involving a total of 363 questions and eight signatures.[64] Liberal leave was also granted, enabling all members of the unit to visit friends and relatives for the last time before boarding a ship for Canada.

The atmosphere in post-war England was tense. Repeated postponements and cancellations of sailings, together with poor accommodations resulting from incompetent administration, had led to rioting by Canadian troops impatiently waiting to go home. The worst incident was at Kinmel Park, Wales, where a two-day rampage in early March left five soldiers dead. There were no fewer than three disturbances at Witley. None involved the disciplined Fighting Tenth, but some of the men later pointed out that the camp was far from ideal. They noted that while the food was "plentiful, it was badly prepared, and there was considerable ill-feeling about it."[65] In mid-April, after the Tenth had departed, the 26th (New Brunswick) Battalion staged a protest over the food, and a subsequent investigation found that the complaints were "justified."[66] The Tenth was assessed a charge of £30 — $147.08 in Canadian funds — for "minor damage to barracks," which was paid in the summer of 1920.[67*]

The Fighting Tenth's turn to leave came in early April. Boarding the liner *Carmania* in Liverpool, the Battalion arrived in Halifax eight days later, on Good Friday, 18 April, after an uneventful voyage.[69]

Calgary was preparing to roll out the red carpet for its returning heroes. On 12 April, Brigadier-General Harold McDonald, the commander of Military District 13, which was headquartered in Calgary, "expressed the hope that something worthy of the occasion would be done in carrying out a welcome which will long be remembered in the city." General McDonald, the Third Brigade staff officer who guided the Tenth into position prior to its famed attack on the wood near Saint-Julien, and who later lost an arm, met with civic officials over the next few days. Plans fell into place, although the exact date of the Battalion's arrival was uncertain — either 22 or 23 April. The train would pull into the CPR depot in downtown Calgary, and the Fighting Tenth would march through the streets to recently completed Mewata Armoury for an official reception and luncheon, and there the men would be discharged. "Every flag staff in the city should have a flag flying," said McDonald, and the mayor, R.C. Marshall, concurred. "All that really

---

* One other unresolved matter concerned a junior officer's account at a London department store. The sum involved was small — £6.17.6, or about thirty Canadian dollars — but it was not settled until November 1920, two months after the unit disbanded.[68]

remains," Mayor Marshall remarked of the planned welcome, "is for the citizens to come out in their thousands and show that they can raise a 'racket' which will always be remembered in Calgary."[70]

The journey from Halifax turned into a triumphal procession for the Fighting Tenth. Some of the more exuberant men chalked phrases in big letters on the sides of their rail cars: "White Gurkhas," "First In, Last Out," "Empire Express, Calgary to the Rhine and Return," and "Who Made Calgary Famous?" While the Battalion was by now considered to be a Calgary unit, it contained men from all parts of Canada, and received "a right royal welcome" at every stop along the way — particularly in Truro, Moncton, and Fort William. Of course, its most enthusiastic receptions were in Western Canada. In Winnipeg, reached at midmorning on Tuesday, 22 April, "a huge crowd of former Calgarians and special admirers of the Fighting Tenth" jammed the platform, but there was disappointment. The schedule permitted a mere half-hour stop in Winnipeg, and a planned official reception had to be cancelled. "A big crowd of citizens was on hand" that afternoon in Brandon, where "there was a band and plentiful cheers" for the Battalion. After a similar greeting in Regina that evening, it was nearly midnight when the train reached Moose Jaw. Here it was met by delegates attending a convention of the Great War Veterans Association, the biggest of the soldiers' organizations which sprouted up after the war. In their forty-five-minute stopover in Moose Jaw, the troops were treated to coffee, sandwiches, and cake, before resuming their westward journey under a starlit prairie sky.[71]

There was one negative note on the Battalion's homecoming. Some of its members had fallen victim to the influenza epidemic which was sweeping across Europe and would soon wreak havoc in Canada. One of the unit's originals, Private Jack Clarke, a CPR fireman in Calgary, had gone through the whole war without a scratch, but contracted the flu just before the Battalion left England and was forced to remain there until he recovered. Two more privates, Paul Soderberg and Stephen Barrett, had fallen ill while travelling through Ontario and been removed to hospitals in North Bay and Kenora, respectively. A fourth soldier, Private Ernie Hinecker, took sick just after leaving Regina, and was rushed to military hospital in Calgary.[72]

Late on Wednesday morning, 23 April, the train carrying the Fighting Tenth pulled into Calgary. It was a grand moment, as Colonel MacDonald declared in an interview with the Calgary Daily Herald. "Today is one of the biggest days of our lives," said the colonel. "There are two outstanding objectives that the men of the Tenth had always kept in view. The first was the crossing of the German frontier, and the second was 'home.' We are glad to have accomplished both."[73]

Warm words of welcome awaited the Battalion. An editorial in the Daily Herald stated: "Alberta prides itself that each of its respective units, and all of its soldiers on the western front, maintained in a glorious way the high traditions of the Anglo-Saxon race; but it was the men of the late Lieut.-Col. R.L. Boyle's unit that first put Canada 'on the map'.... " Mayor Marshall offered his opinion in equal eloquence: "When the history of the great war is written, the name of the Fighting Tenth will be engraved therein in letters that will remain forever immortal." The province's lieutenant-governor, R.G. Brett, sent a message to Colonel MacDonald expressing regret that "I am unable to be present in Calgary to welcome the 'Fighting Tenth.' Please tell them I am glad to welcome them. They have won for themselves honour and glory upon the battlefields of the greatest war in the history of the world, and they have added fame and renown to the Dominion of Canada."[74]

Calgary in 1919 was much smaller, both in size and in population, than today's sprawling prairie metropolis. Bounded on the north by 48th Avenue, and by 50th Avenue on the south side of the Bow River, it was flanked by the separate communities of Forest Lawn and Bowness, where the local airfield was located. Its population was only about 60,000, but there was no mistaking Calgary's patriotism. Despite its modest size, Calgary raised $5.2 million in Victory Loans in 1919, and every passing troop train received an enthusiastic reception. For example, a bright-eyed six-year-old named Jack Peach, who later rose to prominence as a historian, recalled that the CPR station was packed when Edmonton's 49th Battalion passed through Calgary. To young Peach, whose father was a member of the 49th, "It seemed that the whole city turned out" to cheer the returning soldiers.[75]

The scene which greeted the Tenth Battalion was unprecedented in Calgary's history, and rarely equalled since. "As the train entered the depot," reported the Morning Albertan, "the guard of honor of the veterans, many of them Tenth men who had previously returned, led the cheering, and cheer after cheer burst from the throats of the assembled thousands."[76] IMPRESSIVE WELCOME FOR THE TENTH, read the banner headline on the front page of the Herald, with a smaller headline below: "Glorious Reception to Men Who Helped Keep the World Safe."

Never before in the history of public demonstrations in Western Canada did a crowd lend more enthusiasm to a welcome than to that accorded the Tenth Battalion upon their arrival in Calgary this afternoon. With flags, bunting, and banners waving furiously in a heavy wind, thousands of people cheered themselves hoarse along the main thoroughfares of the city as the gallant fighters of Canada's famous regiment marched from the train down Centre street to Eight avenue and

205

thence west to the armouries in Mewata Park.[77]

It was, appropriately, the fourth anniversary of the Fighting Tenth's baptism by fire, an event immortalized a year earlier, with the unveiling of a plaque at City Hall.* With temperatures in the high fifties, it was a pleasant day, and a smiling Colonel MacDonald led his Battalion on the march. They had difficulty getting out of the station, due to the crush of friends and families and one of the unit's most popular officers, Captain William Corrigan, was carried from the train on the shoulders of his men.

The procession finally formed up and moved off. At the head was a mounted detachment of Lord Strathcona's Horse, twenty-two other ranks under Lieutenant H.G. Ritson-Bennett. Behind came more than a hundred young boys with tin cans as drums, in column of fours and marching "in perfect time." A stuffy official attempted to prevent the boys from taking their place in the procession, but his protests were overruled.[78]

Then came the Fighting Tenth, 316 strong.[79] As the Battalion marched through the streets of downtown Calgary, "the noise was deafening," according to one observer, W.R. Gayner. The emotion was contagious. Gayner watched as a young lad dashed from the crowd to march beside his big brother, and an elderly man with flags in his hat proudly limped alongside his son in the ranks.[80]

Among the thousands lining the streets were veterans of the Battalion, some missing limbs, others sightless, and still others recuperating from war wounds. Every soldier, past and present, knew that he was fortunate to be here for this occasion. Sergeant John Porter, who won the MM at the D-Q Line, was quick to remind reporters of that fact, declaring, "Lots braver men than we are never coming back."[81]

The final scene was played at the spacious new Mewata Armoury. People were literally hanging from the rafters to watch as the men of the Fighting Tenth, bayonets fixed, assembled for the last time as a regiment on war footing.

"Parade! Unfix bayonets."

Colonel MacDonald then dismissed the Battalion. Pay and discharge papers were issued, "and the men reverted to civil life in record time." Lunch followed, served by the Ladies' Auxiliary of the Great War Veterans Association. On white table cloths bedecked with daffodils, the men feasted on their first meal as civilians — pork and ham, dressing, bread and butter, cake, and tea. Afterwards, they dispersed. The majority faced the prospect of another journey by train to other parts of the country, but it was much simpler for Calgarians in the Tenth. There were 121 of them, and they just walked out the door of the armoury to waiting automobiles for the short ride home.[82]

Two of the lucky locals walked out together. "Which way?" one asked the other.

"Me for Crescent Heights," came the reply.

"Mount Royal," said his friend. "See you t'morrow, old boy."[83] Another Calgarian who was happy to be home was Sergeant Arthur Barlow. The proud bearer of the DCM and the MM and bar, all won during 1918, Sergeant Barlow rushed out to meet his wife and the three-year-old son he had never seen before.[84]

That night, a smoker was staged at the armoury. Attended by the Battalion's officers and prominent members of the community, this was one of the social events of the year in Calgary, and a highlight of the evening was a speech by the youthful Colonel MacDonald:

My heart is too full for me to even attempt to express adequately my appreciation of the wonderful reception accorded the officers and men of my battalion by the people of Calgary this afternoon. Let me say, however, that the memory of the event will be long cherished by all of us.

I want to avail myself of the opportunity to ask the people of Alberta to be patient with the returned soldiers. These men have been enduring hardships and facing dangers of the most appalling nature for over four years. Many of them would still be at school or college if they had remained at home. They have come back men, but it cannot be expected that they will at once resume their places in civil life as though the great happenings in which they have played such a noble part have made no impression upon them. Give them a helping hand.[85]

Another highlight was the introduction of Laura Boyle, the widow of the Battalion's first commanding officer. Mrs Boyle was given a bouquet of flowers and

---

* The plaque, which can still be seen today at the main entrance to the sandstone structure, was dedicated on 21 April 1918. It reads:

IN MEMORY OF
Lt COL. R.L. BOYLE
OFFICERS N.C.O.s
& MEN OF THE
TENTH BATTn
WHO FELL AT THE
SECOND BATTLE OF
YPRES
APRIL 22nd
1915
ERECTED BY SURVIVING
MEMBERS OF THE BATTALION

"a tremendous ovation."[86]

The evening ended with the playing of "God Save the King." The military men and civilians gradually departed, and the echoes of talk and laughter faded. Soon only the lingering odour of cigar smoke hinted at the memorable events of the day.

The Fighting Tenth had come home at last.

Epilogue

A NEW BEGINNING

With its demobilization completed upon returning to Calgary, the Tenth Battalion awaited word on its future. Born, bred, and bled during the greatest war the world had known, the Battalion had served its purpose in magnificent fashion. The next step, to formally disband, occurred in the autumn of 1920. But before that happened, the veterans of the Tenth fought one final battle. This time, they tangled with Ottawa bureaucrats instead of German *feldgrau*, and they used words instead of bullets, but their victory was as satisfying as any won during the war.

The winds of change were blowing through the Canadian armed forces. Only a handful of Canada's combat units had been formed around pre-war militia regiments, and now that the war was over, there were far too many formations to be comfortably accommodated within the tightened fiscal arrangements that had to be expected. A government-appointed committee under Major-General Sir William Otter toured the country in 1919, gathering input and considering alternatives for reorganizing the military. General Otter's committee visited Calgary in October of that year.

One man who had no doubts about the reorganization was General Currie, the former Canadian Corps commander who came home in August to be appointed inspector-general of the army. Currie felt that Canada's interests would be best served by a small permanent force whose "chief mission," he said, would be "the training of our Militia." A proponent of compulsory service, which he freely admitted was not practicable, he argued that the militia should be provided with "proper armouries, proper equipment, and proper staff to supervise their training." His goal was "not only to give Canada a good militia system but to exert an influence towards the building up of a National sentiment, truly Canadian." The best way to achieve this, he felt, was to perpetuate the overseas battalions in the post-war militia. "The traditions and 'Esprit de Corps' built up and developed by the Corps, and its composite units, during the war are far too valuable an asset to the Dominion of Canada to be lightly discarded and scattered to the four winds of Heaven."[1]

While awaiting a decision on its fate, the Fighting Tenth maintained a high profile. The first opportunity to do this came on 19 July, 1919. "Peace Day" was the celebration of the signing of the Treaty of Versailles which formally ended the war. It was a hot, sunny day, and 25,000 Calgarians attended a peace picnic on St. George's Island. There they were treated to free ice cream and drinks and a variety of activities, including a beauty contest, three-legged races, and a bonfire. Four thousand others jammed Mewata Armoury for the main ceremony, which featured speeches by General McDonald, commanding Military District 13, and Lieutenant-Governor R.G. Brett.[2]

Following a prayer and the singing of "O Canada," Brett declared that this was "probably the most important day in the history of the British Empire." The lieutenant-governor went on to recount Germany's "great mistake" in underestimating the Empire. "They twisted the lion's tail but forgot about the claws. They also forgot about the cubs. And the cubs of the mother hurried to her aid when war sounded. From all parts of the Empire they came, showing their loyalty to the mother land and loyalty and integrity to the Empire, that it might be preserved." General McDonald, in turn, described the many battlefield exploits of the Canadian Corps before his speech was interrupted by a noon salute fired by field guns outside the armoury. "I call upon you as soldiers," he concluded, "not to forget your sixty thousand comrades who rest in France, and to carry on your patriotism. Don't forget the sacrifice of manhood and the suffering of womanhood, but carry on the memory of this great thing."[3]

When the speeches ended, the Tenth became the focal point of another ceremony. One of the unit's original officers, Major Lee Redman, who had been wounded in the attack on Kitcheners Wood near Saint-Julien and returned to Calgary to win a seat in the House of Commons, led a parade to Knox Presbyterian Church (now Knox United). Here the King's Colour was deposited.

Infantry battalions were entitled to two colours. The regimental was adorned by the unit's badge and battle honours, and the sovereign's was a large, fringed Union Jack often emblazoned with the unit's badge. The Tenth had no Regimental Colour at this time, and its King's Colour was not, in the strictest sense, a King's Colour, although it served as such. The flag deposited at Knox Church was the simple Union Jack that the Battalion had carried across the Rhine the previous December.

The Tenth Battalion column was headed by a band provided by the Great War Veterans Association and an honour guard under Lieutenant George Guthrie, who carried the Colour with assistance from the former regimental sergeant-major, Duncan Stuart. The parade followed Seventh Avenue to First Street West, then proceeded along Sixth Avenue to the church, which was filled to overflowing with veterans.

Major Redman presented the Colour "as a token of gratitude to Almighty God, by whom alone victory is secured, for His providential care and gracious benediction granted them in the discharge of duty." The Colour, he said, would serve as "a memorial to the men of all ranks" who served under it, and "afford an inspiration for patriotic service and sacrifice for all who may worship here for some time to come."[4]

The pastor, the Reverend J. Macartney Wilson, accepted the Colour "for the glory of God and in the memory of those who were faithful, many of them even unto death." After another rendition of "O Canada," the escort presented arms, and the Colour was deposited at the front of the church. The Calgary Daily Herald called it "a most impressive ceremony, which those who witnessed it are not likely to forget."[5]

The Battalion was back in the news that fall. On Friday, 2 October, the Tenth Canadian Infantry Battalion, C.E.F., Association was formed, with forty members in its original enrolment. Serving as president was Lieutenant-Colonel Charlie Stevenson, who had gone overseas with the Tenth as a lance-corporal in 1914, and ended the war as an MC-winning major, after being wounded four times. The Association's vice-president was the old sergeant-major, Duncan Stuart, while Captain David Tomlinson MBE was named secretary.[6]

A hint of the Battalion's future was revealed on 21 November, when the Otter Committee released its proposed reorganization of Alberta's military units. If the committee's recommendation was accepted, the 103rd Calgary Rifles would disappear, replaced by The Calgary Regiment, composed of two active battalions. The First Battalion of The Calgary Regiment would perpetuate the Fighting Tenth, while the Second Battalion preserved the traditions of another local combat unit, the 50th Battalion.[7]

This was the organization eventually adopted by the department of militia and defence. But there was controversy in the spring of 1920, when General Currie introduced his own plan. "One does not expect that it will please everyone," he admitted,[8] and he was correct. Calgarians, particularly veterans of the Fighting Tenth, were anything but pleased, and with good reason.

The bombshell landed on 15 March, when the militia department issued the general orders reorganizing the armed forces. General Order 29 concerned

Military District 10, in Manitoba. The pre-war militia unit, the 106th Winnipeg Light Infantry, was to be replaced by a new organization, the Winnipeg Light Infantry, composed of one active and four reserve battalions; the active battalion was to perpetuate the Fighting Tenth. General Order 32 dealt with the reorganization of Military District 13. The 103rd Calgary Rifles, which had been founded on 1 April 1910, would be replaced by The Calgary Regiment, perpetuating the 50th, 56th, 82nd, and 137th battalions. Only the 50th was a combat unit; the others were reinforcement battalions.

The ensuing uproar was predictable. In describing the army's reorganization plans to its readers on 30 March, the Calgary Daily Herald remarked: "The fact that the 10th Battalion will not be perpetuated in a Calgary unit will be a great disappointment to many members of that unit in the city."

"Disappointment" was hardly the word for it. Calling the decision "an insult to the many hundreds of Alberta and Calgary men who fought and fell under this unit in the field," the Tenth Battalion Association launched a campaign to reclaim the Fighting Tenth for the southern Alberta city. A protest rally was staged at Mewata Armoury where the angry veterans passed an indignant resolution: "Be it resolved that the 10th Battalion protests against having the 10th Battalion re-organized in Winnipeg, owing to the fact that 75 per cent of its personnel was sent from Alberta to reinforce this unit in the field during the period of the Great War. Therefore the 10th Battalion should be re-organized in this province." The strongly worded resolution was delivered on 9 April to the provincial legislature by Lieutenant-Colonel William Nasmyth, one of the Tenth's originals, while a copy went to Brigadier-General A.H. Bell, General McDonald's successor in command of the local military district.[9]

Seeking an explanation for the militia department's ruling, the Association dispatched a telegram to Ottawa, addressed to Major Lee Redman, the former Tenth Battalion officer who was also the MP for Calgary East. After making inquiries, Major Redman limply replied that the unit's officers had not displayed much interest in the matter the previous October, when the Otter Committee came to Calgary.[10]

The protest gained momentum. A meeting of the Tenth Battalion Association on 8 April discussed various methods of publicizing the cause. Besides seeking the aid of municipal authorities in Calgary, Lethbridge, and Medicine Hat — the latter two cities had sent notable numbers of recruits to the Fighting Tenth — someone came up with the idea of holding an annual reunion dinner on 22 April to commemorate the Battalion's first battle at Saint-Julien in 1915.[11]

Hasty arrangements were made, and the first commemorative dinner was held on the fifth anniversary of the Battalion's historic action. In addition to

Laura Boyle, the widow of the Tenth's beloved first commander, a glittering array of senior civic, provincial, and military officials gathered, despite the short notice. Even the premier, Charles Stewart, agreed to attend, although he had to cancel at the last moment.

The reunion, held at the Elizabethan Dining Room at the Hudson's Bay Company, provided a platform for the Association's fight to keep the Tenth Battalion in Calgary. The gruff sergeant-major, Duncan Stuart, proposed a toast, "To the 10th Battalion," and remarked, "May history eventually make the fame of the men of St. Julien an inseparable part of Canadian history." But the real reason for the gathering was thinly disguised. The mayor, R.C. Marshall, declared "that Calgary was the real home of the Fighting Tenth," while the Association's secretary, Captain David Tomlinson, commented that "the Manitobans have no more right to it than Fort McMurray."[12]

In Ottawa, the militia department scrambled to respond to the Calgary protest. The bureaucrats were surprised, even mystified, by the reaction from the western city. "When General Otter's Committee visited the West," the department grumbled, "Winnipeg claimed the battalion; Calgary seemed to know it not."[13]

A subsequent investigation vindicated the Calgarians. The militia department's "most careful research" showed that the Tenth had enlisted more than three times as many men from Calgary as Winnipeg. "The obvious conclusion," said the department, "is that Calgary has a better claim than Winnipeg." Accordingly, General Currie recommended in May "that the 10th Bn. C.E.F. be transferred to the Calgary Regiment from the Winnipeg Light Infantry."[14]

The Tenth Battalion had once again prevailed, although a year passed before the militia department worked out a solution to the Calgary-Winnipeg dilemma. The department was in a quandary: Calgary deserved to perpetuate the Fighting Tenth, but Winnipeg had already been awarded that honour. The matter was finally resolved by a compromise: dual perpetuation. Under General Order 32, dated 1 April 1921, both The Calgary Regiment and the Winnipeg Light Infantry were allowed to perpetuate the Tenth, and both would be entitled to carry its battle honours. However, The Calgary Regiment was designated as the senior unit because its pre-war forerunner, the 103rd Calgary Rifles, was senior to the 106th Winnipeg Light Infantry, by virtue of the fact that the 103rd Calgary Rifles were senior to the 106th

Winnipeg Light Infantry in the pre-war militia.*

The Calgary Regiment adopted the organization proposed by the Otter Committee, with its First Battalion perpetuating the Fighting Tenth, and the Second perpetuating the 50th Battalion, along with three reserve units intended to preserve the memories of the 56th, 82nd, and 137th reinforcement battalions. The Calgary Regiment was commanded by Lieutenant-Colonel R.B. Eaton, and the First Battalion was, appropriately, placed under the veteran, Colonel Stevenson, who had to revert to major in order to accept the position. The unit's authorized peacetime strength was 541 all ranks, and five horses.[15]

By this time, the Tenth Battalion had officially ceased to exist. It had been disbanded under General Order 149, issued on 15 September 1920. A formality which had long been expected, it must have been a melancholy occasion for the veterans who had served it so faithfully and well. However, their sadness was tempered by the arrival of a distinguished visitor. The Prince of Wales arrived in Calgary on Sunday morning, 14 September, and members of the Tenth were part of the honour guard which welcomed him at the CPR station. A procession was formed, and the Prince proceeded to the Calgary Exhibition grounds, where 35,000 cheering citizens awaited him. The future King Edward VIII inspected the guard and shook hands with the commander of the Tenth's contingent, Colonel Stevenson.[16]

It was the Fighting Tenth's last hurrah. But, far from being the end of the unit, it marked a new beginning, for the controversy-ridden reorganization ensured that the Tenth formed the basis of what would become one of Canada's most distinguished regiments, The Calgary Highlanders.

The transformation to a Highland unit came in the fall of 1921. General Order 254 of 15 September read: "The Calgary Regiment into a Highland (Kilted) Unit with designation '1st Bn., (10th Bn., C.E.F.) Calgary Highlanders, The Calgary Regiment' is authorized." Why a kilted unit? At first glance, the decision seems odd, given the facts that Calgary's militia had no Highland traditions and that the expenses involved were substantially higher than those associated with other infantry units. According to Major W. Ashton Cockshutt, a Tenth Battalion original officer who became a company commander in the new regiment, the main reason was "to encourage recruitment of the many Scottish people" living in the Calgary area.[17]** It was also favoured by a majority of the officers, many of whom were of Scottish descent.

---

* The Winnipeg Light Infantry ceased to exist in 1955, when the regiment amalgamated with the Royal Winnipeg Rifles, under the latter's name.

** Cockshutt remained a Highlander until 1922, when he was transferred to Edmonton as branch manager of the Cockshutt Plow Company. He presently resides in Brantford, Ontario, where he was born in 1892.

The financial concerns were alleviated by "several prominent Calgarians" who, reported the Calgary *Daily Herald*, "promised donations which will go to defray the cost of extra equipment which cannot be supplied by the militia department."[18] One of these wealthy benefactors was the Honourable Richard Bedford Bennett, the future prime minister, who later accepted the appointment as the new unit's honorary colonel.[19]

The ties between past and present were strong. Popularly known as the "Tenth Battalion, Calgary Highlanders," the regiment utilized the Tenth's cap badge for the time being, and it was estimated that 80 per cent of the Highlanders were former members of the Fighting Tenth.[20]

In October, the kilts arrived, setting the stage for the unit's public debut. On Sunday, 13 November, The Calgary Highlanders showcased themselves, parading through downtown Calgary to Knox Presbyterian Church during the annual Armistice Day service. "The battalion ... caused a good deal of favorable comment as it swung down Eighth avenue led by its bagpipe band," reads the *Daily Herald's* report. "Although this was the first time that the Calgary Highlanders appeared in public they all 'swung a wicked kilt' which synchronized perfectly with the Scotch music. All knees were shined in the approved Highland fashion."[21]

The Regiment's first commanding officer was Harold McDonald, the former commander of Military District 13, who reverted to lieutenant-colonel in order to accept the appointment. Colonel McDonald's second-in-command was Major Lee Redman, who had been among the first to enlist in the new Highland unit. Although his tenure was brief (he handed over to Redman in April 1922), McDonald had a measurable impact. Presiding over The Highlanders' first mess dinner, held at the Palliser Hotel's Grill Room on 15 December 1921, he proposed the toast to "The Glorious Memory of the Twenty-second of April," which remains one of The Calgary Highlanders' most cherished traditions. The dinner was a grand success, as the Calgary *Daily Herald* commented: "The evening was marked by a spirit of good fellowship, and the programme, which contained many Scotch numbers, was very popular."[22]

The following summer, The Highlanders provided their first guard of honour for a visiting dignitary. The occasion was the arrival in Calgary of the governor-general, the Right Honourable Baron Byng of Vimy, the former commander of the Canadian Corps. When Lord Byng's train pulled into the CPR depot at 10:15 a.m. on Tuesday, 4 July, he was met by The Highlanders' guard, 100 strong, all veterans of the Fighting Tenth under the second-in-command, Major Stevenson, who was also an alderman at this time. Byng was very moved by the bearing of these veterans of the Tenth, a unit which he had so greatly admired during the war. "I cannot express my gratification on such a splendid turn out," he remarked, calling it "one of the finest" on his cross-Canada tour. "You are looking just as fit as when we campaigned together in France and Belgium," Byng told the fine-looking veterans. "You look me straight in the eye as you did then."[23]

Yet another indication of the governor-general's regard for the Tenth came in September 1923, when Lieutenant-Colonel Lee Redman, commanding The Calgary Highlanders, was appointed an honorary aide-de-camp.

In 1924, Calgary's militia units were reorganized once again. Under General Order 68 of 15 May, The Calgary Highlanders and The Calgary Regiment became separate units; the latter is known today as The King's Own Calgary (14th Armoured) Regiment.

The Highlanders effectively perpetuated the memory and traditions of the Fighting Tenth. Successive senior officers had seen war service with the Tenth, and the Regiment made it a custom to hold an annual parade on the Sunday nearest 22 April, involving a service at Knox Church and a wreath-laying ceremony at the bronze memorial tablet at City Hall.

There were other reminders of links to the past, notably the presence of Brigadier-General Dan Ormond, the former commander of the Tenth Battalion who had played such an important part in its wartime performance. General Ormond returned to Calgary several times, including a four-year stint, from 1928 to 1932, as the commander of Military District 13. Ormond, who was promoted to major-general upon his retirement from the permanent force in 1932, attended several reunions of the Tenth Battalion Association which remained active until it merged with The Calgary Highlanders' Association on 22 April 1970, the fiftieth anniversary of its first reunion. (The Association was presented with a standard in 1945. The crimson flag, emblazoned with the regimental badges, was turned over to the Glenbow Museum in 1969, where it remains today.)

The annual reunions proved to be popular. Held at the Palliser Hotel, the pre-Second World War dinners and dances usually attracted two hundred people. For men like Ernie Crowe, these were memorable occasions. "Heck, we'd have forty or fifty guys that would come back, and we used to have a lot of fun. I'd see Ormond and Walter Critchley and guys like that, that I knew personally, and [it was a] pretty nice fraternity." But Crowe, who had enlisted shortly after his sixteenth birthday in December 1915, and was one of the Battalion's last survivors, found that the fun gradually went out of these gatherings, "so I just quit going."[24]

It was fitting that Dan Ormond also played a prominent part in a long overdue ceremony involving the Tenth Battalion's Colours. Since 1919, the solitary

Union Jack which served as its King's Colour had hung in Knox Church. The church offered, in the mid-1920s, to present a Regimental Colour, but "it was considered advisable to postpone the acceptance of your kind offer until we were advised as [to] the Battle Honours which were to be awarded."[25] Battle honours were awarded in the autumn of 1929, but nothing was done until 1950, when the Tenth Battalion Association decided to purchase new Colours at its own expense. Permission was granted by the Department of National Defence, "provided no expense to the public is incurred. The original colour may either be left in its present position undisturbed, the replica being deposited in some other position in the Church, or the original colour may be cremated and the ashes spread over the replica as part of the service of depositing the replica in the Church."[26] The Association chose to cremate the original Colour, and set about designing new colours to replace it. These were ordered in late 1952 for delivery in March 1953.[27]

They were magnificent; the Sovereign's Colour, a fringed Union Jack featuring the regimental badge, although usually described as a "replica," was far more beautiful than the modest original. The Regimental Colour, a dark blue flag, carried the ten battle honours permitted by military regulation: "Ypres, 1915–17," "St. Julien," "Somme, 1916," "Vimy, 1917," "Arleux," "Hill 70," "Passchendaele," "Amiens," "Drocourt-Quéant," and "Hindenburg Line." Marshall Neal, president of the Association, was on safe ground when he told his fellow members that the Colours "will be a source of pride and joy, not only to all those gallant lads who served in the 10th Battalion but [to] their Sons and Daughters for many succeeding generations."[28]

These Colours were deposited on Sunday, 26 April 1953, when Ormond led sixty-two veterans of the Tenth, accompanied by the pipe band of The Calgary Highlanders, to Knox Church. Marching to City Hall afterwards, Ormond watched as Laura Boyle placed a wreath on the bronze plaque commemorating the heroism of her husband and the other members of the Fighting Tenth in their first action at Ypres. Ormond was also the guest speaker at the reunion dinner, and he made a special note of the unit which so ably perpetuated his beloved Tenth. "To have this close association with the Calgary Highlanders," he declared, "is something that must give everyone great satisfaction."[29]

Tradition is the life blood of the military, giving meaning and purpose to the present by linking it to the past. In preserving and promoting the memory of the Tenth Battalion, The Calgary Highlanders pay tribute not only to a magnificent predecessor, but to a rich and rewarding part of Calgary's, Alberta's, and Canada's history.

As a combat unit in the Second World War and as a peacetime militia regiment, The Highlanders have proven themselves to be worthy successors to the Fighting Tenth. That, however, is another story.

APPENDIX A

TENTH BATTALION CASUALTIES

Officers: 165

Other Ranks: 4407

Enemy Fire (less prisoners of war and gas)

Fatal: 55 Officers, 1249 Other Ranks

Non-fatal: 107 Officers, 2701 Other Ranks

Prisoners of War

Wounded (fatal): 2 Other Ranks

Wounded (non-fatal): 2 Officers, 15 Other Ranks

Unwounded: 16 Other Ranks

Gas

Fatal: 3 Other Ranks

Non-fatal: 1 Officer, 116 Other Ranks

Injuries

Fatal: 6 Other Ranks

Non-fatal: 9 Officers, 299 Other Ranks

APPENDIX B

TENTH BATTALION DECORATIONS

(Note: ranks are those held at the time of the award.)

Victoria Cross
Private Harry Brown
Sergeant Arthur Knight

Companion of the Order of St. Michael and St. George
Brigadier-General J.G. Rattray; Brigadier-General Dan Ormond

Officer of the Order of the British Empire
Major FitzRoy George; Captain Charles Robinson

Member of the Order of the British Empire
Lieutenant David Tomlinson

Distinguished Service Order
Captain Geoff Arthur; Major E.J. Ashton; Captain Charles Costigan; Major Walter Critchley; Major Hugh Ferguson; Lieutenant Gordon Graham; Major Eric MacDonald; Lieutenant Norman MacEachern; Lieutenant-Colonel Dan Ormond; Lieutenant-Colonel J.G. Rattray; Major Walt Sparling; Major Alexander Thomson; Captain William Thompson; Major Phil Walker

Bar to Distinguished Service Order
Lieutenant-Colonel Eric MacDonald; Lieutenant Norman MacEachern; Lieutenant-Colonel Dan Ormond

Second Bar to Distinguished Service Order
Lieutenant-Colonel Eric MacDonald

Military Cross
Lieutenant Herbert Andrews; Lieutenant Lewis Balfe; Major William Bingham; Captain David Black; Captain Geoff Burbidge; Captain Leo Carey; Lieutenant Tom Carter; Lieutenant Thomas Chutter; Lieutenant Jack Clark; Major Allan Conners; Captain Frank Costello; Captain Charles Costigan; Lieutenant Thomas Dale; Lieutenant Robert Donald; Lieutenant Walter Duncan; Lieutenant Frederick Easterbrook; Lieutenant Frank Fane; Lieutenant Ralph Feurt; Lieutenant F. St. Clair Fisher; Lieutenant Charles FitzRoy; Lieutenant Stanley Grimble; Lieutenant William Hedges; Lieutenant Stanley Kent; Captain Richard Kenny; Major Hercules Lefebvre; Major Eric MacDonald; Captain David McAndie; Captain Bernard McDaniel; Captain Allen McNair; Captain Jack Miller; Captain Edward Milne; Lieutenant David Milne; Captain Jack Mitchell; Lieutenant William Oliver; Lieutenant Hugh Pearson; Lieutenant Stanley Robertson; Lieutenant Leonard Rowley; Lieutenant Frank Rump; Major Joseph Simpson; Lieutenant Benjamin Skinner; Lieutenant D.W. Stephenson; Lieutenant Charlie Stevenson; Regimental Sergeant-Major Duncan Stuart; Lieutenant Harry Templeman; Lieutenant David Teviotdale; Major Alexander Thomson; Captain William Thompson; Lieutenant Alfred Trimmer; Lieutenant Edward Watling; Lieutenant Charles Watt; Lieutenant Lewis Younger

Bar to Military Cross
Captain Herbert Andrews; Major William Bingham; Lieutenant Charles FitzRoy; Captain Stanley Kent; Captain Jack Mitchell; Lieutenant Leonard Rowley; Lieutenant Frank Rump; Lieutenant Benjamin Skinner; Lieutenant Harry Templeman; Captain Alfred Trimmer; Lieutenant Edward Watling; Lieutenant Charles Watt; Captain Lewis Younger

Distinguished Conduct Medal
Company Sergeants-Major Tom Carter, Jack Nuttall, James Watchman; Sergeants Arthur Barlow, Arnold Budd, Davis Forbes, Charles Jeeves, Samuel Leebody, Percy Legg, Wilfred Malkinson, Dougall Maxwell, David McAndie, Edward Milne, Charles Morrison, Ambrose Oliver, Harry Stone, Ernest Vose; Lance-Sergeants John Palmer, Frederick Shoesmith, Arthur Underwood, John Wennevold; Corporals William Baker, Thomas Bradley, Ralph Brookes, Hugh Caminer, Robert Coates, Thomas Greenwood, George Grover, Edward Hume, Gordon Jones, William King, Nicholas Purmal, Samuel Schultz, Harry Wilson; Lance-Corporals George Allan, Frederick Buddry, Arthur Burnell, William Cooper, Alexander Culgin, Arthur Hayter; Privates

William Beggs, Charles Bloxham, Richard Clark, Frank Cox, John Collins, Charles Cracknell, Norval Curtis, McLeod Fenwick, Thomas Fidgett, Thomas Flynn, Lloyd Graham, Hugh Henry, William Holmes, Joseph Hughes, Michael Kosko, George LaDuke, Alexander Morin, Peter Mattison, Charles Pettengill, Thomas Ross, Frank Sixby, Henry Smith, Gordon Van Valkenburg, Harry Webb, Louis Zuidema

Bar to Distinguished Conduct Medal
Sergeant Edward Milne

Military Medal
Regimental Sergeant-Major Duncan Stuart; Company Sergeant-Major Jack Nuttall; Sergeants Frederick Buddry, Robert Burns, John Campbell (467136), Charles Darwin, William Gilchrist, Byron Greer, Frank Henry, Cornelius Hood, Cliff Malcolm, James McCallum, David McAndie, Hugh McCullough, Alexander McLaughlin, John McNeil, Herbert Mortimer, David Murray, Marshall Neal, George Nuttall, James Parry, Chester Pettit, Jeff Rees, Baset Riseley, William Ritchie, John Seeley, James Shaw, James Smart, George Stone, Sydney Sydenham, Harry Templeman, Arthur Underwood, Leslie Wallace, Richard Waller, Charles White, Walter Whitehurst, Benjamin Whiteley; Lance-Sergeants Edward Arnold, David Connell, Frederick Shoesmith, George Stewart; Corporals Arthur Barlow, Michael Bennett, Frederick Bond, Walter Brown, George Burkett, John Campbell (30867), William Cooper, John Crane, Harvie Currie, Andrew Elliott, Thomas Greenwood, Albert Harvey, Sidney Hatherby, E.R. Hughes, David Irvine, William Keith, Arthur Kendall, Reuben Kilmer, George Leslie, Fred Maiden, Edwin Martindale, Reginald Marvin, Robert McGregor, Frederick Murray, Maurice Oldenburg, Arthur Pinder, John Porter, Lancelot Rimmer, Frank Ringrose, Louis Smith, William Southward, Thomas Steadman, Michael Sullivan; Lance-Corporals Roy Armstrong, Charles Broadbent, Hugh Caminer, Richard Chandler (148157), James Corry, Arthur Courtney, John Evans, William Foley, William Forbes, Frederick Foss, David Hampton, John Hutchinson, William L'Hirondelle, Henry Jervis, George Marcellus, Thomas Markinson, Arthur Maxwell, Albert Nowell, Frederick Rowley, William Smith, Vay Stephenson, Leslie Tate, Norman Thompson, George Vowel, Frank Weldon, Percy Witney, Robert Wilson, William Wilson, Robert Wood; Privates George Adams, Robert Adamson, William Adamson, James Aitken, Norman Armstrong, James Atkinson, Ernest Bach, James Ballantyne, A.E. Bartlett, Ewart Bateman, Harry Baxter, Ernest Beer, Dalton Bell, Ernest Bowering, Edward Bowers-Taylor, George Brooks, George Brown, Luke Brown, James Burbridge, Thomas Campbell, Robert Catte, Richard Chandler (22558), Robert Coates, Thomas Connor, Herbert Connor, Frank Corrall, Norval Curtis, Alfred Daum, Walter DeMarre, Frank Depeau, Roland Dewar, William Dunn, William Dyson, Alfred Eakins, H. Eden, Austin Eide, Frank Enderton, Percy Fairbank, Allan Ferguson, Donald Finlayson, Arthur Fisher, James Fisher, Edward Flynn, Charles Foss, James Fowler, Ewen Fraser, George Fowlie, Robert Gibson, William Gibson, David Gillespie, George Golics, James Gray, Peter Greig, Richard Harrison, Charles Haydon, Herbert Hazelwood, Samuel Hemphill, Daniel Heinrichs, Harry Henry, Hugh Henry, John Hescott, Cecil Hewitt, Walter Holcombe, Walter Holley, Gus Holliday, Frank Honey, William Humphreys, Nathaniel Hunter, T. Hurst, John Hutchinson, Wesley Irwin, Tokutaro Iwamoto, Percy Johnson, James Jones, Urban Jones, Grant Knapp, Frederick Knight, Donald Kyle, Charlie Launder, Thomas Laverson, Charles Lee, Wilfred Longwood, John Lynch, Alexander MacKenzie, William Madge, Alfred Maggs, Percy Main, Wilfred Malkinson, Leonard Mallory, George Martin, Michael Matson, Lemuel McCallum, Alexander McCaughan, Alexander McDonald, Edward McDonald, Hugh McDonald, David McGregor, Alexander McInnes, John McKenzie, Phil McKenzie, George McLanders, Alfred McLatchie, Donald McLean, Frank McMackin, Joe McNaughton, John McPhail, Kenneth McPhee, Leonard Melbourne, Charles Michie, Charles Millar, Thomas Milligan, Joseph Milne, John Milton, Joseph Mitchell, Masumi Mitsui, William Moore, Frank Morrison, William Murray, Gardiner Newton, Arthur Norris, Jack O'Hearne, Paul Oleson, Rennie Paget, Albert Parsons, Thompson Reside, Harold Riker, William Rimmer, Frank Robbins, Frederick Roberts, John Robertson, Sidney Robson, Leonard Rowley, Samuel Simms, Thomas Simpson, Chesley Smith, Elmer Smith, Henry Smith, John Smith, Robert Smith, William Smith, William Stevenson, Walter Stevenson, Percy Stewart, James Sullivan, William Summers, Robert Sutherland, William Tait, Sidney Taylor, John Temperton, William Thompson, Ernest Topp, George Trute, Frederick Tuffnell, James Turnbull, Harry Turvey, Gordon Van Valkenburg, Lawrence Vincent, Harry Webb, George Wigglesworth, Aylmer Williams, Harry Wilson, W. Wiskar, Hugh Wright, Leslie Wright, Ronald Young

Bar to Military Medal

Sergeants Harvie Currie, Percy Fairbank, William Keith, Arthur Kendall, Arthur Pinder, Leslie Wallace, Charles White; Lance-Sergeant Reuben Kilmer; Corporals Arthur Barlow, Ernest Bowering, Maurice Oldenburg, Frank Ringrose, Louis Smith, Thomas Steadman; Lance-Corporal Paul Oleson; Privates George Brooks, Richard Harrison, Charles Lee, Leonard Mallory, Joseph Milne, Rennie Paget

Second Bar to Military Medal

Private Joseph Milne

Meritorious Service Medal

Sergeants-Major Herbert Baker, George Murray, Edmond Rayfield, Matthew Wilson; Sergeants John Campbell, Charles Doig, Ralph Hardwick, Sidney Jacobs, Angus McDonald, Charles McNiven, Robson Thompson, George Vincent, Harry Washford, James Winning; Corporals William Menzies, Herbert Simpson; Private James McTurk, Denis Morris

Mentioned in Despatches

Lieutenant-Colonels Russell Boyle, Eric MacDonald (3), Dan Ormond (2), J.G. Rattray**; Majors E.J. Ashton, William Bingham, Walter Critchley, FitzRoy George, Eric MacDonald, Archibald MacLean,* Joseph MacLaren, Joseph Simpson, Walt Sparling, Alexander Thomson, Phil Walker**; Captains Geoff Arthur, David Black, Geoff Burbidge, Charles Costigan (2), George Craggs, Hugh Ferguson, Jack Miller, William Mitchell, Charles Robinson, William Thompson, Gordon Virgo; Lieutenants Ralph Feurt, Byron Greer, Gordon Graham (2), Stanley Kent, Norman MacEachern (2), Thomas Rutherford, Stanley Robertson, Alfred Trimmer, Lewis Younger; Company Sergeants-Major Herbert Baker,* David McCandie, Edmond Rayfield,* Archie Toole; Sergeants Walter Alderton,* Arnold Budd, Robert Burns, Arthur Courtney, Sydney Cox, James Duff, James Harrison,* Clyde Higgins,* Herbert Jarvis,* Arthur Martin,* Edward Milne, Charles Morrison, Ernest Pitman, Richard Waller, M. Wilson; Lance-Sergeant John Palmer; Corporals William Baker, John Brook, Ralph Brookes, Thomas Dale, Victor Evans, James Hogg,* William Menzies,* David O'Rourke, Thomas Ross, Samuel Schultz, Horatio Smith, Ray Smith (2), Arthur Underwood; Lance-Corporals George Allan, Ralph Browne,* William King; Privates Thomas Baxter,* Thomas Bell,* Charles Bloxham, Harold Butterworth,* Frank Cox, Charles Cutter,* Gerald Fitzgibbons,* Richard Harrison, Thomas Morrison,* Frank Sixby, Albert Tinkess,* Louis Zuidema
(* indicates "Brought to notice of Secretary of State for War for valuable services rendered")

Foreign Awards

Croix de Guerre (Belgium)

Sergeant John Seeley; Corporals Arthur Knight, James Robinson; Privates Albert Grainger, James McTurk, Jesse Webb

Croix de Guerre (France)

Lieutenant-Colonel Dan Ormond; Captain William Mitchell; Sergeant William McIntosh; Corporals William Baker, Ray Smith; Private Percy Main

Médaille Militaire (France)

Sergeants Percy Andrews, Hugh Caminer

Order of St. Stanislas, Third Class, with Swords (Russia)

Major Dan Ormond, Lieutenant Sidney Robson

Order of St. George, First Class (Russia)

Sergeant-Major Robert Good

Cross of St. George, Fourth Class (Russia)

Lance-Corporal Joseph Komich; Privates Theodore Belinski, Harry Koewve, Frederick Mulford, Matakichi Yashikawa

APPENDIX C

TENTH BATTALION BATTLE HONOURS

Battle honours for the Tenth Battalion were issued under General Order 123, 15 October 1929. Oddly, The Calgary Highlanders, who inherited the Tenth's battle honours, received theirs a month before, under General Order 110, issued on 15 September. Although virtually the same, the honours are not identical: the Highlanders were given one for "Arras, 1917, '18," while the Tenth's reads "Arras, 1917."

Ypres, 1915 - 17*
Gravenstafel
Saint-Julien*
Festubert, 1915
Mount Sorrel
Somme, 1916*
Thiepval
Ancre Heights
Arras, 1917
Vimy, 1917*
Arleux*
Hill 70*
Passchendaele*
Amiens*
Scarpe, 1918
Drocourt-Quéant*
Hindenburg Line*
Canal du Nord
Pursuit to Mons
France and Flanders, 1915 - 18

(* indicates one of the ten battle honours on the regimental Colour)

APPENDIX D

OFFICERS COMMANDING, TENTH BATTALION

Russell Lambert Boyle
27 September 1914 – 25 April 1915

A native of Port Colborne, Ontario, Boyle was born on 29 October 1880. At age fourteen, he joined the 7th Battery, Canadian Field Artillery, as a trumpeter, and later served as a sergeant in the South African War, where he was wounded and received the Queen's Medal and three clasps. Moving to Alberta with his father and brother, Boyle homesteaded near Crossfield, acquiring his own 960-acre ranch before his marriage to Laura Wight in July 1906. They had two children, Annie and James. An active Conservative, Boyle took part in local politics and was named a commissioner for oaths and justice of peace in 1905.

At the same time, he was rising through the ranks of the militia. When he moved to Alberta, he joined the 15th Light Horse, eventually commanding the regiment's Crossfield-based A Squadron. When the war broke out, Boyle volunteered his services and travelled to Camp Valcartier, where he helped to organize the newly formed Tenth Battalion. Initially one of its majors, he was promoted to command the unit before its departure for England. After leading the Battalion into combat for the first time, in its attack on the wood near Saint-Julien, Boyle was fatally wounded and died in hospital in Boulogne, France, on 25 April 1915.

He was buried in Poperinghe Old Military Cemetery in Belgium.

John Grant Rattray
22 – 26 September 1914
2 June 1915 – 7 September 1916

Born in Banffshire, Scotland, on 15 January 1864, Rattray came to Canada in 1874 when his family moved to Middlesex County in Ontario. Educated in Strathroy and Ottawa, he headed west in 1888, homesteading near Pipestone, Manitoba, where he later established a hardware business. He served as reeve from 1902 to 1904, before moving to Winnipeg in 1911, joining the staff of the Canada Life Assurance Company as inspector of loans for Manitoba and eastern Canada.

Rattray's military career began in 1906, when he enlisted in the 12th Manitoba Dragoons as a lieu-

tenant. His stature was such that, in 1910, he organized a cavalry regiment, the 20th Border Horse, which he commanded until 1914. When the war broke out, Rattray briefly commanded two battalions at Camp Valcartier, the 6th (Fort Garry Horse) and later the Tenth, which he organized before its departure for England. Serving on the staff at Canadian Division headquarters and then as president of the Permanent Board of Enquiry at Shorncliffe, England, he was reinstated to command of the Tenth on 2 June 1915, an appointment he held until 7 September 1916, when he was promoted to brigadier-general and given command of a training brigade in England. He was awarded the DSO in January 1916, and in June 1918, he was named a Companion of the Order of St. Michael and St. George (CMG).

Rattray's post-war career was eventful. In 1920, he was asked to organize the provincial police force in Manitoba, and he served as its commissioner until the fall of 1922. He later acted as chairman of the Soldiers' Settlement Board in Ottawa, and chaired the War Veterans' Assistance Commission in the 1930s. Rattray died on 23 June 1944, and was buried in Pipestone.

Daniel Mowat Ormond
27 September 1916 – 24 May 1918

A native of Pembroke, Ontario, Ormond was born on 14 August 1885. His family moved to Manitoba three years later, and Ormond eventually rose to prominence as a barrister and solicitor in Portage-la-Prairie. A Liberal and a Presbyterian, he married Annie Laura Cadham in 1910, and they had five children, a son and four daughters.

Ormond joined the militia, serving as an officer first with the 12th Manitoba Dragoons — where he met J.G. Rattray — and then with the 18th Manitoba Dragoons. At Valcartier in 1914, he became the adjutant of the Tenth Battalion, a position he held until August 1915. Placed in temporary command of the 7th (1st British Columbia Regiment) Battalion, he was later invalided sick to England. Spending much of the winter of 1915 - 16 in hospital, Ormond recovered to accept the appointment to command the Canadian Pioneer Training Depot in England in March 1916. Returning to France in September, he took command of the Fighting Tenth on 27 September 1916. Before being promoted to brigadier-general and command of the Ninth Brigade in 1918, Ormond won the DSO and bar, and in 1919 was named a CMG.

After the war, he remained in the permanent force, serving as the officer commanding Military District 12, based in Regina, before renewing acquaintances with veterans of the Fighting Tenth when he was posted to Calgary in command of Military District 13, from 1928 until 1932. Upon his retirement that year, he was promoted to major-general, afterwards serving as the superintendent of penitentiaries in Ottawa, and later as the librarian at the Supreme Court of Canada. Ormond died on 19 November 1974.

Eric Whidden MacDonald
24 May 1918 – 23 April 1919

The son of a noted militia officer and clergyman, MacDonald was born in Amherst, Nova Scotia, on 20 July 1892. Educated at Acadia University, he moved to Calgary in 1913, taking a position with the Canadian Oil Company, where he was working as an accountant when the war broke out.

Joining the Fighting Tenth as a subaltern in the summer of 1915, MacDonald assumed command of the Battalion on 24 May 1918. He ended the war with the DSO and two bars, as well as the MC.

Like Rattray and Ormond, MacDonald became a civil servant after the war. Serving as commissioner of the Nova Scotia provincial police until 1923, he then moved to Ottawa, where he held an administrative post with the Department of National Defence until 1938. MacDonald also acted as the Ottawa representative for General Motors, Dominion Rubber, and Canadian Industries Limited, and had acquired a reputation as an international trader by the time of his accidental death in Ottawa on 12 November 1947.

APPENDIX E

THE OAK-LEAF SHOULDER BADGE

It took thirteen years for The Calgary Highlanders to obtain the special shoulder badge commemorating the April 1915 attack by the Tenth Battalion on the wood near Saint-Julien. The man most responsible for the badge was Lieutenant-Colonel Hugh Urquhart, the officer commanding the Canadian Scottish Regiment, perpetuating the 16th Battalion which accompanied the Tenth in this historic action during the Second Battle of Ypres.

Colonel Urquhart was distressed when, in 1925, the defence department's Battle Honours Committee refused to consider bestowing a battle honour specifically for the assault on Kitcheners Wood. After consulting with the commanders of the two units which perpetuated the Fighting Tenth, The Calgary Highlanders and the Winnipeg Light Infantry, Urquhart wrote Ottawa requesting some special recognition of the attack, if not in the form of a battle honour, then perhaps a mention in despatches or a commendation from the government of France.

In his petition, Urquhart pointed out that not only was the operation "completely successful," but that "the 10th and 16th Bns were the first of any overseas troops to attack the troops of a first-class European Power on European soil, and as a phase of this encounter will the Committee please take note of the fact that the army of that Power was the product of a very high military efficiency, and the units opposed to the 10th and 16th ranked among the best troops in that army."

Urquhart enlisted several prominent generals, both British and Canadian, to endorse his request. These included Canadian commanders General Sir Arthur Currie and Lieutenant-General Sir Richard Turner, VC, and Britishers like Field-Marshal Lord Plumer, General Sir Horace Smith-Dorrien, and Lieutenant-General Sir Edwin Alderson, all of whom wrote letters strongly supporting Urquhart's proposal. The Calgary Highlanders and Winnipeg Light Infantry also joined the fray by sending similar petitions to Ottawa.

The campaign produced the desired effect. In June 1926, the adjutant-general, Major-General H.A. Panet, responded with a counter-proposal stating that, while a battle honour was not feasible, it was possible that "some special distinction might be awarded, and it is under consideration to recommend to the Hon. the Minister that this take the form of some special badge or other distinction in accoutrements or dress." The only condition was that it would have to be common to all three regiments. Colonel Urquhart immediately consulted with his counterparts in The Calgary Highlanders and Winnipeg Light Infantry. In a 25 June 1926 letter to his fellow commanding officers, Urquhart suggested a collar badge: "An Oak leaf (or more than one leaf) and acorn or acorns, on a background of blood red. The Wood was oak and therefore this particular emblem would be appropriate in that respect and the sacrifices incurred on that night being such as really made the Two Battalions concerned — that is, as far as the solid esprit-de-corps and individuality concerned — the blood red would seem likewise appropriate.

Lieutenant-Colonel David Ritchie, the Calgary police chief who commanded The Calgary Highlanders, liked the acorn design but, concerned at the prospect of two collar badges, felt that it would look better on the lower sleeve. The Winnipeg Light Infantry's commander, Lieutenant-Colonel C.M. Ackland, held a similar view, although he preferred to have the badge worn on the upper sleeve. Because all three admired the acorn and oak-leaf design, the colonels submitted their applications to Ottawa, leaving the details to be worked out later.

General Panet responded in January 1927 "that the most suitable emblem would be an oak leaf with one acorn" and "that this should be worn as a collar badge." He pointed out that if the regiments wished to wear it in addition to their existing collar badges, there were at least two precedents in the British army for a double collar badge, in the Seaforth Highlanders and the Royal Irish Fusiliers. Panet also noted that "the award of an honorary distinction of this nature has first to receive the sanction of H.M. The King."

Three years passed. In May 1930, the adjutant-general's office proposed that the three regiments wear the same collar badges as the units they perpetuated, with these badges superimposed on a bronze oak leaf. This counter-proposal was rejected, and more correspondence, and delay, ensued. Finally, in 1933, all parties agreed to a metal shoulder badge, and there were further discussions regarding the actual design.

At that time, both The Calgary Highlanders (Lieutenant-Colonel David Tomlinson) and Canadian Scottish expressed a preference for the full regimental name to be inscribed on their respective badges, while the Winnipeg Light Infantry requested the letters "WLI." The chief of the General Staff, Major-General Andy McNaughton, submitted the matter to the quartermaster-general, Brigadier Clive Caldwell, in January 1934, for the preparation of drawings. Brigadier Caldwell informed the regiments in July that the suggested width of two inches was "rather large," and that 1⅞ inches was preferable.

The resulting badges were similar, but not identical. Authority was granted on 14 September 1934, in General Orders 63 (Canadian Scottish), 64 (The Calgary Highlanders), and 65 (Winnipeg Light Infantry). The two Highland units were authorized to wear an oak-leaf and acorn badge of bronze, 1⅞ inches wide and 1⁵/₁₆ inches high, an annulus inscribed "Calgary Highlanders" and "Canadian Scottish," respectively; the Winnipeg regiment's badge was two inches wide and three-quarters of an inch in height, with the letters "WLI" superimposed on the oak leaf and acorn.

Four more years passed before the badges were delivered, and a further design change had occurred. While the Canadian Scottish and Winnipeg Light Infantry received the authorized emblems, that of The Calgary Highlanders was slightly different by the time it was presented to the Regiment at a ceremony on Sunday, 24 April 1938 at Mewata Armoury. Rather than resembling the Canadian Scottish badge, with the full regimental name inscribed on it, The Highlanders' badge looked like that of the Winnipeg Light Infantry, with the letters "CH" upon the oak leaf. The reason for the change is not clear: it might have been a manufacturer's mistake (the regiment's previous shoulder badge, authorized in 1925, consisted of the letters "CH" in black on bronze), or it could have been a matter of cost.

This unique Canadian unit citation is still worn by The Calgary Highlanders, but it has been a matter of some controversy over the years. During the Second World War, the regiment was politely informed that all Canadian units were required to wear only the standard CANADA shoulder badge. A compromise was subsequently reached, enabling The Highlanders to wear both the cloth CANADA badge and its brass oak-leaf and acorn badge. Uniform changes in the wake of the unification of Canada's armed forces presented another problem. The single-service green uniform adopted at that time had no shoulder straps, and the Regiment was eventually forced to utilize a cloth badge, between 1982 and 1987, when new uniforms with shoulder straps were introduced, allowing the unit to revert to its brass badge. Since the demise of the Winnipeg Light Infantry in 1955, The Calgary Highlanders and the Canadian Scottish Regiment (Princess Mary's) are the sole bearers of this distinctive battle emblem.

APPENDIX F

ORDER OF BATTLE,
CANADIAN ARMY CORPS,
11 NOVEMBER 1918

General Officer Commanding Lieut.-Gen. Sir A.W. Currie

Brigadier-General, General Staff Brig.-Gen. R.F. Hayter

Deputy Adjutant and Quartermaster-General Brig.-Gen. G.J. Farmar

General Officer Commanding, Royal Artillery Maj.-Gen. E.W.B. Morrison

Chief Engineer Maj.-Gen. W.B. Lindsay

General Officer Commanding, Canadian Machine-Gun Corps Brig.-Gen. R. Brutinel

General Officer Commanding, Heavy Artillery Brig.-Gen. A.G.L. McNaughton

CORPS TROOPS

CAVALRY
  Canadian Light Horse
  RNWMP Squadron

ARTILLERY
  Royal Canadian Horse Artillery Brigade
  8th Army Brigade, Canadian Field Artillery (CFA)
  "E" Anti-Aircraft Battery

Corps Heavy Artillery
  1st Brigade, Canadian Garrison Artillery (CGA)
  2nd Brigade, CGA
  3rd Brigade, CGA

Fifth Divisional Artillery
  13th Brigade, CFA
  14th Brigade, CFA

ENGINEERS
  1st, 2nd, 3rd, 4th, 5th Army Troops Companies
  Anti-Aircraft Searchlight Company
  3rd Tunnelling Company
  Corps Survey Section
  1st, 2nd Tramways Companies

MACHINE-GUN CORPS
  1st, 2nd Motor Machine-Gun Brigades

ARMY SERVICE CORPS
  1st, 2nd, 3rd, 4th Divisional Mechanical Transport Companies
  Corps Troops Mechanical Transport Company
  Engineers Mechanical Transport Company
  Motor Machine-Gun Mechanical Transport Company

MEDICAL CORPS
  Numbers 1, 2, 3, 4 Casualty Clearing Stations
  Number 7 (Cavalry) Field Ambulance
  Number 14 Field Ambulance

MISCELLANEOUS
  Canadian Cyclist Battalion
  Corps Signal Company

DIVISIONAL TROOPS

FIRST CANADIAN DIVISION
  First Canadian Infantry Brigade
    1st (Western Ontario) Battalion
    2nd (Eastern Ontario) Battalion
    3rd (Toronto Regiment) Battalion
    4th (Central Ontario) Battalion
  Second Canadian Infantry Brigade
    5th (Western Cavalry) Battalion
    7th (1st British Columbia Regiment) Battalion
    8th (90th Winnipeg Rifles) Battalion
    TENTH CANADIAN INFANTRY BATTALION
  Third Canadian Infantry Brigade
    13th (Royal Highlanders of Canada) Battalion
    14th (Royal Montreal Regiment) Battalion
    15th (48th Highlanders of Canada) Battalion
    16th (Canadian Scottish) Battalion
  1st Brigade, CFA
  2nd Brigade, CFA
  1st Brigade, Canadian Engineers
  1st Battalion, Canadian Machine-Gun Corps
  Numbers 1, 2, 3 Field Ambulances

SECOND CANADIAN DIVISION
  Fourth Canadian Infantry Brigade
    18th (Western Ontario) Battalion
    19th (Central Ontario) Battalion
    20th (Central Ontario) Battalion
    21st (Eastern Ontario) Battalion
  Fifth Canadian Infantry Brigade
    22nd (French-Canadian) Battalion
    24th (Victoria Rifles of Canada) Battalion
    25th (Nova Scotia Rifles) Battalion
    26th (New Brunswick) Battalion
  Sixth Canadian Infantry Brigade
    27th (Winnipeg) Battalion
    28th (Northwest) Battalion
    29th (Vancouver) Battalion

31st (Alberta) Battalion
5th Brigade, CFA
6th Brigade, CFA
2nd Brigade, Canadian Engineers
2nd Battalion, Canadian Machine-Gun Corps
Numbers 4, 5, 6 Field Ambulances

THIRD CANADIAN DIVISION
Seventh Canadian Infantry Brigade
Royal Canadian Regiment
Princess Patricia's Canadian Light Infantry
42nd (Royal Highlanders of Canada) Battalion
49th (Edmonton Regiment) Battalion
Eighth Canadian Infantry Brigade
1st Canadian Mounted Rifles
2nd Canadian Mounted Rifles
4th Canadian Mounted Rifles
5th Canadian Mounted Rifles
Ninth Canadian Infantry Brigade
43rd (Cameron Highlanders of Canada) Battalion
52nd (New Ontario) Battalion
58th (Central Ontario) Battalion
116th (Ontario County) Battalion
9th Brigade, CFA
10th Brigade, CFA
3rd Brigade, Canadian Engineers
3rd Battalion, Canadian Machine-Gun Corps
Numbers 8, 9, 10 Field Ambulances

FOURTH CANADIAN DIVISION
Tenth Canadian Infantry Brigade
44th (New Brunswick) Battalion
46th (South Saskatchewan) Battalion
47th (Western Ontario) Battalion
50th (Calgary) Battalion
Eleventh Canadian Infantry Brigade
54th (Central Ontario) Battalion
75th (Mississauga) Battalion
87th (Canadian Grenadier Guards) Battalion
102nd (Central Ontario) Battalion
Twelfth Canadian Infantry Brigade
38th (Ottawa) Battalion
72nd (Seaforth Highlanders of Canada) Battalion
78th (Winnipeg Grenadiers) Battalion
85th (Nova Scotia Highlanders) Battalion
3rd Brigade, CFA
4th Brigade, CFA
4th Brigade, Canadian Engineers
4th Battalion, Canadian Machine-Gun Corps
Numbers 11, 12, 13 Field Ambulances

ACKNOWLEDGEMENTS

As always, a project of this nature results from the co-operation of a great many people. No one deserves more praise than Honorary Colonel Fred Mannix of The Calgary Highlanders; without his efforts, this book would not exist. I also wish to express my thanks to the four Tenth Battalion veterans who so willingly and generously contributed: Wally Bennett, W. Ashton Cockshutt, Ernie Crowe, and Walter Loudon.

Others I wish to acknowledge, in alphabetical order, include: Barry Agnew, Glenbow Museum; Harry Chritchley; Lieutenant-Colonel Murray Dennis; Colonel John Fletcher; Don Graham; Joseph Harper; Dr. Steve Harris, Directorate of History, National Defence Headquarters; Raymond Hébert, Personnel Records Centre, Ottawa; Colonel Paul Hughes; Barry Hyman, Provincial Archives of Manitoba; Brad Kinmond; Larry MacDonald; Lieutenant-Colonel Alan Maitland of The Calgary Highlanders; Dr. Bill McAndrew, Directorate of History, National Defence Headquarters; George Milne; Margaret O'Kane; Sam Nickle; Jack Peach; Donald L. Redman; Dr. Charles Ross, Knox Church historian; Mark Tennant; Sid Wallace; Major Dick Westbury; Glenn Wright, National Archives of Canada; Jack Zuidema. My editor, Barbara Kwasny, worked hard to make this a better book. However, any errors or omissions that remain are mine alone. The opinions expressed are also mine, and do not necessarily reflect the views or beliefs of The Calgary Highlanders.

Last, but far from least, I pay tribute to Cindy Delisle, for her interest, perseverance, and support in this often trying undertaking. She helps me in ways she can never realize, and my feeble expressions of appreciation are inadequate recompense.

The cover artwork for this publication is an extract from a poster commemorating The Calgary Highlanders 80th year of service. The anniversary poster was printed courtesy of the Department of National Defence, Director of Exhibitions and Displays, Ottawa, Canada.

REFERENCE NOTES

Published sources are identified by the author and, where necessary, by a brief description of the title of the work, followed by a page number. A Roman numeral preceding the page number indicates the volume number. For full details, consult the Select Bibliography.

Unpublished sources involve longer entries. References to "CBC interview" are tape-recorded interviews for the 1964 Canadian Broadcasting Corporation Production, "Flanders Fields," in which two dozen members of the Fighting Tenth were involved; the tapes are housed in the National Archives of Canada. Abbreviations used below include:

DHist   Directorate of History (Ottawa)
GM   Glenbow Museum (Calgary)
NAC   National Archives of Canada (Ottawa)
PAM   Provincial Archives of Manitoba (Winnipeg)

CHAPTER ONE: *Birth of a Battalion*

1. Calgary *Daily Herald*, 22/8/14.
2. CBC interview, n.d.
3. *The Glen*, Spring 1984, 4.
4. Duguid, Appendix 83.
5. Ibid., Appendix 84.
6. Ibid., Appendix 85.
7. Ibid.
8. CBC interview, 4/2/64.
9. *The Glen*, Spring 1984, 4.
10. NAC, RG9 III B3, volume 79, nominal roll, n.d.
11. Duguid, Appendix 85.
12. Rattray speech to Tenth Battalion reunion, n.d.
13. Information from W.A. Cockshutt, 8/6/89.
14. NAC, MG30 D45, M-73, Rattray to J.W. Dafoe, 1/11/15.
15. Calgary *Daily Herald*, 26/4/15.
16. Interview with author, 19/11/87.
17. Ibid.
18. *The Glen*, Spring 1984, 4.
19. Interview with author, 19/11/87.
20. Ibid.
21. Duguid, Appendix 111.
22. NAC, RG9 III D1, volume 4691, folder 49, file 5, Historical Record, Tenth Battalion, n.d.
23. Duguid, Appendices 132, 133.
24. *The Glen*, Spring 1984, 4.
25. NAC, RG9 III C15, volume 4622, C-E-5, Emsley to Director, Chaplain Services, 7/11/19.
26. Interview with author, 19/11/87.
27. NAC, RG9 III C3, volumes 4919 - 21, Tenth Battalion war diary (henceforth, War Diary), 19/10/14.
28. Ibid.
29. NAC, RG9 III C15, volume 4622, C-E-5, Emsley to Director, Chaplain Services, 7/11/19.
30. Ibid., 20,21/10/14.
31. Nicholson, 35.
32. CBC interview, 4/2/64.
33. War Diary, 13/11/14.
34. Duguid, I/142.
35. *Militia Orders, 1915,* Order No. 20, 11/1/15.
36. Ibid., Order No. 71, 8/2/15.
37. NAC, RG 9 III C3, volume 4072, folder 9, file 3, Battalion orders, 14/11/14.
38. Tucker, 11.
39. Duguid, I/134.
40. War Diary, 7/11/14.
41. Interview with author, 19/11/87.
42. War Diary, 25/12/14.
43. NAC, RG9 III C15, volume 4622, C-E-5, Emsley to Director, Chaplain Services, 7/11/19.
44. Ibid., volume 4653, "Honours and Awards, 2", Emsley extract, n.d.
45. NAC, RG9 III C3, volume 4072, folder 9, file 3, B.M. Youill to Tenth Battalion, 1/1/15.
46. Ibid., volume 4051, folder 18, file 5, Boyle to A.W. Currie, 19/1/15.
47. War Diary, 7,27/1/15.
48. *Militia Orders, 1914,* Order No. 464, 19/10/14.
49. War Diary, 29/1/15.
50. Ibid., 17/12/14, 12,16/1/15.
51. Interview with author, 19/11/87.
52. War Diary, 18/1/15.
53. NAC, RG9 III C3, volume 4072, folder 9, file 2, Battalion orders, 15/11/14 to 1/2/15.
54. Roy, 317 - 18.
55. NAC, MG30 E75, volume 2, Currie to E.A.H. Alderson, 4/1/15.
56. Ibid., 16/1/15.
57. War Diary, 20/1/15.
58. NAC, RG9 III C3, volume 4051, folder 18, file 5, Boyle to Currie, 19/1/15.
59. Ibid., Kemmis-Betty to Boyle, 23/1/15.
60. War Diary, 20,21,26,28/1/15.

61. NAC, RG9 III B1, volume 390, B-9–1, Lightfoot to Boyle, 15/11/14.
62. Ibid., Paterson to Currie, 20/11/14.
63. Ibid., MacLaren to Cohoe, 19/12/14.
64. Ibid., Canadian Division to Currie, 31/12/14.
65. War Diary, 9/2/15.
66. Duguid, I/151.
67. War Diary, 7/2/15.
68. NAC, RG9 III C3, volume 4072, folder 9, file 3, Battalion orders, 2/2/15 to 19/2/15.
69. War Diary, 9/2/15.
70. CBC interview, C. Scriven, 25/9/63.
71. *The Glen*, Spring 1984, 4.
72. War Diary, 10,11/2/15.
73. CBC interview, 25/9/63.
74. Ibid., 29/1/64.
75. War Diary, 13,14/2/15.
76. Ibid., 14,17/2/15.
77. *The Glen*, Spring 1984, 4.
78. CBC interview, 25/9/63.
79. NAC, RG9 III C3, volume 4051, folder 18, file 6, J. Sutherland-Brown to Currie, 22/2/15.
80. Ibid., Boyle to Currie, 20/3/15.
81. Ibid., volume 4070, book 1.
82. War Diary, 15 - 17/2/15.
83. Duguid, Appendix 263.
84. War Diary, 21/2/15.
85. Ibid., 22,23/2/15.
86. CBC interview, 27/1/64.
87. Ibid., 4/2/64.
88. Ibid., n.d.
89. Duncan, 9.
90. War Diary, 25,26/2/15.
91. Ibid., 28/2/15-1/3/15.
92. Duguid, Appendix 267.
93. War Diary, 5 - 9/3/15.
94. Ibid., 11 - 13,17/3/15.
95. NAC, RG9 III C3, volume 4070, book 1, Lightfoot/Robinson to Boyle, 15/3/15.
96. NAC, MG30 E75, volume 2, file 3, Currie to E.A.H. Alderson, 16/3/15.
97. Calgary *Daily Herald*, 8/3/19.
98. NAC, RG9 III C3, volume 4073, Battalion orders, 23/3/15, 1/4/15.
99. Ibid., volume 4070, book 1, Lightfoot to Boyle, 15/3/15; Gliddon to Boyle, 15/3/15.
100. War Diary, 14 - 18/3/15.
101. *Letters from the Front*, I/8.
102. CBC interview, 25/9/63.
103. Ibid., 19/11/63.
104. War Diary, 22 - 31/3/15 – 1 - 14/4/15.
105. NAC, MG30 E100, diary, 11/4/15.
106. CBC interview, 27/1/64.
107. War Diary, 12 - 15/4/15.
108. Duguid, I/207.
109. CBC interview, n.d.
110. War Diary, 15/4/15.
111. CBC interview, n.d.
112. War Diary, 15 - 19/4/15.
113. Ibid.,15,16/4/15.
114. NAC, MG30 E100, diary, 15/4/15.
115. Duncan, 14.
116. Calgary *Daily Herald*, 5/5/15.
117. CBC interview, n.d.
118. War Diary, 20,21/4/15.

CHAPTER TWO: Glorious Memory

1. *War Illustrated*, 1747.
2. A.W. Bennett, "An Account of the Second Battle of Ypres," unpublished manuscript (henceforth, Bennett account).
3. *The Glen*, April 1975, 2.
4. War Diary, 22/4/15.
5. Ibid.
6. Ibid.
7. Bennett account.
8. GM, Helen and Eric Adams papers, undated newspaper clipping.
9. NAC, RG9 III C3, volume 4070, book 1.
10. Bennett account.
11. CBC interview, n.d.
12. Bennett account.
13. War Diary, 22/4/15.
14. *The Glen*, April 1975, 2.
15. Calgary *Daily Herald*, 22/4/19.
16. NAC, MG30 E46, volume 1, file 4, "Diary of Operations, 3rd Canadian Infantry Brigade," n.d.
17. NAC, RG9 III C3, volume 4919, file 372(1)/15–4.
18. Calgary *Daily Herald*, 27/5/15.
19. GM, Helen and Eric Adams papers, undated newspaper clipping.
20. Calgary *Daily Herald*, 27/5/15.
21. Scott, 62.
22. War Diary, 22/4/15.
23. *Letters from the Front*, I/10.
24. War Diary, 22/4/15.
25. Calgary *Daily Herald*, 22/4/19.
26. War Diary, 22/4/15.
27. CBC interview, n.d.
28. NAC, MG30 E75, volume 1, Tenth Battalion report, 28/4/15 (henceforth, Battalion report).
29. GM, Helen and Eric Adams papers, undated newspaper clipping.
30. *Letters from the Front*, I/10.
31. Calgary *Daily Herald*, 22/4/19.
32. *With the First Canadian Contingent*, 87.
33. *Letters from the Front*, I/11.
34. Tucker, 95.
35. *With the First Canadian Contingent*, 87.
36. *Letters from the Front*, II/174.
37. Ibid.
38. GM, Helen and Eric Adams papers, undated newspaper clipping.
39. War Diary, 23/4/15.

40. CBC interview, 25/10/63.
41. Ibid., n.d.
42. War Diary, 23/4/15.
43. GM, Helen and Eric Adams papers, undated newspaper clipping.
44. War Diary, 23/4/15.
45. CBC interview, 25/10/63.
46. War Diary, 23/4/15.
47. CBC interview, 29/1/64.
48. Ibid., 25/10/63.
49. Ibid.
50. Urquhart, 39.
51. Calgary *Daily Herald*, 22/4/19.
52. War Diary, 23/4/15.
53. Calgary *Daily Herald*, 22/4/19.
54. Urquhart, 38fn.
55. CBC interview, 29/1/64.
56. Calgary *Daily Herald*, 22/4/19.
57. Ibid.
58. CBC interview, n.d.
59. Ibid., 25/10/63.
60. Calgary *Daily Herald*, 14/8/16.
61. War Diary, 23/4/15.
62. GM, Helen and Eric Adams papers, undated newspaper clipping.
63. *Canadian Daily Record*, 25/7/19.
64. Urquhart, 72.
65. Battalion report.
66. Ibid.
67. Ibid.
68. War Diary, 23/4/15.
69. Ibid.
70. CBC interview, 25/10/63.
71. NAC, RG9 III C3, volume 4070, book 7, Ormond to L.J. Lipsett, 25/7/15.
72. Aitken, I/94.
73. NAC, RG9 III C3, volume 4919, file 372(1)/15–4.
74. War Diary, 23/4/15.
75. Ibid.
76. Ibid.
77. Battalion report.
78. Duguid, I/293.
79. War Diary, 24/4/15.
80. Calgary *Daily Herald*, 23/6/15.
81. CBC interview, 25/10/63.
82. Battalion report.
83. CBC interview, n.d.
84. Battalion report.
85. CBC interview, n.d.
86. Battalion report.
87. War Diary, 24/4/15.
88. CBC interview, 27/1/64.
89. Ibid., n.d.
90. Ibid.
91. Ibid., 25/10/63.
92. Battalion report.
93. CBC interview, n.d.
94. War Diary, 24/4/15.
95. Battalion report.
96. War Diary, 24/4/15.
97. Aitken, I/82–83.
98. Montreal *Daily Star*, 22/4/16.
99. Ibid., 24/4/16.
100. Battalion report.
101. War Diary, 24/4/15.
102. Battalion report.
103. Ibid.
104. Bennett account.
105. Ibid.
106. Ibid.
107. Interview with author, 13/12/84.
108. Bennett account.
109. Ibid.
110. Interview with author, 13/12/84.
111. Ibid.
112. NAC, MG30 E75, volume 1, file 4, "2nd Canadian Infantry Brigade Narrative of Events," n.d. (henceforth, Second Brigade report).
113. CBC interview, 25/10/63.
114. NAC, MG30 E75, volume 1, file 4, "7th Battalion Narrative of Events," 1/5/15 (henceforth, 7th Battalion report).
115. Ibid.
116. Calgary *Daily Herald*, 25/5/15.
117. CBC interview, 27/1/64.
118. Second Brigade report.
119. Ibid.
120. Ibid.
121. NAC, RG9 III C3, volume 4070, book 3, Guthrie to A.W. Currie, 3/5/15.
122. Ibid., Guthrie to Currie, 2/5/15.
123. 7th Battalion report.
124. Montreal *Daily Star*, 25/4/16.
125. CBC interview, 25/10/63.
126. *The Glen*, April 1975, 3.
127. Second Brigade report.
128. Bennett account.
129. Ibid.
130. NAC, RG9 III C3, volume 4070, book 3.
131. Second Brigade report.
132. CBC interview, 4/2/64.
133. Account of R.T. Wilson, n.d., loaned to author.
134. CBC interview, 27/1/64.
135. Bennett account.
136. NAC, RG9 III C3, volume 4070, book 3.
137. CBC interview, n.d
138. Calgary *Daily Herald*, 23/6/15.
139. Ibid., 26/4/15.
140. Second Brigade report.
141. War Diary, 12/5/15.
142. NAC, RG9 III C3, volume 4070, book 3, P.A. Guthrie to A.W. Currie, 2/5/15.
143. Calgary *Daily Herald*, 3/6/15.
144. NAC, RG9 III C3, volume 4070, book 3, Guthrie to Currie, 2/5/15.
145. Montreal *Daily Star*, 24/4/16.

CHAPTER THREE: "The Gates of Hell"

1. Guthrie, 32.
2. NAC, RG9 III C3, volume 4070, book 1.
3. War Diary, 6/5/15.
4. NAC, RG9 III C3, volume 4070, book 1.
5. Ibid.
6. CBC interview, 25/9/63.
7. Bennett account.
8. Duguid, I/455.
9. NAC, RG24, volume 1813, file 4–15K, "Words Spoken to First Canadian Division," n.d.
10. War Diary, 11 - 18/5/15.
11. Duguid, I/460–61.
12. Guthrie, 11.
13. Calgary *Daily Herald*, 10/12/15.
14. Bennett account.
15. Guthrie, 11.
16. Duguid, Appendix 773.
17. Dancocks, *Currie*, 54.
18. Guthrie, 11.
19. Ibid., 31.
20. Ibid., 14–15.
21. Ibid., 15–18.
22. Ibid., 18.
23. Ibid.
24. *Letters from the Front*, I/17–18.
25. Guthrie, 18–19.
26. Ibid.
27. CBC interview, 25/1/64.
28. Ibid., 25/10/63.
29. Interview with author, 19/11/87.
30. Calgary *Daily Herald*, 10/12/15.
31. Guthrie, 25.
32. CBC interview, 25/10/63.
33. *Letters from the Front*, I/31-32.
34. Guthrie, 25.
35. Ibid., 20.
36. War Diary, 22/5/15.
37. Calgary *Daily Herald*, 10/12/15.
38. Bennett account.
39. Guthrie, 22.
40. Ibid., 1.
41. *New York Herald*, 29/7/17.
42. CBC interview, 27/1/64.
43. Ibid.
44. Duguid, I/498.
45. Calgary *Daily Herald*, 10/12/15.
46. War Diary, 26/5/15.
47. *Letters from the Front*, II/24.
48. Duguid, I/499.
49. PAC, RG9 III C3, volume 4070, book 3.

CHAPTER FOUR: War in the Trenches

1. NAC, RG9 III C3, volume 4070, book 5, Rattray to J.L. Regan, 6/6/15.
2. Ibid., book 9, Rattray to Currie, 29/7/15.
3. Ibid., book 5, Rattray to J.S. Brown, 4/6/15.
4. *Letters from the Front*, II/88–89.
5. CBC interview, 25/10/63.
6. War Diary, 14/6/15.
7. Duncan, 73.
8. War Diary, 14,15/6/15.
9. Ibid., 17 - 23/6/15.
10. Bennett account.
11. Cockshutt letter to author, 28/2/89.
12. NAC, RG9 III C3, volume 4919, folder 372–1, Currie to Rattray, 26/6/15.
13. Bennett account.
14. CBC interview, 25/9/63.
15. Ibid., n.d.
16. Duncan, 40.
17. Ibid., 35.
18. NAC, RG9 III C3, volume 4070, book 9, Rattray to Currie, 18/7/15; book 12, Rattray to Currie, 11/9/15.
19. Ibid., book 6, Rattray to E.E.W. Moore, 2/7/15.
20. Ibid., Rattray to Currie, 30/6/15.
21. Ibid., book 16, Rattray to L.J. Lipsett, 30/10/15.
22. Ibid., Rattray to OC, 49th Battalion, 31/7/15.
23. War Diary, 31/7/15.
24. NAC, MG30 E100, diary, 8/8/15.
25. War Diary, 7 - 10/8/15.
26. NAC, MG30 E100, diary, 18/8/15.
27. War Diary, 3 - 7/9/15.
28. Ibid., 10 - 13/9/15.
29. NAC, MG30 E45, M-73, Rattray to J.W. Dafoe, 1/11/15.
30. Bennett account.
31. NAC, MG30 E100, Currie to F.W. Hill, 15/8/18.
32. NAC, MG30 E45, M-73, Rattray to Dafoe, 1/11/15.
33. War Diary, 19 - 24/9/15.
34. NAC, RG9 III C3, volume 4070, book 13, Rattray to Lipsett, 25/9/15.
35. War Diary, 29/9/15 - 4/10/15.
36. Ibid., 5 - 8/10/15.
37. Ibid., 11,12/10/15.
38. Ibid., 15 - 18/10/15.
39. NAC, RG9 III C3, volume 4070, book 16, Rattray to S. Seccombe, 31/10/15.
40. GM, Helen and Eric Adams papers, undated newspaper clipping.
41. War Diary, 19 - 24/10/15.
42. NAC, RG9 III C3, volume 4070, book 10.
43. NAC, MG30 E100, diary, 27/10/15.
44. War Diary, 25/10/15.
45. NAC, MG30 E100, diary, 5/11/15.
46. War Diary, 2,3/11/15.
47. Duncan, 38–39.
48. Dancocks, *Currie*, 67.
49. War Diary, 4 - 7/11/15.
50. Ibid., 8 - 13/11/15.
51. Ibid., 12/11/15.
52. Calgary *Daily Herald*, 22/4/19.
53. War Diary, 18 - 21/11/15.

54. Interview with author, 19/11/87.
55. War Diary, 19 - 23/11/15.
56. NAC, RG9 III C3, volume 4919, file 372(2)/15–11, "Programme of Training," 5/12/15.
57. War Diary, 24/11/15 – 15/12/15.
58. Ibid., 16 - 21/12/15.
59. NAC, RG9 III C3, volume 4919, file 372(2)/15–12, Shannon to J.G. Rattray, 28/12/15.
60. War Diary, 22 - 27/12/15.
61. NAC, MG30 E45, M-73, Rattray to J.W. Dafoe, 1/11/15.
62. Ibid.
63. NAC, RG9 III C3, volume 4919, file 372(2)/16–2, J.G. Rattray to L.J. Lipsett, 7/2/16.
64. War Diary, 28 - 30/12/15.
65. Ibid., 31/12/15.
66. NAC, RG9 III C3, volume 4070, book 21, Rattray to Alderson, 1/1/16.
67. War Diary, 2/1/16.
68. Ibid., 3,4/1/16.
69. Ibid., 5,6/1/16.
70. Ibid., 7/1/16.
71. NAC, RG9 III C3, volume 4919, file 372(2)/16–1, Appendix 3-a, 8/1/16.
72. Rattray speech to Tenth Battalion reunion, n.d.
73. War Diary, 9 - 12/1/16.
74. NAC, RG9 III D1, volume 4691, file 9, folder 49, DJE-4.
75. War Diary, 21/1/16.
76. Ibid.
77. 22 - 27/1/16.
78. Ibid., 27 - 31/1/16.
79. NAC, RG9 III C3, volume 4070, book 17, Rattray to L.J. Lipsett, 10/12/15.
80. Ibid., volume 4919, folder 372(2)/16–2, A.D. Conners report, 6/2/16 (henceforth, Conners report).
81. War Diary, 2,3/2/16.
82. NAC, RG9 III C3, volume 4919, folder 372(2)/16–2, "Report of Minor Offensive Operation...," n.d. (henceforth, Battalion report).
83. Ibid., volume 4070, book 23, Summary of Evidence, 11/2/16.
84. Ibid., volume 4919, folder 372(2)/16–2, S.H. Kent report, 5/2/16 (henceforth, Kent report).
85. Battalion report.
86. NAC, RG9 III C3, volume 4070, book 23, Summary of Evidence, 11/2/16.
87. Battalion report.
88. NAC, RG9 III C3, volume 4071, book 39, D.M. Ormond to F.O.W. Loomis, 5/12/16.
89. Kent report.
90. NAC, RG9 III C3, volume 4919, folder 372(2)/16–2, L. Younger report, n.d.
91. Kent report.
92. Ibid.
93. Ibid.
94. Battalion report.
95. NAC, RG9 III C3, volume 4919, folder 372(2)/16–2, statement by 20187, N. Purmal, n.d.
96. Kent report.
97. NAC, RG9 III, volume 3858, folder 84, file 6, "Narrative by G.O.C., 2nd Canadian Infantry Brigade," 5/2/16 (henceforth, Lipsett report).
98. Ibid.
99. Battalion report.
100. Conners report.
101. War Diary, 7/2/16.
102. Ibid.
103. NAC, RG9 III C3, volume 4919, folder 372(2)/16–2, Rattray to L.J. Lipsett, 7/2/16.
104. Conners report.
105. Lipsett report.
106. Ibid.
107. NAC, MG30 E100, diary, 6/2/16.
108. NAC, RG9 III, volume 3858, folder 84, file 6, Alderson to Second Army, 6/2/16.
109. War Diary, 26/2/16.
110. Battalion report.
111. Jack Zuidema, interview with author, 13/10/88.
112. War Diary, 8 - 14/2/16.
113. Ibid., 14,15/2/16.
114. Ibid., 16 - 19/2/16.
115. Ibid., 20/2/16.
116. Ibid., 23 - 25/2/16.
117. Ibid., 29/2/16.
118. NAC, RG9 III, volume 3858, folder 84, file 11, "Report on Minor Operation by 10th Canadian Battalion on Night of March 1st/2nd, 1916," n.d. (henceforth, Battalion report).
119. Ibid.
120. Ibid., Costigan to J.G. Rattray, 2/3/16 (henceforth, Costigan report).
121. Battalion report.
122. NAC, RG9 III, volume 3858, folder 84, file 11, L. Younger report, n.d.
123. Ibid.
124. Costigan report.
125. Battalion report.
126. War Diary, 2/3/16.
127. Ibid., 3 - 8/3/16.
128. Ibid., 9/3/16.
129. Ibid., 9 - 13/3/16.
130. NAC, RG9 III C3, volume 4919, folder 372(2)/16–3, E.W. MacDonald report, n.d.
131. Ibid.
132. Ibid., C.H. Trotter report, 14/3/16.
133. Ibid., C.W. Stewart report, 16/3/16,
134. War Diary, 15 - 21/3/16.
135. Ibid., 21 - 27/3/16.
136. Ibid., 27 - 29/3/16.
137. Ibid., 30/3/16-3/4/16.

138. Ibid., 4/4/16.
139. Warner, 29.
140. War Diary, 8/4/16.
141. Ibid., 9 - 16/4/16.
142. NAC, RG9 III D1, volume 4691, file 10, folder 49, DJE-4.
143. NAC, RG9 III C3, volume 4919, folder 373(1)/16–4, "Operation Order, 10th Canadian Battalion," 12/4/16.
144. Ibid., S.H. Kent report, 13/4/16.
145. Ibid., Rattray to L.J. Lipsett, 13/4/16.
146. Ibid., J.D. Simpson report, n.d.
147. Duncan, 83.
148. NAC, RG9 III, volume 4073, Battalion orders, 5/8/16.
149. War Diary, 16 - 30/4/16.
150. RG9 III D1, volume 4691, file 11, folder 49, DJE-4.
151. War Diary, 2 - 10/5/16.
152. Ibid., 11 - 18/5/16.
153. Ibid., 18 - 25/5/16.
154. Ibid., 26 - 31/5/16.
155. Ibid., 31/5/16 – 1/6/16.
156. *The Glen*, April 1975, 3.

CHAPTER FIVE: "Dearest Mother, Do Not Weep"

1. NAC, RG24, volume 4689, file 12 - 13, Rattray to D.J. MacDonald, 29/11/28 (henceforth, Rattray letter).
2. CBC interview, 27/1/64.
3. Nicholson, 149.
4. Ibid., 150.
5. PAM, A.W. Morley papers, "2nd Canadian Infantry Brigade, Describing the Operations in the Ypres Salient from June 2nd to June 14th, 1916," n.d.
6. NAC, RG9 III C3, volume 4070, book 28.
7. NAC, RG9 III D1, volume 4691, folder 49, file 12, "Narrative 10th Canadian Infantry Battalion from June 1st to June 16th, 1916," 17/6/16 (henceforth, Battalion report).
8. Ibid., folder 48, file 10, 7th Battalion report, n.d.
9. Battalion report.
10. Ibid.
11. Ibid.
12. Ibid.
13. Ibid.
14. Ibid.
15. Ibid.
16. CBC interview, 27/1/64.
17. *Letters from the Front*, II/411–12.
18. Battalion report.
19. Rattray letter.
20. Battalion report.
21. Ibid.
22. Rattray letter.
23. War Diary, 4/6/16.
24. Ibid., 5 - 7/6/16.
25. Urquhart, 141.
26. *Letters from the Front*, II/440.
27. War Diary, 8 - 10/6/16.
28. Rattray letter.
29. Dancocks *Currie* 70.
30. War Diary, 11/6/16.
31. Edmonds, 241.
32. Urquhart, 143.
33. Rattray letter.
34. War Diary, 13/6/16.
35. Urquhart, 150.
36. CBC interview, 26/11/63.
37. Rattray letter.
38. Calgary *Daily Herald*, 21/6/15.
39. War Diary, 14/6/16.
40. Ibid., 15/6/16.
41. Ibid., 15 - 29/6/16.
42. Rattray speech to Tenth Battalion reunion, n.d.
43. War Diary, 29/6/16 – 5/7/16.
44. Ibid., 5/7/16 – 26/8/16.
45. Nicholson, 160.
46. War Diary, 27 - 30/8/16.
47. Macphail, 68.
48. *Canada in the Great World War*, 14.
49. Nicholson, 155.
50. NAC, RG9 III D1, volume 4691, file 49–5, Ormond to W.M. Aitken, 29/11/16.
51. NAC, RG9 III, volume 3876, folder 6, file 2, Rattray to Loomis, 9/11/15; Rattray to First Division, 10/11/15; First Division to Rattray, 12/11/15; Carson to Rattray, 24/2/16; Rattray to Carson, 18/3/16.
52. Ibid., H.D.E. Parsons to War Office, 18/3/16.
53. NAC, RG9 III C3, volume 4073, Battalion orders, 18/6/16.
54. J.H. Harper, letter to author, 29/1/89.
55. NAC, MG30 E100, Currie to V.W. Odlum, 11/9/16.
56. War Diary, 1 - 6/9/16.
57. Nicholson, 155.
58. War Diary, 9/9/16.
59. NAC, MG30 D45, M-73, Rattray to J.W. Dafoe, 1/11/15.
60. Rattray speech to Tenth Battalion reunion, n.d.
61. NAC, RG9 III C3, volume 4070, book 20, Rattray to Currie, 1/1/16.
62. Rattray speech to Tenth Battalion reunion, n.d.
63. Urquhart, 162.
64. Williams, 134.
65. War Diary, 10/9/16.
66. Ibid., 11/9/16.
67. *Letters from the Front*, I/337.
68. War Diary, 12 - 22/9/16.
69. Ibid., 23/9/16.
70. Ibid., 24,25/9/16.
71. NAC, RG9 III C3, volume 4919, "Narrative of Operations, 10th Canadian Infantry Battalion," n.d. (henceforth, Battalion report).

72. CBC interview, 27/11/63.
73. PAM, A.W. Morley papers, "Report of 2nd Canadian Infantry Brigade, Action of 26th and 27th September, 1916," 28/9/16 (henceforth, Second Brigade report).
74. Ibid.
75. Battalion report.
76. NAC, RG9 III, volume 4918, 8th Battalion report, 30/9/16 (henceforth, 8th Battalion report).
77. Interview with author, 6/12/88.
78. Battalion report.
79. Ibid.
80. NAC, RG9 III, volume 4916, 5th Battalion report, 27/9/16.
81. Second Brigade report.
82. Battalion report.
83. CBC interview, 29/1/64.
84. Second Brigade report.
85. Interview with author, 6/12/88.
86. Battalion report.
87. Ibid.
88. War Diary, 26,27/9/16.
89. Ibid., 1/10/16.
90. Ibid., 2 - 7/10/16.
91. McKenzie, 33–34.
92. War Diary, 8 - 11/10/16.
93. Interview with author, 6/12/88.
94. NAC, RG9 III C3, volume 4071, book 37, Ormond to Loomis, 27/10/16.
95. *The Glen*, April 1975, 3.
96. Ibid.
97. Ibid.
98. War Diary, 16/10/16.
99. 8th Battalion report.
100. Nicholson, 198.
101. CBC interview, n.d.
102. War Diary, 17 - 27/10/16.
103. NAC, RG9 III C3, volume 4073, file 9, Second Brigade to Tenth Battalion, 27/10/16.
104. Ibid., 28 - 30/10/16.
105. NAC, MG30 E100, diary, 30/10/16.
106. War Diary, 30/10/16-5/11/16.
107. Berton, 73.

CHAPTER SIX: A Ridge Named Vimy

1. Swettenham, 146.
2. War Diary, 6 - 9/11/16.
3. Ibid., 10 - 13/11/16.
4. NAC, RG9 III C3, volume 4051, file 8 - 19, Ormond to Loomis, 15/11/16.
5. War Diary, 14 - 17/11/16.
6. Ibid., 18/11/16 – 4/12/16.
7. NAC, RG9 III C3, volume 4071, book 37, Ormond to Guthrie, Ormond to Loomis, 29/11/16.
8. Don Graham, letter to author, 21/2/89.
9. Loudon to author, n.d.
10. War Diary, 3 - 5,25,28/12/16.
11. Ibid., 4 - 12/12/16.
12. Ibid., 12 - 18/12/16.
13. Ibid., 19 - 31/12/16.
14. Ibid., 25,28/12/16.
15. Ibid., 29 - 31/12/16.
16. Ibid., 1/1/17.
17. Ibid., 2 - 18/1/17.
18. Ibid., 18 - 24/1/17.
19. NAC, RG9 III C3, volume 4919, file 373/17–2, "Defence Scheme," 20/2/17.
20. War Diary, 24 - 30/1/17.
21. Letter to author, 16/12/88.
22. War Diary, 31/1/17-4/2/17.
23. Ibid., 5 - 11/2/17.
24. Ibid., 11 - 16/2/17.
25. Ibid., 17 - 22/2/17.
26. NAC, RG9 III C3, volume 4071, file 4, book 41, Ormond to Loomis, 23/2/17.
27. War Diary, 23 - 27/2/17.
28. Ibid., 28/2/17-2/3/17.
29. Ibid., 4 - 11/3/17.
30. Berton, 78.
31. War Diary, 14,18/3/17.
32. Ibid., 14 - 19/3/17.
33. Ibid., 20 - 23/3/17.
34. NAC, RG9 III C3, volume 4071, book 41, Ormond to Loomis, 23/3/17.
35. Ibid., 26/2/17-23/3/17.
36. Ibid., 21/3/17.
37. War Diary, 24 - 26/3/17.
38. NAC, RG9 III C3, volume 4071, book 41, Ormond to Loomis, 24/3/17.
39. War Diary, 29 - 31/3/17.
40. CBC interview, n.d.
41. Roy, 318.
42. CBC interview, n.d.
43. NAC, RG9 III C3, volume 4051, file 19–11, "2nd Canadian Infantry Brigade, Instructions No. 3," 26/3/17.
44. Ibid., volume 4919, file 373(2)/17–3, Order No. 32, 30/3/17.
45. Ibid., B.M.A. 213, 24/3/17.
46. CBC interview, n.d.
47. Ibid.
48. NAC, RG 9 III C3, volume 4919, file 373(2)/17–4, S.H. Kent report, 5/4/17.
49. Ibid., "Observation Posts," 31/3/17.
50. CBC interview, n.d.
51. Ibid.
52. Ibid.
53. Ibid.
54. NAC, RG 9 III C3, volume 4919, file 373(2)/17–4, Appendices A, B, C to "Operations on Morning of 8/4/17," n.d.
55. Ibid.
56. CBC interview, n.d.
57. NAC, RG9 III C3, volume 4919, file 373(2)/17–4, Order No. 34, 5/4/17.

58. Ibid., "Report on Operations, 9th/20th April 1917," 24/4/17 (henceforth, Battalion report).
59. Ibid., volume 4071, book 41, Ormond to Loomis, 26/2/17.
60. Ibid., volume 4919, file 373(2)/17–4, Order No. 35, 7/4/17.
61. Ibid., volume 4071, book 62, Ormond to Loomis, 27/5/17.
62. W.A. Loudon, interview with author, 6/12/88.
63. NAC, RG9 III C3,, volume 4919, file 373(2)/17–4, Ormond to Loomis, 19/4/17 (henceforth, Ormond report).
64. CBC interview, 25/1/64.
65. Battalion report.
66. Ormond report.
67. NAC, RG9 IIIC3, volume 4071, book 65, Ormond to Mrs. P. McPherson, 1/7/17.
68. Interview with author, 6/12/88.
69. Letter to author, 7/12/88.
70. *Letters from the Front*, II/477.
71. Ormond report.
72. *Letters from the Front*, II/388,400.
73. Battalion report.
74. Ibid.
75. Ibid.
76. Ibid.
77. Ibid.
78. Ormond report.
79. CBC interview, n.d.
80. Ormond report.
81. Battalion report.
82. Ibid.
83. Ormond report.
84. CBC interview, 25/1/64.
85. Ibid., n.d.
86. Don Graham, letter to author, 27/3/89.
87. Battalion report.
88. Ibid.
89. Ibid.
90. CBC interview, 25/9/63.
91. Battalion report.
92. Ormond report.
93. Ibid.
94. CBC interview, 25/1/64.
95. War Diary, 11/4/17, Appendix 73.
96. Ormond report.
97. War Diary, 14 - 23/4/17.
98. Ibid., 24,25/4/17.
99. NAC, RG9 III C3, volume 4919, file 373(2)/17–4, "2nd Canadian Infantry Brigade, Preliminary Operation Order," 18/4/17.
100. Ibid., B.M.A. 363, 18/4/17.
101. Ibid., "2nd Canadian Infantry Brigade Instructions for the Attack on Arleux (No. 2)," 27/4/17.
102. Ibid.
103. Ibid.
104. Dancocks, *Currie,* 95–96.
105. NAC, RG9 III C3, volume 4919, file 373(2)/17–4, B.M. 419, 27/4/17.
106. Ibid., Thomson to Ormond, 3/5/17 (henceforth, Battalion report).
107. War Diary, 27/4/17.
108. Ibid.
109. Battalion report.
110. Ibid.
111. Ibid.
112. Ibid.
113. Ibid.
114. Ibid.
115. NAC, RG9 III C3, volume 4071, book 41, Ormond to R.H. Kearsley, 30/4/17 (henceforth, Ormond comments).
116. Battalion report.
117. Ibid.
118. NAC, RG9 III C3, volume 4919, file 373(2)/17–4, Appendix 121.
119. Ibid., Appendix 140.
120. Ibid., Appendix 127.
121. Ibid., Appendix 128.
122. Battalion report.
123. Ibid.
124. CBC interview, 20/11/63.
125. NAC, RG9 III C3, volume 4045, folder 2, file 3, First Division to Second Brigade, 6/7/16; Reserve Army to Second Brigade, 13/9/16.
126. Battalion report.
127. Ibid.
128. Ibid.
129. Ibid.
130. Ibid.
131. Ibid.
132. Ormond comments.
133. CBC interview, 20/11/63.
134. Ibid.
135. Duncan, 78.
136. War Diary, 1/5/17.
137. Ibid., 1 - 5/5/17.
138. Ibid., 6 - 23/5/17.
139. Ibid.
140. *The Glen*, Spring 1986, 4.
141. War Diary, 1 - 8/6/17.
142. CBC interview, 27/1/64.
143. Interview with author, 6/12/88.
144. War Diary, 9 - 21/6/17.
145. Ibid., 22/6/17.
146. Ibid., 23 - 30/6/17.
147. Ibid., 4 - 13/7/17.
148. Ibid., 13,14/7/17.
149. Ibid., 15,16/7/17.
150. Ibid., 16 - 23/7/17.
151. Ibid., 24 - 26/7/17.
152. CBC interview, 20/11/63.
153. War Diary, 27 - 29/7/17.
154. Ibid., 31/7/17.

CHAPTER SEVEN: Victoria Cross Hill

1. War Diary, 29 - 31/7/17.
2. Ibid., 1 - 4/8/17.
3. CBC interview, 20/11/63.
4. Ibid., 29/11/63.
5. War Diary, 5 - 12/8/17.
6. Ibid., 13,14/8/17.
7. NAC, RG9 III C3, volume 4920, file 376(1)/17–8, "Operations, Vicinity of Hill 70, 14 - 16 August 1917," 22/8/17 (henceforth, Battalion report).
8. Ibid.
9. Ibid.
10. Ibid.
11. CBC interviews, 20/11/63.
12. NAC, RG9 III C3, volume 4920, file 376(1)/17–8, Carey to "Pelican," 15/8/17.
13. Battalion report.
14. Ibid.
15. Ibid.
16. Ibid.
17. Ibid.
18. Ibid.
19. NAC, RG9 III C3, volume 4920, file 376(1)/17–8, Templeman to "Pelican," 15/8/17.
20. Battalion report.
21. NAC, RG9 III C3, volume 4920, file 376(1)/17–8, Thompson to "Pelican," 15/8/17 (No. 54).
22. Ibid., (No. 63).
23. CBC interview, 20/11/63.
24. Letters from the Front, II/431.
25. NAC, RG9 III C3, volume 4920, file 376(1)/17–8, Templeman to "Pelican," 15/8/17.
26. Battalion report.
27. Ibid.
28. NAC, RG9 III C3, volume 4920, file 376(1)/17–8, Pearson to "Pelican," 15/8/17.
29. Ibid., volume 4070, book 28.
30. Battalion report.
31. Ibid.
32. NAC, RG9 III C3, volume 4920, file 376(1)/17–8, Templeman to "Pelican," 16/8/17.
33. CBC interview, n.d.
34. Battalion report.
35. Ibid.
36. NAC, RG9 III C3, volume 4920, file 376(1)/17–8, Thompson to "Pelican," 16/8/17.
37. Interview with author, 9/12/88.
38. CBC interview, 26/11/63.
39. Battalion report.
40. CBC interview, 29/11/63.
41. Battalion report.
42. "A war hero dishonoured," Maclean's, 20/5/85.
43. Ibid.
44. Ibid.
45. CBC interview, 26/11/63.
46. Battalion report.
47. CBC interview, 29/11/63.
48. Ibid., n.d.
49. Ibid., 26/11/63.
50. Battalion report.
51. Ibid.
52. Ibid.
53. Ibid.
54. CBC interview, 19/11/63.
55. Battalion report.
56. Ibid.
57. Ibid.
58. Interview with author, 9/12/88.
59. Letter to author, 12/12/88.
60. Battalion report.
61. Ibid.
62. Letters from the Front, II/380.
63. CBC interview, n.d.
64. Morning Albertan, 23/4/19.
65. CBC interview, John Matheson, 27/1/64.
66. NAC, RG24, volume 2538, file S 1822, part 2 (henceforth, Alexander file).
67. Ibid.
68. Alexander file.
69. Babington, 12-13.
70. NAC, RG24. Volume 2537, HQS-1822/1, "Some Notes Regarding the Award and Confirmation of Sentences of Death on Canadian Soldiers in the Great War, 1915-1918," 16/2/22 (henceforth, MacBrien report).
71. Alexander file.
72. Babington, 14-15.
73. MacBrien report.
74. Ibid.
75. NAC, RG9 III C3, volume 4072, book 73, Ormond to F.O.W. Loomis, 2/10/17.
76. MacBrien report.
77. NAC, RG9 III D3, Volume 4839, J. Sutherland Brown to APM, Second Brigade, 16/10/17; RG 24 Volume 2537, HQS-1822/1, "Points to Which Attention Should be Paid by Officers Charged with the Carrying Out of a Death Sentence," n.d.
78. Ibid.
79. Scott, 214-16.
80. NAC, RG24, volume 2537, HQS-1822/1, A.M. Alexander to Militia Dept., 6, 22/12/17.
81. War Diary, 18/8/17 – 3/9/17.
82. Ibid., 27/8/17.
83. Duff Cooper, II/149.
84. War Diary, 3 - 13/9/17.
85. Ibid., 13 - 17/9/17.
86. Ibid., 17 - 19/9/17.
87. Ibid., 20,21/9/17.
88. Ibid., 21/9/17-3/10/17.
89. NAC, RG9 III C3, volume 4072, book 77, Ormond to Loomis, 5/10/17.
90. Ibid., 3 - 12/10/17.
91. Duncan, 39.

92. Ibid., 42.
93. Interview with author, 9/12/88.
94. Duncan, 87-88.
95. Ibid.
96. Ibid., 103.
97. Ibid., 43-45.

CHAPTER EIGHT: "A Useless Waste of Life"

1. CBC interview, n.d.
2. War Diary, 21 - 31/9/17.
3. CBC interviews, 1/12/63, 26/11/63.
4. McKenzie, 113-14.
5. War Diary, 2 - 6/11/17.
6. Ibid., 7/11/17.
7. CBC interview, 29/11/63.
8. War Diary, 8,9/11/17.
9. CBC interview, 1/12/63.
10. War Diary, 9/11/17.
11. NAC, RG9 III C3, volume 4920, file 379/17–11, Ormond to Second Brigade, n.d. (henceforth, Battalion report).
12. CBC interviews, 1/12/63, 27/11/63.
13. Ibid., n.d.
14. NAC, RG9 III C3, volume 4920, file 379/17–11, Order No. 68, 8/11/17.
15. Battalion report.
16. NAC, RG9 III C3, volume 4052, folder 21/2, 7th Battalion report, 19/11/17.
17. Battalion report.
18. Ibid.
19. CBC interview, 25/9/63.
20. Battalion report.
21. Ibid.
22. Ibid.
23. CBC interview, n.d.
24. Ibid., 26/11/63, 1/12/63.
25. Battalion report.
26. Ibid.
27. Ibid.
28. CBC interviews, 19/11/63, 27/11/63.
29. Ibid., n.d.
30. Ibid., 1/12/63.
31. Battalion report.
32. Ibid.
33. CBC interviews, 26/11/63, 1/12/63.
34. Ibid., 26/11/63.
35. Ibid., 19/11/63.
36. Reid, 165.
37. CBC interview, 25/9/63.
38. Ibid., 26/11/63, 29/11/63.
39. Ibid., n.d.
40. RG9 III C3, volume 4052, folder 21/2, 5th Battalion report, n.d.; 8th Battalion report, 18/11/17.
41. Battalion report.
42. Ibid.
43. Ibid.
44. Ibid.

45. Ibid.
46. Ibid.
47. Ibid.
48. Ibid.
49. Aitken, II/58.
50. War Diary, 11/11/17.
51. Battalion report.
52. War Diary, 12/11/17.
53. CBC interview, n.d.
54. Ibid., 25/9/63.
55. NAC, RG9 III C3, volume 4045, folder 3, file 7.
56. Ibid., volume 4070, book 31, G. Craggs to Second Brigade, 11/4/16.
57. Calgary *Daily Herald*, 10/11/17.
58. War Diary, 12 - 18/11/17.
59. Ibid., 19 - 21/11/17.
60. Ibid., 22 - 30/11/17.
61. Ibid., 1 - 7/12/17.
62. Ibid., 8 - 11/12/17.
63. Ibid., 12 - 15/12/17.
64. *Calgary Eye Opener*, 24/11/17.
65. Ottawa *Journal*, 20/2/18.
66. *War Diary*, 16 - 20/12/17.
67. Ibid., 24 - 27/12/17.
68. Ibid., 27 - 31/12/17.
69. Ibid., 1/1/18.
70. Ibid., 2 - 14/1/18.
71. CBC interview, n.d.
72. War Diary, 18 - 25/1/18.
73. Ibid., 26 - 31/1/18.
74. Ibid., 1 - 8/2/18.
75. NAC, RG9 III C3, volume 4071, book 65, Ormond to T.G. Roberts, 24/6/17.
76. Ibid., book 73, Ormond to Armstrong, 19/9/17.
77. Ibid., Ormond to Messrs. Boosey & Co., 25/9/17.
78. War Diary, 8/2/18.
79. Ibid., 8 - 16/2/18.
80. Ibid., 17 - 24/2/18.
81. Ibid., 24/2/18-1/3/18.
82. CBC interview, n.d.
83. War Diary, 4 - 10/3/18.
84. NAC, RG9 III C3, volume 4921, file 379/18–3, Operation Orders, 10/3/18.
85. *The Glen*, April 1981, 3.
86. Ibid.
87. War Diary, 12,15/3/18.
88. Ibid.
89. Ibid., 31/3/18.
90. Ibid., 20 - 22/3/18.
91. Ibid., 23/3/18.
92. Ibid., 24 - 26/3/18.
93. Ibid., 27/3/18.
94. CBC interview, n.d.
95. War Diary, 27/3/18-5/4/18.
96. Ibid., 5 - 7/4/18.
97. CBC interview, n.d.
98. War Diary, 8 - 11/4/18.
99. Ibid., 12/4/18.

100. Ibid., 13/4/18.
101. Ibid., 14 - 17/4/18.
102. Ibid., 18 - 20/4/18.
103. Ibid., 21 - 26/4/18.
104. Ibid., 27/4/18-1/5/18.
105. Ibid., 1 - 3/5/18.
106. *Letters from the Front*, II/477.
107. CBC interview, 7/2/64.
108. War Diary, 4/5/18.
109. Ibid., 5,6/5/18.
110. Ibid., 6 - 25/5/18.
111. Ibid.
112. NAC, RG9 III C1, volume 4047, folder 6, file 1, Second Brigade to Tenth Battalion, 19/5/18.
113. War Diary, 23,24/5/18.
114. Ibid.
115. Ibid., 25/5/18-1/6/18.
116. NAC, RG9 III C3, volume 4051, folder 18, file 6, MacDonald to Loomis, 11/6/18.
117. War Diary, 1 - 28/6/18.
118. Ibid., 29/6/18.
119. Ibid., 9,17/6/18.
120. Ibid., 1/7/18.
121. Ibid., 3/7/18.
122. Ibid., 13 - 16/7/18.
123. Ibid., 17/7/18.
124. Ibid., 17,18/7/18.
125. Ibid., 18 - 22/7/18.
126. Ibid., 26/7/18.
127. NAC, RG9 III C3, volume 4921, file 379/18–7, P. Walker report, 27/7/18.
128. War Diary, 26/7/18.
129. Calgary *Daily Herald*, 23/4/19.
130. War Diary, 28,29/7/18.
131. Ibid., 30/7/18-1/8/18.

CHAPTER NINE: "Pure Bloody Murder"

1. War Diary, 1 - 3/8/18.
2. Ibid., 4/8/18.
3. Ibid.
4. Ibid.
5. CBC interview, 7/2/64.
6. War Diary, 4,5/8/18.
7. Ibid.
8. Ibid., 6/8/18.
9. CBC interview, 7/2/64.
10. NAC, RG9 III C3, volume 4921, file 380/18–8, Second Brigade B.M. 235, 5/8/18.
11. Ibid., B.M. 255, 6/8/18.
12. War Diary, 7/8/18.
13. CBC interviews, 7/2/64, 29/11/63.
14. NAC, RG9 III C3, volume 4921, file 380/18–8, Tenth Battalion report, 14/8/18 (henceforth, Battalion report).
15. CBC interview, 7/2/64.
16. Ibid.
17. Ibid.
18. Battalion report.
19. Nicholson, 398fn.
20. Battalion report.
21. CBC interview, 7/2/64.
22. Battalion report.
23. CBC interviews, 1/12/63, 7/2/64.
24. Ibid., 7/2/64.
25. Nicholson, 400.
26. Battalion report.
27. Goodspeed, 238.
28. Nicholson, 401fn.
29. Battalion report.
30. NAC, RG9 III D1, volume 4691, file 49–7, Tenth Battalion Honours and Awards, n.d. (henceforth, Honours list).
31. CBC interview, 27/11/63.
32. Battalion report.
33. Honours list.
34. Ibid.
35. Ibid.
36. Battalion report.
37. CBC interview, 7/2/64.
38. Honours list.
39. Battalion report.
40. Ibid.
41. Ibid.
42. CBC interview, 7/2/64.
43. Battalion report.
44. *Letters from the Front*, I/298.
45. CBC interviews, 27/11/63.
46. Battalion report.
47. War Diary, 9/8/18.
48. CBC interviews, 7/2/64, 27/11/63.
49. War Diary, 9/8/18.
50. CBC interview, 7/2/64.
51. War Diary, 10/8/18.
52. Ibid., 10 - 16/8/18.
53. Ibid., 15/8/18.
54. CBC interview, 7/2/64.
55. War Diary, 15/8/18.
56. Ibid., 16/8/18.
57. Ibid., 16,17/8/18.
58. NAC, RG9 III C3, volume 4921, file 380/18–8, Patrol Report, 19/8/18.
59. War Diary, 19/8/18.
60. Ibid., 20 - 25/8/18.
61. Ibid., 26/8/18.
62. Ibid., 26 - 29/8/18.
63. Ibid., 29 - 31/8/18.
64. 1/9/18.
65. CBC interview, 27/11/63.
66. NAC, RG9 III C3, volume 4052, folder 22, file 6, Tenth Battalion report, 6/9/18 (henceforth, Battalion report).
67. Ibid.
68. Ibid.
69. CBC interview, 19/11/63.
70. Battalion report.
71. CBC interview, 4/1/64.

72. Ibid.
73. Ibid., 19/11/63.
74. NAC, RG24, volume 1827, file GAQ 7–11, Tenth Battalion historical record, n.d.
75. *Surrey Mirror and County Post*, 27/9/18.
76. CBC interview, 27/11/63.
77. Ibid.
78. *Letters from the Front*, I/298.
79. NAC, RG9 III C3, volume 4921, file 380/18–9, "List of Ordnance," 12/9/18.
80. Battalion report.
81. War Diary, 4/9/18.
82. Battalion report.
83. War Diary, 3/9/18.
84. Ibid., 4 - 20/9/18.
85. NAC, RG9 III C15, volume 4649, "Biographies, 1."
86. War Diary, 20/9/18.
87. NAC, MG30 E5, volume 3, file 18, "Statement of Strength," 22/9/18.
88. War Diary, 25/9/18.
89. Hahn, 172-76.
90. War Diary, 25 - 26/9/18.
91. CBC interview, 4/1/64.
92. NAC, MG30 E5, volume 3, file 18, "Statement of Strength," 22/9/18.
93. NAC, RG9 III C3, volume 4921, file 380/18–10, Tenth Battalion report, 4/10/18 (henceforth, Battalion report).
94. CBC interview, 29/1/64.
95. Ibid.
96. Battalion report.
97. Ibid.
98. CBC interview, 29/11/63.
99. Battalion report.
100. Ibid.
101. Ibid.
102. NAC, RG9 III D2, volume 4809, file 195, First Division report, n.d. (henceforth, First Division report).
103. Battalion report.
104. CBC interviews, 27/11/63, 19/11/63.
105. Battalion report.
106. Ibid.
107. CBC interview, 19/11/63.
108. Battalion report.
109. CBC interview, 19/11/63.
110. Ibid., 29/1/64.
111. Ibid.
112. Battalion report.
113. Scott, 314.
114. Ibid., 29/1/64.
115. NAC, RG9 III C15, volume 4649, "Biographies, 1."
116. Scott, 314-15.
117. Ibid., 315.
118. Ibid., 316.
119. Battalion report.
120. CBC interview, 4/1/64.
121. First Division report.

CHAPTER TEN: Homecoming

1. War Diary, 5 - 7/10/18.
2. Ibid., 8/10/18.
3. NAC, RG9 III C3, volume 4921, file 380/18–10, Tenth Battalion report, n.d.
4. Ibid.
5. Ibid.
6. Ibid.
7. War Diary, 15,16/10/18.
8. NAC, RG9 III C3, volume 4921, file 381/18–10, Operation Order No. 50, 17/10/18.
9. Ibid., Tenth Battalion report, 20/10/18 (henceforth, Battalion report).
10. Ibid., Operation Order No. 50A, 18/10/18.
11. Battalion report.
12. Ibid.
13. Ibid.
14. Ibid.
15. War Diary, 19/10/18-10/11/18.
16. Duncan, 52.
17. War Diary, 24/10/18, 1,6,11/11/18.
18. Ibid., 11/11/18.
19. CBC interview, 27/11/63.
20. Ibid., 4/1/64.
21. NAC, RG24, volume 1827, GAQ 7–11, Historical record.
22. DHist, HQ 1451–603/07.
23. Duncan, 113.
24. *The Glen*, Spring 1986, 4.
25. Ibid.
26. Duncan, 111.
27. *The Glen*, Spring 1986, 4.
28. NAC, RG9 III C3, volume 4072, book 80, MacDonald to F.O.W. Loomis, 31/10/17.
29. CBC interview, 25/9/63.
30. NAC, RG9 III C3, volume 4072, book 73, Ormond to Loomis, 25/9/17.
31. CBC interviews, 4,29/1/64.
32. War Diary, 12 - 17/11/18.
33. Ibid., 18,19/11/18.
34. Ibid., 21 - 26/11/18.
35. Ibid., 27/11/18-2/12/18.
36. CBC interview, 4/1/64.
37. War Diary, 4,5/12/18.
38. NAC, RG9 III C1, volume 3894, folder 57, file 31.
39. War Diary, 6/12/18.
40. Goodspeed, 270.
41. CBC interview, 27/11/63.
42. War Diary, 7 - 12/12/18.
43. NAC, RG9 III C3, volume 4921, file 381/18–12, Operation Order No. 73, 12/12/18.
44. J.H. Harper, interview with author, 7/11/88.
45. Ibid.
46. Calgary *Daily Herald*, 22/4/19.

47. CBC interview, J. Sproston, 4/1/64.
48. War Diary, 13/12/18 – 2/1/19.
49. Ibid., 25/12/18.
50. CBC interviews, 27/11/63.
51. War Diary, 31/12/18.
52. Ibid., 1,2/1/19.
53. Ibid., 2 - 7/1/19.
54. NAC, RG9 III C3, volume 4921, file 381/19–1, Second Brigade B.M. 191, 6/1/19.
55. War Diary, 7,8/1/19.
56. Calgary *Daily Herald*, 22/4/19.
57. NAC, RG9 III C1, volume 3894, folder 57, file 31.
58. War Diary, 9,10/1/19.
59. Ibid., 25/1/19.
60. Ibid., 10/1/19 – 28/2/19.
61. NAC, RG9 III C3, volume 4921, file 381/19–1, "Educational Syllabus, 10th Canadian Infantry Battalion," n.d.
62. War Diary, 23/1/19, 4,19/2/19.
63. Ibid., 15,22,23,25,28/2/19.
64. Dancocks, *Spearhead,* 227.
65. Calgary *Daily Herald*, 23/4/19.
66. Dancocks, *Spearhead,* 229.
67. NAC, RG24, volume 1717, HQ 683–490–2.
68. Ibid.
69. Calgary *Daily Herald*, 12,17/4/19.
70. Ibid.
71. Ibid., 22–24/4/19.
72. Ibid., 22,23/4/19.
73. Ibid., 24/4/19.
74. Ibid., 22,23/4/19.
75. Interview with author, 15/12/88.
76. *Morning Albertan*, 25/4/19.
77. Calgary *Daily Herald*, 23/4/19.
78. Ibid., 24/4/19.
79. *Morning Albertan*, 25/4/19.
80. Ibid.
81. Ibid.
82. Ibid.
83. Ibid.
84. Ibid., 23/4/19.
85. Ibid., 24/4/19.
86. Ibid.

EPILOGUE: A NEW BEGINNING

1. Dancocks, *Currie,* 203 – 4.
2. Calgary *Daily Herald*, 21/7/19.
3. Ibid.
4. Ibid.
5. Ibid.
6. Ibid., 4/10/19.
7. Ibid., 22/11/19.
8. Dancocks, *Currie,* 204.
9. Calgary *Daily Herald*, 6,9/4/20.
10. Ibid., 9/4/20.
11. Ibid.
12. Ibid., 23/4/20.
13. DHist, HQ 1451/603/C7.
14. Ibid.
15. *Militia Orders*, No. 262, 21/7/20.
16. Calgary *Daily Herald*, 15/9/20.
17. Cockshutt to author, n.d.
18. Calgary *Daily Herald*, 6/9/21.
19. Cockshutt to author, n.d.
20. Farran, 7.
21. Ibid., 14/11/21.
22. Calgary *Daily Herald*, 16/12/24.
23. Ibid., 5/7/22.
24. Interview with author, 9/12/88.
25. GM, M1957, D. Ritchie to J.E.A. MacLeod, 1/2/30.
26. DHist, WC 1175–4, W.H.S. Macklin to HQ, Western Command, 6/6/50.
27. GM, M369, Neal to Association, 18/11/52.
28. Ibid.
29. Calgary *Daily Herald*, 27/4/53

INDEX

Barrett, Pte Stephen, 205
Bartlett, Pte A.E., 73, 215
Bateman, Pte Ewart, 132, 215
Battersea Farm, 82
battles: Amiens, 166-80; Arleux, *116*, 117-20, 121; Artois, 61; Cambrai, 159; Canal du Nord, 187-92; Champagne, 61; Drocourt-Quéant Line, 181-86; Festubert, 43-53, 63, 102; First Ypres, 15-16; Hill 70, 124-36, 137-38, 184; Loos, 60, 62; Marne, 15; Mount Sorrel, 78-86, 94, 137; Neuve-Chapelle, 17-18, 60; Passchendaele, 143-55, *150*, 174, 184, 197; Second Ypres, 22-43, 56, 62, 134, 206fn, 220; Somme, 85, 87-95, 100, 112; Third Ypres, 142-43; Verdun, 85, 87, 112; Vimy Ridge, *101*, 110-15, 119, 121, 137
Bay of Biscay, 14
Baxter, Pte Harry, 132, 155, 215
Baxter, Pte Thomas, 216
Beaufort, 178-79, 180
Beaverbrook, Lord, 66fn, 81, 154
Bedford House, 77
Beer, Pte Ernest, 133, 215
Beggs, Pte William, 153-54, 155, 164, 215
Belinski, Pte Theodore, 216
Bell, BGen A.H., 209
Bell, Pte Dalton, 136, 215
Bell, Pte Thomas, 216
Bellevue, 147
Bennett, Cpl Michael, 215
Bennett, Pte Wally, 1, 7, 9, 11, 12, 14, *27*, 46, 56-57; at Second Ypres, 22, 26, 39-49, 42-43; at Festubert, 50, 52; wounded, 66
Bennett, Richard Bedford, 27, 211
Berlin, 16
Berlin Wood, 20
Berneville, 160
Berthnoval, 102
Berton, Pierre, 104
Bertram, Maj W.R., 153
Bethune, 83, 103, 135
Bilsland, Lt William, 122
Bingham, Maj William, *44*, 64, 150, 155, *156*, 165, 216; MC, 76, 184, 214; hospitalized, 187; returns, 195
Bingham, Pte Charles, 10
Birrell, Pte Alexander, 34
Black, Capt David, 90, 94, 109, 117, 120, 214, 216
"Black Marias", 17
Bloxham, Pte Charles, 18, 36-37, 41, 43, 215-16
Bois des Cuisiniers, 20. *See also* Kitcheners Wood
Bond, Cpl Frederick, 129, 215
Bonn, 200, 202
Bonner, Sgt "Blondy", *45*
Booth, Lt Herbert, *156*, 202
Borden, Sir Robert, 8, 157fn, 164
Borre, 15
Bouilly-Grenay, 103, *153*, 158, 159
Boulogne, 43
Bourlon, 187
Bowering, Cpl Ernest, 113, 118, 120, 215-16
Bowers-Taylor, Pte Edward, 136, 215
Boyd, Pte John, *45*

Boyle, Laura, 43, *201*, 206-7, 210, 212
Boyle, LCol Russell, 2, 6-7, 54, 205, 206; biography, 218; at Salisbury, 10, 11, 13, 14; in trenches, 18, 19, 21; at Second Ypres, 22, 26 28; death of, 33, 43
Bradford, Pte Herbert, 34
Bradley, Cpl Thomas, 191, 214
Bramshott, 158, 188fn
Brandhoek, 145, 154, 156
Brandon, 205
Braquemont, 158
Brett, R.G., 205, 208
Briand, Aristide, 112
Brielen, 76
Bristol, 14
Broadbent, LCpl Charles, 179, 190, 215
Brook, Cpl John, 216
Brookes, Cpl Ralph, 52, 214, 216
Brooks, Pte George, 186, 191, 215-16
Brown, Cpl Walter, 86, 215
Brown, Pte Elsdon, *45*
Brown, Pte George, 155, 215
Brown, Pte Harry, *126*; and VC, 134-35, 164, 184, 214
Brown, Pte Harry L., 202
Brown, Pte John, 66
Brown, Pte Luke, 191, 215
Browne, LCpl Ralph, 216
Bruille-lez-Marchienne, 195
Brunay, 140, 157
Brutinel, BGen Raymond, 84
Bryan, Pte George, 17
Budd, Sgt Arnold, 71-72, 214, 216
Buddry, Sgt Frederick, 82, 115, 214, 215
Buissy, 191
Buissy Switch Line, 181, 184-86
Bulford Camp, 65-66, 68, 69, 70, 75
Burbidge, Capt Geoff, 59, 92, 95, 109, 117-20, 214, 216
Burbridge, Pte James, 136, 215
burial detail, 119
Burkett, Cpl George, 113, 215
Burland, LCol W.W., 38
Burns, Sgt Robert, 136, 215-16
Burnell, LCpl Arthur, 191, 214
Burrow, Pte Thomas, 18
Burtonville, 200
Butterworth, Pte Harold, 216
Byng of Vimy, Baron, *78*, 122, 159fn; command of Canadian Corps, 81; praise for Tenth, 87, 121, 211

Cagnicourt, 187
Caix, *173*, 175-76, 180
Caldwell, Brig Clive, 221
Calgary, 1, 3, 105, 111, 137, 138, *199*; welcomes Tenth, 204-7; post-war era, 208-12
Calgary *Daily Herald*, iii, 1, 43, 65, 140, 155, 205, 209, 211
Camblain l'Abbé, 95
Cambrai, 180, 187, 191-92, 194. *See also* battles
Cambrai-Douai road, 187-91, 191, 194
Caminer, Sgt Hugh, 95, 114, 214-16
camouflet, 76
Camp E, 86
Campeen-Amienois, 166

Foss, LCpl Frederick, 215
Foss, Pte Charles, 136, 215
Fosse 2, 124
Fosse 7, 122
Fosse 10, 103, 158, 160
Fosse Way, 82
Fowler, Pte James, 136, 215
Fowlie, Pte George, 120, 215
Franco-Prussian War, 15
Fraser, Pte Ewen, 215
Frasnes-lez-Gossellies, 198
French, Sir John, 11, 15, 60, 62
Fresnes-Rouvroy Line, 180
Fresnoy-en-Gohelle, 116, 119, 121
Frost, HCapt Francis, 187, 190, 191fn
Fryer, Capt Thomas, 34
Fuller, J.F.C., 16
Furnston, Pte Charlie, 36

Gallipoli, 60
Galloway, Pte Victor, 100
Gaspé Bay, 9
Gayner, W.R., 206
Gembloux, 198
Genappe, 198
Gentelles, 166
Gentelles Wood, 180
George V, King, 8, 11, 14, 60, 64, 72, 122
George, Maj FitzRoy, 93, 214, 216
Gericht, 85
Gibaut, Lt Alfred, 109
Gibson, Pte Robert, 136, 215
Gibson, Pte William, 136, 215
Gilchrist, Sgt William, 186, 215
Gillespie, Pte David, 191, 215
Gilmore, Pte George, 22
Gilson, LCol William, 187
Givenchy, 53, 54, 56, 96, 97
Glanfield, Lt Stanley, 6, *44*
Glasgow, Pte Allan, 50
Gleam, Lt Alexander, 132, 138
Gliddon, Capt George, 18, 22, 42
Glover, LCpl James, *45*
Goddard, Pte William, *45*
Godden, Lt Bertram, *156*
Godeswaersvalde, 75
Golics, Pte George, 136, 215
Good, Lt Robert, 43, *44*, 56, 59, 216
Goodfellow, Sgt Walter, *33*, 34
Gordon, Lt David, 30
Gouelzin, 195
Gough, Gen Sir Hubert, 146
Gouy Servins, 141
Graham, Capt Gordon, *156*, 165, 183, 214, 216
Graham, Lt John, 56, 59
Graham, Pte Lloyd, 160, 215
Grainger, Pte Albert, 216
Gravenstafel, 19, 20, 36, 41
Gravenstafel Ridge, 20, 37, 38, 40-41, 42
Gray, Pte James, 136, 215
Great War Veterans Association, 205, 206, 209
Green, Pte Robert, 69

Greenwood, Cpl Thomas, 165, 176, 214, 215
Greer, Lt Byron, 86, 215-16
Gregg, LCol H.T.R., *201*
Greig, Pte Peter, 186, 215
grenades, 56, *61*, 73
Griffiths, Pte Norman, *45*
Griffiths, Pte William, 43
Grimble, Lt Sidney, *156*, 165, 214
Grover, Cpl George, 214
Guillaucourt, 180
Guthrie, LCol Percy, 38, 41-42, 43, *44*, 102, 197; at
    Festubert, 46-52
Guthrie, Lt George, *156*, 161, 209

Hague Convention, 21, 28
Haig, Sir Douglas, 17, 60-61, 62, 77, 81, 87, 92, 103,
    157, 181, 194; plans for 1916, 85; conflict with
    Lloyd George, 112-13, 174-75; plans for 1917, 116,
    127, 142-43, 146, 154; and executions, 137;
    opinion of Canadians, 140
Halifax, 204, 205
Hall, Pte George, 21
Hamel, 192
Hamilton, Lt William, *156*, 161
Hampson, LCpl Sydney, 165fn
Hampton, LSgt David, 136, 186, 215
Hannebeek, 40
Harber, Pte Ephraim, 164
Hardwick, Sgt Ralph, 216
Harrison, HCapt Ralph, *156*, 187
Harrison, Lt Albert, *45*
Harrison, Pte Richard, 86, 114, 215-16
Harrison, Sgt James, 216
Hartman, Pte William, *45*
Hart-McHarg, LCol William, 40fn
Harvey, Cpl Albert, 191, 215
Hatcher, Cpl Charles, 14, 31, 33, 93
Hatherby, Cpl Sidney, 179, 215
Hautain Laval, 198
Haydon, Pte Charles, 215
Hayman, Pte Alexander, *45*
Haynecourt, 187-89, 191
Hayter, LCpl Arthur, 82, 214
Hazebrouck, 15, 87
Hazlewood, Pte Herbert, 134, 215
Hawkins, Pte Albert, 21
Haydon, Pte Charles, 155
Hedges, Lt William, *156*, 189, 191, 214
Heinrichs, Pte Daniel, 136, 215
Hellenthal, 200
Hemphill, Pte Samuel, 92, 151, 175, 178, 180, 215;
    wounded, 184-86; armistice, 196; in Germany,
    200-202
Henderson, Lt Norman, 153, 155, 161
Henry, Pte Harry, 136, 215
Henry, Pte Hugh, 109, 111, 119, 215
Henry, Sgt Frank, 115, 119, 215
Hersin, 103, 124, 158
Hescott, Pte John, 186, 190, 215
Hessian Trench, 92, 93
Hewitt, Pte Cecil, 186, 190, 215
Higgins, Sgt Clyde, 216

248

2. Formations, Units, and Corps

CANADIAN

Pre-war units

Post-war units

Canadian Expeditionary Force

Others:
    2nd London Heavy Battery, 31, 34

FRENCH

First Army, 166
11th Division, 19
173rd Regiment, 180
26th Battalion, Chasseurs à Pied, 72fn

GERMAN

Fourth Army, 28
XIII Württemburg Corps, 81
2nd Prussian Guards, 31
11th Prussian Reserve Regiment, 83
16th Bavarian Reserve Regiment, 29
234th Bavarian Regiment, 31